Discover a Watershed:
The Colorado
Educators Guide

Discover a Watershed

Project
WET
Water Education for Teachers
INTERNATIONAL

ISBN 1-888631-19-8

Front cover photo credits:
Grand Canyon Sunset © Digital Vision/Getty Images
Flash Flood © Michael Collier
Colorado River Delta © Michael Collier

Back cover art credits:
Green River Lakes © Christine Newell
Grand Canyon © Christine Jaworsky
Delta Avocets © Maria Goodin

Project WET International is an award-winning nonprofit science, natural resources, and heritage education program and publisher located in Bozeman, Montana, U.S.A.

Established in 1989, Project WET International works with visionary sponsors, educators, resource professionals, business leaders, policy makers, and citizens in the creation, development, and implementation of their projects. Project WET International responds to the needs of many diverse groups and relies on public and private partnerships to accomplish its work.

Project WET International reaches millions of people each year through its international delivery network. This extensive grassroots support is a hallmark of Project WET International.

Discover a Watershed

Project WET International Foundation
Discover a Watershed Series
PO Box 847
Bozeman, Montana 59771
www.discoverawatershed.org
www.projectwet.org

Word Usage, Grammar, and Writing Style
The writing style within the guide follows *The Chicago Manual of Style, 15th edition*; spelling is based on *The Random House Unabridged Dictionary, 2nd edition*. The term ground water is presented as two words based on the recommendation of the United States Geological Survey (USGS), the primary water management data agency for the United States.

Printed on recycled paper.

Dedication

Jim Richardson

The future of this great watershed
depends on
   knowledge,
      commitment,
         cooperation.
Cherish the water, for it is life—
   our life,
      nature's life,
         our planet's life.

      Our future depends on it.

V. G.

How to Use This Educators Guide

This Educators Guide is divided into three sections. **Part I** presents an overview of the watershed and its water resource management issues. It includes maps, photographs, quotations, and charts. This section is written in a narrative style and describes an expedition through the watershed. **Part II** is a collection of lesson plans (activities) that present creative, hands-on teaching methods to teach about water users and water management, ecosystems, geology, hydrology, geography, history, and cultures of the Colorado River Watershed. Each activity includes a detailed background section that complements information presented in Part I. Internal references help make connections between Part I and Part II. **Part III** includes cross-reference charts that correlate the activities to National Science Standards for the United States, cross-reference charts that identify subject areas to which each activity applies, a glossary, a bibliography, and an index. A full-color wall map illustrates the geography of the watershed.

Note to the reader: Project WET has done everything possible to present information in an unbiased manner and takes responsibility for the manuscript and content. This is a guide for educators and should not be mistaken as a government policy document or position statement. The project has been reviewed by individuals, agencies, and organizations representing extremely diverse interests and geographic locations. The future of the Colorado River is in the hands of the citizens of the basin, elected officials at all levels, and a huge number of local, state, regional, national, and international agencies and organizations. If a student gains a better understanding of the Colorado River and its watershed when participating in an activity led by a teacher or a resource manager, we have reached our objective. If information is found to be incorrect, it will be changed. Thank you.

—*Project WET International*

Common Units of Water Measurement		
1 acre-foot (af)	=	1 acre (.405 hectares) covered with a foot of water
	=	325,851 gallons
	=	43,560 cubic feet
	=	1233.482 cubic meters
	=	About the amount of water that a family of four in the United States uses each year
1 cubic foot/second (cfs)	=	7.481 gallons/second
	=	449 gallons/minute (gpm)
	=	646,320 gallons/day
	=	.028 cubic meters/second
1 cubic meter/second (m³/s)	=	35.315 cubic feet/second

Table of Contents

Activity Summaries

the negotiations leading up to the 1944 treaty between the United States and Mexico. (Grade Level: 9–12)

Activity Format

Grade Level:
Suggests appropriate learning levels, for example, grades 3–5; 6–8; or 9–12.

Subject Areas:
Disciplines to which the activity applies.

Duration:
Preparation time: The approximate time needed to prepare for the activity. NOTE: Estimates are based on first-time use. Preparation times for subsequent uses should be less.
Activity time: The approximate time needed to complete the activity.

Setting:
Suggested site.

Skills:
Skills applied in the activity.

Vocabulary:
Significant terms defined in the glossary and/or in the activity.

Summary
A brief description of the concepts and skills learned during the activity.

Objectives
The qualities or skills students should possess after participating in the activity. NOTE: Learning objectives, rather than behavioral objectives, were established for activities. To measure student achievement, see Assessment.

Materials
Supplies needed to conduct the activity.

Background
Preparatory information for the educator about activity concepts or teaching strategies.

Procedure
Warm Up
Prepares everyone for the activity and introduces concepts to be addressed. Provides the instructor with pre-assessment strategies.

The Activity
Provides step-by-step directions to address concepts. NOTE: Some activities are organized into "parts." This divides extensive activities into logical segments. All or some of the parts may be used, depending on the objectives of instruction. In addition, a few activities provide "options." These consist of alternative methods for conducting the activity.

Wrap Up
Brings closure to the lesson and includes questions and activities to assess student learning.

Assessment

Presents diverse assessment strategies that relate to the objectives of the activity, noting the part of the activity during which each assessment occurs. Often suggests ideas for assessment opportunities that follow the activity.

Extensions

Provides additional activities for continued investigation into concepts addressed in the activity. Extensions can also be used for further assessment.

Resources

Lists references providing additional background information. NOTE: This is a limited list. Several titles are suggested, but many other resources on similar topics will serve equally well.

e-Links

Provides links to Web sites with relevant information for further study.

Acknowledgments

Sponsors
Discover a Watershed: The Colorado Educators Guide was published through a partnership between public and private sponsors and Project WET International. Sponsors include:

Valerie Gates
Mission: To invest in the healthy future of our planet through the education of our children.

Bureau of Reclamation, Upper and Lower Colorado Regions
Mission: To manage, develop, and protect water and related resources in an environmentally and economically sound manner in the interest of the American public.

Mexican Institute of Water Technology
Mission: To carry out research, develop, adapt, and transfer technology; provide technological services; and prepare qualified human resources for water management, conservation, and restoration, in order to contribute to the sustainable development of Mexico.

Gonzalo Río Arronte Foundation
Mission: To support projects in water resources, health, and other programs with social impact that will significantly benefit the population.

Southern Nevada Water Authority
Mission: To manage the region's water resources and develop solutions that will ensure adequate future water supplies for the Las Vegas Valley.

Other contributors include:
Imperial Irrigation District; National Park Service, Dinosaur National Monument; National Park Service, Glen Canyon National Recreation Area; National Park Service, Grand Canyon National Park; Museo Sol del Niño of Mexicali; U.C. Davis Desert Research and Extension Center; Upper Gulf of California and Colorado River Delta Biosphere Reserve; Utah State Parks; Fort Lewis College, The Center for Southwest Studies; Daniel Graber; Outdoor Adventure River Specialists (O.A.R.S).

Publication Team and Contributors

Publisher
Dennis L. Nelson

Project Managers and Authors
Elisabeth Howe, Justin Howe

Contributing Authors and Researchers
Dennis Nelson, Savannah Barnes, Christine Jaworsky, Rita Vazquez del Mercado, Rosalinda Uribe Visoso, John Etgen, Gary Cook, Rab Cummings, Linda Hveem, Stephanie Ouren

Expedition Team Members and Student Researchers
Larissa Conte, Paul Formisano, Maria Goodin, Karen Hyun, Christine Jaworsky, Craig Maier, Carlota Monroy Lopez, Christine Newell, Lynn Peesel, Bárbara Peralta Zúñiga, Mauricio Torres Santillan, Paul Viosca

Sponsoring Agency Representatives
Bureau of Reclamation: Joe Whittaker (Upper Colorado Region); Tina Mullis (Lower Colorado Region)
Mexican Institute of Water Technology: Rita Vazquez del Mercado (Director, Project WET Mexico)

Leadership Team
José Campoy Favela, Director, Upper Gulf of California and Colorado River Delta Biosphere Reserve/CONANP–SEMARNAT
Valerie Gates, Sponsor
Judy Maben, California Project WET State Coordinator, Water Education Foundation
Tina Mullis, Water Conservation Coordinator, Bureau of Reclamation, Lower Colorado Region
Martha Román Rodriguez, Biologist, Sonora Institute for Environment and Sustainable Development (IMADES)
Kerry Schwartz, Project WET State Coordinator, University of Arizona Water Resources Research Center
Rosalinda Uribe Visoso, Project WET Mexico
Rita Vazquez, Director, Project WET Mexico
Joe Whittaker, Hydrologic Technician and Education Specialist, Bureau of Reclamation, Upper Colorado Region

Publications Coordinator
Savannah Barnes

Editorial Services
Liz Gans and Rick Newby *Zadig, LLC*

Designer
Geoffrey Wyatt *Wyatt Design*

Cover Design
Bryan Knaff *Gingerbee Creative*

Logo Designer
Ivy Davis *StudioID*

Illustrator
Claire Emery

Cartographer
Tony Thatcher *DTM Consulting*

Financial Management
Stephanie Ouren, Gro Lunde

Project WET International Staff
Dennis Nelson *Executive Director*
Linda Hveem *Assistant to the Executive Director*
John Etgen *Associate Director of Development and International Network Coordinator*
Savannah Barnes *Publications Director*
Elisabeth Howe *Co-coordinator, Discover a Watershed: The Colorado*
Justin Howe *Co-coordinator, Discover a Watershed: The Colorado*

Writing Workshop Participants and Reviewers

Arizona

Michael Collier

*Hilary Cummings, University of Arizona Maricopa County Cooperative Extension

*Jacob Fillion, Grand Canyon National Park

Lenore Grover-Bullington, Grand Canyon National Park

*Deborah Johnson, Maricopa County Regional Schools

*Robin Kropp, Arizona-Sonora Desert Museum

*Daniel Lopez, Tohono O'odham Community College

*†Craig Maier, Northern Arizona University

*Jim Manley, Northern Arizona University Center for Excellence in Education

*Annie Morrison, Scottsdale Public Schools

*†Christine Newell, Prescott College

Andre Potochnik, Grand Circle Field School

*Kerry Schwartz, Project WET State Coordinator, University of Arizona Water Resources Research Center

Crystal Thompson, Central Arizona Project

Baja California

*Catalina Lozano Álvarez, Colegio de Bachilleres de Baja California

*Martha Leticia Beltrán López, Colegio de Bachilleres de Baja California

Maria Concepción Díaz Sontona, Escuela Secundaria Mat. y Vesp. Numero 56

Gerardo Cesar Díaz Trujillo, Universidad Autónoma de Baja California

*Ana Rosa López Hernández, Museo Sol del Niño

Cesár Iván Manríquez Castero, Pro Esteros

Jesús Manuel Marquez, Escuela Secundaria Numero 56 T. UESP

*Laura Martinez Ríos del Rio, Pro Esteros Instituto del Medio Ambiente y el Desarrollo Sustentable del Estado de Sonora

Griselda Morales Sanders, Museo Sol del Niño

*Martin G. Morales Valdez, Colegio de Bachilleres de Baja California

Valentine Moreno Sánchez, Escuela Secundaria Numero 56

*Samuel Peraza Quintero, Escuelas de San Felipe

Jorge Ramírez, Universidad Autónoma de Baja California

*Arnulfo Rodríguez Jimenez, Universidad Autónoma de Baja California

*José Francisco Rodríguez Valdez, Secretaría de Educacion y Bienestar Social

Jesús Adolfo Román Calleros, Universidad Autónoma de Baja California

*†Mauricio Torres Santillan, Universidad Autónoma de Baja California

Carlos Yruretagoyena, Oceanólogo y Educador Ambiental

California

*†Larissa Conte, Stanford University

*Matthew Huffine, Lewis Center for Education Research

*†Karen Hyun, Stanford University

*Judy Maben, California Project WET State Coordinator, Water Education Foundation

*Julie Miller, Metropolitan Water District of Southern California

John Nyhoff, Lewis Center for Education Research

Helen Scantlin, Lewis Center for Education Research

*Nancy Wade, U.C. Davis Desert Research and Extension Center

Colorado

*Linda Baker, Southern Ute Indian Tribe

Maggie Cason, Fort Lewis College

*Margie Connolly, Crow Canyon Archaeological Center

*†Maria Goodin, Fort Lewis College

Ashley Hillmer, Escalante Middle School

Gregory Hobbs, Jr., Colorado State Supreme Court

*Pat Page, Bureau of Reclamation

David Robbins, Robbins and Hill PC

*Peter Roessman, Colorado River Water Conservation District

*Valerie Gates

*†Paul Viosca, Fort Lewis College

*Mike Wilde, Glenwood Springs High School

New Mexico

*Katie Gilbert, Kirtland Central High School

*Bryan Swain, Project WET State Coordinator, New Mexico State University Waste Management Education and Research Consortium

*Colleen Welch, New Mexico Department of Game and Fish

Kathy Willcutt, Los Alamos Public Schools

Nevada

*Phil Aurit, Bureau of Reclamation

Joe Kahl, Bureau of Reclamation

Tina Mullis, Bureau of Reclamation

*Valerie Robinson, Clark County Public Schools

*Hilarie Robison, Southern Nevada Water Authority and Nevada Public Education Foundation

Sonora

*Armando Aceves Pino, Escuela de Riíto

*Jorge Aceves Zavala, Escuela de Riíto

*Daniel Alemán Ruiz, Escuela El Golfo de Santa Clara

María de los Ángeles Preciado, Instituto Kino de San Luis A. C.

* José Campoy Favela, Director, Upper Gulf of California and Colorado River Delta Biosphere Reserve/CONANP–SEMARNAT

Mario Corral Duarte, Escuela Miguel Hidalgo y Costilla

Fernando Figueroa Dávila, Ejido Michoacán Riito

Lucila Gallardo E., Instituto Kino de San Luis A. C.

Carlos Ham Lugo, Escuela de Luis B. Sánchez

José Inés Mejía, Instituto del Medio Ambiente y el Desarrollo Sustentable del Estado de Sonora

María Jesús Martínez Contreras, Reserva de la Biosfera Alto Golfo de California y Delta del Río Colorado

Claudia Mena Johnston, Instituto Kino de San Luis A. C.

*†Carlota Monroy Lopez, Centro de Estudios Superiores del Estado de Sonora

*†Bárbara Peralta Zúñiga, Centro de Estudios Superiores del Estado de Sonora

Isaúl Rentaría Guerrero, Instituto Kino de San Luis A. C.

* Martha Román Rodriguez, Biologist, Sonora Institute for Environment and Sustainable Development (IMADES)

Utah

*David Dawson, Utah State Parks

*†Paul Formisano, Brigham Young University

*Andreé Walker, Project WET State Coordinator, Utah State University Water Quality Extension

*Joe Whittaker, Bureau of Reclamation

Wyoming

*Sue Perin, Project WET State Coordinator, Teton Science School

*Cathy Scheer, Lincoln Middle School

Project WET International Reviewers

Rab Cummings, Project WET U.S.A.

Gary Cook, Project WET U.S.A.

Jeanne Moe, Project Archaeology

Kristi Neptun, Project WET Montana State Coordinator

Christine Gmitro, Administrative Assistant, Project WET International

Mexican Federal Institutions

Javier Aparicio Mijares, Instituto Mexicano de Tecnología del Agua

Julio Navarro, Comisión Nacional del Agua

*Guadalupe Pardo Camarillo, Centro de Educación para el Desarrollo Sustentable, SEMARNAT

*Rosalinda Uribe Visoso, Instituto Mexicano de Tecnología del Agua and Project WET Mexico

*Rita Vazquez del Mercado, Director of Project WET Mexico, Instituto Mexicano de Tecnología del Agua and Project WET Mexico

Project WET International's Discover a Watershed Series

The Discover a Watershed Series

The Discover a Watershed Series is a broad watershed education program of Project WET International designed for anyone interested in learning about rivers and watersheds. Each project in the series contains the following three core components researched and developed specifically for an individual watershed: publications, education events, and support services.

Mission Statement

To reach children, young adults, teachers, parents, and communities through water education.

Goal

To facilitate and promote the awareness, appreciation, knowledge, stewardship, and understanding of watershed topics and issues from an unbiased perspective that crosses political, cultural, economic, and national boundaries.

Consistent with the core beliefs of Project WET International, the Discover a Watershed program is grounded in the following:

- Water is important for all water users (e.g., energy production, farming and ranching, fish and wildlife, manufacturing, cultural use, recreation, and rural and urban communities).
- Wise water management is crucial for providing tomorrow's children social and economic stability in a healthy environment.
- Awareness of, and respect for, water resources can encourage a personal, lifelong commitment to responsible and positive community participation.

Audience

The Discover a Watershed Series is for anyone interested in learning and teaching about the watershed in which they live:

- Upper elementary through secondary school teachers.
- University professors.
- Local, state, national, and international watershed managers.
- Nature center, zoo, aquaria, park, and museum educators.
- Community groups, NGOs, and conferences.
- Citizens.

Our Approach

The Discover a Watershed Series is a comprehensive program before, during, and after the publication of our materials. We are committed to the following:

- Building connections throughout watersheds.
- Involving diverse stakeholders within the watershed throughout the process from research and writing to training and implementation.
- Connecting educators with water resources management agencies and leaders.
- Investigating watersheds irrespective of political boundaries.
- Linking educators and students within and among watersheds.

Publications

Project WET International is an award-winning educational publisher. In cooperation with visionary sponsors, education leaders, and water managers, the Discover a Watershed Series was launched in 1996. It includes publications on the Everglades, Lake Patzquaro, the Rio Grande/Rio Bravo, the Missouri, and the Colorado. Other watersheds are now under consideration.

The Watershed Manager Educators Guide
19 activities / 200 pages / maps / photos / illustrations / glossary / resources / full-color wall map

This adaptable guide provides an introduction to watersheds for educators of middle school through adult students. Content includes defining and profiling watersheds, investigating basic water principles, characterizing water users, identifying and analyzing issues, and exploring management strategies. Science-based, multidisciplinary, classroom-ready activities are included that can be tailored to any watershed—large or small, local or international. Learners use critical thinking skills to deliberate real world watershed management challenges and opportunities. A full-color wall map of selected rivers and watersheds of North America is included with the guide and also sold separately.

At a minimum, each watershed project has two core publications:

Discover a Watershed KIDs (Kids in Discovery Series)
These colorful sixteen-page activity booklets are written and illustrated for readers ages eight through twelve. These informative, inexpensive booklets explore specific watersheds through creative and hands-on investigations, demonstrations, science experiments, educational games, and stories. They make excellent handouts to complement school curriculums and the *Educators Guide*, or they can stand alone as a fun introduction to a watershed.

Discover a Watershed: Educators Guide
300–400 pages / photos / illustrations / charts / maps / graphs / appendices / index / glossary / resources

Each guide contains activities and reference material covering hydrology, geology, cultural traditions, plant and animal communities, water management systems, basin economy, priority issues, and future scenarios. Special features include a "String of Pearls" and "One River,

Many Voices" and extensive photos, illustrations, and maps. Selected projects also have a full-color wall map of the basin included. All activities are cross-referenced to National Science Standards for middle school through adult students. Further research into the topics is encouraged via Web site lists. Each science-based, multidisciplinary activity brings the particular watershed to life through hands-on projects that make watershed education engaging and accessible.

Project WET International

In addition to active networks in every state of the United States, Project WET International materials are used in American Samoa, Argentina, Cameroon, Canada, Dominican Republic, Japan, Mexico, Nigeria, N. Marianas Islands, Palau, Philippines, Togo, Uganda, and Ukraine. An additional twenty-three countries are under consideration. Project WET International has official partnerships with UNESCO CATHALAC (Caribbean and Latin America) and the U.S. Peace Corps (Global). It has developed professional partnerships with RAMSAR: Global Convention on Wetlands, International Water Resources Association (World Water Congress), World Water Council (World Water Forum), and UNESCO-IHE (United Nations "Water Family" Meeting).

Project WET International's motto is "No Boundaries in Water Education." Its mission is to reach children, parents, educators, and communities of the world with water education. Project WET trains facilitators and educators through six-hour to three-day workshops and seminars. Educators can opt for the minimum introduction to using the guide, or choose advanced study into wetlands, ground water, water conservation, water monitoring, and other topics of local and national interest. To find out more, visit www.projectwet.org.

Maps

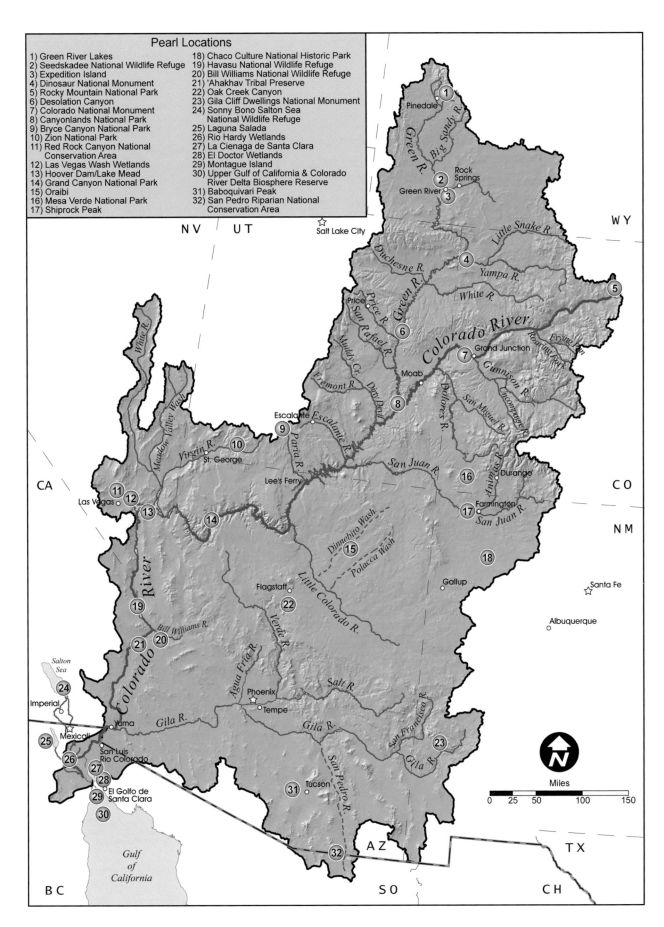

Pearl Locations

1) Green River Lakes
2) Seedskadee National Wildlife Refuge
3) Expedition Island
4) Dinosaur National Monument
5) Rocky Mountain National Park
6) Desolation Canyon
7) Colorado National Monument
8) Canyonlands National Park
9) Bryce Canyon National Park
10) Zion National Park
11) Red Rock Canyon National Conservation Area
12) Las Vegas Wash Wetlands
13) Hoover Dam/Lake Mead
14) Grand Canyon National Park
15) Oraibi
16) Mesa Verde National Park
17) Shiprock Peak
18) Chaco Culture National Historic Park
19) Havasu National Wildlife Refuge
20) Bill Williams National Wildlife Refuge
21) 'Ahakhav Tribal Preserve
22) Oak Creek Canyon
23) Gila Cliff Dwellings National Monument
24) Sonny Bono Salton Sea National Wildlife Refuge
25) Laguna Salada
26) Rio Hardy Wetlands
27) La Cienaga de Santa Clara
28) El Doctor Wetlands
29) Montague Island
30) Upper Gulf of California & Colorado River Delta Biosphere Reserve
31) Baboquivari Peak
32) San Pedro Riparian National Conservation Area

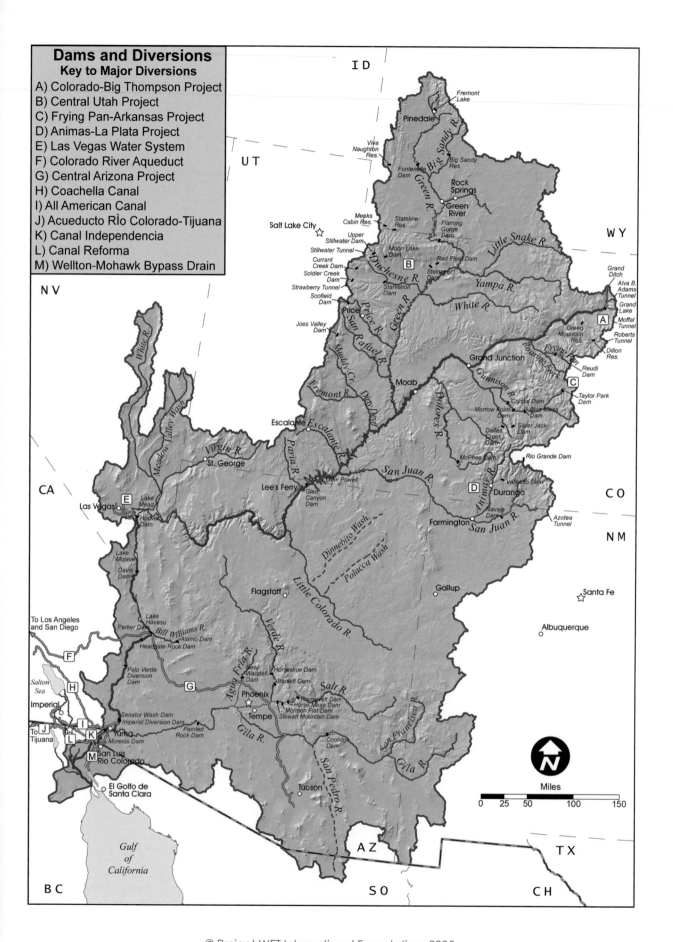

Dams and Diversions
Key to Major Diversions

A) Colorado-Big Thompson Project
B) Central Utah Project
C) Frying Pan-Arkansas Project
D) Animas-La Plata Project
E) Las Vegas Water System
F) Colorado River Aqueduct
G) Central Arizona Project
H) Coachella Canal
I) All American Canal
J) Acueducto Rìo Colorado-Tijuana
K) Canal Independencia
L) Canal Reforma
M) Wellton-Mohawk Bypass Drain

Eight Largest Reservoirs in the Colorado Watershed			
Reservoir	State	Basin	Active Capacity (million acre-feet)
Lake Mead	AZ, NV	Lower	25.9
Lake Powell	AZ,UT	Upper	24.3
Flaming Gorge	WY	Upper	3.75
Mohave	AZ, NV	Lower	1.81
Navajo	NM	Upper	1.7
Strawberry	UT	Upper	1.1
Blue Mesa	CO	Upper	.83
Havasu	AZ, CA	Lower	.62

(Data from: Pontius, 1997)

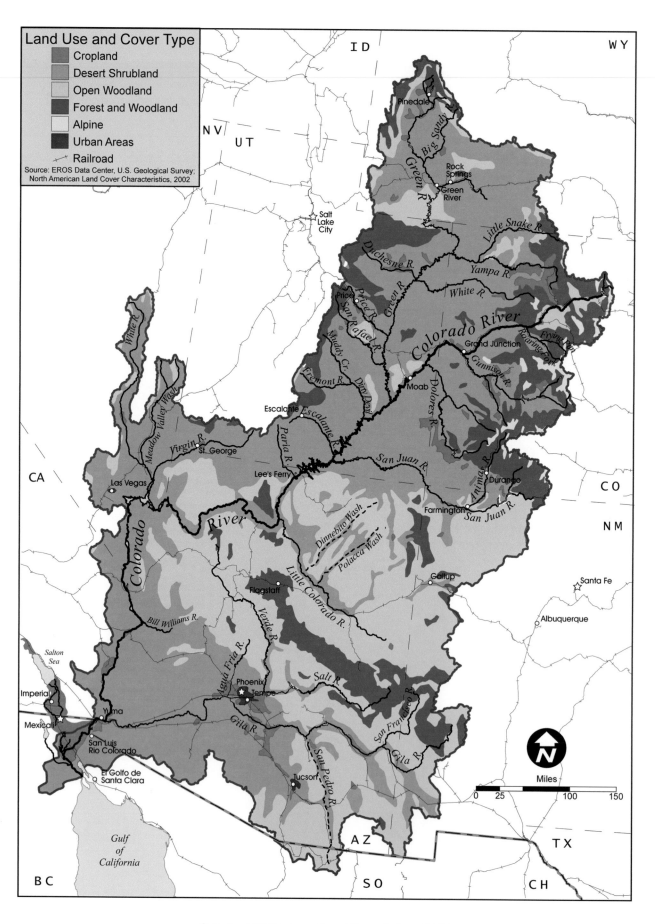

Land Use and Cover Type

- Cropland
- Desert Shrubland
- Open Woodland
- Forest and Woodland
- Alpine
- Urban Areas
- Railroad

Source: EROS Data Center, U.S. Geological Survey;
North American Land Cover Characteristics, 2002

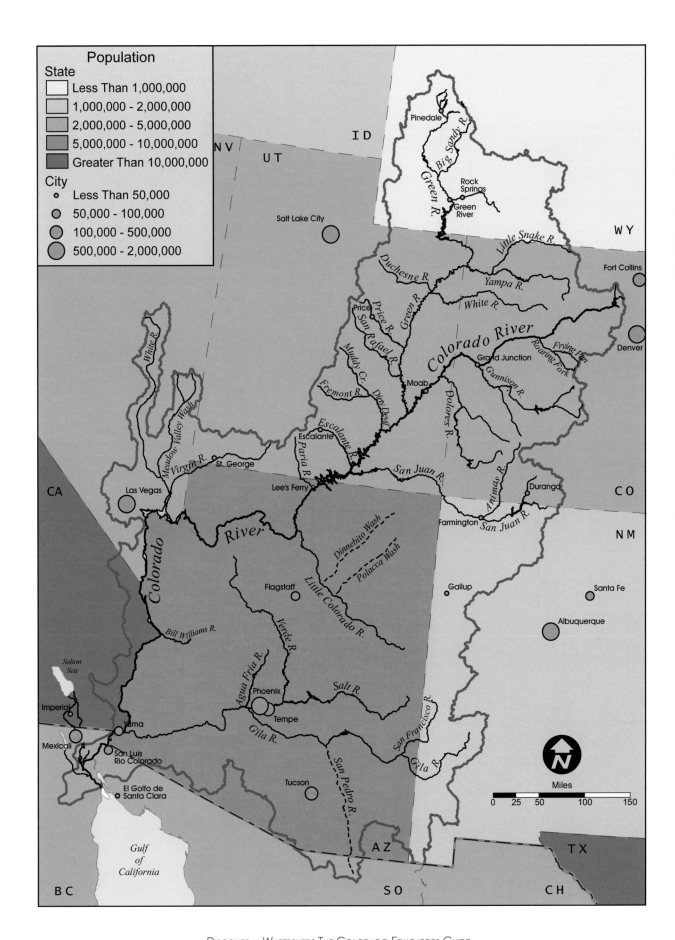

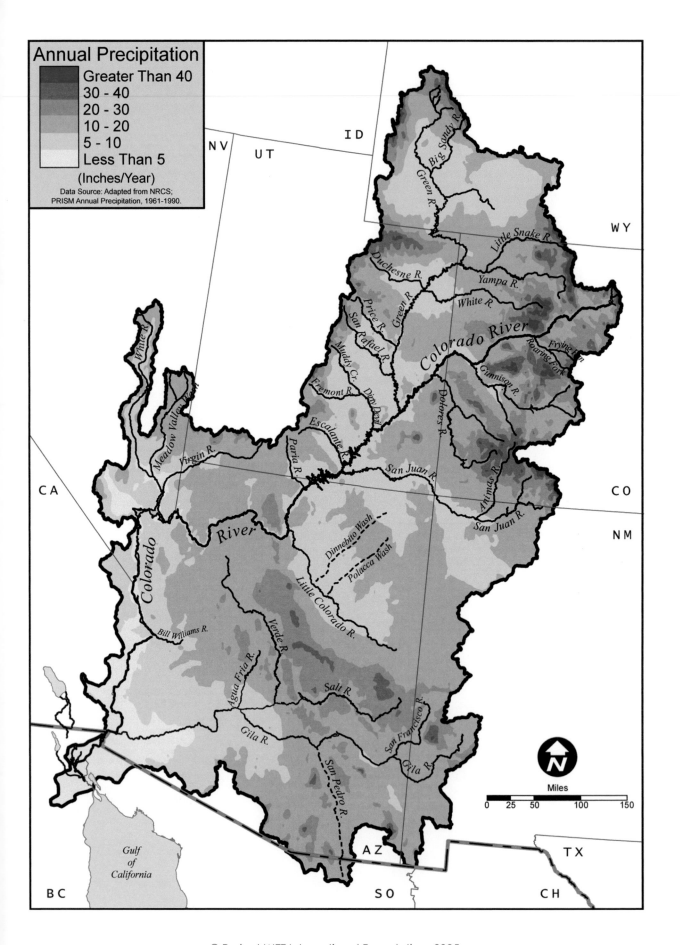

Annual Precipitation

Greater Than 40
30 - 40
20 - 30
10 - 20
5 - 10
Less Than 5
(Inches/Year)

Data Source: Adapted from NRCS;
PRISM Annual Precipitation, 1961-1990.

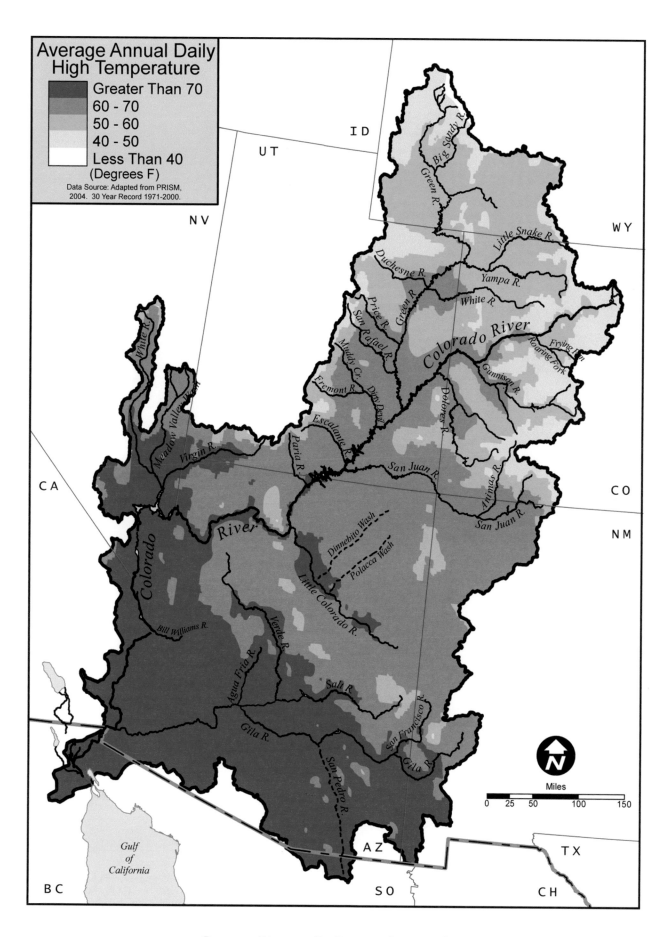

Average Annual Daily High Temperature

Greater Than 70
60 - 70
50 - 60
40 - 50
Less Than 40
(Degrees F)

Data Source: Adapted from PRISM, 2004. 30 Year Record 1971-2000.

I D

U T

N V

W Y

White R.

Big Sandy R.

Green R.

Little Snake R.

Duchesne R.

Yampa R.

Price R.

Green R.

White R.

Colorado River

San Rafael R.

Frying Pan

Muddy Cr.

Roaring Fork

Fremont R.

Dirty Devil

Gunnison R.

Escalante R.

Dolores R.

Meadow Valley Wash

Paria R.

San Juan R.

Animas R.

C A

Virgin R.

San Juan R.

C O

N M

River

Dinnebito Wash

Polacca Wash

Colorado

Little Colorado R.

Bill Williams R.

Verde R.

Agua Fria R.

Salt R.

San Francisco R.

Gila R.

Gila R.

San Pedro R.

N

Miles
0   25   50   100   150

Gulf of California

B C

A Z

S O

T X

C H

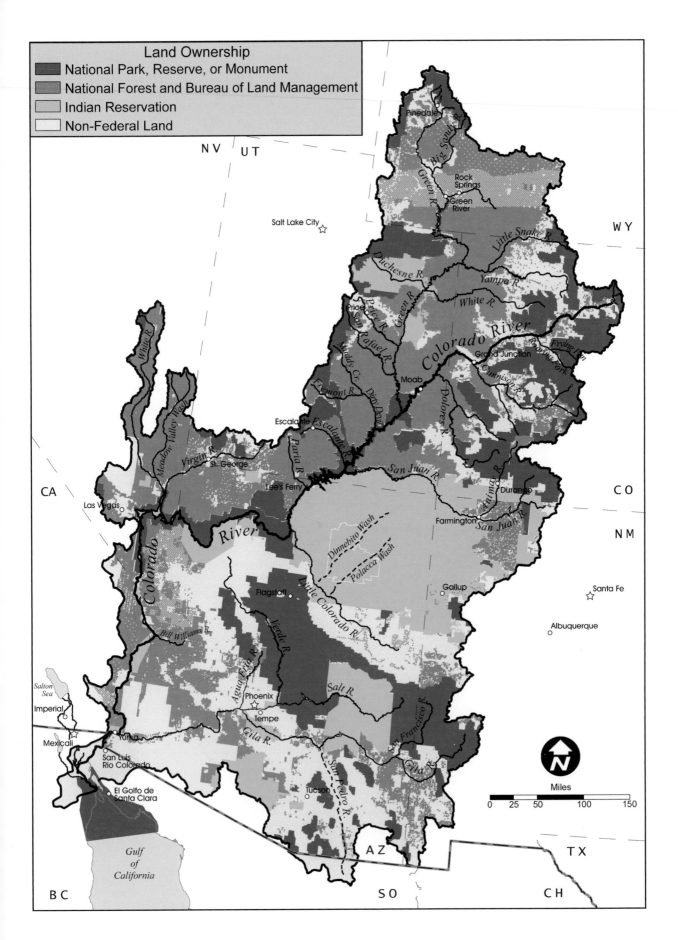

Land Ownership
- National Park, Reserve, or Monument
- National Forest and Bureau of Land Management
- Indian Reservation
- Non-Federal Land

NV   UT

Pinedale

Big Sandy R.

Green R.

Rock Springs

Green River

WY

Salt Lake City

Little Snake R.

Duchesne R.

Yampa R.

White R.

Price

San Rafael R.

Green R.

Colorado River

Grand Junction

Roaring Fork

Frying Pan

Moab

Gunnison R.

White R.

Muddy Cr.

Dirty Devil

Fremont R.

Dolores R.

Escalante

Escalante R.

Paria R.

San Juan R.

Lee's Ferry

Animas R.

Durango

CO

Meadow Valley Wash

Virgin R.

St. George

Las Vegas

Farmington

San Juan R.

NM

CA

Colorado   River

Dinnebito Wash

Polacca Wash

Gallup

Santa Fe

Flagstaff

Little Colorado R.

Albuquerque

Bill Williams R.

Verde R.

Agua Fria R.

Salt R.

Phoenix

Tempe

San Francisco R.

Salton Sea

Imperial

Gila R.

Gila R.

Mexicali

Yuma

San Luis Rio Colorado

San Pedro R.

El Golfo de Santa Clara

Tucson

Miles
0   25   50   100   150

AZ

TX

BC

Gulf of California

SO

CH

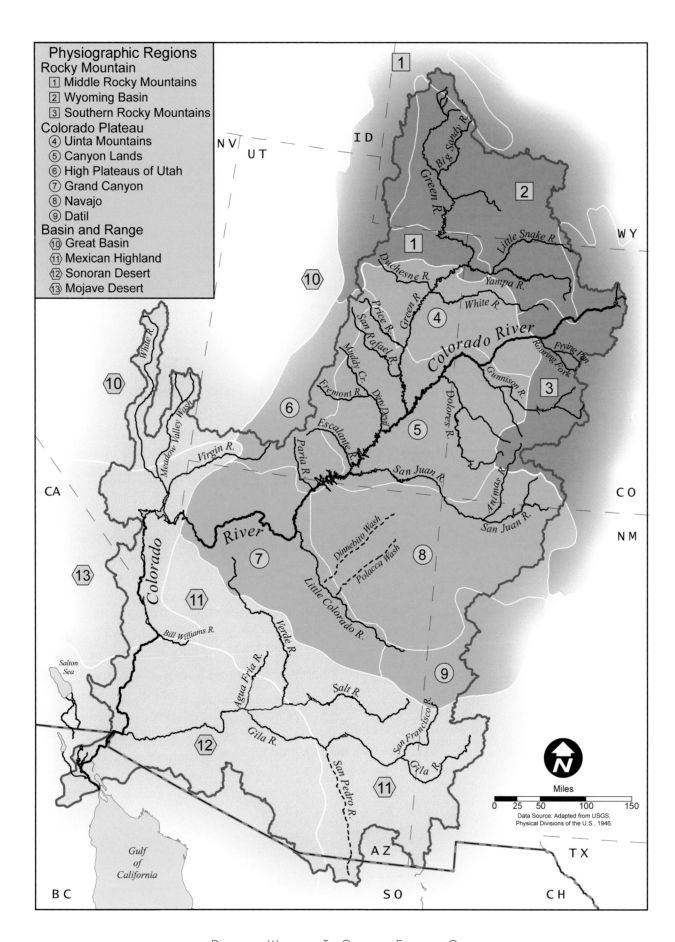

Physiographic Regions

Rocky Mountain
1. Middle Rocky Mountains
2. Wyoming Basin
3. Southern Rocky Mountains

Colorado Plateau
4. Uinta Mountains
5. Canyon Lands
6. High Plateaus of Utah
7. Grand Canyon
8. Navajo
9. Datil

Basin and Range
10. Great Basin
11. Mexican Highland
12. Sonoran Desert
13. Mojave Desert

Miles
0   25   50   100   150

Data Source: Adapted from USGS;
Physical Divisions of the U.S., 1946.

Timeline of Human History in the Colorado River Watershed

23,000–11,000 years before present (B.P.) Possible human arrival in the watershed.

2,500 B.P. Humans begin growing corn in the watershed.

1,000 B.P. Hohokam and Ancestral Puebloan Indians develop elaborate water distribution systems.

A.D.

1100 Hopi village of Oraibi is established, now thought to be the oldest continuously occupied settlement in the United States.

1539 Spanish explorer Francisco de Ulloa sails to the mouth of the Colorado River.

1540 Francisco Vásquez de Coronado travels through the watershed to present-day Zuni Pueblo, seeking the legendary Seven Cities of Cibola. This begins the Spanish colonial period, which lasts until 1821.

1690 Missionary Father Eusebio Francisco Kino observes vast acreages of irrigated native land along the Santa Cruz and Gila Rivers.

1821 Mexico gains independence from Spain.

1847 Mormons arrive in Utah and begin cultivating farmland.

1848 Mexico and the United States sign the Treaty of Guadalupe Hidalgo, ending the Mexican-American War and ceding Mexican territory to the United States.

1854 Gadsden Purchase acquires 29,640 square miles of Mexican land south of the Gila River for the United States.

1869 John Wesley Powell begins exploration of the Colorado and Green Rivers.

1902 U.S. Reclamation Service (now Bureau of Reclamation) is established.

1908 U.S. Supreme Court rules in favor of American Indian tribes to create the Winters Doctrine, which sets aside water for reservations and other federally reserved lands.

1919 Grand Canyon National Park is established.

1921 The Grand River, which begins in Rocky Mountain National Park and joins the Green River to form the Colorado River, is renamed "The Colorado."

1922 Colorado River Compact is negotiated between seven U.S. basin states.

1925 All U.S. states except Arizona sign compact.

1935 Construction of Hoover Dam is completed.

1944 The U.S.–Mexico Water Treaty is ratified, allocating 1.5 million acre-feet per year to Mexico.

1963 Glen Canyon Dam is completed.

1964 U.S. Supreme Court Decree in *Arizona v. California,* formalizes allocation between Lower Basin states and authorizes the construction of the Central Arizona Project.

1969 Endangered Species Act is passed.

1973 Minute 242 is added to the 1944 Treaty, regulating salinity of water delivered to Mexico.

1993 Central Arizona Project (CAP) is completed.

1993 Upper Gulf of California and Colorado River Delta Biosphere Reserve is created to protect 2 million acres of habitat.

2000 Minute 306 is added to the 1944 Treaty, providing a conceptual framework for managing Colorado River Delta ecosystems.

2003 The Quantification Settlement Agreement (QSA) is signed, paving the way for reducing California's water use to its allocated 4.4 million acre-feet.

Prologue

The Colorado River and its tributaries carry the water that makes life in the arid southwestern United States and northwestern Mexico possible. These rivers are essential to the functioning of diverse ecosystems, communities, and economies throughout a vast region.

About 244,000 square miles are drained by the Colorado River. This area is referred to as the Colorado River Watershed (or basin). It stretches from the mountains of Colorado and Wyoming south and west through the American states of Utah, New Mexico, Arizona, Nevada, and California. In Mexico, it encompasses parts of Sonora and Baja California.

The Colorado River travels 1,450 miles from headwaters to delta, flowing through a variety of ecosystems on its way. In its mountainous headwaters, snowy tundra and pine-covered slopes are habitat for elk, bear, beaver, and other animals. The river's middle section winds along high plateaus and through deep gorges, including the Grand Canyon in northern Arizona. Further south, the river flows through the Mojave and Sonoran Deserts before reaching its mouth at the Gulf of California in Mexico.

About 85 percent of the Colorado's water originates in the mountains of Colorado, yet communities and ecosystems as far south as Mexico rely on its flow. More than 25 million people in Denver, Phoenix, Las Vegas, Los Angeles, Tijuana, and other cities use its water, as do people in rural areas. The river irrigates 1.8 million acres of land, producing 15 percent of U.S. crops; over 80 percent of the winter vegetables eaten in the United States are grown with its water. In most years, its entire flow is stored in reservoirs or consumed and does not reach the Gulf of California.

Every drop of the river has been allocated, and

The Colorado's modern notoriety . . . stems not only from its wild rapids and plunging canyons but from the fact that it is the most legislated, most debated, and most litigated river in the entire world. It also has more people, more industry, and a more significant economy dependent on it than any comparable river in the world.

Marc Reisner, *Cadillac Desert*

resource managers face the challenge of balancing a multitude of sometimes-conflicting demands for its water. As human populations grow, this becomes increasingly difficult.

The watershed's diversity of ecosystems, climates, communities, cultures, and economies contributes to its compelling character. Yet throughout the human history of the watershed, this complexity has led to conflict as different people's values and needs interact. From these interactions, the Law of the River (a dynamic body of laws and policies governing how the river is managed) has developed. It continues to grow as needs and values shift.

At the heart of these laws and policies is a river whose natural beauty inspires human achievement in art, literature, architecture, and culture. The landscapes and ecosystems it creates are beyond price. These fundamental, intrinsic values can connect us—education has the power to communicate this.

The goal of *Discover a Watershed: The Colorado* is to foster a deeper understanding of how this watershed connects individuals and communities irrespective of political boundaries. Through creative, educational activities, this guide seeks to communicate what the watershed is, whom it affects, and how it is impacted by human activities. It seeks to inspire teachers and students to connect to their watershed, use its water wisely, and work to develop sustainable water management solutions. With science-based activities that cross disciplines, students will gain a heightened understanding of the Colorado River Watershed and its management. It is our hope that they will be encouraged to make a positive difference through personal actions and future leadership.

This educators guide is a core element of the

Discover a Watershed: The Colorado education program. It was developed using a collaborative writing process that involved peer-nominated educators and resource managers from Mexico, the United States, and several American Indian tribes. Project WET held a curriculum development workshop to design teaching methods and identify key issues to be discussed. This approach has helped make the guide relevant to geographically and culturally diverse parts of the watershed.

In order to build a stronger connection to the watershed and to facilitate research for the guide, Project WET organized a learning expedition. The expedition led a group of Mexican and American university students on a six-week journey through the basin. On their way from headwaters to delta, the team met with water users and managers to

Justin Howe

Expedition team members at the end of their six-week trip from the headwaters to the delta of the Colorado River. Back row: Craig Maier, Larissa Conte, Justin Howe, Lissa Howe, Carlota Monroy, Maria Goodin, Bárbara Peralta. Front row: Paul Viosca, Paul Formisano, Mauricio Torres Santillan, Chrissy Jaworsky, Karen Hyun, Chris Newell.

develop a broad understanding of the issues associated with this watershed. They experienced ice-cold streams at the headwaters and swam in warm waters of the Gulf of California. To be able to simultaneously hold in their minds these contrasts was the essence of this educational journey.

The results of the expedition exceeded expectations. For the expedition's members, listening to stories of the watershed's people; exploring its mountains, canyons, and deserts; and discussing its management challenges created a new depth of connection to the watershed. Deeply moved by their experiences, the expedition's members developed a sense of stewardship for this important resource. Not only did the expedition strengthen their connections to the river, but also to communities with whom they interacted during the journey.

In the following pages, we attempt to communicate the impact of the expedition experience through a narrative describing our journey through the watershed (Part I). We also offer (in Part II) multidisciplinary lesson plans designed to help educators teach about the watershed and present issues relating to managing and protecting the watershed. We begin this story at the river's end, where the results of complex management decisions and competing water uses from the entire watershed are distilled. This perspective, we hope, will provide context for the knowledge we gained during our watershed journey.

To develop a more comprehensive portrait of the watershed, we have included a collection of contemporary and historic perspectives from water managers, farmers, teachers, students, scientists, and others. These "River Voices" communicate the diverse ways in which people relate to and rely on the Colorado River and its tributaries. The quotations include writing from well-known authors and historic figures as well as from people who were inspired to write specifically for this publication. These River Voices, and more, can be found in a more complete form in the activity, "One River, Many Voices of the Colorado Basin" (page 350), along with biographical information about the authors.

In addition to River Voices, we present specific information about some of the special places—the "Pearls"—of the watershed. These places were identified by people who feel a strong connection with the watershed. Like a cord binding a string of pearls, the Colorado River and its tributaries are the link between these places and perspectives. What we offer here is only a beginning. Each person has his or her own River Voice and Pearl based on his or her own experience. They may be as big as the Grand Canyon or small as a backyard ditch—what makes them special are their connections to our hearts, minds, history, and cultures.

Part I

A Journey Through the Colorado River Watershed

Justin Howe

Beginning at the River's End: Context for the Watershed Journey

We shall not cease from exploration
And the end of all our exploring
Will be to arrive where we started
And know the place for the first time.

T. S. Eliot, *Four Quartets*

Upper Gulf of California and Colorado River Delta Biosphere Reserve, Sonora and Baja California

- The Mexican government created this reserve in 1993 to protect marine and terrestrial environments in the delta and upper Gulf of California.
- It protects critical habitat for birds and fish.
- It is one of the most important marine fisheries for Mexico.
- Species found here include Yuma clapper rails, California brown pelicans, totoaba, gulf corvina, vaquita marina, and several species of clam.
- Because of dams and diversions built on the Colorado River, little fresh water reaches this once verdant landscape. Today, most water in the area comes from tidal shifts in the Gulf of California.

A fishing net in El Golfo de Santa Clara, Sonora, is poised to catch fish the next time the tide comes in.

Watersheds are areas of land that drain water to one place, but they are much more than that. They are home to humans, plants, and animals that live together, supported by water from streams and rivers, snow and rain, springs and aquifers. Water that falls as rain or snow in the headwaters may flow to support life for users in the delta. In this sense, residents of a watershed are bound together, irrespective of political and cultural boundaries. Actions taken upstream have impacts that may be felt downstream. For this reason, we begin the story of our expedition through the Colorado River Watershed at its delta, where the effects of a multitude of uses and management decisions can be seen; this perspective will provide context for the rest of the journey.

Justin Howe

A small aluminum boat seems out of place in the dry delta.

Upper Gulf of California, Baja California and Sonora

Holding on tight in the back of a rusty pickup, we bounce across sandy beaches near the Mexican fishing community of El Golfo de Santa Clara, on the northeastern coast of the Gulf of California. Behind us drags a twenty-four-foot fishing boat, known as a *panga*. Its outboard motor balances precariously on the stern, ready to power us to the mouth of the Colorado River.

We are here to prepare for a six-week expedition that will take a group of American and Mexican college students from the Colorado River's headwaters to its delta. José Campoy, director of the Upper Gulf of California and Colorado River Delta Biosphere Reserve, has joined us today to discuss life at the end of one of the hardest-working rivers in the world.

The delta is a place of extremes, and temperatures can range from near freezing to 130 degrees F. Travelers on the dusty roads may drive for hours without seeing another person, and water from the Gulf of California periodically floods the region as tides rise and fall more than twenty feet in a single day. The Colorado River Delta seems an impossible

place for life to thrive, yet the sky is full of pelicans and gulls, and we can see several fishing boats already on the water.

We drive on the beach for a quarter mile before arriving at the edge of the Gulf of California (also known as the Sea of Cortez). The *panga* slides into the water where gentle waves lift it from the sand, then deposit it back on the earth. The tide is coming in with remarkable speed. In the few minutes it takes to load the boat, water creeps past our knees.

With a quick pull of the starter cord, the outboard springs to life. Soon we are bouncing across the shallow gulf waves. Bottle-nosed dolphins swim nearby and surface occasionally to watch our progress. They are fishing for gulf corvina and other fish that live in these waters. Only thirty miles to the south, shrimp boats troll the gulf.

José Campoy points to a group of swimming gulls, and we notice that the clear water has become brown and sediment-filled. So much silt is suspended that the water looks like *café con leche* (coffee with milk). The sediment has washed from

In most years, the Colorado River does not reach the Gulf of California, but in 1996, above-average precipitation helped the river to flow its entire length, as shown in this photo of Montague Island at the river's mouth.

Michael Collier

down the river.

José explains that, during high tide, seawater in the river channel may extend fifty miles into the heart of the delta. Before dams and diversions altered the flow of the Colorado River, steamboats traveled here, powering up the river as far as Black Canyon, just below where Hoover Dam stands today.

Even without fresh water flowing in the Colorado, the river's power can be felt. We are surrounded by its massive delta, which encompasses several million acres in southeastern California, southwestern Arizona, northeastern Baja California, and northwestern Sonora. These barren salt flats that once held the world's largest desert wetland ecosystem are a footprint that reminds us of what the river is capable of. Slowly, we turn back south, imagining what this wetland and estuary looked like one hundred years ago.

It is October. The next time we visit this place, hot July sunshine will greet us at the end of a six-week expedition through the Colorado River Watershed (see Prologue).

the delta where the Colorado River had deposited it in layers thousands of feet deep. Now that the river rarely reaches the gulf, new sediment is no longer being deposited and tidal action is eroding and redistributing the old deposits.

After an hour, we reach Montague Island, which marks the mouth of the Colorado River. Our captain motors to the northernmost point, and for the first time we see the main river channel. A green river of salt grass fills the channel, swaying in the waves and wind. The water here is seawater, easing northward with the tide, unopposed by fresh water flowing

© Claire Emery and Project WET International

The vaquita marina is endemic to the Upper Gulf of California and is the most rare marine mammal in the world—fewer than six hundred individuals make up the population. An estimated forty to sixty are killed in fishing nets each year (see www.vaquitamarina.org for more information).

Rocky Mountain National Park, Colorado

Look out on the western side of the Great Divide from the heart of Rocky Mountain National Park. You're at the top of the watershed destined for the Sea of Cortez. All that lies before you, all you can hope for, is a chance to serve, to be of use, to share tumbling through the sublime. This is what it means to be the Colorado River.

Gregory Hobbs, Colorado Supreme Court Justice

Like so many other things in the Colorado River Watershed, even the location of the headwaters can be debated. The river named the Colorado finds its headwaters within Rocky Mountain National Park, near Grand Lake, Colorado. However, the point in the watershed that is furthest from the Gulf of California is on the Green River, near Pinedale, Wyoming. Talk to locals in Grand Lake or Pinedale, and they will insist that theirs is the true headwaters of the Colorado River. Our expedition will focus on both places, and for this reason it can be said to have two beginnings—one at the headwaters of each river.

Our first beginning is in Rocky Mountain

The Never Summer Mountains in Rocky Mountain National Park gather snowmelt that becomes the headwaters of the Colorado River.

National Park Service

Headwaters: Rocky Mountain National Park

It's late June and at the Continental Divide in Rocky Mountain National Park, the snow pack is higher than my head. It's been months since I last saw snow on the San Francisco Peaks in Flagstaff—and none of the Mexican participants have ever seen snow before.

As we hike the high, alpine Poudre Pass trail I am mindful of what a rare opportunity I have to step outside the daily routine of my work—to temporarily suspend my role as an environmental advocate on the Colorado Plateau and to simply be a person, adventurous and inquisitive, traveling the length of the river listening closely to the stories of the land, of the water, and of the people.

My intention for the trip is to be simply and fully present where I am at each moment, in each place. Perhaps the greatest gift of this journey is the ability to listen without having to respond. To listen to and attempt to understand so many different perspectives on the same place. How often are we afforded the honor of simply listening to another's story?

Christine Newell participated in the 2003 Expedition. She is a student in the teacher education program at Prescott College and lives in Flagstaff, Arizona.

Justin Howe

Justin Howe

National Park, at the headwaters of the named Colorado River. June 16 finds us high in the Never Summer Mountains where icy snowmelt drips from drifts and depressions, combining into rivulets that gather to form the beginning of the Colorado River. Below, gray cliffs and scree fields give way to slopes covered in ponderosa pine and then to verdant valleys of grass, sedge, and willow. As we descend along the headwaters, we hike through conifer forests, seeing signs of deer, elk, marmots, and pika. Our conversation is filled with talk of treaties, environmental ethics, water management, and conservation.

Rounding a corner on the Colorado River Trail, there is a sign reading, "Trail Closed for Repairs." We are not surprised. Jim Capps, ranger and interpreter for Rocky Mountain National Park, had informed us that morning that a section of the Grand Ditch had recently overflowed, washing out the trail and uprooting acres of trees.

Rocky Mountain National Park, Colorado

- The headwaters of the Colorado River begin here, in the Never Summer Mountains.
- During winter, snowpack is often more than twenty feet deep.
- The Grand Ditch is the first diversion from the Colorado River.
- The highest point in the watershed, 14,259 feet above sea level, can be found here.

Justin Howe

Bighorn sheep (upper left), mule deer (lower right), pikas, and other wildlife depend on habitats in Rocky Mountain National Park.

This is the lesson I learn today: take a deep breath, enjoy the ride, slow down, speed up, cherish the journey. The destination will take care of itself. Like the river, I have little knowledge of what will lie around the next bend, but the certainty of moving downstream is a constant reminder that the journey has begun!

Mike Wilde, Glenwood Springs, Colorado,
high school science teacher

The Grand Ditch is the first diversion from the Colorado River. Constructed at high elevation, above tree line, the ditch collects snowmelt before it reaches the Colorado and diverts it over a pass in the Continental Divide. Water bound for the Gulf of California is instead diverted into the watershed of the Cache La Poudre River, destined eventually for the Gulf of Mexico. This water will be used in farms and communities on Colorado's eastern slope (see page 277, "Plumbing the Colorado").

On the river's edge we measure water temperature: 42 degrees F; just five degrees cooler than the water we'll swim in through the Grand Canyon, but nearly 40 degrees colder than the river when it ends in Mexico, almost 1,500 miles downstream.

Justin Howe

Expedition member Maria Goodin takes a photograph of wetlands at the headwaters.

I always refer to the Law of the River as a fabric and that you're weaving additional portions. Those weaving tools . . . can be or have been compacts, laws, contracts, court decrees, agreements, treaties, administrative actions, and regulations.

Dennis Underwood, Vice President, Colorado River Issues, Metropolitan Water District of Southern California

Negotiators sign the 1922 Colorado River Compact at Bishop's Lodge in Santa Fe, New Mexico.

David Robbins, a water lawyer from Denver, talks to our group about American water law and the "Law of the River." The Law of the River is a framework that has evolved over time in order to manage the multitude of demands on the Colorado River. It is the body of laws, compacts, treaties, court decisions, policies, and regulations dealing with the operation and management of the river.

With his well-kept handlebar mustache and polished cowboy boots, David Robbins looks like he would be equally comfortable riding the range and in a big city courtroom. His knowledge of water law is deep, and he first explains to us the principles upon which water law in the western United States is based: prior appropriation and beneficial use (see page 287, "First Come, First Served"). He then describes the historic context and circumstances that led to the signing of the Colorado River Compact among U.S. basin states in 1922.

During the western expansion of the United States and into the early 1900s, growing populations in the southwestern states (especially California) demanded ever-greater amounts of water. The Colorado River, as the single largest river in this desert region, was an obvious source. Canals, dams, and diversions were built to deliver water to cities and irrigation districts. As the number of diversions increased, flow in the Colorado decreased and states, cities, and individuals sought to guarantee rights to its water.

In November 1922, the Colorado River Compact created a legal division that divided the U.S. portion of the Colorado River into Upper and Lower Basins. This helped ensure that, regardless of which "basin" (Upper or Lower) grew fastest, the other would still be guaranteed its share of river water. The dividing line was established at Lee's Ferry, Arizona, just above the Grand Canyon (see page 244, "Sharing the Shed").

We live in a Colorado transformed. Once labeled the "Great American Desert," Colorado now abounds with wetlands, riparian areas, meadows, and farms. We have streams that historically ran dry in summer and fall that now sustain valuable fisheries year-round. There is one thing that has made this transformation possible—water storage.

Greg Walcher, former Director of the Colorado Department of Natural Resources

The Colorado River Aqueduct carries water out of the Colorado's watershed to coastal cities from Los Angeles to San Diego.

Green River Lakes, Wyoming

- Located in the Bridger-Teton National Forest and the Bridger Wilderness.
- Glacial meltwater—from the headwaters of the Green River—carries fine sediment that makes the lakes appear turquoise.
- The lakes are just a few miles from Knapsack Col, the point in the Colorado River Watershed that is farthest from the Gulf of California.
- Moose, mountain lion, wolves, grizzly bear, black bear, and other wildlife inhabit the forests of the Wind River Mountains.

Based on available stream-flow data, negotiators of the compact estimated that the average annual flow of the Colorado River was 17 million acre-feet per year. Fifteen million acre-feet were divided evenly between the Upper Basin (Colorado, Wyoming, Utah, and New Mexico) and the Lower Basin (Arizona, Nevada, and California). The remaining 2 million acre-feet were left unallocated for eventual water settlements with Mexico and American Indian tribes.

Although it had been working to formalize rights to Colorado River water since the end of the Mexican–American War (in 1848), Mexico was not included in the 1922 Compact negotiations. The Colorado is an important source of fresh water for the states of Baja California and Sonora, and Mexico feared that the United States would use all of the river's water before it reached the border (see page 244, "Sharing the Shed").

The completion of Hoover Dam in 1935 increased Mexico's concern, as the structure gave

The Colorado River basin: a place where two countries and many cultures have met, clashed, and intermingled, giving rise to an interdependent and transboundary civilization. A civilization so closely linked to a precious and scarce resource: water. A resource that has been debated upon and fought over, and that has fueled the development of a desert, transforming it from an inhospitable territory into a prosperous land.

A resource that has been used and abused, exploited and overexploited, almost to its last drop; jeopardizing the sustainability of the basin and of the ecosystems that depend on the supply of the liquid in sufficient quantity and quality. Amongst those, most notably, the ecosystems located at the river's delta and beyond it, at the Sea of Cortez (Gulf of California).

The river system is the sustenance of life in the basin and therefore, metaphorically, constitutes its bloodstream. Accordingly, it is almost poetic that the river conveys water with a reddish color, given by the minerals contained in the sediment that it transports, hence the name "Colorado," which means red in Spanish.

Only a vision based on public awareness and common will, geared towards the conservation, preservation, and sharing of water and other natural resources related to it, may protect the blood of this arid but living land. Educators will play a critical role in instilling and spreading such vision among the present and future generations. Therein lies the Colorado's hope.

Dr. Alvaro Aldama is Director of the Instituto Mexicano de Tecnología del Agua (Mexican Institute of Water Technology).

Prior to the Mexican-American War, most of the Colorado River Watershed was Mexican Territory; after the war, only 10 percent of the watershed remained in Mexico. However, it became clear during the expedition that Mexican culture is still at the heart of many local traditions throughout the watershed.

the United States the ability to stop the entire flow of the Colorado. At the same time, Mexico could see the benefits of Hoover Dam. Like Americans living downstream from the dam, Mexicans were protected from devastating floods that had previously washed down the Colorado. In addition, regulated flow made it easier to divert water for use in houses and on farms. By 1938, Mexicans were farming about 180,000 acres in the Colorado Delta.

Finally, in 1944, a treaty governing the division of the Colorado River between the United States and Mexico was established. The treaty allocated 1.5 million acre-feet of Colorado River water to Mexico per year (with an additional 200,000 acre-feet available during high flow years). This brought the total amount of water allocated to states and nations to 16.5 million acre-feet (see page 244, "Sharing the Shed").

Colorado River Water Allocation and Actual Use in Year 2000 (acre-feet)

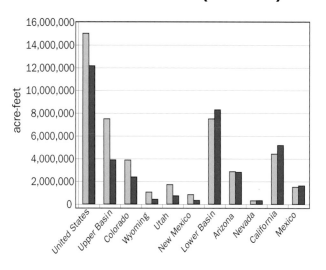

☐ Allocation (from 1922 Compact and 1944 Treaty)
■ Actual Usage in Year 2000

Upper Basin figures from www.usbr.gov/uc/library/envdocs/reports/crs/crsul.html

Lower Basin figures from www.usbr.gov/lc/region/g4000/use.txt

Allocated water and actual usage for the year 2000. In this year (as in most years), the entire flow of the Colorado was either used or stored in reservoirs. None of its flow reached the Gulf of California. Each state's water use varies yearly depending on climate and other factors. Annual flow of the river is also quite variable. The lowest recorded annual flow for the Colorado is 5 million acre-feet (maf); its highest is 24 maf. Average annual flow is thought to be 12.5–13.5 maf—the river may be over-allocated by 4 maf.

Colorado River Water Allocation and Year 2000 Usage (acre-feet)

	Allocation (from 1922 Compact)	Actual Usage
United States	15,000,000	12,156,257
Upper Basin	7,500,000	3,869,300
Colorado	3,855,000*	2,377,300
Wyoming	1,043,000*	425,000
Utah	1,714,000*	729,900
New Mexico	838,000*	337,100
Lower Basin	7,500,000	8,286,957
Arizona	2,850,000	2,802,759
Nevada	300,000	321,983
California	4,400,000	5,162,215
Mexico	1,500,000	1,623,163
Total	16,500,000	13,779,420

* These figures are estimates based on the 7,500,000 acre feet allocated to the Upper Basin. This water is divided according to percentage of water available to the Upper Basin each year. Arizona recieves 50,000 acre-feet of Upper Basin water in addition to its Lower Basin allocation. The remaining 7,450,000 acre-feet of Upper Basin water are allocated as follows: Colorado, 51.75%; Wyoming, 14%; Utah, 23%; New Mexico, 11.25%.

The waters of the Colorado River have been divided and diverted to meet the many needs of its users, yet everyone who uses Colorado River water is connected by a common need for an adequate and dependable supply of clean water. Listening to David Robbins in Grand Lake, Colorado, Mexico seems a world away, but the water in our drinking glasses speaks of our connection to everyone else within this international watershed.

On the morning after our conversation with David Robbins, we leave Grand Lake and follow the Colorado southwest. Along the way we meet with farmers, ranchers, and irrigators in western Colorado. Near the Utah border we turn north to follow the Green River to its headwaters in the mountains of Wyoming.

Until recently, over-allocation has not been a major issue, since several U.S. states have not used all the water to which they are entitled. States needing more water have been able to use the surplus water from other states. Increasing population and drought are changing this dynamic as more states are predicted to eventually use their full water allocation.

Over-Allocation of the River

The data used in 1922 to determine the amount of water available in the river overestimated its average annual flow. In recent decades, paleontological studies of tree, clamshell, and fishbone growth patterns have extended our climate and streamflow records back several centuries. These data indicate that the long-term average annual flow of the Colorado River is closer to 12.5–13.5 million acre-feet per year. They also reveal that the data used in 1922 to allocate the river were based on two of the wettest decades in the last five hundred years. The Colorado River is over-allocated by about 4 million acre-feet per year (see page 146, "Reading the Rings").

Annual Series and 20-Year Moving Average of Reconstructed Flow of the Colorado River at Lee's Ferry, Arizona, 1520–1961

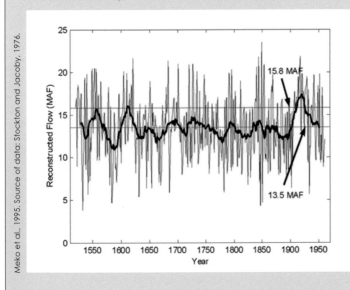

Meko et al., 1995. Source of data: Stockton and Jacoby, 1976.

Reconstruction of annual flow in the Colorado River from 1520–1961, based on tree-ring research. The heavy black line shows the 20-year average flow over time and helps portray overall fluctuations in streamflow. The average annual flow, based on this data, is 13.5 million acre-feet per year. The line representing 15.8 million acre-feet shows measured flow between 1902 and 1932.

Green River Lakes, Wyoming

The cool temperatures and ample water that characterize Rocky Mountain National Park in early summer are echoed in Wyoming's Wind River Range, the headwaters of the Green River. We camp on the shores of Green River Lake in the shadow of Squaretop Mountain. It is easy to see how the Green River got its name; the supple river flowing out of these glacier-fed lakes is emerald green from the glacial till (eroded material) it carries. The rugged peaks of the Wind Rivers surround the lakes, which perch above a wide valley filled with sagebrush.

Wyoming is famous for its unpredictable and often wintry weather, and we are, after all, camped in mountains that host the largest number of glaciers in the lower forty-eight states. On June 21 we awaken to a snowstorm that blankets wildflowers and transforms the landscape into another season.

Beneath the beating of the wind I can hear the river beginning. Snow rounds into water, seeps and trickles, splashes and pours and clatters, burnishing the shattered gray rock, and carols downslope, light and sound interwoven with sunlight. The high saddle upon which we stand, here in the Wind River Mountains, is labeled Knapsack Col on the map, a rim left where two opposing cirques once enlarged toward each other. It defines the head of a rock-strewn valley less than a mile wide and some two miles long. This valley, hung like a hammock between twelve- and thirteen-thousand-foot peaks, is weighted down the middle with a lead-blue line: the first vein of the Green River.

Ann Zwinger, *Run, River, Run: A Naturalist's Journey Down One of the Great Rivers of the American West*

Christine Newell

An abandoned homestead stands on the shore of Green River Lake, Wyoming.

Squaretop Mountain is dramatic above Green River Lakes.

June wildflowers color the landscape at Green River Lake, Wyoming.

Standing atop Mansface Rock and gazing across the vast landscape carved by the forces of weathering, I rejoice—I'm present! Spectacular are these moments in time along the Green River.

Cathy Scheer, Pinedale, Wyoming, middle school science teacher

Justin Howe

The Green River winds its way through Seedskadee National Wildlife Refuge, Wyoming.

Seedskadee National Wildlife Refuge, Wyoming

- This refuge is an important stopover place for birds migrating along the Green River during travel between summer and winter homes.
- Visitors frequently see osprey, white pelicans, Canada geese, and other birds.
- Sagebrush covers the low rolling hills that surround the river.
- The National Fish and Wildlife Service has created wetland habitat by diverting water from the Green River onto the river's floodplain and nearby fallow fields.
- American Indian tribes in this area once used cliffs above the river to capture buffalo and other large game.

South of Green River Lakes, glacial mountains give way to rolling hills and sagebrush prairie. Wild horses, deer, and antelope climb bluffs above the river. In the town of Green River, Wyoming, we stop at Expedition Island where American explorer John Wesley Powell began his expeditions through the Colorado Watershed more than 130 years earlier (see page 232, "Colorado River Timeline").

Powell's expedition down the Green and Colorado Rivers was a landmark event in the history of this watershed. The vast area of canyons and deserts through which the rivers flow was a blank spot on the maps of that time, and Powell's mission was to survey and map the geology of the country. His account of this trip, *The Exploration of the Colorado River and Its Canyons*, contains detailed descriptions and illustrations of geology, ecology, and native cultures in the region as well as accounts of hardships encountered.

In 1878, Powell published his *Report on the Lands of the Arid Region of the United States*. Based on his observations, Powell cautioned that homesteads in areas without irrigation would struggle due to lack of

The 1871 river expedition led by John Wesley Powell launches at Expedition Island in Green River, Wyoming.

rainfall. Despite his concerns, homesteaders moved into the desert and many farms failed (see "Desert Gardens," available online; see page IV for Web address). Those that remained built new communities. Since that time, infrastructure has been built that carries water to regions that previously had little water. Today, some of the fastest-growing cities and most productive agricultural areas in the United States and Mexico are located in the desert—supported by the Colorado River and its tributaries. As our expedition moves south, we observe that, while the land gets drier, the number of people living on it increases.

Farming and ranching were not the only things that drew settlers to the watershed. Beginning in 1540, more than three centuries before Powell's river expeditions, rumors of gold and other mineral wealth brought Spanish explorers into the basin. The quests of Spanish explorers were followed by those of miners, who extracted gold, silver, copper, and other minerals throughout the watershed.

Artist's depiction of the Powell Expedition on their voyage through the watershed.

Mineral and energy resources are still a central part of the basin's economy. Gold, silver, and copper in Colorado, Arizona, and New Mexico; uranium in Utah and Arizona; coalmines, oil wells, and natural gas wells in nearly every state; geothermal plants in California and Baja California—all testify to the importance of what lies beneath the soil. The geology of the watershed, first described by Powell, is one of its most prominent features both visually and economically.

Dramatic erosion patterns and sparse vegetation make it impossible to ignore the geology that surrounds us. Jagged mountain cliffs and smooth river rock illuminate how water has shaped the landscape. From shale beds deposited on the bottoms of ancient seas, to sandstone desert dunes, the rock layers exposed in the canyons of the Colorado Basin tell a story of shifting environments and the perpetual forces of erosion and deposition.

Irrigation's Long History in the Watershed

Many cities in the watershed were started as farming communities, relying on irrigation canals to carry water from rivers to fields. Some of the canals they used were first developed by native farmers hundreds of years before. Around 500 A.D., the Hohokam people built several large canals in central Arizona, including one that irrigated an estimated eight thousand acres. Ancestors of the Paiute, Zuni, Hopi, Tohono O'odham, Pima, and others began building irrigation canals two to three thousand years ago along the San Pedro River in southern Arizona. Early irrigation canals are also found at Chaco Culture National Historic Park in New Mexico and at Montezuma's Well in Arizona. The Pima maintained an estimated six hundred miles of canals until they lost water to white settlers.

Spanish missionaries arriving in northern Mexico and the southwestern United States quickly learned the importance of irrigation and modeled their own systems after canals developed by tribes in the region. In the 1840s, members of the Church of Jesus Christ of Latter-day Saints (Mormons) expanded the

We live in a desert, and that makes the waters of the Colorado Watershed as important to all of us today as they were to the Hohokam one thousand years ago—may we be as thankful and conservative of those waters and the watershed ecosystems as they were!

Deborah Johnson, professional archaeologist and high school teacher in Phoenix, Arizona

Ancient Hohokam irrigation canal near Phoenix, Arizona.

Marjie Risk

practice of irrigation throughout the western United States.

In 1902, the United States government established the Reclamation Service (later renamed the Bureau of Reclamation), an agency whose purpose was to develop and manage irrigation systems in the western United States. One of the Reclamation Service's first major projects was constructed on the Salt River, a tributary to the Colorado located in Arizona. Roosevelt Dam was built to control floods and to store water for use in irrigation. Water stored by the dam and hydroelectric power produced there still supply farms, houses, and businesses in the Phoenix area. Many of the canals through which this water is delivered were first used by the Hohokam.

Irrigation in Mexico also has a long history. Cultures throughout the country have been diverting water for crops for thousands of years. Modern management of irrigation in Mexico began in 1926 when a new national irrigation law and the National Irrigation Commission were developed, leading to the construction of significant irrigation infrastructure. On the Colorado River, Morelos Dam was completed in 1950. Morelos diverts water to irrigate crops and supply water to homes and businesses in northern Baja California and Sonora. In 1989, the National Water Commission was established. Two of its primary goals are to maintain irrigation delivery structures and to develop water planning that establishes economic and social benefits while conserving water resources.

(See pages 287, 299, and 307, "First Come, First Served," "Irrigation Calculations," and "Many Happy Return Flows.")

Justin Howe

Colorful rock layers are exposed at Flaming Gorge Reservoir on the Utah/Wyoming border.

The Atlas Uranium Mine, Moab, Utah

Justin Howe

Bill Hedden, Director of the Grand Canyon Trust, an environmental advocacy group that supports efforts to clean up the Atlas tailings pile, talks to the expedition team while on a hike up sandstone terraces high above Moab, Utah.

The development of mineral and energy resources brings economic benefit to communities and is demanded by American consumers, but there are environmental and social concerns associated with it. Towns such as Rock Springs, Wyoming, Moab, Utah, and Price, Utah, have endured economic boom-and-bust cycles associated with mining, as well as environmental problems that persist beyond the life of the local mining industry.

One place of concern is the Atlas uranium tailings (mining waste) pile near Moab, Utah. The 130-acre tailings pile is left over from mining operations between 1956 and 1984 and contains 13 million tons of mill waste contaminated with radioactive material and hazardous chemicals, including uranium, radium, and mercury. The tailings pile is situated within the floodplain of the Colorado River, and increased concentrations of these elements have been found in ground water and in the river.

Uranium levels in river water increase by 1,660 percent at the Atlas site (Utah Department of Environmental Quality report: "Intensive Water Quality Sampling of the Colorado River at the Atlas Uranium Tailings Site, January 1997"). Scientists, resource managers, and policymakers are developing plans to move the tailings pile to a location where ground and surface water will be protected from the hazardous material.

Justin Howe

Walking on petrified sand dunes near Moab, Utah.

Expedition Island, Wyoming

- Located in the town of Green River, Wyoming.
- This is the place where famous explorer, John Wesley Powell, began his 1869 river expedition through the Colorado River Watershed.
- Today, the island is a community gathering place and destination for kayakers who come to paddle the river's whitewater kayak course.

Justin Howe

Flaming Gorge Dam was built for the purposes of water storage. It also provides hydro-electric power and recreational opportunities. Since the 1980s, the dam has been operated to minimize impacts to the endangered fish species that live in the Green River below the dam (see page 211, "Chillin' with the Chubs").

Canyon Country

In Dinosaur National Monument, geology again takes center stage. The Yampa and Green Rivers have carved beautiful canyons here, exposing twenty-six different rock formations and luring hikers, rafters, and kayakers. We spend a morning talking with David Whitman, chief interpreter at the monument. He has worked extensively to promote environmental education in the area, focusing not only on the large-scale subjects of geologic history and ecosystems, but also on life forms at a small scale. Whitman leads our group into the cold waters of the Green, where we capture and study macro-invertebrates living on the gravelly river bottom. Biologists use macro-invertebrates, which are sensitive to changes in water quality, as indicators of stream health.

Dinosaur National Monument is famous, of course, not for its thriving macro-invertebrates but for its ancient dinosaur fossils. A huge, partially excavated dinosaur quarry is on display inside the visitors' center. Thousands of bones are exposed for viewing. Paleontologists think that the dinosaur bones preserved here were gathered and then buried by river floods about 150 million years ago (see page 114, "Rock Sandwich, Stone Soup").

The Green River continues to carve impressive canyons as it cruises southward towards its confluence with the Colorado. John Wesley Powell named one of these canyons Desolation. With its steep cliffs and cottonwood-shaded riverbanks, Desolation Canyon is one of the most remote areas in the United States. The Green finally meets the Colorado in Canyonlands National Park, another stunning example of geology on display.

Justin Howe

Desolation Canyon, in Utah, still lives up to the name that was given to it in the late 1800s by Powell's expedition.

The Green River carves deep canyons on its way to its confluence with the Colorado River in Canyonlands National Park, Utah.

The red and white sandstone and shale formations of Canyonlands reveal the story of ancient environments—deserts, seas, and swamps advancing and receding through the millennia. They also hold reminders of the long human history in this area. We see petroglyphs pecked into cliff walls by past human residents a stone's throw from dinosaur tracks preserved in sandstone.

Human history in the canyon country of southern Utah, northern Arizona, and western Colorado and New Mexico is deep. Ancient dwelling and sacred sites overlap with contemporary communities. We hike into a steep, red canyon in Navajo National Monument, near Kayenta, Arizona, to visit Betatakin, an Ancestral Puebloan ruin that was occupied between about 1250–1290 A.D. The elaborate, well-preserved stone buildings fill a massive alcove ringed by seeps and springs.

The canyon bottom is lush with aspen trees, scrub oak, and wildflowers. This dwelling has been abandoned for hundreds of years, yet there is a paradoxical feeling of "newness" in the ancient stone structures. Our guide, a sixteen-year old Navajo, quietly points out features of the ruin. He tells us that this place is highly important to some Hopi clans, descendants of the Betatakin builders.

Many groups of people have lived in this area. Archaeologists find artifacts that show Paleo-Indian and Archaic hunter-gatherers hunted game and harvested wild plants here 10,000–12,000 years ago. From A.D. 600–1300, Ancestral Puebloans built permanent (and often elaborate) structures, developed sophisticated agricultural practices, and traded with other groups from as far south as Central America. The Pueblo people who now live in northwestern New Mexico and northeastern

Justin Howe

Petroglyphs on sandstone in Desolation Canyon, Utah.

Arizona are thought to be descendants of these ancient desert dwellers.

Another ancient culture, the Hohokam, established a civilization in southern Arizona that closely mirrored the Aztec in Mexico. Both the Ancestral Puebloans and Hohokam are thought to have migrated northward from Mexico and Central America. More recent migrations in the canyon country region include the arrival of Ute people in the last thousand years and the arrival of Navajo people (Diné) 300–500 years ago. All of these cultures adapted to the arid environment and developed traditions, religions, and art that reflect the importance of the natural world. Today, thirty-four tribes live in the Colorado River Watershed. (See page 232, "Colorado River Timeline" as well as "Desert Gardens" and "Colorado Art Festival" [available online; see Table of Contents for Web address]).

Justin Howe

Church Rock, near Kayenta, Arizona. The harsh desert environments of the canyon country hold a unique beauty, shaped by wind and water over time, and containing human stories from thousands of years ago to the present.

The Zuni are recognized as experts in soil conservation techniques. The waffle gardens shown in this 1926 photo help grow crops in the desert by holding soil and water where crops are planted. Some farmers still use this technique to grow crops in arid regions.

Desolation Canyon, Utah

- The Green River carved this deep and wild canyon.
- There are no roads into this canyon for almost two hundred miles.
- During spring runoff, water flow can reach thirty thousand cubic feet per second (cfs).
- Mustangs and bighorn sheep are often sighted along the river.
- Much of the canyon is within the Uintah–Ouray Indian Reservation of the Northern Ute Tribe.

Come Into the Shade (excerpt)

Q: Where are you from?
A: Where I'm from is like this
Hard summer rains
leave hollow beads
of moisture in the dust.
My mother says each fall:
We have to husk this corn
and throw it on top of the shed
then we'll shell it when it dries.
It's really good in the winter.
The dogs raise a racket
every time someone comes
home—
it's never quiet here.
Sometimes the chickens join
in
then the babies wake up
wanting to play.
My father—a thin slightly
bent figure—a shovel over
his shoulder coming home
from the fields. Come into
the shade by the house.

Luci Tapahonso is a Navajo writer who grew up near Shiprock, New Mexico. She has published numerous award-winning stories, poems, essays, and articles and is currently a professor at the University of Arizona in Tucson.

Courtesy National Park Service

Ancient stone structures at Chaco Canyon in New Mexico were built in alignment with solar and lunar cycles.

Chaco Culture National Historic Park, New Mexico

- This park preserves structures built by Ancestral Puebloans about six hundred years ago.
- Complexes with hundreds of rooms were built by thousands of people, but it is likely that food and supplies had to be imported to this remote area.
- The function of the structures at Chaco is not known, but many archaeologists believe that they were built in alignment with cycles of the sun and moon.

Summer sunset illuminates the Hopi mesas, Arizona.

The canyon country is special and we spend time with people who know it deeply. Jane and Eric Polingyouma, Hopi elders and historians, welcome us to their home in Kykotsmovi and share stories as well as feather-light piki bread (a flaky bread cooked on a hot stone) made from their blue corn. One of the current issues that we discuss is coal mining on Black Mesa, which is located on Hopi and Navajo land.

The Black Mesa mines, operated by Peabody Energy Company, supply coal for power production in Page, Arizona, and Laughlin, Nevada. They are a cornerstone of the local economy and produce power for millions of people throughout the western United States. To transport coal 273 miles to the Mojave Generating Station in Laughlin, it is pulverized and mixed with pure water pumped from the Navajo Aquifer (N-Aquifer). About 3,500–4,000 acre-feet of water are used each year. Many tribal members are concerned that the pumping is depleting the aquifer and impacting seeps and springs that have cultural and economic importance (see page 140, "Basin in a Bottle").

The Black Mesa controversy is complicated because the Navajo and Hopi tribes rely on revenues from the mine's royalties, but at the same time are concerned about impacts on their water supply. Our conversations with Hopi and Navajo people as well as spokespeople from Peabody Energy reveal deep divisions about coal and water extraction in the region. Peabody's scientists have concluded that the rate of aquifer depletion is not significant and that drought is instead to blame for the loss of springs. Potential alternatives to using water from the N-Aquifer have been considered, including pumping ground water from an aquifer with lower water quality.

The Black Mesa Coal Mine, operated by Peabody Energy Company. Land disturbed by the mining process is re-vegetated with native plants. The mine supplies coal to power plants that provide electricity to millions of people.

Shiprock Peak, New Mexico

- Shiprock rises out of the desert floor and looks like a ship on the ocean.
- This mountain is sacred to the Navajo who call it *"Tsé bit' a 'í'* (Rock with Wings).
- According to Navajo stories, the rock was once a giant bird.
- Geologists say the rock is a remnant of an ancient volcano.

The Black Mesa controversy is better understood within the broader context of American Indian water rights. Maria Goodin, an expedition member who has studied the history of American Indian water rights, leads the discussion as we sit in the shade of tamarisk trees in a dry wash near the river at Lee's Ferry, Arizona.

When American Indians were forced onto reservations in the late 1800s, the United States government said that tribes "should have the means to enable them to become self-supporting, as a pastoral and agricultural people. . ." (FindLaw U.S. Supreme Court 207 *U.S.* 564). However, much of the land set aside for reservations was non-arable desert land with limited access to water. This made pursuing an agricultural lifestyle difficult and, in some cases, impossible.

The Winters Doctrine

In 1908 the United States Supreme Court issued a ruling in Winters v. United States that allocated water to American Indian reservations. The ruling has been applied to set aside water rights for national parks, national monuments, protected areas, and any other land that is reserved from the public domain. The water rights for these lands are tied to the date they were established.

This is significant because, in the Colorado River Watershed and most of the western United States, the Doctrine of Prior Appropriation is used to allocate water. Under prior appropriation, the right to use water is tied to the date a water right was established. During dry years, water users with "senior" water rights can use water before "junior" users even if that means that there is none left for the junior users.

In the United States, American Indian reservations were established before most white settlers claimed water rights. This means that American Indians on reservations have senior water rights on many rivers. This does not mean that they have access to water. Many tribal water rights have not been quantified, existing on paper rather than as "wet water." Lack of delivery infrastructure, a historic lack of political clout to enforce water rights claims, small populations, and other issues have resulted in tribes not receiving water, although this has begun to change in recent years.

Since the establishment of reservations, tribes have not only struggled to maintain traditional cultures and languages, but have been fighting for water rights.

Most of the thirty-four tribes in the basin have been using water from the Colorado River and its tributaries for centuries. The water rights of all tribes are legally protected by the 1908 Winters Doctrine (see sidebar), but were not included in the 1922 allocation of the Colorado River. Negotiators of the 1922 Compact did, however, recognize that these water rights would need to be addressed in the future. For this reason, they expressly stated that nothing in the compact would affect the United States' obligation to the tribes.

In the last 50 years there has been some progress in quantifying water rights and delivering water to Colorado Basin tribes. Some of the first federal irrigation projects that benefited tribes were built on the Colorado River Indian Tribes reservation in the Lower Basin. When Parker Dam was authorized in the 1930s, its purpose included expanding irrigation on Colorado River reservations. While the dam helped provide water to some tribes, the reservoir it formed (Lake Havasu)

Canyonlands National Park, Utah

- Sedimentary sandstones eroded by the Colorado and Green Rivers have formed a colorful landscape of mesas and buttes.
- People have lived in this area for more than 10,000 years. Some of them have left elaborate petroglyphs and pictographs.
- River rafters float the Colorado River through Cataract Canyon.
- The Green and Colorado Rivers meet here.

flooded the Chemehuevi Reservation, forcing the relocation of many families.

In 1963, when Arizona quantified its Colorado River allocation in order to obtain federal funding for the Central Arizona Project, five American Indian groups along the lower Colorado River asserted their water rights (the Fort Mojave Indian Tribe, the Chemehuevi Indian Tribe, the Colorado River Indian Tribes, the Quechan Tribe of the Fort Yuma Reservation, and the Cocopah Indian Community). A quantification process was established and the tribes' water rights were confirmed, setting a precedent for future American Indian water rights claims. Since that time, the Gila River Indian Community has also had its water right quantified. Some tribal leaders, including Mary Thomas,

My Grandfather already knew that it was going to be like this. He said that someday the language (Tohono O'odham) *is going to be gone. It is like traveling and then you hit something. And then you turn back and remember what the old people say. They will look for it, but they can't find it because it is going to be gone. It's about time now. My grandchildren, my great-grandchildren don't even talk Indian. That's what he meant, but I didn't understand.*

Francis Manuel, Tohono O'odham elder

Zion National Park, Utah

- Water has carved deep, narrow canyons in this park.
- Utah's highest plant diversity can be found here.
- Green cottonwood trees along the Virgin River contrast with colorful red and gold canyon walls.

Bryce Canyon National Park, Utah

- Named after a Mormon settler, this park is famous for its unique geology: dramatic towers or "hoodoos" and narrow "slot" canyons.
- The colorful rock formations have prompted visitors to compare it to a maze.
- High air quality allows visitors to see up to two hundred miles.

Lieutenant Governor of the Gila River Indian Community, have advocated a return to agricultural values.

The Navajo, Southern Utes, Ute Mountain Utes, Jicarilla Apache, and Northern Utes have also achieved full or partial quantification of water rights claims. However, this does not mean that they have received water. Quantification exists on paper, but they still need infrastructure to deliver the water. The Ak-Chin Indian Community and Tohono O'odham are currently engaged in water rights settlement proceedings, and litigation is likely to continue for many years. Some water experts estimate that Indian water settlements in Arizona may soon give tribes rights to more than half of Arizona's allocation of Colorado River water. When the expedition reaches Mexico, we will learn about how the Cucapá, a tribe whose livelihood is based on fishing, are struggling to make a living without adequate water.

Christine Newell

Expedition member Carlota Monroy climbs into a slot canyon in the Navajo Nation. Slot canyons are formed when rushing water erodes rapidly through rock layers.

Justin Howe

The Animas–La Plata Project, under construction near Durango, Colorado, will benefit the Southern Ute Tribe, Ute Mountain Ute Tribe, and Navajo Nation. The project involves pumping water from the Animas River to a 120,000-acre-foot off-stream reservoir. A pipeline has also been authorized that will deliver water to the Navajo Nation near Shiprock, New Mexico.

Mesa Verde National Park, Colorado
- This park is famous for its large cliff dwellings built under overhangs in cliffs.
- Ancestral Puebloans built some of the first water control structures in the watershed here.
- Most of the seven hundred years of occupation are represented in the archaeological record.
- Mesa Verde was abandoned in the late 1200s.
- Many American Indian tribes have ancestral connections to sites here.

Glen Canyon Dam and Lake Powell, Arizona

Throughout the arid West, the scarcity of water and the demand for it run head on into each other. [U.S. Bureau of] *Reclamation and other water agencies are committed to working with the various water interests to ensure that the precious water supply is managed in a way that maximizes the benefits to all users. It is a challenge that won't go away—it will only grow.*

Pat Page, Water Management Team Leader,
U.S. Bureau of Reclamation's Western Colorado Area Office

Glen Canyon Dam and the reservoir it forms (Lake Powell) help store water in wet years for use in dry times. They also provide recreational opportunities and produce hydroelectric power. Critics of the dam and its reservoir argue that it should be removed to restore the river's natural environment. Whether a person believes the dam should remain or be decommissioned, it cannot be denied that it has become an important component of human life in the arid Colorado River Basin, the western United States, and northwestern Mexico.

We are fortunate to meet with several stakeholders who frame the Glen Canyon Dam issue from different perspectives. Our first meeting is with Chris Peterson, director of the Glen Canyon Institute. His organization advocates decommissioning the dam in order to restore ecosystems in Glen Canyon and Grand Canyon and prevent evaporative water loss. He argues that the water

storage provided by Lake Powell could be accommodated by Lake Mead, downstream.

Several days later, Ken Rice, manager of Glen Canyon Dam for the Bureau of Reclamation, leads us on a tour of the facility. Security is tight, and we are limited to viewing a few public areas. Lake Powell, which sprawls through canyons in both Arizona and Utah, can store roughly 24 million acre-feet (active capacity), or about three years of river flow. The dam and its reservoir are used for power generation, flood control, water storage, and recreation. According to Rice, without Lake Powell as a water "bank account," the Upper Basin states would not be able to deliver to the Lower Basin the amount of water required by the 1922 Colorado River Compact. He also argues that, if Glen Canyon Dam were removed and more water stored in Lake Mead, during drought years Lake Mead would have to be mostly drained to satisfy needs.

Lake Powell, formed by Glen Canyon Dam, can store about 24 million acre-feet of water (active capacity). This is enough water to serve the needs of about 6,750,000 people for one year. Water managers estimate that about 3 percent (750,000 acre-feet) of reservoir storage is lost to evaporation each year.

Glen Canyon Dam altered the Grand Canyon ecosystems. No longer subject to scouring spring floods, more plants—many of which are non-native—have established themselves along the riverbank. Beaches built by sand carried into the system during flood events are shrinking because the reservoir captures sediment before it can be deposited in the canyon. Archaeological sites, once protected by periodic deposition of sediment, are being eroded. Fish such as the humpback chub and razorback sucker are close to extinction because of changes in water temperature, sediment load, and competition from introduced species (see page 211, "Chillin' with the Chubs," and page 224, "An Invited Guest in the Colorado Watershed").

Some of the impacts have been beneficial. As a result of increased vegetation in the canyon, the diversity of bird species has increased; the clear and cold water flowing from Glen Canyon Dam has created a world-class trout fishery; and predictable river flow has made it possible for the multi-million-dollar-per-year whitewater rafting industry to become established. Each year Lake Powell draws almost 3 million visitors who boat, camp, and fish at the reservoir and bring economic benefits to the region.

River Flow Before and After Construction of Glen Canyon Dam

Before dams were built on the Colorado, river flow sometimes reached several hundred thousand cfs. A springtime occurrence, such floods usually ended by mid summer, leaving the river with much less water during the rest of the year, with the exception of intermittent summer flash floods (see page 126, "Go with the Flow," and page 211, "Chillin' with the Chubs"). Today, river flow in the Grand Canyon rarely exceeds 20,000 cfs, and water stored in the dam is managed to maximize power production, protect water supplies, and mitigate negative environmental effects of the dam.

In order to maximize power production from Glen Canyon Dam, most of the water released from the dam is run through the hydroelectric power generators and flow fluctuates with energy demand.

In 1996, the Interior Department conducted a flooding experiment that officials hoped would wash away nonnative vegetation and move sand from the river bottom to its banks, re-establishing beaches. They opened Glen Canyon Dam's floodgates, letting out enough water to raise the Colorado by as much as thirteen feet. At first the experiment seemed a success, with new sand deposition visible in the canyon. But within a few years, the new beaches were gone. Without a constant inflow of new sediment, the river simply moved the sand through the canyon where it was deposited in Lake Mead.

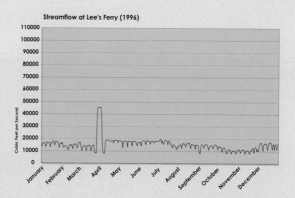

Hydrograph showing the spike in Colorado River flow that resulted from the 1996 experimental flood designed to mimic flood patterns before the construction of Glen Canyon Dam.

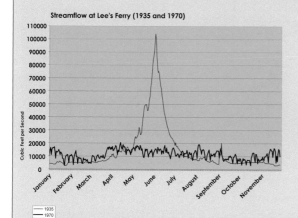

Hydrographs showing Colorado River streamflow at Lee's Ferry, Arizona, before and after the completion of Glen Canyon Dam in 1963.

Beaches in the Grand Canyon are disappearing due to lack of sediment, which is trapped behind Glen Canyon Dam.

It took a few years to convince me that the Lake [Powell] *could replace the beauty of "my" Glen Canyon, but the more I explored newly accessible canyons, the more people I showed this great lake to, I had to admit that there was no body of water nor scenic area that could today compare to Lake Powell.*

Art Greene, early Colorado River and Lake Powell tourist guide, Marble Canyon, Arizona

Art Greene, Earl Johnson, and Irene Johnson help Colorado River passengers onto a tour boat in 1943. Greene continued operating river and lake tours after the construction of Glen Canyon Dam, twenty years later.

Adaptive Management in the Grand Canyon

The Adaptive Management Work Group is an advisory group to the U.S. Secretary of the Interior; the group is made up of a variety of Colorado River stakeholders. Its purpose is to make management recommendations to limit the negative impacts of Glen Canyon Dam while maintaining the benefits of the facility. Members include representatives from the hydroelectric power industry, the recreation industry, state and federal agencies, tribes, environmental groups, and the seven U.S. basin states. The workgroup develops experiments that test how changes in dam operations affect water users, for example, the 1996 experimental flood flow.

The Paria River near its confluence with the Colorado. The Adaptive Management Work Group plans to time flood releases from Glen Canyon Dam with natural floods from the Paria. It is hoped that this action will help deposit sediment from the Paria on beaches in the Grand Canyon.

Justin Howe

Grand Canyon National Park, Arizona

- More than 4 million people visit this park each year.
- The 1,217,403-acre park was designated a national park by an act of Congress in 1919.
- One of the deepest canyons in the world, it is about one vertical mile from canyon rim to river.
- The rocks on the rim are about 270 million years old.
- The rocks at the bottom of the canyon are about 1.7 billion years old.

The Grand Canyon, Arizona

If the river didn't teach me all that I know, at least it put everything into perspective.

Michael Collier, geologist, professional photographer, physician, author, and former Grand Canyon river guide, Flagstaff, Arizona

As we travel south and west, the multitude of demands on the river becomes increasingly clear. Cities, farms, power plants, ecosystems, and recreation industries all rely upon this fluid network. Humans strive to control and make predictable this vital resource, but its nature remains *un*predictable—governed by climate and other forces beyond our control. The soaring cliffs of Grand Canyon are testimony to its power.

We gain a new connection with the river during a research river trip through the canyon. From the launch at Lee's Ferry to the take-out at Diamond Creek seventeen days later, our flotilla of three rubber rafts and two hard-hulled dories descends deep into the rock. Winding our way past side canyon washes and through deep, rushing rapids, our passage is guided by vermillion sandstone, black schist, and millions of years of geologic history (see page 114, "Rock Sandwich, Stone Soup").

Justin Howe

Deep in the Grand Canyon, a boatman guides his dory to shore.

Justin Howe

A dory gracefully maneuvers waves in Granite Rapid, Grand Canyon.

First, as always, is the roar. "Forward," shouts Megan. We drop from calm into havoc, attacking Hermit's wave-train head on. One, two, three, four giant waves lift us. . . . Then comes the fifth wave. We climb up and up, but we do not cut through. The wave grows.

It's a demon curling above us. Its foaming dragon breath is distinct as a Japanese painting, alive. . . . The raft is hanging vertical in air. Then the crest breaks. We are thrown back. The boat flips. We are flying.

Annick Smith, from *Writing Down the River: Into the Heart of the Grand Canyon*

Alternating between noisy rapids and quiet calm, our moods shift with the river's. Rushing rapids bring bursts of adrenaline that punctuate long hours of quiet reflection. It is unbelievably hot, and we arrange our activities around the temperature, with strenuous activity during the early morning and shaded rest in the heat of the day. We are dependent upon the river for our survival. We travel on it, drink it, cool ourselves in it. The river water has just been released from the depths of Lake Powell and is about 47 degrees F. Side canyon streams are the perfect temperature, and we take every opportunity to explore places with names like Shinumo Creek, Elves Chasm, Vasey's Paradise, Nankoweap Creek, and Matkatamiba.

Lower Elves Chasm

Amid the towering tri-colored walls,
Honed smooth by wind and water,
Is a place of unexpected earth magic: Elves Chasm.

Here water races down a precipitous slope,
Plunging over three enormous pock-marked boulders,
Standing toppled end on end.

Luscious green maiden hair fern,
Columbine with its dainty stemmed flower,
And moist slimy moss, drape the smooth slide.

The frothy, white, raging water winds through
Twists and turns down this natural labyrinth.
As it reaches the bottom,
The gushing water transforms into
A dozen elegant, elongated streams

But with not a second to tarry,
The strings of droplets dance their grand finale.
One final splash and the tumultuous journey is over.

The once raging water
Quietly succumbs to the gentle ripple
Of the aqua pool below.

Maria Goodin

Vasey's Paradise is an oasis in the desert. It is one of only two places where the endangered Kanab amber snail is found.

Lenore Grover-Bullington is a Natural Resource Specialist for Grand Canyon National Park. She has worked on Colorado River management issues for most of her career. Lenore participated in a nine-day Grand Canyon river trip with the 2003 Colorado River Expedition.

August 13.—We are three quarters of a mile in the depths of the earth, and the great river shrinks into insignificance as it dashes its angry waves against the walls and cliffs that rise to the world above; the waves are but puny ripples, and we but pigmies, running up and down the sands or lost among the boulders.

Major John Wesley Powell, *The Exploration of the Colorado River and Its Canyons*

Maria Goodin

The brilliantly blue waters of the Little Colorado River are part of what makes its confluence with the Colorado River a special and sacred place. During floods the river turns dark brown.

Oraibi, Arizona

- This community is thought to be the oldest continuously inhabited settlement in North America.
- Hopi people have lived here since at least 1100 A.D.
- Farming techniques practiced here have been in use for hundreds of years.
- The people living here are descendants of the Ancestral Puebloans who lived in the Mesa Verde area.
- One of the most sacred sites for Hopi people is near the confluence of the Little Colorado and Colorado Rivers.

Christine Jaworsky

This watercolor painting captures the view of the Grand Canyon from an overlook near Nankoweap Creek.

Tracing the footsteps of previous explorers, we float past waterfalls bursting from towering cliffs, play frisbee in an alcove the size of a stadium, and explore slot canyons so narrow and deep that, while we cannot see the rim, our arms span the width. We attempt to capture our experiences by writing in journals and watercolor painting the Muav limestone deposits, clear sky, and sparkling river.

Justin Howe

Matkatamiba Canyon (named for a Havasupai family) is a beautiful side canyon that can be accessed from the river in Grand Canyon.

Red Rocks Canyon National Conservation Area, Nevada

- More than forty springs attract humans, plants, and animals to this area.
- As many as six prehistoric cultures may have lived here.
- About 65 million years ago, geologic faults developed in the area, forcing older geologic deposits on top of younger ones.
- The red rocks that give this canyon its name are fossilized sand dunes that contain high concentrations of iron oxide.

Matkat

my pink whorls and wrinkles
have cooled against the smooth
gray blue
curves of bedrock canyon floor

Muav and I exposed to the sky,
algae and the little teeth of
cottonwood leaves

I am a half-naked mammal
animal
asleep in the chill July trickle of
Matkatamiba Creek

dreaming
of water seducing rock
and discovering

as limestone has
her irresistible eloquence
and waiting to break—
like the fierce knots
of calcium and carbonate—
to break allegiance

and follow the river to
where the water will.

Craig Maier participated in the 2003 Colorado River Expedition. He is a geologist and graduate of Northland College.

Justin Howe

Much of our time is spent exploring the magic of the canyon, but we also have work to do. We are helping with two National Park Service studies. The first involves eradicating tamarisk, a non-native plant species that has invaded waterways throughout the basin (see page 211, "An Invited Guest in the Colorado Watershed"). Previous work teams have hiked up most of the side canyons to manually pull the smaller tamarisk trees and use mechanical and chemical (herbicide) methods on larger trees. Our job is to document re-growth and to identify any tamarisk that may have been overlooked by previous crews. Our findings will be used to direct future eradication efforts.

The second project involves recording the impacts of camping on canyon beaches. With thousands of people camping on a limited number of beaches, there can be significant accumulation of human waste, destruction of vegetation, proliferation of trails through sensitive habitat, and damage to archaeological sites. During our monitoring we collect anything from tiny pieces of eggshell to human feces. We discover that, while the Grand Canyon seems beyond the scale of human activities, it is dramatically affected by people.

This view of the Grand Canyon, taken from the South Rim, is one of the most-photographed landscapes in the watershed.

Justin Howe

Condors Get a Second Chance in the Colorado River Watershed

California condors are among the most endangered species in the world. They are the largest birds in North America, and their wingspans can reach nine and a half feet. Condors use thermal updrafts to fly and frequently travel more than one hundred miles in a single day.

During the Pleistocene epoch (1.8 million–11,000 years ago), California condors were found throughout northern Mexico, North America, and into British Columbia. They fed on carcasses of large animals including mastodon. As the Pleistocene ended with the decline of these large mammals, condor populations also decreased. By A.D. 1890 only about 600 remained.

Condors lay their eggs in caves on the bare ground. Exposure to the pesticide DDT caused the birds to lay eggs with weak shells, which would break on contact with hard rock. Lead poisoning exacerbated this problem, and by 1987 only 22 birds remained. Several captive breeding programs have been established to recover condor populations. In 2003 there were 220 birds living in California and Arizona. A few of these birds are nesting in the wild. In 2003, one pair nesting near the Grand Canyon hatched the first condor born in Arizona in more than eighty years.

© Claire Emery and Project WET International

California condors are the largest bird in North America. Their wingspans can reach nine and a half feet.

Justin Howe

One of the many non-human residents of the Grand Canyon

Paul Viosca

Canyon walls drawn by artists on Powell's expeditions remain virtually unchanged, 130 years later.

Tracks of the Colorado

Something magnificent
has occurred on our planet . . .
the Grand Canyon of the Colorado,
in the United States,
is an example of water's power over
rocks.

The Colorado River, which runs
through the canyon,
has lingered millions of years carving
it.

How marvelous to appreciate this
natural action
so important for millions of people.

Armando Aceves Pino is a teacher in Riíto, Sonora, where eroded sediment from the Grand Canyon has been deposited in the delta.

Justin Howe

Waterfalls and riparian vegetation in Deer Creek Canyon, a side canyon of the Grand Canyon.

Gila Cliff Dwellings National Monument, New Mexico

- This park protects artifacts and dwellings made by the Mollogon culture between 1280 and 1300 AD.
- Visitors can see the dwellings much as they were while inhabited.
- The cliff dwellings are located on the edge of the Gila Wilderness, which was the first wilderness area established in the United States.

From Canyon to City: Las Vegas, Nevada

This ancient willow tree grows on the banks of the Colorado River in the southern end of the Grand Canyon. It is a sacred tree to Hualapai people, whose land encompasses much of the Grand Canyon rim.

Dawn on the last day of our Grand Canyon river trip finds our group navigating a lazy, sinuous river current. Our way is marked by golden eagles and peregrine falcons in flight. Soft in the hazy morning air, music drifting from a boatman's wooden flute carries memories of ancient ruins, crashing rapids, and echoing waterfalls hidden in the canyon behind us. Distant cliffs are framed by those towering above us. A final turn reveals the Diamond Creek take-out, and like a velvet curtain, cliffs close behind us leaving only memories of our canyon adventure.

Our first contact with the outside world is the sight of two men taking river flow measurements from a cable car suspended high above the river. Positioned above the middle of the river, they lower a measurement probe into the current. The results of their test will be used to estimate the amount of water arriving in the Lower Basin as well as the amount of sand eroded from the Grand Canyon.

The serenity we felt in the canyon abruptly ends the moment our boats touch the ramp at Diamond Creek and we rush to unload our gear and clear the ramp for other groups. In less than two hours, we are loaded and begin the drive to Las Vegas, Nevada—five hours and a world away from the canyon.

The contrast we experience during the transition from the rhythms of the river to those of casinos is dramatic. Neon lights take the place of moonlight; river sounds become rushing traffic noise; and the energy of the bustling city replaces the serenity of the immense canyon.

River flow is measured at the Diamond Creek gaging station.

Patricia Mulroy is general manager of the Southern Nevada Water Authority (SNWA), water provider for Las Vegas and the surrounding area. We meet with her at the headquarters of the SNWA to discuss water planning in the Las Vegas area. SNWA has responded to recent droughts by encouraging a decrease in residential water use and is working to secure water supplies for an additional fifteen years of growth in the region. This has not been easy. According to Mulroy, the average Las Vegas family of four uses about 340,000 gallons of water per year and some residential users use multiples of that.

When asked why SNWA does not simply raise water rates to help limit use, she laughs and says, "I have [one residential customer] who uses more than 17 million gallons of water per year. His front door handles cost $500,000. His bathtub cost $6 million! What would you like me to charge him?" Her candid assessments of water and growth issues in the area leave us with a greater understanding of the complexities of water management, and an appreciation for the responsibility that individual water users bear as they make decisions about personal water use.

Nowhere is water so beautiful as in the desert, for nowhere else is it so scarce. By definition, water, like a human being or a tree or a bird or a song, gains value by rarity, singularity, isolation.

Edward Abbey, *Desert Solitaire*

Courtesy of Bellagio Hotel and Casino

The fountain at Bellagio Hotel and Casino uses well water rather than Colorado River water. At nearby Treasure Island Hotel and Casino, a water recycling plant cleans up to 100,000 gallons of gray water per day. The treated water is used for landscaping and fountains at the Treasure Island and Mirage resorts.

Justin Howe

The golf courses, palm trees, and decorative ponds of the Lake Las Vegas development use treated water drawn from Lake Mead.

Residential Water Use in the Colorado Watershed

Many people think of water use in terms of how much water their family uses at home. Residential water use in the basin varies greatly. In Nogales, Sonora, the average single-family residence uses about 40 gallons per person. This compares to 200 gallons in Nogales, Arizona, on the other side of the border. In Tucson, Arizona, the average single-family residence uses about 107 gallons of water per person per day. In Las Vegas, Nevada, a family of the same size uses more than twice that amount. Indoor water use includes showers, faucets, appliances, toilets, and air conditioners. However, the greatest factor in urban water use is the amount of water used outdoors for landscaping and swimming pools (see page 320, "Faucet Family Tree"). In Tucson, many yards are planted with drought-tolerant (mostly native) plants, including grasses, shrubs, trees, and cacti. This landscaping technique is referred to as Xeriscaping™. In the southern basin, where it is warm year-round, lawns planted with Kentucky bluegrass and other water-loving plants may require up to 40–60 inches of water per year.

In Mexico, fewer houses are landscaped with turf and outdoor water use is lower than in the United States. One major outdoor use of urban water is dust control. Many roads are unpaved, and the reduced air quality has caused health problems. To combat this, some residents and business owners wet roadways to reduce dust.

Average Per Capita Water Use Per Day	
City	**Gallons of Water per Capita per Day**
Nogales, SON	40
Tijuana, BC	54
Mexicali, BC	88
Tucson, AZ	107
Albuquerque, NM	136
Phoenix, AZ	144
San Diego, CA	151
Los Angeles, CA	155
Denver, CO	159
Grand Junction, CO	182
Taylorsville, UT (Salt Lake City suburb)	193
Nogales, AZ	200
Tempe, AZ	211
Las Vegas, NV	230

Data from: San Diego County Water Authority (www.sdcwa.org); Situación del Agua Potable y Saneamiento, 2001 (www.cna.gob.mx); Smart Water Report, 2003; Metropolitan Water District of Southern California (www.mwd.dst.ca.us); Natural Resources Journal, 2000 (vol. 40).

Courtesy City of Las Vegas

The city of Las Vegas was first built around ground water springs in the area. Today, 88 percent of its water comes from the Colorado River. According to the Law of the River, Las Vegas is entitled to 300,000 acre-feet plus 4 percent of any excess Colorado River water annually. The little water to which Las Vegas is entitled must be stretched, as it serves millions of residents and tourists each year (see page XXV, Population Map; page 46, Per Capita Water Use Chart; and page 307, "Many Happy Return Flows").

Las Vegas Wash Wetlands, Nevada

- This is the primary channel through which storm drain and treated wastewater from the Las Vegas area returns to the Colorado River.
- A large wetland creates habitat for many species and naturally filters the water.
- Increased return flow from the growing Las Vegas area has eroded the wash in some areas, causing the wetlands to shrink.
- Local water agencies are building erosion control structures to stop soil loss and rebuild wetlands.

Hoover Dam and Its Companion Projects

When I stand over the star chart built into the top of [Hoover] dam that marks its day of dedication, I think that the hubris of that dam-building generation was tempered by the knowledge that nothing is permanent. Like hieroglyphics on the pyramids, they wanted to leave a sign that said, "We were here once, and look what a fabulous thing we made."

Judy Maben, Education Director, Water Education Foundation, Sacramento, California.

Forty-five minutes southeast of Las Vegas stands Hoover Dam. Once the largest man-made structure in the world, it is the key structure in the series of dams and diversions that manage flow in the Colorado River. It was built to control floods, store water, reduce sedimentation, and generate electricity. More than five thousand men worked for five years to complete the project, which forms Lake Mead (see page 244, "Sharing the Shed"). In 1935, the last bucket of concrete was poured into the gracefully curving arch that is Hoover Dam. At that moment the character of the Colorado River changed dramatically. From Hoover Dam to the Gulf of California, ecosystems adapted to fluctuating river flows were altered.

Justin Howe

Hoover Dam intake towers as viewed from Arizona. The towers were built with the functional purpose of releasing water from the reservoir through power turbines. Like many other parts of the dam, they were designed for aesthetic appeal—a walk across the dam reveals rails of solid brass, carved stone statues, and other artistic details. Lake Mead has about 26 million acre-feet of active capacity water storage.

Justin Howe

The solid concrete tailbay [water outlet] *at the base of Hoover Dam is the one place in the structure where the uncontested power of water can best be felt. The force of the 30,000 cfs of water* [spinning] *seventeen turbines makes the entire tailbay and powerhouse quiver and hum with energy. Huge boils and eddies swirl where swimming pools full of water jet out of the turbine draft tubes every second.*

Phil Aurit, Environmental Awareness Specialist,
U.S. Bureau of Reclamation,
Boulder City, Nevada.

Lissa Howe and Phil Aurit stand at the tailbay of Hoover Dam where water used to generate electricity is released back to the Colorado River.

Hoover Dam/Lake Mead, Nevada and Arizona

- This 726-foot dam was once the largest man-made structure in the world.
- The dam's primary purpose is to regulate floods and store water.
- Its hydroelectric generators produce 2 million kilowatts of electricity.
- The dam forms Lake Mead, which can hold almost 26 million acre-feet or more than three years flow of the Colorado River.
- Water pressure at the base of the dam is 45,000 pounds per square inch.
- In 1991, water stored in Lake Mead irrigated more than 840,000 acres on 7,500 farms, with economic benefits of about 1.3 billion dollars per year (U.S. Bureau of Reclamation).

The construction of Hoover Dam and its companion projects (including Parker Dam, built in 1938) removed the uncertainty of water supply in the Lower Basin, catalyzing population growth. Communities throughout the basin developed projects to divert water from the river, including the coastal California cities of Los Angeles and San Diego. The Metropolitan Water District of Southern California (MET) has been a major Colorado River water user since the completion of Hoover and Parker Dams. MET draws water from Lake Havasu (formed by Parker Dam). This water is transported via the Colorado River Aqueduct, which carries it across the desert and out of the watershed to the coast, where it helps fuel one of the world's largest economies.

By 1960, more than 600,000 acres were under cultivation in California's Imperial and Coachella Valleys alone. All of the water for this development is delivered through the All American Canal, the construction of which was facilitated in part by the flood control provided by Hoover Dam. Hoover Dam also helped irrigators in Arizona. Farmers in the Yuma Valley withdraw water from the All American Canal to irrigate more than 150,000 acres. In Mexico, irrigators benefit from the dam's regulation of the destructive floods that previously inundated the delta region. Several hundred thousand acres are now watered there using Colorado River water.

Across Lake Havasu from the MET intake, the Central Arizona Project's intakes pump reservoir water into the system of pipes and canals that will lift it thousands of feet and carry it hundreds of miles for use in Phoenix, Tucson, and surrounding areas.

Justin Howe

On the eastern shore of Lake Havasu, the intake for the Central Arizona Project (CAP) withdraws up to 1.5 million acre-feet of Colorado River water for urban, agricultural, and industrial use in central Arizona.

Havasu National Wildlife Refuge, Arizona and California

- This refuge is located on the upper end of Lake Havasu.
- One of its most dramatic features is Topock Gorge, with dramatic cliffs that rise from the banks of the river.
- The Chemehuevi and Mojave Indians have sacred sites within the refuge.
- It is a popular destination of boaters and naturalists.

Jim Richardson

The Metropolitan Water District of Southern California (MET) withdraws up to 1.3 million acre-feet of water from Lake Havasu each year. The water is transported to Southern California coastal cities, from Los Angeles to San Diego.

The 4.4 Plan

The Colorado River supplies water for many water users in Southern California, including several large irrigation districts and Southern California cities from Los Angeles to San Diego. Under the 1922 Colorado River Compact, California is entitled to 4.4 million acre-feet of Colorado River water per year, but annual usage has been closer to 5.2 million acre-feet. This has been possible because some states have not used all the water to which they are entitled. California has used this "surplus" to meet its water needs.

California's use of surplus Colorado River water has become contentious as other states in the basin fear that California's reliance on surplus water could make it difficult for them to develop their own water rights in the future. In an effort to bring California water use within its allocated 4.4 million acre-feet, the seven U.S. basin states and the federal government have negotiated the California Colorado River Water Use Plan, colloquially known as the "4.4 Plan." Under the plan, California will be allowed to continue to use surplus water until 2016, during which time programs will be implemented to reduce the state's annual usage of Colorado River Water to 4.4 million acre-feet.

Implementation of the 4.4 Plan has been complicated by the need for the Imperial and Coachella Irrigation Districts to quantify their use of Colorado River water. Finally, in October, 2003, California stakeholders approved a plan that quantified Imperial and Coachella's water rights (the Quantification Settlement Agreement) and addressed environmental mitigation and other issues. With that agreement, the 4.4 Plan could be put into action.

Water in Arizona

Our expedition route keeps us close to the Colorado's main stem on the western border of Arizona, but more than 90 percent of the state drains to the Colorado River. Arizona is entitled to 2.8 million acre-feet from the Colorado, 1.5 million of which are delivered by the Central Arizona Project (CAP).

Several of the Colorado's major tributaries flow through the state, but almost all of their water is used before it reaches the Colorado. (In the Lower Basin, water in Colorado River tributaries is not part of state allocations. As a result, these waters can be used without affecting Colorado River allocation.) Arizona is entitled to 7.24 million acre-feet of surface, ground, and reclaimed water.

The Salt, Verde, and Gila Rivers cross central and southern Arizona, their desert waters (along with ground water and CAP water) giving rise to Phoenix, one of the fastest-growing metropolitan areas in the United States. The Salt River Project supplies water and power to farmers, ranchers, and municipalities. Humans have been using water from these rivers for millennia; canals built by the Hohokam thousands of years ago have been updated to meet modern water demands.

As in other parts of the basin, Arizona's ground water is as important as its rivers. Several major aquifers are tapped for urban and agricultural use, and these are actively managed by the Arizona Department of Water Resources. The Arizona Water Banking Authority, formed in 1996, directs unused CAP water into underground aquifers to store for future use. Ground water banking allows

Arizona Daily Star, Nacho Ibarra

A subsidence crack along the Arizona/New Mexico border. Subsidence cracks are caused by over-pumping of aquifers. When water is removed from aquifers faster than it is replaced, the earth can settle, causing cracks to form at the edge of the settling area.

Oak Creek Canyon, Arizona

- A spring-fed stream, Oak Creek flows year-round through a beautiful red sandstone canyon in the Coconino National Forest.
- Oaks, sycamores, cottonwoods, and pines fill the canyon, attracting wildlife and birds.
- Visitors can explore the overgrown remains of an abandoned early-1900s settlement and orchard near the West Fork trailhead.
- The scenic beauty and cool temperatures of the canyon attract thousands of visitors each year.

Arizona to use its full entitlement of 2.8 maf of the Colorado River's water.

In Tucson (in the south) and near the headwaters of the Little Colorado River (in the north), there is no year-round supply of surface water. With the exception of rain runoff, all water must be piped, pumped, or directed through canals to reach water users. In times of drought, it is difficult to get water to all users. In wet times, it can be difficult to get people to plan for the next drought.

As Herb Guenther, Director of the Arizona Department of Water Resources, has said, "Every time we start planning, putting together a drought plan, it starts to rain. And when it starts to rain, everybody packs up and goes home."

On the expedition we are struck by the multitude of competing water users in this arid region, and we discuss the difficulty of meeting the sometimes-conflicting needs of diverse water user groups.

The Central Arizona Project (CAP)

On Lake Havasu's eastern shore stands the intake and pumping plant that withdraws up to 1.5 maf per year of the Colorado's water. This is the beginning of the Central Arizona Project, a 336-mile-long series of canals, tunnels, pipelines, and siphons that delivers water to cities, irrigation districts, and tribes in three of Arizona's largest and most populated counties (Maricopa, Pima, and Pinal Counties).

When the U.S. Supreme Court confirmed Arizona's 2.8 maf allocation of the Colorado in 1964, the way was paved for the construction of the $4 billion conveyance system. The Bureau of Reclamation began work on the project in 1973.

Bureau of Reclamation

The CAP winds across the desert of Arizona. Pumping stations lift the Colorado's water from an elevation near sea level at Lake Havasu to almost 2,900 feet at the highest point. Some of the water is stored in a ground water recharge basin.

Lower Colorado River Agricultural Valleys, California and Arizona

My grandfather was a farmer and my father and son are farmers, working the same land as my grandfather near Casa Grande, Arizona. I was born and raised there and remember watching my grandfather irrigate. When my hands were big enough to cover the end of a siphon hose, my father taught my sister Patty and me how to start hoses. He gave us irrigation boots and showed us how to build up furrows if they should become weak or broken. During times of drought there was no water available and sometimes we would lose crops.

Nancy Wade, Education Coordinator, U.C. Davis Desert Research and Extension Center, El Centro, California

From Hoover Dam south, the river becomes increasingly engineered. Davis, Parker, Imperial, and Morelos Dams interrupt its flow in the remaining 250 miles of its course. These dams help put the waters of the Colorado to work making more hydropower, growing more vegetables, and supplying more cities. To be able to simultaneously hold in our minds the image of the Colorado rumbling through Gore Canyon in northern Colorado, and pooling in desert reservoirs, is the essence of this educational journey.

The wild character of the river has not vanished in its lower section. Havasu National Wildlife Refuge (Topock Marsh), Bill Williams River National Wildlife Refuge, and the 'Ahakhav Tribal Preserve on the Colorado River Indian Tribes Reservation are places where fragments of the historic Colorado's riparian ecosystems have been recreated and preserved, although the once-mighty flow of the lower river is a thing of the past.

In the half-light before dawn, the water is calm and black. It's chilly out here [in Topock Gorge], *not a breeze. The birds are calling and have been for a while. The marsh wren buzzes and chatters as he moves about the cattails and bulrushes advertising his territory. The little fellow with the black mask, the common yellowthroat, calls out from his spot in the marsh. Pied-billed grebes, coots, great-tailed grackles, red-winged and yellow-headed blackbirds along with an occasional Virginia rail, least bittern, and hopefully an endangered Yuma clapper rail are all adding their voices to the dawn chorus. It's quite a way to greet the day.*

Joe Kahl, Biological Science Technician, U.S. Bureau of Reclamation, Boulder City, Nevada

Justin Howe

The Bill Williams River National Wildlife Refuge is a haven of biodiversity, one of the last remnants of natural wetlands along the Lower Colorado. Cottonwood forest transitions into Sonoran Desert habitat, providing a mosaic of habitat types for insects, birds, reptiles, bats, and other mammals.

Bill Williams River National Wildlife Refuge, Arizona

- This refuge preserves one of the last cottonwood-willow forests along the lower Colorado River.
- Floods of up to 200,000 cfs sometimes rush down the Bill Williams River.
- More than 280 bird species are found here.
- Species associated with both the Mojave and Sonoran Deserts live here.
- The Bill Williams River was named for a missionary and mountain man who traveled the area in the early 1800s.

Southwest of Lake Havasu lie great expanses of Mojave Desert—cracked soil, creosote bushes, and miles without a tree. Across this dry openness, the Colorado River Aqueduct carries the river's water over mountains to California's coastal cities, from Los Angeles to San Diego. Highway 62 parallels the aqueduct, and seeing this water so far beyond its watershed is a tangible reminder of the scope of the river's importance.

Driving south from Joshua Tree National Monument, we descend through several elevation zones, beginning in high desert country covered with cholla cactus, Mojave yucca, ocotillo, and other native plants. Suddenly, we are surrounded by the vivid green of vineyards and orchards in neat rows with water from cement-lined irrigation ditches binding it together: the Coachella Valley. We continue south along the west side of the Salton Sea under hot and hazy skies.

From this point south, agriculture will remain a focus of the expedition as we meet with farmers, water managers, scientists, and educators in the Imperial, Yuma, Mexicali, and San Luis Valleys. This region of the watershed produces most of the United States' winter vegetables and uses about 35 percent of the river's water. Lettuce, wheat, alfalfa, broccoli, cotton, and asparagus are just a few of the crops that grow here. Dairy farms dot the landscape.

Agriculture is a cornerstone of the economy in this region, and when farmers suffer from failed crops or low prices for their products, so too do communities. To help ensure the economic stability of the area, farmers are continually working to develop techniques that allow them to grow more crops and make a living.

On a visit to the UC–Davis Desert Research and Extension Center, the expedition team learns about the potential for growing sugar cane in the Imperial Valley for the production of ethanol. Several test plots have been planted, and the tall, green stocks are a stark contrast to the dry soil surrounding them.

Water conservation and quality are important topics to everyone living in this vast desert garden. The issue of salinity in the river came to the forefront in 1972 when U.S. farmers began using ground water to flush salt from soils in the Wellton-Mohawk Irrigation and Drainage District. The irrigation district irrigates 62,500 acres of land just east of Yuma, Arizona. Water used for flushing became too saline for reuse and was directed back to the Gila and Colorado Rivers. This caused the salinity of Colorado River water flowing into Mexico to spike and made it difficult to use the water.

Mexico argued that the United States was obligated to send water that is suitable for human use and asked that salinity in the Colorado be managed. As a result, the United States and Mexico established Minute 242, which amends the 1944 treaty. Minute 242 establishes salinity standards for Colorado River water being delivered to Mexico, requiring that it fall within 115 +/- 30 parts per million (ppm) of the annual average salinity measured at Imperial Dam (see page 63, La Ciénaga de Santa Clara). This is important, because water that is too saline cannot be used by humans without expensive desalination.

'Ahakhav Tribal Preserve, Arizona

- Colorado River Indian Tribes have restored native vegetation by removing invasive species and planting native cottonwood, willow, and mesquite.
- Visitors can now walk through native forests where nonnative species including arrundo (a giant grass that can grow to twelve feet) and tamarisk were once impenetrable.
- Wetland habitats are being restored along the river.
- In 2004, the Colorado River Indian Tribes, along with tribes on other Arizona reservations, controlled 44 percent of the state's Colorado River water allocation. This water can be used for agriculture and other purposes.

The Paradox of the Salton Sea

The Salton Sea is not technically in the watershed, but its existence is closely tied to the Colorado River and the Gulf of California. The bottom of the Salton Sea (also known as the Salton Sink) is about 260 feet below sea level. It was once connected to the Gulf of California, but sediment deposited by the Colorado River has formed a barrier that separates it from the ocean. Because of this, it is considered part of the Colorado River Delta.

Periodically, the Colorado River has flowed into the Salton Sink. The most recent filling was facilitated by human activity when, in 1905, an irrigation diversion carrying water from the Colorado River to the Imperial Valley burst. The entire flow of the river flowed into the basin for sixteen months before engineers could return it to the channel that leads to the Gulf of California. During that flooding, many farms were submerged in up to eighty feet of water, a new riverbed was formed which flows north from Mexico, and a four-hundred-square-mile freshwater lake was created.

Since that time, agricultural, urban, and industrial runoff from the United States and Mexico have continued to flow into the sea. Pollutants in the runoff (including pesticides, fertilizers, and sewage), combined with the warm temperatures of the sea, can cause problems. Fish in the sea have been introduced and, at certain times in its history, have produced a thriving commercial and sport fishery. In recent years, algal blooms have resulted in massive fish die-offs, which in turn lead to epidemic botulism for birds eating the dead fish. Officials in the United States and Mexico are working to reduce pollutants in the sea by building sewage treatment plants and cleaning the water using man-made wetlands.

Salinity is another issue. It is estimated that the Colorado River at the U.S./Mexico border carries about one ton of salt per acre-foot of water. Some of this water is diverted to the Salton Sea after being used for irrigation. High evaporation rates have steadily increased the concentration of salt in the sea. Today, its water is 25 percent saltier than the ocean.

Changes in salinity have altered the sea's ecology from a freshwater to a saltwater ecosystem. Biologists fear that, without intervention, the salinity may eventually kill most fish species. If that were to happen, millions of birds that winter at the sea, eating fish and other aquatic organisms, would lose habitat. This issue has become more important since the loss of wetland habitat in the Colorado River Delta (see page 193, "Flight without Borders").

As water needs shift in Southern California, some irrigation water is being transferred to urban use. This reduces the amount of fresh water reaching the sea. This could allow Salton Sea salinity to increase more rapidly. Mitigating the environmental impacts of these water transfers is a major challenge facing water managers in this region.

Visit www.saltonsea.water.ca.gov for more information.

Salinity and the Colorado River

The story of agriculture in the Colorado Basin is connected to salt; the Colorado River carries about 9 million tons of it every year. Millions of years ago, much of the land in the watershed was submerged beneath an inland sea. As the sea dried up, salts (e.g. sodium chloride, calcium carbonate, calcium sulfate, magnesium chloride), minerals, and elements that had once been suspended in the ocean were precipitated, leaving deep deposits of shale with accompanying salts.

In areas where irrigation is used, salts and minerals in soils are dissolved at a greater rate than would naturally occur. This is because more water comes in contact with them. The water carries these minerals to rivers through surface and ground water.

When a farmer or homeowner waters a field or lawn, water soaks into the soil, is taken up by plants, runs off, or evaporates. When the water evaporates, salts are left behind. The next time the land is irrigated, salts left behind are again dissolved and carried into the soil. This process may be repeated dozens of times, each time resulting in water with higher salinity.

To remove salt from the soil, large volumes of water must be flushed through the soil to dissolve and carry away the salts. By the time the Colorado River reaches Imperial Dam, just north of the U.S./Mexico border, salinity in the Colorado River is the highest measured in a U.S. river.

Justin Howe

A variety of programs have been developed to prevent minerals (especially salts and selenium) from reaching rivers. Canals are being lined, farmers are changing irrigation techniques, and researchers are using plants (such as these hybridized poplar trees) to remove harmful elements from water (see the U.S. Bureau of Reclamation's Web site for information about the Colorado River Salinity Control Program: www.usbr.gov/dataweb/html/crwq.html).

Sonny Bono Salton Sea National Wildlife Refuge, California

- This refuge is important winter habitat for waterfowl and shorebirds.
- Over 375 species of birds are found here, including several endangered species.
- As many as 90,000 ducks and geese live here from November through February.
- The refuge is located on the south end of the Salton Sea. The sea's water comes from municipal, industrial, and agricultural runoff.

Mexicali and San Luis Valleys, Baja California and Sonora

The Colorado River that flows into Mexico appears disconnected from the clear, churning streams at its headwaters. The river is broad and shallow, winding its way along levees and past diversions. The water is warm and the current hard to see on its flat surface.

The temperature is 116 degrees F when our group steps onto Morelos Dam, the only Mexican-controlled dam on the Colorado. There we catch our last glimpse of the flowing river. Morelos is a diversion structure; its purpose is to direct Mexico's share of Colorado River water into irrigation canals and urban water systems. The majority of the water is used to irrigate crops in Sonora and Baja California. The remainder is used by the communities of Mexicali, San Luis Rio Colorado, Los Algodones, Riíto, Tijuana, and Rosarito, to name a few. A red line painted on the top of the dam marks the international border. From there, the states of California, Arizona, Sonora, and Baja California can be seen, and the river's link between

Morelos Dam on the U.S./Mexico border diverts Mexico's share of the Colorado River into canals to be delivered to cities and farms in the delta region.

the two countries seems stronger than the political division represented by the fading line.

Looking north toward the cities of Los Algodones and Yuma, we watch the river meet Morelos Dam, change its course, and enter the Canal Independencia. South of the dam, the Colorado is a trickle, filled only by water leaking through the structure and seeping from ground water. Watching the river reach this abrupt end is moving. After six weeks of traveling along it, drinking its water, and sleeping with river sounds in our ears, we feel strongly connected to the Colorado.

While the river no longer flows in the channel, its water sustains life elsewhere. All along the border, cities are booming. Attracted by low wage rates and easy access to U.S. markets, domestic and foreign companies have moved to the area, bringing with them hundreds of thousands of jobs. Towns along the border are some of the fastest growing in Mexico. Without water from the Colorado River, such growth would be impossible.

Baboquivari Peak, Arizona

- This peak is the religious center for the Tohono O'odham people. It is called *Waw Kiwulik* in O'odham, which means "narrow at the middle."
- According to Tohono O'odham stories, the spirit *I'itoi* (Elder Brother) lives in the mountain.
- *I'itoi* is a mythical figure who lives on Baboquivari Peak. He is often depicted in jewelry and basketry as a man entering a maze. The maze is an allegory about the decisions and changes that humans experience during their lives.
- The peak's sheer cliffs are 7,734 feet above sea level. Because of its high elevation, clouds and mist often cover this southern Arizona mountain.

In most years, the entire flow of the Colorado is used before it reaches the Gulf of California.

Montague Island, Sonora and Baja California

- This island is located at the mouth of the Colorado River and was formed by sediment carried by the river.
- The northernmost point is sometimes referred to as the "Y" because the river channel splits and water flows around the island.
- Today, the river rarely reaches the island. This has caused plants and animals that rely on the mixing of salt and fresh water to become extinct.
- Now the island is alive with clams and crabs adapted to the saltwater environment that surrounds the island.
- Eight species of birds nest on the island in salt grass and middens of *Mulinia coloradoensis*.

Just north of the border, the All American Canal diverts water from the Colorado River for use in California's Imperial and Coachella Valleys. Some of the water is also used in the Yuma and Wellton-Mohawk irrigation districts (near Yuma, Arizona) and sent to Mexico to satisfy requirements of the 1944 treaty (see page 244, "Sharing the Shed"). On its way from its diversion point at Imperial Dam, the canal crosses a twenty-three-mile stretch of sand dunes. The porous sand allows an estimated seventy thousand acre-feet per year to seep from the canal. In Mexico this water is pumped back to the surface for agricultural and municipal uses. Mauricio Torres, an expedition member who has researched this ground water, explains that while the water is not part of Mexico's Colorado River allocation, it is an important part of Mexican agriculture in the region. The high-quality ground water is used to irrigate cotton, wheat, and other crops. Some of it is directed to Mexicali for use as drinking water.

In recent years, the Imperial Irrigation District has been under pressure in the United States to reduce water loss from the canal. Plans are underway to line it with concrete. This will increase the amount of water available in the Imperial Valley, but it will stop the ground water flow into Mexico. Despite protests from Mexican officials, it is likely that the section will be lined by 2010. The economic effect on Mexico will be negative, as thousands of acres currently under cultivation may have to be fallowed due to lack of water.

A few miles downstream from Morelos Dam is the city of San Luis Rio Colorado. On the out-

Expedition member Bárbara Peralta and agronomist Jésus Román Calleros discuss how lining the All American Canal will affect agriculture in Mexico.

skirts of town, our group stops on a bridge over the Colorado River channel. Tractor-trailers loaded with lettuce and alfalfa (grown using Colorado River water) thunder past, carrying crops to be sold in the United States and other countries.

During the peak growing season, the river here sometimes fills with irrigation return flows. Natural floods can also bring water. In 1983, above-average spring runoff caused the Colorado River to swell. Flood-control dams upstream were filled, and managers quickly released water to make space for additional flow. When these releases reached Mexico, the river channel overflowed, inundating parts of the Mexicali and San Luis Valleys. Today, the river channel is filled with sand. The only water visible to us is saline agricultural runoff carried in the cement-lined Wellton-Mohawk canal. It is flowing toward La Ciénaga de Santa Clara, where we will make camp tonight.

Pointing across the dry channel, Jesus Román, an agronomist from the Universidad Autónomo de Baja California, shows us a canal that supplies

Laguna Salada, Baja California

- Before dams were built on the Colorado River, this lagoon frequently filled with river and ocean water.
- When water does reach the lagoon, it fills and becomes habitat for many fish species.
- It is the traditional fishing ground of the Cucapá Indians.
- Most of the Laguna is part of the Cucapá communal land given to the tribe by the Mexican government in 1973.

Colorado River water flows under the bridge near San Luis Rio Colorado, Sonora, but it is in an irrigation drainage canal rather than in the river channel.

The All American Canal (foreground) flows across the Algodones Dunes on the U.S./Mexico border. Plans are underway to line the canal with concrete to stop water from seeping into the sand. This will reduce the amount of ground water available for agricultural use on the Mexican side of the border.

In August 2003, Mexico's Comisión Nacional del Agua (National Water Commission) and Baja California's Comisión Estatal de Agua (State Water Commission) approved a program that will line irrigation canals in the Mexicali area. It is estimated that about 10 percent of water currently used in the Mexicali Valley will be saved by preventing seepage from the canals. This water will be transferred to the Pacific coast for use in the communities of Tijuana, Tecate, and Rosarito.

most of the water for this part of the delta. Eight feet deep and one hundred feet wide, it carries an impressive volume of water. From where we stand, several smaller canals can be seen pulling water from the larger one. Cascading water rushes into the smaller canals, and we imagine tributaries that had joined in the headwaters finally parting ways in the delta.

The hundred-mile drive from the border to the Gulf of California takes about two hours. On the way we pass hectare after hectare (one hectare equals 2.47 acres) of fields growing asparagus, cotton, sugar beets, and onions. Many of these crops will be sold in the United States. Countless canals crisscross the landscape.

La Ciénaga de Santa Clara, Sonora

La Ciénaga de Santa Clara, a wetland marsh in the Mexican delta, is formed by salty return flows from irrigation districts in southwestern Arizona. At La Ciénaga, the stories of salinity, return flows, habitat loss and restoration, and human water needs intersect.

José Campoy, director of the Upper Gulf of California and Colorado River Delta Biosphere Reserve, meets us at the marsh at dawn. The oppressive and still air of the night before has been replaced by a relentless, hot wind. We paddle canoes into the marsh to look for birds and learn more about the ecology and history of this unique place. José explains the events that led to the creation of this wetland.

Justin Howe

The twelve-thousand-acre Ciénaga de Santa Clara provides a glimpse of the former Colorado River Delta, a 2-million acre wetland before dams and diversions stopped the Colorado's water from reaching it.

On the map the Delta was bisected by the river, but in fact the river was nowhere and everywhere, for he could not decide which of a hundred green lagoons offered the most pleasant and least speedy path to the Gulf. So he traveled them all, and so did we. He divided and rejoined, he twisted and turned, he meandered in awesome jungles, he all but ran in circles, he dallied with lovely groves, he got lost and was glad of it, and so were we. For the last word in procrastination, go travel with a river reluctant to lose his freedom to the sea.

Aldo Leopold, *A Sand County Almanac, and Sketches Here and There*

The Yuma Desalination Plant was built to reclaim salty irrigation runoff, but it has not been used because the high costs of operating it have exceeded benefits. As water grows more scarce, operating the plant may become feasible.

Inside the Yuma Desalination Plant, reverse-osmosis filters are designed to remove salts from water.

La Ciénaga de Santa Clara, Sonora

- This twelve thousand-acre cattail marsh is the largest remaining wetland in the Colorado Delta.
- It is formed by saline irrigation wastewater flowing from fields in Arizona and Sonora.
- Thousands of migratory birds use the wetland as a stopover place during migration and in the winter.
- It has the largest population of the endangered Yuma clapper rail and is one of the last refuges for the desert pupfish.
- Residents of the nearby community of Ejido Johnson have developed an ecotourism business to teach visitors about the marsh.

When the United States and Mexico signed Minute 242, it was agreed that the United States would take the steps necessary to limit the amount of salty water entering Mexico via the Colorado River. As part of the solution, a series of cement-lined canals were built to direct salty water from the Wellton-Mohawk Irrigation and Drainage District (WMIDD) to Yuma, Arizona, where the salt would be removed by a desalination plant.

The Bureau of Reclamation completed the Yuma Desalination Plant in 1992, but the plant has not been used due to the high operation costs. Instead, runoff water from the WMIDD flows into the Wellton-Mohawk Bypass Drain, which carries it about fifty miles south into Sonora. This water is not suitable for drinking or irrigating and thus is not considered part of Mexico's Colorado River allocation. Near the town of Riíto, Sonora, additional return flows from local fields enter the canal.

At the end of the Wellton-Mohawk Bypass Drain, water is spread onto non-arable land in the Colorado River Delta. At the release location, the twelve-thousand-acre wetland known as La

Revelation at La Ciénaga

When our two vehicles rolled to a stop at the edge of La Ciénaga de Santa Clara, I entered a world foreign to me. Our team had traveled for six weeks from the high Rocky Mountains and glacier-carved Wind Rivers, through deep sandstone canyons and blazing deserts, to eventually arrive at the marsh where we'd make our last camp.

Stepping onto the dark, moist earth, I could hear the rustling of wind through the cattail rushes. Behind me, creosote bushes dotted the barren landscape, swaying in time with reeds at the water's edge. To my right, a lookout tower reached towards the sky inviting my curious eyes. Climbing the ladder, I saw the Ciénaga stretch into the distance until it finally disappeared in the hazy light of dusk. The heavy, humid air brushed my cheek and my mind filled with images of our journey down the Colorado.

For six weeks I had lived closely with the Colorado, and the natural world had become something I belonged to, not just a place for recreation. At La Ciénaga there was earth, water, creosote bush, cattail, and me. With suntanned skin and dusty clothes, I was part of the landscape as much as the ants and pelicans. This revelation came only after weeks under the bright azure sky, towering peaks, and narrow canyons of the watershed. At La Ciénaga, on my last night under the stars, I found once again where I'm most at peace.

Justin Howe

Paul Formisano participated in the 2003 Colorado River Expedition. He is a graduate of Brigham Young University and is pursuing a master's degree at the University of Nevada, Reno.

Ciénaga de Santa Clara has formed. The wetland is a maze of cattails. Paddling through its channels in a canoe brings Aldo Leopold's words describing "the green lagoons" of the historic delta to life.

La Ciénaga de Santa Clara is critical habitat for birds such as the California brown pelican, Yuma clapper rail, and others. Hundreds of thousands of birds use the wetland as a stopover place during migration along the Pacific Flyway. As we canoe through a patchwork of cattail islands, our guide, Juan Butrón, tells how the *ciénaga* (wetland) has become part of his life and livelihood. He lives in the nearest town, Ejido Johnson, and leads tourists and scientists on tours of the marsh. It is clear that he loves the place, and we watch his eyes light up upon hearing an elusive Yuma clapper rail.

In the dry delta, the wet *ciénaga* is like a breath of fresh air—full of life. In July, a time when most wildlife has left in favor of cooler climates to the

north, the air still hums with wings of pelicans, terns, rails, plovers, and swallows. Juan discusses the importance of this green oasis and how drought and growing water demand may lead water managers in the United States to operate the Yuma Desalination Plant. If this were to happen, the habitat at La Ciénaga would all but disappear.

We ask Juan if he feels the Mexican government could take action to protect this habitat. "No," he says. "This water is not part of Mexico's allocation. In my opinion, if La Ciénaga is to survive, it will be because of actions taken by the American government."

José Campoy has hope for the wetland. Nongovernmental organizations and other groups in the Mexican delta region have been discussing opportunities to buy or lease water for the habitats of La Ciénaga in the event that flows from the Wellton-Mohawk canal decline.

La Ciénaga de Santa Clara provides habitat for pelicans and many other species of birds and fish. If flows from the Wellton-Mohawk canal stop, the wetland will shrink to a small fraction of its current size.

Rio Hardy Wetlands, Baja California

- The Rio Hardy is a tributary of the Colorado River. About two hundred thousand acre-feet of agricultural and industrial runoff flow down it each year.
- A wetland is formed along the river by natural and man-made levees. This wetland has shrunk in the last twenty years as flooding has washed out natural levees and man-made ones have been moved north.
- Along with the Rio Mayor, which connects the Laguna Salada to the rest of the delta, the Rio Hardy has been an important fishing ground for the Cucapá people.

The Gulf of California and the Mouth of the Colorado River

Each time that I cross the bridge on my way to Mexicali my heart sinks. I see the dry river and hear my little son, Emiliano, say, "Look Mama, the Colorado River!" My imagination flies to the headwaters and back to the delta. I think about Lake Mead, Lake Powell, and Lake Havasu and I am certain that the delta was a paradise with plenty of water when the river flowed freely to the sea.

I would like to see my river marching sand to the sea as it did before the dams, just as the old people that live from Yuma, Arizona, to El Golfo de Santa Clara, Sonora, saw in their youth. I think that if the river were as it was before dams, shrimp and totoaba would thrive.

The most surprising thing about the dammed Colorado River is that it still brings life. Its delta is noble—with only a small amount of fresh water, it can maintain life for birds, fish, mesquite, and for people . . . my people here in the delta and in the Upper Gulf of California . . . here in Sonora and Baja . . . here in Mexico.

Martha Román Rodriguez has worked to support conservation in the Upper Gulf of California and Colorado River Delta region for fourteen years. She and her family live in San Luis Rio Colorado, Sonora.

Justin Howe

Sunset near El Golfo de Santa Clara, Sonora.

In the small fishing village of El Golfo de Santa Clara, the tide is in and the gulf waves splash against the sea wall. This is the most southern point of our journey. Although the river has reached its end, its water (or lack thereof) still affects marine ecology in the Gulf.

In the northern (upper) part of the Gulf of California, nutrients in silt deposited by the Colorado River feed plankton, shrimp, and other small organisms. These are in turn eaten by marine species including totoaba, corvina, and stingray.

Marine mammals including bottle-nosed dolphins, blue whales, and the endangered vaquita marina are at the top of the food chain.

Most of the silt that swirls in the tides of the Upper Gulf was deposited before upstream dams could trap it and when the river still flowed to the ocean. The nutrients it contains still support life, but without the river to bring fresh water and sediment to its delta and estuary, the ecosystems are changing.

The Cucapá and Fishing in the Delta Region

Fishing has long been a part of human life in the Colorado River Delta. When European explorers arrived, the Cucapá people (Cocopah in the United States) were fishing the mouth of the river and intertidal zone. One of their major fishing grounds was the Laguna Salada, a low-lying area west of present-day Mexicali. When the Colorado flooded and tides were high in the Gulf of California, the Laguna Salada filled with water. As the waters would recede, indigenous groups living there gathered fish using large nets.

"We are the people of the river," says Monica Gonzalez Portillo, a Cucapá who lives in the village of El Mayor (Bergman 2002). Despite historic and cultural connections to the Colorado River, the Cucapá struggle to maintain ties with it. Look towards the river from El Mayor, and you will see only desert—the dry riverbed far in the distance.

In order to support traditional ways of life, the Cucapá are seeking the right to fish in the Upper Gulf of California and Colorado River Delta Biosphere Reserve. The core area of the biosphere reserve (near the mouth of the Colorado) has been closed to all fishing to protect endangered marine species living there. The Cucapá argue that their cultural survival depends on their ability to continue fishing there.

Outside of the reserve, commercial and private fishermen troll the waters of the Gulf of California for fish and shrimp. Scientists are studying the effects of flow from the Colorado River on fish stocks in the Gulf of California. Preliminary studies show that populations of aquatic organisms spike after flows from the Colorado reach the gulf. Resource managers are seeking ways to manage the effects of reduced flow from the Colorado (see page 172, "Hunting for Habitats in the Colorado Watershed," and page 211, "Chillin' with the Chubs").

Recently, citizens in the United States and in Mexico have become more aware of the importance of delta and upper gulf ecosystems and their potential for restoration. In the 1980s and 90s, wet winters resulted in surplus water flowing down the Colorado all the way to the gulf. This limited amount of fresh water had a significant impact, producing new growth of native plant species as well as increasing shrimp and fish populations in the gulf. Scientists believe that even limited freshwater flows to the gulf would have substantial benefits to the ecosystem. This in turn would have a positive economic impact on the region by improving commercial fishing in the gulf. The difficulty lies in finding ways to make fresh water available in a river system that is already over-allocated.

Fossil beds near El Golfo de Santa Clara, Sonora, hold remains of giant sloths, saber-toothed tigers, and other animals from thousands of years ago.

The otherworldly appearance of the delta research station is best captured in paintings.

The Biosphere Reserve field research station at El Golfo de Santa Clara.

Reduced Colorado River flow has decreased the diversity of life in the delta by an estimated 95 percent. Since the completion of Hoover Dam in 1935, many species have become extinct or are in danger of extinction. Sixty years ago, *Mulinia coloradoensis* (an endemic species of mollusk) thrived in the upper gulf, living in the intertidal zone and feeding on the rich sediment carried by the Colorado. Shell deposits miles long and many feet deep reveal their former abundance. The construction of Hoover Dam rapidly reduced the volume of fresh water reaching the intertidal zone. This fresh water was important to the survival of *Mulinia coloradoensis*. Today, its niche in the ecosystem has been claimed by clam species better suited to saltier conditions, and *Mulinia coloradoensis* is thought to be extinct.

At low tide, miles of mudflats separate the dunes of El Golfo from the water. We decide to walk to the water in the soft light of sunset, but firm sand gives way to thick mud that sticks to the bottom of our sandals, forcing us to abandon them in favor of bare feet. With each step, clams squirt water out of knee-deep holes and crabs scurry from under us. On the horizon, *la igriega* ("the Y," see photo on cover of this book) reflects a hazy blue sky and flocks of white pelicans trail into the distance. Recognizing that we will not reach the water's edge, we wander back to the dunes above. The tide will bring the water to us soon enough.

Christine Newell

Exploring the desert landscape near the shore of the Upper Gulf of California.

Flowers of the Desert

Wasted and hostile the panorama extends . . .
indomitable and dry the land groans,
and its lacerating voice that implores
submerges itself in the anguish of its drama.

And the water drops that it reclaims,
when merged into its blood, are bartered
in the savia that ascends through the hollowed,
thirsty vein of the shriveled branch.

And when the hefty pitahayo blooms,
or the biznaga, of lonesome stem,
trembling amongst its rough thorns,
purple flowers break their calyx,

and in its sprout, barely opened,
wet is the blood of the desert!

María Cárdenas. 1983. From *Panorama Historico de Baja California*. Ed. David Piñera Ramírez, trans. Rita Vázquez and Emilio García. Mexicali, Baja California: Centro de Investigaciones Históricas UNAM–UABC.

Justin Howe

Mudflats at low tide on the eastern coast of the Upper Gulf of California.

El Doctor Wetlands, Sonora

- This ten-mile strip of freshwater springs forms an important "oasis" ecosystem in the Colorado River Delta.
- The wetlands are an important stopover for more than one hundred species of neotropical migratory birds.
- More than twenty species of aquatic plants grow here.
- The springs are the most important refuge for the desert pupfish, the only native fish in the Mexican portion of the watershed.

Río Colorado, to be here with you, to listen to life, and interact with everyone who lives here: to be here is to feel happiness, love, energy, spirituality. It is to feel all the goodness that we have.

Why do we not know you? Because we have forgotten love. Because we have lost our equilibrium.

Río Colorado, you carry in your name the color of our blood that boils in each turn and in each part of you. This colored blood that runs through our body and in each special place—this marvelous river. Each rock formed in these great mountains invites us to

dream and imagine and is an important part of everything. Everything that we have begun to break apart with egotism, ambition, and malice.

Everything that lives in this paradise shows us how to be civilized and we have not taken the time to listen to them and to learn from these things; because in our desperation to advance and become more civilized we have forgotten them and ourselves.

Río Colorado, give me time to listen to you and to each of my brothers that lives with you, leave me with a sense of love, happiness, spirituality, and everything good that you carry.

Justin Howe

Carlota Monroy Lopez participated in the 2003 Colorado River Expedition. She studies tourism at the Centro de Estudio Superiores del Estado de Sonora in Hermosillo, Sonora.

San Pedro Riparian National Conservation Area

- The San Pedro River is the only tributary in the Colorado River Watershed that begins in Mexico and flows into the United States. Another nearby river, the Santa Cruz, begins in the United States, flows into Mexico, and returns to the United States at the border towns of Nogales, Sonora, and Nogales, Arizona.
- Near its headwaters, the river flows during much of the year, providing habitat for plants and animals.
- More than half of the bird species found in North America have been seen here.
- Cottonwood, willow, and other riparian plants thrive along the river. Desert species such as mesquite and creosote bush grow on the hills above the river.
- Ground water pumping from aquifers surrounding the San Pedro River has lowered the water table. Irrigation diversions also remove water. In most years the waters of the San Pedro River soak into the ground before reaching the Gila River.

A Full Glass

Mountains cradling a watershed
Rushing water cradling the dust of those mountains
Porous rock cradling sacred tribal water
Swirling water cradling oxygen for gills
Sand flats cradling the memory of a vibrant estuary
Dwarfing canyon walls
A dwarfing concrete wall
Concrete-lined veins
Blooming cities
Blooming plants
A coal plant
Fuel for different kinds of life   *Rocket Fuel*
A motor   *An oar*   *A paddle*
Arms   *Fins*
A great blue heron taking to wing
Travel-weary wings looking for a place to stop
A Sea that formerly wasn't seen
Salt
Salt cedar
A journey   *A tear*   *A smile*
What are the stories in your glass of water?

Larissa Conte is shown here with fellow expedition member Bárbara Peralta. Larissa participated in the 2003 Colorado River Expedition. She is a recent graduate of Stanford University, where she studied Earth Systems.

Epilogue

In the red delta, the smell of moist clay and salty water mixes with the dryness of the desert. More than eight thousand miles of driving, several hundred miles on the river, and many miles on foot have brought us to our journey's end. From here, we can see the effects of water law, use, and flow distilled.

We have seen how dams are managed and endangered fish are studied, which type of lawn uses the least amount of water, how to paint a sunset over water. The myriad of issues we've discussed, places we've explored, and people we've talked with during the expedition combine to create a portrait of this watershed. The lessons learned have helped us build a heartfelt connection to the river that will form the foundation for stewardship and leadership.

The Colorado River sustains life in an arid region, but its flow is limited. Competing values and water needs can lead to conflict, yet the very conflicts that divide us illustrate how the river connects us as citizens of the same watershed. We are all neighbors, and this is a shared resource—our challenge is to continue developing creative and sustainable solutions to the water management problems that we face.

The river is our teacher and learning is a journey. By exploring the watershed, we all can gain appreciation for the fundamental element that connects us: our mutual need for its water. This sense of connection can be extended as teachers carry the excitement, respect, and adventure of the educational journey into their classrooms and beyond.

Dry and dusty, green and vibrant, the trials and triumphs of the Colorado culminate in the delta, forming a great punctuation mark at the end of this beautiful river.

Justin Howe

I see the world now through water goggles.

"Swim goggles, you mean?"

No, I mean water goggles. These are not for swimming. They are goggles that shape the way I look at water. After our intimate expedition along the Colorado River Watershed, I no longer see just the spray from the showerhead or the firing of a lawn sprinkler. Instead I envision the rush of snowmelt at the headwaters and the dry river channel in Mexico. When I drive past green alfalfa fields, I see canals and diversions from the river to crops. When I start up my laptop, I feel the power coursing through dam turbines harnessing the work of the river. And when I see inefficiencies in water use, I see a cause to be championed. Conservation despite scarcity shall brand my goggles.

"Water glasses, you mean?"

No, I mean water goggles. These are not for clarity. They are goggles that blur the boundaries we have created. If the expedition has taught me anything it is that an understanding of a watershed requires an open mind. For we can delineate a distinction between the Upper Basin and the Lower Basin, but how helpful is this line if we do not share in a common ethic of water conservation? Similarly, the political boundary between the United States and Mexico ought to be blurred to share in a common ethic of water quality. My goggles are not transparent, for the solutions to these water issues must be looked at through a different lens.

"Well then what are your goggles made of?"

My water goggles are made of the voices of those we've interviewed, with an appreciation of their local knowledge. They contain a strong glue of education that gives these voices a megaphone within the watershed. And they are framed with hope: a hope that the importance of water will be conscious in the minds and intertwined in the lives of the people in the watershed

"Can I try them on?"

Justin Howe

Karen Hyun participated in the 2003 Colorado River Expedition. She is a Fulbright Scholar and has a master's degree from Stanford University, where she studied Earth Systems.

Part II

The Activities

Rab Cummings

Introductory

Seeing Watersheds and Blue Beads: The Colorado River

What is a watershed? How do you find one? How do you measure the water in one?

Grade Level:
6–12

Subject Areas:
Geography, Earth Science, Environmental Science, Math

Duration:
Preparation time: 20 minutes
Activity time: 90–110 minutes

Setting:
Classroom and Outdoors

Skills:
Compare and Contrast, Demonstrate, Simulate, Interpret, Map Reading, Graph, Calculate

Vocabulary:
acre-foot, adjudicated, basin, branching pattern, confluence, cubic feet per second (cfs), delineate, drainage basin, drainage divide, ground water, headwaters, hydrograph, main stem, mouth, precipitation, rivulet, runoff, snowpack, streamflow, tributary, watershed

Summary
Students use maps and activities to identify the Colorado River Watershed and learn key water management terms: acre-feet and cubic feet per second (cfs). Students simulate the flow of water through a watershed during different seasons.

Objectives
Students will:
- locate the main stem, tributaries, and headwaters of the Colorado River Watershed;
- outline the boundaries of the watershed;
- apply skills to a more detailed map;
- demonstrate the movement of water through a watershed during different seasons;
- describe the major components of a watershed;
- learn water management terms (acre-feet and cubic feet per second [cfs]);
- compare and convert gallons and acre-feet.

Materials
- For *Seeing Watersheds*:
  - Copies of **Seeing Watersheds** *Student Copy Page* (1 per student)
  - *Blue, red, green, orange, and purple markers*
- For *Blue Beads*:
  - *About 100 each of several colors of beads, beans, marbles, or similar objects*
  - *1 five-gallon bucket or similar container*
  - *One-quart containers* (one for each headwaters stream)
  - *Large ball of string or yarn*
  - *Optional: signs on sticks with pictures representing snow, rain, sun, and each of the seasons*

Background

Seeing Watersheds

Glance at a map of the western United States and northern Mexico. Can you see the Colorado River Watershed? Most people don't know where the boundaries of their watershed are. In fact, a recent national survey showed that only 20 percent of respondents were able to select the correct definition of a watershed from a list of possible answers. One reason the concept of a watershed is difficult to understand is that we seldom see the boundary of our watershed on a map—more often streams, lakes, roads, and political boundaries are labeled.

Seeing watersheds on a map is as easy as tracing a line. You will need a map that shows rivers and smaller tributaries (see page 87, **Seeing Watersheds Student Copy Page**). It begins with finding the Colorado River on a map. Watersheds are named after the river into which tributaries drain (the Colorado, in our case). The Colorado River Watershed encompasses parts of nine states in the western United States and northern Mexico. It is defined as the land that is drained by the Colorado River. So, any river that flows into the Colorado River is a tributary and is part of the watershed. Similarly, any smaller stream flowing into the tributary is part of the watershed.

Streams (flowing bodies of water of any size) often start on ridge tops and flow to the lowest point, driven by gravity. That point may be thousands of miles away. In the case of the Colorado River, the distance from its northernmost tributary to its mouth is about 1,700 miles. As the tributaries flow, they join other small streams, growing larger and more powerful. Eventually they reach the main stem, which will carry them to the ocean. This pattern is found elsewhere in nature: trees in winter, fingers on our hands, stemming patterns on leaves, webs, or arteries, vessels, and capillaries in our bodies. It is an intricate system of the small feeding into the large to keep the entire system functioning.

To trace the branching pattern found in a watershed, use a map to follow the main stem to a tributary and the tributary to its source or sources.

By doing this for each tributary, you will begin to see the shape of the watershed. The source of the tributaries will be on ridgelines that separate river basins (e.g., the Continental Divide). Trace the ridgelines surrounding the basin to see the shape of the watershed.

Blue Beads

Water flow in the Colorado River Watershed is extremely varied. During winter, most precipitation is stored as snow in snowpack (accumulated snow that is condensed and compressed by its own weight). In the headwaters of the Colorado River, snow may be twenty feet deep. Very little water flows into streams in the winter.

With the arrival of spring and warmer temperatures, the snowpack begins to melt. For several weeks this water—often referred to as the spring runoff—saturates the ground and fills streams. If enough water runs off at once, flooding can occur. As the snowpack disappears during the late spring and summer, streamflow diminishes. By fall, some streams have very little water in them. Some desert streams dry up entirely. Only ground water supplies (springs and subterranean flow), remaining snowmelt, and precipitation keep water in the streams. With the return of winter, the process repeats itself as it has for millennia.

Justin Howe

The Green River Overlook in Canyonlands National Park is a perfect place to see the patterns formed by tributary streams flowing to the river's main stem.

Procedure

Preparation

1. **For *Seeing Watersheds*: Make copies of the *Colorado River Watershed Map Student Copy Page*.**

2. **For *Blue Beads*: Divide beads or other similar material into small buckets.**

Warm Up

1. **Review the definition of "watershed" with the class, if necessary.** Compare watersheds to other naturally branching items such as trees, leaves, and blood vessels. Ask the students if they know which watershed they live in. They may say the Colorado River Watershed or a tributary such as the Gila, Animas, Green, or Little Colorado. Ask if they can name several features of the watershed such as the states it encompasses, highest and lowest points, several cities, tribal lands, and national parks. Tell the class that the only way to answer these questions is to first know the watershed's boundary.

2. **Show students a map of the western United States and northern Mexico.** Ask if they can see the boundary of the Colorado Watershed. Brainstorm methods to find the boundary (e.g., looking at the map of the Colorado River Watershed included with this book, looking up the watershed online, flying over it in a plane, etc.).

Snowpack in the San Juan Mountains of southwestern Colorado may eventually find its way to the delta in Mexico.

The gaging station at Lee's Ferry in Arizona is used to measure river flow between the Upper and Lower Basins.

Watersheds are divided by ridgelines. All water in a watershed flows to the same outlet.

3. **Return attention to the map.** Ask why it might be important to know the boundary of a watershed. There could be a wide range of ideas such as learning who or what is affecting the water supply, how much water is available to different towns, where the water is coming from, or how water use in one place may affect water quality and quantity in another.

The Activity
Seeing Watersheds

1. **Tell the class that they will learn how to see watersheds on a map that shows rivers.** Distribute copies of the *Seeing Watersheds Student Copy Page* to each student. Make sure each student has a set of markers (blue, red, green, orange, and purple).

2. **Instruct students to use the blue marker to trace the main channel (main stem) of the Colorado River from its mouth at the Gulf of California to the headwaters in Rocky Mountain National Park in Colorado.**

3. **Have students use the red marker to trace the tributaries of the Colorado River.** To do this, they can start at the Gulf of California again. Each time they encounter a river connecting to the Colorado they should follow that river from its mouth to its headwaters (the farthest they can get from the Gulf of California).

4. **With a green marker, repeat the process for any smaller tributaries following the ones marked in Step 2.**

5. **Now it is time to find the drainage divides.** Remember that streams flow from the higher elevations to the lower. Thus, each tributary or stream actually begins at some point on the land above the headwaters, usually a hill, mountain, or some other high point dividing this watershed from the one(s) next to it. Find a spot above the top of each river and mark it with an orange dot to indicate the divide.

6. **Complete the process of seeing the divide by connecting the dots with a purple marker.** Start at the mouth of the Colorado River and move in a clockwise direction around the main stem. Continue to connect the dots all the way around until the purple line meets itself back at the mouth of the river.

7. ***Optional:*** **using a new color, have the students mark the sub-basins for major tributaries within the Colorado Watershed using the same methods used above.**

Blue Beads
Part I

1. **Ideally, assemble students on a gently sloping hill to help reinforce the idea that water flows from higher to lower elevations.** If a hill is unavailable, students can assemble on gymnasium bleachers or a similar location.

2. **Assemble students in a branching formation in order to simulate streams in a watershed (see *Forming Watersheds Teacher Copy Page*).**

3. **Headwaters streams: at the top of the hill, have two or three students form a short line (fingertip to fingertip, close enough to easily pass beads) leading down the slope.** Form a second line of two or three students next to the first with the two "lowest" students fingertip to fingertip (see page 88, ***Forming Watersheds*** *Teacher Copy Page*). Explain that these students represent the streams that capture precipitation at the highest elevation in the watershed. Depending on the number of students participating, assemble two or

three additional "headwaters streams" a short distance from the first group.

4. **Tributary streams: starting where the headwater streams join, assemble a line of students leading down-slope to represent tributary streams.** These tributaries should touch fingertips and "flow" towards each other but not connect as a whole yet.

5. **Main stem of river: ask students what element of a watershed is still missing.** How will all the headwaters and tributaries join? Have the remainder of the students line up fingertip to fingertip in an S-shaped line starting at the topmost tributary and connecting the remaining tributaries as it winds downhill. Explain that these new students represent the Colorado River and that all tributaries flow toward it and connect. Have everyone touch fingertips. Where headwaters, tributaries, and the main stem connect, have two lines connect to form one "confluence."

6. **At the top of each headwater stream, place a container of beads.**

7. **At the bottom of the main stem, place an empty five-gallon bucket or other container to receive the beads.**

8. **Ask one student from the mouth of the river to step out of the line.** This student will measure the "flow" of the river by counting the number of beads that reach the mouth during each season. Have them record their "measurements" on a piece of paper.

9. **To help connect "Seeing Watersheds" to "Blue Beads" pass a string around all the students.** Explain that this string represents the ridges that separate this watershed from the ones next to it.

Part II

1. **To help students understand what will happen during this activity, instruct those at the top of the headwaters stream to pick one bead and hand it to the person below them.** Have students continue to pass the bead "downstream" until it travels down through the tributaries and the main stem and is deposited in the bucket representing the Gulf of California.

2. **Explain that the students will now simulate the flow of water through a watershed during different seasons.** Then begin the flow scenarios (spend the same amount of time in each season). (*Optional:* make large signs with symbols for snow, rain, sun, and each of the seasons. Attach these signs to sticks and hold them up to indicate/emphasize each scenario).

3. **Winter: Students at the top of the headwater streams begin to pass the beads slowly to simulate the very low flows typical of streams in winter.** (They could count to three before passing each bead on.) Remember, during this time of year, precipitation is stored in its frozen form, snowpack.

4. **Spring: Spring Melt!** Temperatures rise and begin to melt the winter snowpack. Have the "headwaters" students pass beads quickly. "Tributary streams" and the "main stem" will need to pass beads as quickly as they can. Don't worry about dropped beads. They represent flooding that occurs when a stream channel exceeds its capacity. (The student who is counting beads may find it hard to keep up. If this happens, just make note of that fact on the hydrograph [see *Wrap Up* below].)

5. **Summer: The winter snowpack has melted off and streamflow decreases.** Instruct "headwaters" students to slow down and pass beads at a leisurely pace. Instruct "tributary" and "main stem" students to pick up beads that dropped during flooding and pass them downstream. This represents floodwaters receding and flows returning to normal. Simulate an isolated summer storm by having one "headwaters" stream quickly pass beads for twenty seconds. What did this do to the rest of the system? Many people are surprised to learn

that a storm can drop significant amounts of water in one part of the watershed while other parts remain dry.

6. **Fall: Streams generally have low flows during the fall months.** Have students pass beads slowly, but not quite at the winter pace (counting one or two instead of three).

Wrap Up

1. **Gather students and have them describe their location in the watershed.** What is it like to be a headwaters stream? What is the importance of a tributary? What is the role of the main stem in the watershed? What are the challenges for each component? Which section does the class think works the hardest? How do seasons and weather influence the flow of water through the watershed? If time permits, have students switch places and repeat the activity.

2. **Ask students to compare "Seeing Watersheds" with "Blue Beads."** How was the watershed they created similar to the Colorado River Watershed as shown on maps? How was it different?

3. **Return to the classroom.**

4. **Have the student who recorded the streamflow write his or her findings on the chalkboard.** Have students make a hydrograph (graph of water flow) on their own sheets of paper using the season as the X-axis and the number of beads reaching the Gulf of California as the Y-axis. Have them plot the stream measurements and draw a line connecting them. How does the resulting graph reflect the flow of beads through the "watershed?" Does the graph reflect actual river flow on the Colorado River? It does mimic the amount of water flowing in the system, but dams and diversions built on the river have altered the flow, making streamflow more constant (i.e. a graph of actual river flow through a year would be more flat than the one on the board.)

5. **Explain that measuring streamflow is important because it tells water managers how much water will be available for irrigating fields, drinking, and washing clothes, among other things.** In the activity we used the number of beads as a measurement unit. Water managers use cubic feet per second (cfs) and acre-feet to measure flow. One hundred cfs means that 100 cubic feet of water pass a given point each second. Each cubic foot of water contains 7.48 gallons. One acre-foot is the amount of water it takes to cover one acre of land (about the size of a football field) with one foot of water. It is equal to 325,851 gallons. One cfs flowing for twenty-four hours equals 1.983 acre-feet. If each bead that reached the bucket at the end of the "watershed" represents 100,000 gallons, how many gallons passed through the system? How many acre-feet is this?

Assessment

Have students:

- compare the shape of watersheds to other branching patterns in nature (***Warm Up***, Step 1);
- identify the main stem and tributaries of the Colorado River (*Seeing Watersheds*, Steps 2–4);
- show drainage divides of the Colorado River Watershed (*Seeing Watersheds*, Steps 5–6);
- show sub-basins within the Colorado River Watershed (*Seeing Watersheds*, Step 7);
- explain the parts of a river system (*Blue Beads, Part I*, Steps 1–4);
- demonstrate the movement of water through a watershed during each season (*Blue Beads, Part II*, Steps 3–6);
- demonstrate how local weather can affect stream systems in a watershed (*Blue Beads, Part II*, Step 5);
- discuss how water moves through a watershed (***Wrap Up***, Step 1);
- create a hydrograph showing flow patterns during each season (***Wrap Up***, Step 4);
- convert gallons to acre-feet (***Wrap Up***, Step 5).

Extensions

As a class, build a large watershed model using cardboard, plastic pipe, wood, or other material. Simulate water movement through the model using marbles, golf balls, water, etc.

Use different color beads to represent water flowing from different tributaries.

Find out if there is a volunteer watershed-monitoring program for your local river that students could participate in.

Resources

The Watercourse. 1995. *Project WET: Curriculum and Activity Guide.* Bozeman, MT: The Watercourse.

The Watercourse. 2002. *Discover a Watershed: Watershed Manager Educators Guide.* Bozeman, MT: The Watercourse.

e-Links

Mexican Institute of Water Technology
Information about water resources in Mexico.
www.imta.mx

United States Environmental Protection Agency Watersheds Site
Allows you to locate your watershed using maps, keywords, or codes.
www.epa.gov/surf

United States Geological Survey
Streamflow and other data for rivers in the United States.
http://water.usgs.gov

Seeing Watersheds

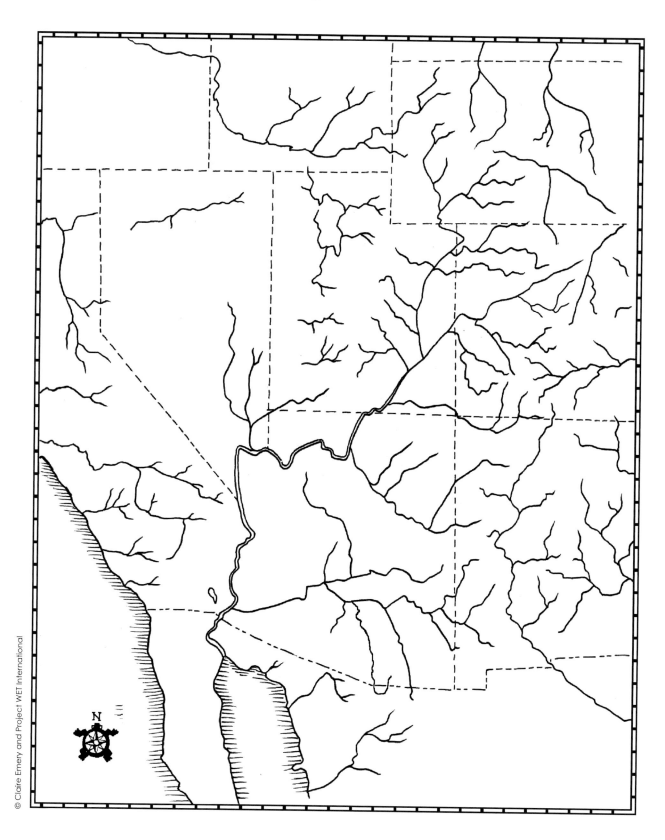

Forming Watersheds

Incredible Journey of the Colorado River

How is evaporation from the Gulf of California connected to a snowstorm in Colorado?

Grade Level:
4–9

Subject Areas:
Art, Geography, Earth Science

Duration:
Preparation time: 90 minutes
Activity time: two 60-minute periods

Setting:
Large Room or Playing Field

Skills:
Gather, Organize, Interpret, Present, Simulate, Discuss

Vocabulary:
atmosphere, condensation, evaporation, ground water, herbaceous, hydrologic cycle, precipitation, recharge, respiration, runoff, sediment, silt, snowpack, topography, transpiration, vapor

Summary
Students play a game to simulate the movement of water in the Colorado Watershed water cycle.

Objectives
Students will:
- describe the water cycle;
- identify and categorize water users in the Colorado Watershed;
- identify the states of water as it moves through the water cycle.

Materials
- ***A map of the Colorado River Watershed***
- ***Copies of the water cycle diagram*** *(1 per student)*
- ***Incredible Journey of the Colorado Box Sides*** *Teacher Copy Page*
- ***Incredible Journey of the Colorado Water User Cards*** *Teacher Copy Pages* (9 sets, place 1 set at each station.)
- *9 pieces of paper*
- *Marking pen*
- *9 boxes, about six inches (fifteen centimeters) on a side.*
- *Audible signal such as a bell, whistle, or buzzer*
- *Optional:*
  - *Beads, 9 different colors* (see *Part 1*, Step 8)
  - *9 small containers* (to hold beads)
  - *Twine or string* (cut in twelve-inch [thirty-centimeter] lengths, 1 per student)

Snowy mountains above the Animas River, Colorado.

Background

The pathways that water follows are part of an incredible journey known as the hydrologic cycle. Water evaporates from oceans, rivers, lakes, and soil; water transpired from plants also rises into the air. Cooled in the atmosphere, it condenses and falls to the earth as rain, snow, or hail. There it can seep into the ground, evaporate again, be used by plants, animals, and humans, or flow in rivers toward the sea.

During its journey from the ocean, water can assume solid, liquid, or vapor (gas) form. Partnered with gravity and other forces, water as a solid, liquid, or gas is a powerful agent of change as it constantly arranges and rearranges the planet. Expanding when it freezes, water exerts enough pressure to fracture rock. Raindrops can release tremendous energy. During rainstorms, droplets falling on unprotected lands can loosen tons of soil. Runoff carries these sediments into streams and riv-

ers that may eventually find their way to the sea. Much of the silt that forms the Colorado River Delta may be traced to landforms more than one thousand miles away.

Water's most dramatic movements take place in its vapor phase. Water is constantly evaporating—changing from a liquid to a gas. As a vapor, it travels through the atmosphere over Earth's surface. In fact, water vapor surrounds us all the time. Where it will condense and return to Earth depends on loss of heat energy, gravity, and the topography of the earth's surface.

In the Colorado River Watershed, most moisture begins as evaporation from the Pacific Ocean and the Gulf of California. Westerly winds carry the moisture onto land. The first major obstacles it meets are the Sierra Madre Mountains in California and Baja California. Humid air hits the mountains and is thrust upward where cooler air causes some of the moisture to condense and pre-

Justin Howe

Dragon-shaped willow tree in the Grand Canyon.

cipitate on the western slopes. After crossing the Sierra Madres, the air returns to a lower elevation and warms again. This results in less condensation and precipitation.

By the time the air enters the Colorado River Watershed, it has warmed enough so that it can hold the remaining moisture. Little precipitation occurs as air moves across the area east of the Sierra Madres. It is not until the Rocky Mountains force the air upward and cool it that more of the moisture evaporated from the Pacific Ocean and Gulf of California again begins to precipitate. This is why more than 95 percent of the water in the Colorado River system may be traced to the mountains of Colorado, Wyoming, and Utah.

Although an inch of snow contains much less water than an inch of rain, snowpack functions like a water bank and is important in the water cycle. When snow in the high country of Utah, Wyoming, and Colorado melts in late spring, the runoff swells streams and rivers and recharges ground water. Snowfields at the highest elevations may melt more slowly, releasing their water into streams throughout the summer months.

Water that runs as surface water is used by plants, animals, and humans. A few of the major tributaries to the Colorado River are the Green, Gila, San Juan, and Little Colorado. Today, humans use most of the water in these rivers for irrigation, drinking, and cleaning, among other

uses. As a result, water in the Colorado River usually does not make it to the Gulf of California (see page 277, "Plumbing the Colorado").

The water cycle connects all living and nonliving things on Earth. Living organisms help move water. Humans and other animals carry water within their bodies and transport it from one location to another. Water is either directly consumed by animals or is removed from foods during digestion. Water is excreted as a liquid or leaves the body as a gas, usually through respiration. When water is present on the skin (for example, as perspiration), evaporation may occur.

Plants such as willow, cottonwood, and creosote bush also play a role in the hydrologic cycle. Water makes up 80 to 90 percent of the weight of herbaceous (green leafy) plants, and about 50 percent of the weight of woody plants. Where temperatures favor plant growth, the availability of water is one of the main factors that determine the distribution of plants. Through transpiration, plants give off water to the atmosphere through pores on their leaves. Most plants give up 95 percent of the water they absorb; the remaining 5 percent is used for growth and maintenance. Plants are the greatest movers of water among living organisms.

In addition to the natural pathways within the water cycle, humans have created pathways for water to follow in its journey on the planet. For example, water is often supplied for urban use by a public water supply system. Water is withdrawn from large wells or is removed from surface waters such as lakes or rivers. This water is generally treated regardless of where it comes from (surface or ground water). The water treatment process kills microorganisms that may occur in water lines. However, if surface water is used and it contains silt, algae, microorganisms, or other materials, a more elaborate and costly cleaning process is required. Man-made structures such as reservoirs and canals become part of the water cycle in a particular place, as water evaporates from their surfaces and seeps into the ground beneath them.

Within the Colorado Watershed, the river and its tributaries serve many users:

- irrigation
- municipalities
- ecosystem services (water- and air-quality improvement by wetlands and forests, erosion and flood control by vegetation and wildlife [beavers], soil conservation, maintenance of biodiversity, and other natural functions)
- industry and manufacturing
- transportation
- pollution disposal
- fish production
- energy production (coal-fired power plants, hydroelectric power plants, etc.)

- grazing and logging
- spiritual and cultural uses by American Indians and others who feel a connection with the river
- development
- recreation
- fish, wildlife, and vegetation

As water moves through natural and man-made systems, we recognize the need that all water users have for water of the right quality and quantity, at the right time and cost. As all water users recognize their dependence on this resource, protecting water quality and quantity makes good sense, socially, economically, and ecologically.

Procedure

Preparation

1. **Use gift boxes to make nine game cubes.** (Gift boxes used for coffee mugs work well; inquire at your local mailing outlet.) There will be one box per station in the activity. Label each box according to the ***Incredible Journey of the Colorado Water Cycle Table***. You can use the images provided on the ***Incredible Journey of the Colorado Box Sides***, create your own images, or have students create artwork.

Students play "The Incredible Journey of the Colorado."

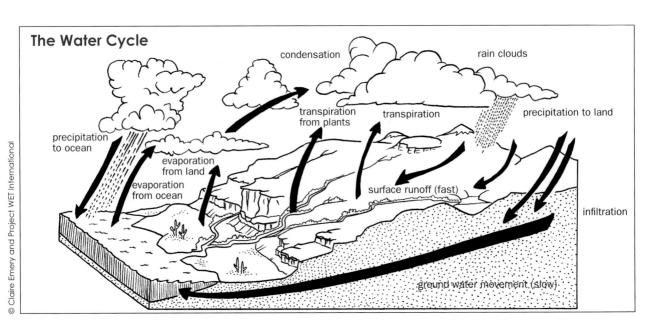

2. **Create station labels to match the game cubes you have made.** Place these labels and the cubes around the classroom.

3. **Make copies of the *Water User Cards* and place one set at each station.**

Warm Up

1. **Ask students to take out a piece of paper and illustrate how they think water moves on the planet.** Ask them to identify the different places water can go as it moves through and around the earth and to indicate the processes that occur (condensation, evaporation, precipitation, transpiration). Remind them to include not only the "natural" cycle, but also where humans have added to that cycle. Ask them to be specific, naming rivers, types of plants, and other features of their watershed if they can.

2. **Have students discuss the different forms water can take and where it can be found.** For example, most moisture in the Colorado Watershed starts in liquid form in the Pacific Ocean and the Gulf of California. The sun heats ocean water and some of it evaporates (becomes vapor). The water stays in clouds until the air cools enough to allow it to precipitate as rain or snow. In the Colorado Watershed, most of this precipitation happens over mountain ranges in Colorado. Where does the rain and snowfall go once it reaches the earth (rivers, lakes, reservoirs, underground, etc.)? Point out that in the Colorado Watershed, where temperatures can be very high, much of the water evaporates and becomes vapor once again.

The Activity

1. **Tell students that they are going to simulate water molecules moving through the water cycle.**

2. **Show students a map of the Colorado Watershed.** You may want to point out specific locations shown on the map. Discuss the different phases of the water cycle in terms of the Colorado Watershed. During what phase of the cycle would water be contained within the basin? In most cases, surface water moves within the bounds of the watershed (this is how watersheds are defined), but in the Colorado Basin, humans have created canals and pumping systems to move water to cities and farms outside the watershed. When water is in the vapor phase of the cycle, it is not contained within the Colorado's watershed; in this way, watersheds all over the globe are connected.

3. **Use the list of places that water can move that was generated in the *Warm Up* to categorize those places into nine stations.** Brainstorm specific examples if some of the categories are lacking them.

Station	Example
Rivers	Gila River, Yampa River
Plants	Sagebrush, alfalfa, creosote bush, ponderosa pine
Oceans	Gulf of California
Snowpack	Mountains of Colorado, Wyoming, and Utah
Animals	People, coyote, antelope, javelina, dairy cow
Ground water	Navajo Aquifer, Coconino Aquifer, Phoenix Aquifer, Colorado River Delta Aquifer
Lakes/Reservoirs	Lake Mead, Lake Powell, Lake Havasu
Cloud	
Soil	Colorado Basin agriculture

4. **Write these station names (Rivers, Plants, Oceans, and so forth) on nine large pieces of paper and post them in locations around the playing area.** Briefly mention the specific examples of water places and users in the list above. Students may want to illustrate the station labels.

5. **Assign an even number of students to each station.** The cloud station can have an uneven number. Ask the students at each station to identify the different places water can go from their station in the water cycle and explain the conditions that cause them to move. This discussion may require an explanation of how water movement depends on energy from the sun, gravity, and other forces. The students can be given the cube for each station, which will help them check that they have covered all the places water can go. The *Water Cycle Table* provides an explanation of water movements from each station. After students have come up with their lists of where and how they could move from their station, ask them to share their work with the entire group. For example, students at the river station can remain in the river current, flow into a lake, be pulled by gravity into the soil, flow into the Gulf of California, be used by an animal, or evaporate.

6. **Have students discuss the form in which water moves from one place to another (i.e., solid, liquid, or gas).** In most cases water will be moving in its liquid form. However, any time water moves to the clouds, it is in the form of water vapor, with molecules moving rapidly and apart from each other.

7. **Tell students that they will be demonstrating water's movement from one location to another.** When they move as liquid water, they will be moving in pairs to represent many water molecules bonded together in a water drop. When they move to the clouds (evaporate), they will separate from their partners and move alone as individual water molecules. When

water condenses and rains from the clouds, each student will grab a partner and move to the next location.

8. **In this game, a roll of the cube indicates where the water will go.** Students line up behind the cubes at the nine different stations. At the cloud station, they should be in single file; at all other stations, they should line up in pairs. Students roll the cube and go to the location indicated on the label facing up. If they roll "stay," they move to the back of the line.

9. **When students arrive at the next station, they get in line.** When they reach the front of the line, they roll again and move to the next station (or proceed to the back of the line if they roll "stay"). In the clouds, students roll the cube individually, but if they leave the clouds they grab a partner (the person immediately behind them) and move to the next station; the partner does not roll the cube.

10. **Students should keep track of their movements.** They do this by keeping a journal or note pad to record each move they make, including stays. Another approach is to place a container with beads of a certain color at each station. For example, offer blue beads at the ocean station, white beads at snowpack, and so forth. Provide lengths of twine on which to string the beads. As students move from station to station, have them keep track of their movements by picking up beads and stringing them on the twine.

11. **Students should pick up a *Water User Card* at each station they move to.** These cards should be kept with their journal or map until the end of the game.

12. **Tell students that the game will begin and end with the sound of a bell, buzzer, or whistle.** The game usually lasts about ten to fifteen minutes. Begin the game.

Wrap Up

1. **Have students study either their journal or string of beads.** Ask them what conclusion they can draw about the water cycle based on what they have observed. Could they have predicted the exact pattern of water's movement through the Incredible Journey? Did any of the "molecules" (students) follow exactly the same pathway?

2. **What *Water User Cards* did the students collect?** Did any of the students get one of each card? How does the water cycle affect these water users?

3. **Discuss the following: How does an understanding of how water moves through the Colorado Watershed contribute to the idea that we must be good neighbors to both upstream and downstream water users?** How are all water users connected in a watershed? As water users, do we have any responsibility for the quality or quantity of water we use?

4. **Ask students to turn over the paper on which they first drew how water moved on the planet (from *Warm Up*).**

5. **Now that they have run the simulations, ask students to illustrate or create a model of the water cycle.** Ask students to compare and contrast their original and final impressions of the water cycle.

Assessment

Have students:
- draw a picture or create a model of how water moves on the planet (***Warm Up** and **Wrap Up***);
- identify the states of water as it moves through the cycle (Step 2);
- role-play water as it moves through the water cycle (Step 12);
- discuss patterns of water movement (***Wrap Up***, Step 3).
- discuss the responsibility of water users for the quantity and quality of water from the Colorado River (***Wrap Up***, Step 3).

Extensions

Have students compare the movement of water during different seasons in the watershed and at different locations around the globe. They can adapt the game (change the pictures on the cubes, add alternative stations, and so forth.)

Have students make and illustrate the game cubes before playing.

Resources

Alexander, Gretchen. 1989. *Water Cycle Teacher's Guide*. Hudson, NH: Delta Education, Inc.

DeYonge, Sandra Chisholm. 2000. *Spring Waters, Gathering Places*. Bozeman, MT: The Watercourse.

Mayes, Susan. 1989. *What Makes it Rain?* London: Usborne Publications.

Schmid, Eleonore. 1990. *The Water's Journey*. New York: North-South Books.

Incredible Journey of the Colorado Box Sides

Copy these pages, enlarging them to fit the
sides of your boxes, as necessary. Cut or paste
the artwork onto the six sides of each box. Or
have students create their own illustrations for
the boxes.

Incredible Journey of the Colorado Water User Cards

Make nine copies of these pages and cut up the cards. Place one set of cards at each Water Cycle station (Soil, Plant, River, Clouds, Ocean, Lake, Animal, Ground Water, Snowpack). Alternatively, work with the class to create their own water user cards.

Earth Systems	Plants, Fish, and Wildlife
The wetlands and forests in the Colorado Basin provide important services to people and all other living things. Wetlands help to purify the water that flows through them. Forests help to remove pollution from the air. Natural vegetation helps to control erosion and keep water from running off too quickly.	The river and its tributaries provide habitats, water, and food for residents of the watershed and migratory species. The great extent of the Colorado Watershed includes numerous, diverse plant and animal communities, from the Rocky Mountains to the Sonoran Desert.
Commercial	**Logging and Grazing**
Water is needed for motels, restaurants, office buildings, and civilian and military institutions in towns and cities of the watershed. Water is used for golf courses and other commercial development.	Logging and grazing are economically important land uses in much of the Colorado Basin, especially in Colorado and Wyoming.
Mining	**Power Plants/Energy Production**
Water is used to carry and wash rock materials during the mineral removal processes (for example, at the Peabody Coal Mine in northern Arizona, water is mixed with coal to make a slurry that can be transported by pipeline). Also, water is important for sand and gravel companies for preparing sand and gravel for cement and road construction, and much of that sand and gravel is mined from riverbeds.	Water from the Colorado and its tributaries is used in the production of electric power at coal-fired generating plants such as the Four Corners Power Plant and the Mojave Generating Station. Dams built on the river can be used to produce electricity. Glen Canyon Dam in Arizona and Hoover Dam in Nevada/Arizona (among other dams) provide hydroelectric power to cities and towns.

Incredible Journey of the Colorado Water User Cards

Make nine copies of these pages and cut up the cards. Place one set of cards at each Water Cycle station (Soil, Plant, River, Clouds, Ocean, Lake, Animal, Ground Water, Snowpack). Alternatively, work with the class to create their own water user cards.

Irrigation	**American Indians and Other Groups Closely Connected to the River.**
Farmers and ranchers in Colorado, Wyoming, Utah, Nevada, New Mexico, Arizona, California, Sonora, and Baja California irrigate crops with water from the Colorado River and its tributaries. Several reservoirs, including Lake Havasu and Flaming Gorge Reservoir, provide water for irrigation.	Water is used for fishing, spiritual, and cultural uses, as well as domestic, irrigation, industrial, and commercial uses. More than thirty tribes are located within the Colorado Watershed, including the Hopi, Navajo, Ute Mountain Ute, Southern Ute, Paiute, Cocopah (Cucapá), Tohono O'odham, Chemehuevi, Apache, Hualapai, Havasupai, Zuni, Pima, and many others.
Municipal Water Use	**Industry and Manufacturing**
Many cities in the watershed depend upon the river and its tributaries for drinking water, landscaping, and other needs. Rivers can help recharge ground water, which is also important for municipal uses.	Water is needed for the production of all goods. Especially in its lower basin, the Colorado provides water for factories that manufacture everything from paper to computer chips.
Recreation	**Rural Water Use**
Many people enjoy the river for fishing, boating, swimming, and other recreational uses. The Colorado River is famous for its whitewater, and many people enjoy rafting and kayaking through its canyons. Whitewater rafting is also popular on the San Juan, Green, Yampa, Dolores, and other tributaries of the Colorado. The Colorado River has numerous reservoirs that provide recreational opportunities.	People in rural areas depend upon the river to satisfy their water needs. (Water is needed for domestic uses, livestock, gardens, etc).

Incredible Journey of the Colorado Water Cycle Table

Station	Die Side Labels	Explanation
Soil	one side *plant* one side *river* one side *ground water* two sides *clouds* one side *stay*	Water is absorbed by plant roots. The soil is saturated, so water runs off into a river. Water is pulled by gravity; it filters into the soil. Heat energy is added to the water, so the water evaporates and goes into the clouds. Water remains on the surface (perhaps in a puddle or adhering to a soil particle).
Plant	four sides *clouds* two sides *stay*	Water leaves the plant through the process of transpiration. Water is used by the plant and stays in the cells.
River	one side *lake* one side *ground water* one side *ocean* one side *animal* one side *clouds* one side *stay*	Water flows into a lake. Water is pulled by gravity; it filters into the soil. Water flows into the Gulf of California. An animal drinks the water. Heat energy is added to the water, so the water evaporates and goes into the clouds. Water remains in the current of the river.
Clouds	one side *soil* one side *glacier* one side *lake* two sides *ocean* one side *stay*	Water condenses and falls on soil. Water condenses and falls as snow onto a glacier. Water condenses and falls into a lake. Water condenses and falls into the ocean. Water remains as a droplet clinging to a dust particle.
Ocean	two sides *clouds* four sides *stay*	Heat energy is added to the water, so the water evaporates and goes into the clouds. Water remains in the ocean.
Lake or Reservoir	one side *ground water* one side *animal* one side *river* one side *clouds* two sides *stay*	Water is pulled by gravity; it filters into the soil. An animal drinks the water. Water flows into a river. Heat energy is added to the water, so the water evaporates and goes into the clouds. Water remains within the lake or reservoir.
Animal	two sides *soil* three sides *clouds* one side *stay*	Water is excreted through feces and urine. Water is respired or evaporated from the body. Water is incorporated into the body.
Ground Water	one side *river* two sides *lake* three sides *stay*	Water filters into a river. Water filters into a lake. Water stays underground.
Glacier	one side *ground water* one side *clouds* one side *river* three sides *stay*	Ice melts and water filters into the ground. Ice evaporates and water goes into the clouds. Ice melts and water flows into a river. Ice stays frozen in the glacier.

String of Pearls: The Colorado Watershed

What are the "jewels" of the Colorado River Watershed?

Grade Level:
6–12

Subject Areas:
Geography, History, Ecology

Duration:
Preparation time: 20 minutes
Activity time: 90 minutes

Setting:
Classroom

Skills:
Organize, Analyze, Apply, Interpret, Create, Symbolize

Vocabulary:
agriculture, alignment, archaeology, brackish, browse, closed basin, evaporation, glacial till, headwaters, hydroelectric, marine, mouth of stream, Mojave Desert, petroglyph, pictograph, runoff, sediment, Sonoran Desert, terrestrial

Summary

By playing this geography game, students learn about some of the natural and cultural landmarks (the "Pearls") of the Colorado River Watershed.

Objectives

Students will:
- identify the basin's unique geographic features (landforms and life forms);
- synthesize information about different sites in an effort to identify them;
- recognize that there are a variety of unique sites throughout the watershed.

Materials

- *1 copy per group of the **Pearls Locations Map** (page XXI) with the key covered*
- *1 copy per group of the Student Copy Pages: **Clue Cards, Score Cards, and Game Rules***
- *A number cube (or have students draw numbers [1–6] written on pieces of paper)*
- *1 "buzzer object" per group (e.g. chalkboard, eraser, small ball, or other similar object)*
- *1 copy per student of the **String of Pearls Fact Sheet** Student Copy Pages*
- *Scissors*
- *Pencils*
- *Paper*
- *Sculpting clay of various colors (air-drying or oven-drying)*
- *Blue yarn or fishing line*

Background

The Colorado River is a highly diverse river, cascading from mountains and flowing across deserts in nine states in the United States and Mexico. About 25 million people and countless plants and animals rely on the water it carries.

The river passes through many ecosystems including alpine tundra, subalpine forests, Navajoan Desert, Mojave Desert, and Sonoran Desert. The river is a lifeline in the arid region, and life gathers at its banks. Animals visit watering holes, plants grow in wetlands, and people use the water for irrigation, industry, recreation, and their households.

A trip through the Colorado River Watershed reveals countless special places. They are special because of ecological, aesthetic, emotional, and spiritual reasons, among other things. There are as many "Pearls" in the Colorado River Watershed as there are people, as each person has his or her own special places. The Pearls identified here are geographically, historically, and biologically diverse, but they are only a starting point for learning about the String of Pearls linked by the Colorado River and its tributaries.

Procedure

Preparation

1. **Make copies of the *String of Pearls Student Copy Pages* (one per group of the *Pearls Locations Map* (page XXI), *Clue Cards*, *Score Card,* and *Answer Key,* and one per student of the *String of Pearls Fact Sheet*).** Cover the key (legend) on the *Pearls Locations Map* before making copies. This will be the game board (note that there are additional Pearls on this map that are not included in the game).

2. **Gather "buzzer objects" (such as an eraser, small ball, or similar object), and number cubes, spinners, or bags with pieces of paper numbered 1–6 (one of each per group).**

Warm Up

Introduce the concept of a String of Pearls to students and ask for volunteers to discuss special places they have visited in the world. Then invite students to describe the Pearls (precious places of

Green River Lakes near the headwaters of the Green River in Wyoming.

Ocotillo is a distinctive plant of the Sonoran Desert.

ecological, historical, or cultural significance) in the Colorado River Watershed that they have visited. What were the special features of these places? Was the area wet or dry? Have the students name and describe any animals or plants that they remember seeing. Challenge students to mark several cities and other reference points on the *Pearls Locations Map*.

The Activity
Part I
1. **Have students read the *String of Pearls Fact Sheet Student Copy Page*.**

2. **Pass out and explain the *Rules of the String of Pearls Game*.**

3. **Pass out the *Clue Cards*, *Answer Key*, buzzer objects, and number cubes.**

4. **Challenge students to play a round of the game, then mix up teams and have them play again.** (You may ask students to put away the *String of Pearls Fact Sheet* during the game, or you may allow them to use it.)

Part II
In *Part I*, students learned about pre-selected Pearls, chosen and described by others. In *Part II*, each student will select his or her own Pearl, research it if necessary, and present information on it to classmates. Students will create a String of Pearls keepsake.

Option I (Individual Student Keepsake Bracelet or Necklace)
1. **Have students select a Pearl within the Colorado River Watershed.** Their Pearl can be well known or it can be relatively unknown, special only to them. Students should avoid selecting Pearls that have already been highlighted in *Part I*.

2. **Have students do research on their Pearl.** Their research should include many of the clue topics from *Part I*, including water, animals, plants, landscape, culture, and location.

3. **Ask students to create an original trinket with sculpting clay to represent their Pearl.** The trinket should have a hole in it so yarn can pass through. Tell students that their trinket should represent their Pearl, but it doesn't need to replicate it. Encourage them to use symbolism when making it.

4. **Have students give short presentations to their classmates about their Pearl.** Students can pass string through the hole to make a keepsake necklace or bracelet representing their Pearl.

Option II (Class Keepsake)
1. **Repeat the steps for *Option I*, but have students combine their Pearls into one class necklace.** If desired, have students present geographically, starting at the headwaters and finishing at the river delta.

2. **Place the class keepsake on display in the classroom or in the school library.** Have students write a brief (one-sentence) description of what their Pearl represents, and display these descriptions with the necklace.

Wrap Up
Have students compare and contrast the Pearls of the Colorado River Watershed. How does the landscape affect the way humans, plants, and animals interact with the land and river? What are the Pearls of their local communities (from this game, or that they would like to nominate)? How do they compare with other Pearls of the Colorado Basin?

Assessment
Have students:
- use the **String of Pearls Fact Sheet** to recognize specific Pearls of the Colorado River Watershed (*Part I*, Step 1);
- demonstrate that they can identify and locate Pearls of the Colorado River Watershed

according to their attributes (*Part I*, Step 3);

- research an individual Pearl and create a keepsake trinket to represent it (*Part II, Options I and II,* Step 1–4 and 1–2);
- identify Pearls of their community and compare them with those of others along the Colorado River and its tributaries (***Wrap Up***).

Extensions

Ask students to make ***Clue Cards*** for their individually researched Pearls. They should include information about flora, fauna, and other identifying elements found there. Students can combine the new cards into the game. This activity may help to demonstrate how communities throughout the watershed are connected. Students could also make a class book of personal Pearls.

Resources

Durham, Michael. 1990. The *Smithsonian Guide to Historic America: the Desert States; New Mexico, Arizona, Nevada, Utah.* New York: Stewart, Tabori & Chang.

Kennedy, Roger. 1998. *The Smithsonian Guide to Historic America: The Rocky Mountain States.* New York: Stewart, Tabori & Chang.

e-Links

City of Green River, Wyoming
Information about Expedition Island and the city of Green River.
www.cityofgreenriver.org/aboutus/powell.asp

Conservation International
Information about critical habitats in the Colorado River Delta and around the world.
www.conservation.org

United States Bureau of Reclamation: Hoover Dam
Historic information and facts about Hoover Dam.
www.usbr.gov/lc/hooverdam

National Park Service
Information on national parks and monuments.
www.nps.gov

Pinedale, Wyoming, Web Site
Information about the area around Pinedale, Wyoming, including Green River Lakes.
www.pinedaleonline.com

U.S. Fish and Wildlife Service
Links to wildlife refuges in the United States.
http://refuges.fws.gov

Vaquita Marina
Information about the status of vaquitas in the Gulf of California.
www.vaquitamarina.org

String of Pearls Clue Cards

Pearl # 1
Water Clue: The headwaters of the Colorado River are here.
Animal Clue: Elk, deer, bear, and beaver can be seen in this place.
Plant Clue: Spruce trees and aspen cover the mountainside.
Landscape Clue: The highest peak in this park is 14,259 feet above sea level.
Culture Clue: Cattle ranchers and skiers live near this place.
Location Clue: It is located near Grand Lake, CO.

Pearl # 2
Water Clue: The Yampa and the Green Rivers join here.
Animal Clue: Colorado pikeminnows swim where dinosaurs once walked.
Plant Clue: Desert shrubs like sagebrush and greasewood thrive in this dry climate.
Landscape Clue: Lodore Canyon cuts through the middle.
Culture Clue: River rafters now float where Arapaho and Apache once hunted.
Location Clue: It is located in northwestern Colorado and northeastern Utah.

Pearl # 3
Water Clue: They are located near the farthest point from the Gulf of California within the Colorado River Watershed.
Animal Clue: Moose are commonly seen here browsing on willow branches.
Plant Clue: Plants adapted to deep snow and cold winters are found here.
Landscape Clue: Large glaciers cover mountain valleys above.
Culture Clue: Trading rendezvous were held near here during the 1800s.
Location Clue: It is located fifty miles from Pinedale, WY.

Pearl # 4
Water Clue: It is located on the Green River.
Animal Clue: Fish swim in pools made for kayaking.
Plant Clue: Cottonwoods, willows, and Russian olives line the shore.
Landscape Clue: It is an island.
Culture Clue: Powell launched his explorations here in 1869 and 1871.
Location Clue: Look in the town of Green River, WY.

Pearl # 5
Water Clue: This was the first major dam built on the Colorado River.
Animal Clue: Razorback suckers are raised in hatcheries just downstream.
Plant Clue: Creosote bush and other desert plants live near this structure.
Landscape Clue: It forms Lake Mead.
Culture Clue: It protects Lower Basin residents from floods and drought.
Location Clue: It is located near Boulder City, NV.

Pearl # 6
Water Clue: Many people who live near this mountain haul water to their houses.
Animal Clue: Golden eagles soar over this mountain that looks like a large boat.
Plant Clue: Piñon, rabbitbrush, and other desert plants grow here.
Landscape Clue: It is located in the Navajoan Desert in New Mexico.
Culture Clue: Its Navajo name means "rock with wings."
Location Clue: A town also bears the name of this mountain.

String of Pearls Clue Cards

Pearl # 7 **Water Clue:** Little water flows where thousands of people visited long ago. **Animal Clue:** Rabbits, deer, and coyotes are found here. **Plant Clue:** Large-scale agriculture would have been difficult due to poor soil and dry climate. **Landscape Clue:** Buildings found here are aligned with the sun and moon. **Culture Clue:** Ancestors of the Hopi, Zuni, and other Puebloans lived here. **Location Clue:** It is located south of Farmington, NM.	**Pearl # 8** **Water Clue:** The confluence of the Green and Colorado Rivers is found in this park. **Animal Clue:** Bighorn sheep climb steep cliffs above rivers and streams. **Plant Clue:** Plants here are adapted to the canyon environment. **Landscape Clue:** Rock formations have inspired people to name part of this park "Island in the Sky." **Culture Clue:** Rock art shows the deep cultural history of this area. **Location Clue:** It is located near Moab, UT.
Pearl # 9 **Water Clue:** Water carved deep canyons here, including "the Narrows." **Animal Clue:** Pallid bats are commonly found here. **Plant Clue:** This park contains the highest diversity of plants in Utah. **Landscape Clue:** It lies on the edge of the Colorado Plateau. **Culture Clue:** Its name is a Hebrew word meaning "place of refuge or sanctuary." **Location Clue:** It is located in Utah along the Virgin River.	**Pearl # 10** **Water Clue:** The Colorado River carved this deepest canyon in North America. **Animal Clue:** Endangered humpback chub live here. **Plant Clue:** Century plants bloom here. **Landscape Clue:** The distance from rim to river is more than one mile. **Culture Clue:** The Havasupai are the only American Indian tribe still living in this canyon. **Location Clue:** It is found in northwestern Arizona.
Pearl # 11 **Water Clue:** It is located on a tributary to the Colorado that is known for large floods. **Animal Clue:** More than 280 species of birds are found here. **Plant Clue:** Saguaro and Mojave yucca grow with cottonwood and mesquite. **Landscape Clue:** It lies on the edge of the Sonoran desert. **Culture Clue:** Chemehuevi and Mojave tribes have lived here. **Location Clue:** It is located just above Parker Dam.	**Pearl # 12** **Water Clue:** The water here is 25 percent saltier than the ocean. **Animal Clue:** Brown pelicans and other birds spend their winters here. **Plant Clue:** Crops grown nearby include alfalfa and corn. **Landscape Clue:** It is about 230 feet below sea level. **Culture Clue:** Irrigation runoff is the main source of water for this closed basin. **Location Clue:** The Coachella and Imperial Valleys surround it.

String of Pearls Clue Cards

Pearl # 13 **Water Clue:** It is located on the north end of the lake formed by Parker Dam. **Animal Clue:** Desert tortoises live here. **Plant Clue:** Cattail marshes have been formed by the reservoir to the south. **Landscape Clue:** Topock Gorge cuts through the refuge. **Culture Clue:** On weekends, visitors race powerboats along the river here. **Location Clue:** It is located near the town of Lake Havasu, AZ.	**Pearl # 14** **Water Clue:** It is formed by irrigation runoff from Arizona. **Animal Clue:** Migratory birds winter here. **Plant Clue:** It is a cattail marsh. **Landscape Clue:** It covers twelve thousand acres. **Culture Clue:** The nearby community of Ejido Johnson guides birdwatchers and ecologists through the wetland. **Location Clue:** It is found in Mexico at the end of the Wellton-Mohawk canal.
Pearl # 15 **Water Clue:** Its name means "salty lagoon." **Animal Clue:** When the Colorado River floods, fish and birds thrive here. **Plant Clue:** Tamarisk trees grow on its banks, but little grows within. **Landscape Clue:** It is usually dry. **Culture Clue:** It is the traditional fishing ground for the Cucapá Indian tribe. **Location Clue:** It is located between two mountain ranges in the Colorado River Delta.	**Pearl # 16** **Water Clue:** Ocean tides here can move inland fifty miles in a single day. **Animal Clue:** This reserve provides critical habitat for birds in winter. **Plant Clue:** Plant diversity diminished when Hoover Dam was built. **Landscape Clue:** It includes ocean and delta habitat. **Culture Clue:** It was created to protect wildlife. **Location Clue:** It is located in the Sonoran Desert in Mexico.

String of Pearls Score Card

	Name	Tallies	Total Score
Player 1			
Player 2			
Player 3			
Player 4			
Player 5			
Player 6			

String of Pearls Game Rules

How many players?
- 2–6

What do I need?
- Each group must have:
  - o one copy of the ***Pearls Locations Map,*** a full set of ***Clue Cards,*** a ***Score Card,*** an ***Answer Key,*** "buzzer object" (such as an eraser, small ball, or similar object), and a number cube, spinner, or bag with pieces of paper numbered 1–6.
- Each player must have:
  - o one ***String of Pearls Fact Sheet.***

What is the object of the game?
- Players compete to identify and locate Pearls of the Colorado River using information given on ***Clue Cards.***

How does it work?
- One player draws the top card from the stack of clue cards and reads the clues one by one to other members of the group, while each player tries to be the first one to identify the Pearl.
- When a player has an answer, he or she picks up the buzzer object and gives the answer.
- If the person is correct, place a mark next to his or her name on the ***Score Card.*** He or she can earn an extra point by showing the Pearl's location on the ***Pearls Locations Map*** (note: there are more Pearls shown on the map than those included in this game).
- If the answer given is **not** correct, the buzzer object is replaced. The reader continues to read clues until a player who has taken possession of the buzzer object gives the correct answer.
- Players should write the name of each correctly identified feature next to the numbered location on their game board.
- Once a Pearl has been identified or all clues from a card have been read, the player sitting to the reader's left should pick the next card and read the clues to the rest of the group.
- Pearls that go unnamed should be set aside to solve later.
- The cycle is continued until all cards have been read.
- At the end of the game, players should work together to identify Pearls that were not identified.
- The player with the most tallies on the scorecard is the winner.

String of Pearls Fact Sheet

Rocky Mountain National Park, Colorado

This high mountain park is located at the headwaters of the Colorado River. Deer, beaver, pine marten, black bear, and mountain lion live here in the spruce forests and aspen groves that grow on the mountains. During winter, deep snow blankets peaks up to 14,259 feet. The area around the park is known for cattle ranching and skiing. After a day of viewing wildlife, playing in the snow, and hiking, visitors can visit the nearby town of Grand Lake, Colorado.

Dinosaur National Monument, Colorado and Utah

The Yampa and Green Rivers join in this national monument located in northwestern Colorado and northeastern Utah. Endangered Colorado pikeminnows and razorback suckers are found here. The monument was created because of large finds of dinosaur remains. At the visitor center, you can see the remains of hundreds of prehistoric animals still in the hillside. Millions of years ago, the climate would have been warm and humid. Today it is dry. Plants like sagebrush and greasewood grow in the desert landscape. Once a hunting ground of Apache and Arapaho people, it has become a destination for river rafters and hikers. Beautiful Lodore Canyon cuts through the middle.

Green River Lakes, Wyoming

Although the headwaters of the Colorado River are found in Rocky Mountain National Park, the Green River Lakes are almost as far as you can get from the mouth of the Colorado River and still be in the watershed. The lakes are only a few miles from the headwaters of the Green River. The water is azure blue from glacial till (a fine powder of rock crushed by the weight of glaciers). Moose browse (chew) on willow branches and aquatic plants. The plants that grow here are adapted to deep snow and cold winters. Located fifty miles from Pinedale, Wyoming, the lakes are near where trappers and traders held rendezvous during the 1800s.

Expedition Island, Wyoming

This is where the famous explorer, John Wesley Powell, launched his explorations in 1869 and 1871. The island is located in the town of Green River, Wyoming. The river flowing around it has been altered to form a whitewater kayaking course. Cottonwood trees, Russian olives, and willows line the shore and shade rainbow trout in the water below.

Hoover Dam, Nevada/Arizona Border

This was the first major dam constructed on the Colorado River. At the time of its construction, it was the largest dam ever built. It is designed to reduce flooding and protect against drought in the southern basin. It is also a major hydroelectric power generation facility. Water stored by the dam forms Lake Mead.

Shiprock Peak, New Mexico

This jagged mountain rises out of the flat desert like a ship on the ocean. According to Navajo stories, the mountain was once a giant bird. This is why they call it *Tsé bit' a 'i'* (rock with wings). The land around the mountain is dry, and many people living here have to haul water from miles away. The area is sometimes referred to as the Navajoan Desert. Rabbitbrush, piñon, and other desert plants are found here.

String of Pearls Fact Sheet

Chaco Culture National Historic Park, New Mexico

Much about the ancient culture that lived at Chaco Canyon is a mystery. Giant structures (some of which were four stories high) were built by thousands of people, yet the dry desert around it has few places to grow crops or hunt for food. People that were living here likely hunted rabbits, deer, and other small animals, as well as grew small fields of beans and corn. In the evening, coyotes can be heard howling on the mesa. Archaeologists believe that the buildings here were designed to be in alignment with the movements of the sun and moon. The ancestors of the Hopi, Zuni, and other Puebloans lived here. It is located south of Farmington, New Mexico.

Canyonlands National Park, Utah

This park is known for deep canyons and towers of stone. On cold mornings, clouds settle into the valleys and high points stick out of the clouds like islands in the sky. The Green and Colorado Rivers join here. Bighorn sheep climb high cliffs, and plants living here are adapted to the rugged canyon environment. Petroglyphs and pictographs (or rock art) may be seen on rock walls near the river. They are evidence of the deep human history in the area. Canyonlands is located near Moab, Utah.

Zion National Park, Utah

Zion is known for deep, narrow canyons and colorful rock formations. Like much of the region, it is the home of small mammals including pallid bats. Located on the margin of the Colorado Plateau and Mojave Desert, it is home to plant species from both ecological regions. More than nine hundred plant species are found here. It is located along the Virgin River in Utah. Zion is a Hebrew word meaning "place of refuge or sanctuary."

Grand Canyon National Park, Arizona

The Grand Canyon is more than one mile deep from canyon rim to river and is the deepest canyon in North America. The combination of depth, width, length, and variety of rock exposed make it special. It is one of the only places where the endangered humpback chub is found. Hikers in the canyon will see century plants, which send up a tall blossom once about every twenty-five years. People have been living in the canyon since at least 800 A.D. Today, the Havasupai village of Supai is the only town located within the canyon. More than four million people visit Grand Canyon National Park each year. It is located in northwest Arizona.

Bill Williams River National Wildlife Refuge, Arizona

The ecosystem surrounding the Bill Williams River is one of the last places in the Lower Basin where tamarisk (an invasive species) is not the dominant plant growing along the river. This is due in part to occasional large floods that clear them out. The Bill Williams is located on the edge of the Sonoran Desert, which contributes to species diversity. Within the reserve, cottonwood trees, Mojave yucca, saguaro cacti, and mesquite all thrive. More than 280 bird species are found there. The Chemehuevi and Mojave tribes once lived there. The Bill Williams River flows into Lake Havasu, just above Parker Dam.

String of Pearls Fact Sheet

Salton Sea, California

The Salton Sea is located near the delta of the Colorado River. It is about 230 feet below sea level—just a few feet higher than Death Valley. It is separated from the Gulf of California by deep deposits of sediment left by the Colorado River over millions of years. The Colorado River has periodically flowed into the Salton Basin. The Salton Sea was filled most recently when an engineering mistake allowed the river to flow into the basin for about two years. Since that time, it has been an inland sea, kept filled by irrigation runoff from the Imperial and Coachella Valleys. Crops grown nearby include alfalfa and corn. It is a closed basin, which means that water cannot flow out of it and is only lost through evaporation. Since minerals cannot evaporate, they remain in the water. As a result, the sea, which started as a body of fresh water, has become salty. Today it is about 25 percent saltier than the ocean. Located in the middle of the desert, it is important habitat for brown pelicans and other bird species.

Havasu National Wildlife Refuge, California

This refuge is located on the north end of Lake Havasu, which is formed by Parker Dam. Many animals live on its shores, including big brown bats, desert tortoises, and great blue herons. Cattail marshes along the river provide habitat in some places. It is a destination for many boaters. On weekends, hundreds of powerboats speed through Topock Gorge. It is near the towns of Needles, California, and Lake Havasu, Arizona.

Laguna Salada, Baja California

Laguna Salada (which means "salty lagoon" in Spanish) is the traditional fishing ground of the Cucapá Indians. Water only reaches the lagoon when the Colorado River floods and tides in the Gulf of California are high. When this happens, it becomes valuable habitat for fish and birds alike. Because it fills and evaporates periodically, the soil in the lagoon is extremely salty. As a result, very few plants grow within the lagoon. Tamarisk trees and other salt-tolerant plants live on its edge. It is located between two mountain ranges in the Colorado River Delta.

Upper Gulf of California and Colorado River Delta Biosphere Reserve, Baja California and Sonora

In 1993, the Mexican government created this reserve to protect the marine and Sonoran Desert environment of the Colorado River Delta. An oasis in the desert, it provides critical habitat for birds in winter. As a result of the construction of dams on the Colorado River, plant diversity in the delta has diminished. Dry sand and salt now blow where large lagoons were once filled with water from the Colorado River. Today, most water in the reserve comes from tidal shifts in the Gulf of California, which can carry seawater fifty miles inland. Part of the reserve is in the Gulf of California, home to the vaquita, the world's rarest marine mammal.

La Ciénaga de Santa Clara, Sonora

This twelve-thousand-acre cattail marsh forms a complex maze of lagoons and pools. It is part of the Upper Gulf of California Biosphere Reserve and is formed by brackish (somewhat salty) agricultural runoff flowing from the Wellton-Mohawk canal. The canal starts in the United States near Yuma, Arizona, and flows more than fifty miles into Mexico. Thousands of birds, including pelicans, avocets, and terns, spend their winters at the wetland. It is one of the last remaining habitats for the endangered Yuma clapper rail. Guides from the community of Ejido Johnson lead visitors to La Ciénaga de Santa Clara through the marsh.

Answer Key to Pearls of the Colorado River

1. Rocky Mountain National Park, Colorado
2. Dinosaur National Monument, Colorado and Utah
3. Green River Lakes, Wyoming
4. Expedition Island, Wyoming
5. Hoover Dam, Nevada/Arizona Border
6. Shiprock Peak, New Mexico
7. Chaco Culture National Historic Park, New Mexico
8. Canyonlands National Park, Utah
9. Zion National Park, Utah
10. Grand Canyon National Park, Arizona
11. Bill Williams River National Wildlife Refuge, Arizona
12. Salton Sea, California
13. Havasu National Wildlife Refuge, California
14. La Ciénaga de Santa Clara, Sonora
15. Laguna Salada, Baja California
16. Upper Gulf of California and Colorado River Delta Biosphere Reserve, Baja California and Sonora

Geology

Rock Sandwich, Stone Soup

What do a sandwich and the Grand Canyon have in common?

Grade Level:
6–9

Subject Areas:
Earth Science, Geography, Art

Duration:
Preparation time: 20 minutes
Activity time: 90 minutes

Setting:
Classroom

Skills:
Interpret, Explain, Construct, Apply, Draw, Discuss, Write

Vocabulary:
deposition, erosion, fault, geologic formation, the Great Unconformity, headward erosion, igneous intrusion, igneous rock, lithification, magma, metamorphic rock, plate tectonics, precipitate (from solution), Principle of Cross-cutting Relationships, Principle of Original Horizontality, Principle of Superposition, rock cycle, sedimentary, weathering

Summary
Students learn basic principles of geology and how to interpret rock layers by building sandwich models. They learn the rock sequence of the Grand Canyon, create timelines to show how the environment changed over geologic time, and explain how geology can be used to reconstruct the history of the landscape.

Objectives
Students will:
- discover basic principles of geology that can be used to interpret landscapes (the Principle of Original Superposition, the Rock Cycle, etc);
- construct and interpret sandwich models representing a sequence of geologic events using basic principles of geology;
- apply their understanding of geology to the Grand Canyon;
- create timelines depicting the different environments in which Grand Canyon rock formations originated;
- explain how Grand Canyon geology relates to geology in other parts of the watershed, especially the delta.

Materials
- *Copies of* **Grand Canyon Geology** *Student Copy Page*
- *Overhead transparency or student copies of* **The Rock Cycle** *Teacher Copy Page*
- *Peanut butter* (one-half cup per 5 students)
- *Jelly* (one-half cup per 5 students)
- *Bread* (1 slice per student)
- *Cheese (thin slices)* (2 slices per 5 students)
- *Mayonnaise or soft butter in "squeezable" plastic containers* (1–2 bottles per 10 students)
- *Paper cups* (2 per 5 students)

- *Paper plates* (1 per 5 students)
- *36" x 12" sheets of white butcher paper* (1 per 5 students)
- *Markers or colored pencils*
- **Colorado River Watershed Wall Map**
- *Optional: If you don't want to use food to build the models in this activity, you can instead use different colors of modeling clay, fabric, foam, cardboard, etc.*

Background

The Colorado Watershed is home to numerous national parks and monuments that showcase unique and stunning rock formations. Arches National Park (NP), Canyonlands NP, Bryce Canyon NP, Zion NP, Dinosaur National Monument (NM), Navajo NM, Colorado NM, and Grand Canyon NP are among the most well-known parks in the watershed. Native people have long revered the natural beauty of these landscapes, and observations of geology are incorporated into their understanding of the relationships between different realms of the natural and spiritual world. The dramatic geology of the watershed also sparked the interest of early explorers like John Wesley Powell. In more recent times, geologic formations in the basin have been highly valued for their minerals, including coal, oil, natural gas, gold, silver, copper, gypsum, and uranium.

The geologic history of the Colorado River and its Grand Canyon is still a subject of study and debate. Geologists know that the lower section of the river (below Grand Canyon) began to drain to the Gulf of California about 4–5 million years ago, and it gradually carved an increasingly larger valley northward. (The process by which a stream erodes further up its course, becoming longer, is called headward erosion.) What is now the upper section of the river

was separated from the lower section by the high Kaibab Plateau in northern Arizona. What isn't clear is how (and why) the upper section of the river cut through the Kaibab Plateau to form the Grand Canyon instead of flowing around the high plateau.

One theory suggests that the ancestral Colorado River originally flowed northeastward across the Kaibab Plateau, before the plateau was uplifted by the mountain-building forces that pushed up the modern Rocky Mountains (about 65 million years ago). This river created its own "ancestral Grand Canyon," and when the Rocky Mountains uplifted to the east, the river reversed its course and began to flow southwest through the original canyon. Because the canyon was already incised into the plateau, it was the easiest path for the river to take. When another major tectonic shift occurred about 5 million years ago and the Gulf of California began to rapidly open, the upper drainage basin integrated with the lower drainage basin and the modern Colorado River drainage network began to become established.

While the entire basin displays interesting geology, the Grand Canyon provides a great "classroom" for an introduction to geology concepts. The

A layer of petrified mud buried below thousands of feet of sandstone is evidence of an ancient streambed or pond.

erosive power of the river has exposed an incredible depth of rock layers, representing over 1 billion years of Earth's history. The three basic types of rock (sedimentary, igneous, and metamorphic) can all be observed within the Grand Canyon.

The Rock Cycle (see *Teacher Copy Page*) illustrates the relationships between the different rock types and the processes that lead to the formation of each type. Sedimentary rocks are formed in three ways: 1) sediments are deposited and become lithified (turn to rock), 2) minerals precipitate out of solution, or 3) the remains of plants or animals become consolidated. Sandstone, limestone, and coal are examples of sedimentary rocks formed in each of the three ways listed above, respectively. Sedimentary rocks are often recognizable by their layered appearance.

If sedimentary rock (or any other type of rock) is deeply buried and subjected to high temperatures and pressures, its structure changes and it becomes metamorphic rock. Examples of metamorphic rock are slate, marble, and schist. Metamorphic rocks often appear to have crystals that are aligned in the same direction, and they may have swirls of minerals that have separated from other minerals in the rock.

Solid rock can melt in a number of situations found deep under the earth's surface, forming liquid rock, called magma. If the magma cools and crystallizes below the earth's surface, it becomes intrusive igneous rock such as granite, with large mineral crystals throughout the rock. If it cools at the earth's surface, as lava from a volcano, it is called extrusive igneous rock. Basalt, pumice, and obsidian are examples of extrusive igneous rock, which cools too rapidly for crystals to form.

All of the different rock types, when exposed to water, frost, wind, and other environmental factors, will begin to break down over time. This process is called weathering. Through weathering, sediments are produced that can be moved and deposited and become new sedimentary rocks—and the cycle begins again.

Rocks on the surface are constantly undergoing change, from weathering and from large-scale forces such as plate tectonics and faulting. Rock layers that were originally laid down horizontally may be tipped, tilted, bent, folded, or broken through faulting and the uplift of underlying molten rock. Plate tectonics is the movement of large slabs of the earth's crust due to forces generated from within the earth.

Geologists face the challenge of reconstructing the history of a landscape by studying its rock formations. The following three basic principles help geologists interpret a sequence of rock layers:

- Layers were originally laid down one on top of the other with the oldest layer on the bottom (the geologic Principle of Superposition).
- Layers were originally horizontal, but may have been later folded, bent, tilted, or overturned by geologic forces like faulting (the geologic Principle of Original Horizontality).
- Where melted igneous rock has forced its way into existing rock and hardened, the igneous intrusion is younger than the rock it intruded (the geologic Principle of Cross-cutting Relationships).

In addition to interpreting the sequence of events and relative age of different rock layers, geologists are often able to determine the environment in which sedimentary rocks formed. They use clues such as the type of sediment (sand or clay), fossils (marine or terrestrial), presence of plant material, and structural patterns to help determine whether a specific rock formed in a windblown desert or at the bottom of a shallow sea.

The Grand Canyon displays layers of sedimentary rock that formed in a variety of environments (see **Grand Canyon Geology** *Student Copy Page*). A famous geologic feature in the canyon is the Great Unconformity, where almost 1 billion years of the rock record are missing. Rock layers below this point were tilted and eroded before the huge stack of younger horizontal layers was deposited on top of them. The metamorphic Vishnu Schist and intrusive Zoroaster (zo-raster) Granite are part

Justin Howe

Desert washes in the Colorado Delta near El Golfo de Santa Clara, Sonora, reveal layers of river gravels deposited by the Colorado thousands of years ago.

and is especially famous for its fossils. The canyons near El Golfo de Santa Clara, Sonora, contain a great diversity of fossils, including mammals such as giant sloths and saber-toothed tigers.

Procedure

Preparation

Important note: *Some students may have food allergies to ingredients used in this activity.*

1. **For *Warm Up:* Make a peanut butter and jelly sandwich (two slices of bread, one thick layer of peanut butter under one thick layer of jelly).** Flip the sandwich over and put it on a plate (layers from top to bottom will be: bread, peanut butter, jelly, bread).

2. **For *Activity Part I:* Divide peanut butter and jelly into paper cups so that each group of five students will have half a cup of each.** For each group, prepare: one paper plate, five slices of bread, two slices of cheese, peanut butter, and jelly. Groups can share the mayonnaise and/or butter bottles.

Warm Up

1. **Show your students the sandwich and tell them that you are going to ask them some simple questions about it.** Tell them that you made it by adding one layer at time in sequence.

   a. What layer of the sandwich do they think was in place first?

   b. Which came next?

   c. What layer was last?

2. **If they answer correctly (that you flipped the sandwich over after you made it, so the top layer is really the "oldest"), ask them how they figured it out.** (It is easier to spread jelly on top of peanut butter than the other way around, so it makes sense that the peanut butter was spread first.)

3. **If they answer incorrectly, tell them that the basis for their answer was logical (the**

of the oldest group of rocks in the canyon. New studies show that some of the rock layers in Grand Canyon may be 20 million years older than was previously thought.

The massive amounts of sediment that were removed by the Colorado River over time to form the canyon were carried downstream. In the last 5 million years, most were deposited at the river's mouth in the Colorado Delta. Sedimentary layers in the delta region contain the eroded particles of rock layers found in the Grand Canyon and elsewhere in the watershed. The geology of the delta is unique sandwich was built from the bottom up, so the top layer was added last, i.e., is the "youngest"). However, they need to look more closely to see if there are any other possibilities. If necessary, flip the sandwich back over to help them see that there are two different possible sequences.

4. **Hand out the cross-section of the Grand Canyon rock layers (*Grand Canyon Geology Student Copy Page*).** Explain that the logic they used to figure out the simple questions about the sandwich is the same logic that geologists use to interpret rock layers. Geologists are interested in knowing which layers of rock are older than others, how old they are, how the rock formed, and what may have happened after the rock was formed to change it. Answering these questions and others can help them figure out where ancient rivers flowed, how long ago volcanoes erupted, what ancient climates were like, and when different plants and animals thrived in a certain area.

   Geologic time can be a difficult concept because its magnitude is so great. Discuss the difference between 1 million and 1 billion to help students grasp relative amounts of time (1 million seconds is about twelve days; 1 billion seconds is about thirty-two years!). Geologic time is divided into Eras, Periods, and Ages that have certain characteristics. This division is similar to dividing time into centuries, decades, years, etc.

The Activity
Part I

1. **Show students the overhead transparency of the Rock Cycle (*The Rock Cycle Teacher Copy Page*) and guide them through the cycle.** Explain that all rocks on Earth are part of the never-ending cycle through sedimentary, metamorphic, and igneous phases. Give several examples of each rock type (e.g., sedimentary=sandstone, metamorphic=marble,

igneous=granite), and ask them to think of rock formations that they have seen that fit into one of those categories. For example, Shiprock in northern New Mexico and Picacho Peak in southern Arizona are formed of igneous rock, while Arches National Park features sedimentary formations.

2. **Ask them to think about the sandwich example again.** What can you assume about rock layers that you see, for example, in the Grand Canyon or along a roadcut? Guide them to come up with the following "rules" and write them on the board:

   - Layers were originally laid down one on top of the other with the oldest layer on the bottom (the geologic Principle of Superposition).
   - Layers were originally horizontal, but may have been later folded, bent, tilted, or overturned by geologic forces like faulting (the geologic Principle of Original Horizontality).
   - Where melted igneous rock has forced its way into existing rock and hardened, the igneous intrusion is younger than the rock it intruded (the geologic Principle of Cross-cutting Relationships).

3. **Tell students that they will use the three rules above to make their own geologic puzzle.** They will work in groups of five to create a sandwich that represents rock layers, and then switch sandwiches with another group to see if they can figure out the sequence of geologic events that the sandwich represents. For example, a group could first put a layer of bread on their plate (oldest layer). Then they may add a layer of cheese, and fold both layers in half before adding a layer of peanut butter. They may add an igneous intrusion by making a hole in the bread layer and squirting in mayonnaise. When they exchange with another group, that group will have to figure out the sequence and list the "rock" layers in order of their age.

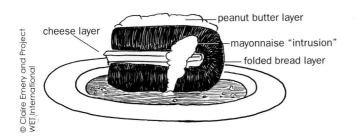

cheese layer — peanut butter layer

mayonnaise "intrusion"

folded bread layer

© Claire Emery and Project WET International

This illustration shows an example of a sandwich model depicting geologic events.

4. **Divide into groups of five.**

5. **Give each group the plate with sandwich items that you prepared in advance.**

6. **Tell the groups that they will have ten minutes to make their sandwich, and encourage them to think of ways to make it a challenging puzzle for the group that will decipher it.** Remind them that they have to follow the three rules or principles above when making their sandwiches.

7. **Have one student in each group make a list of the sequence of events for their sandwich (e.g., 1] bread layer is laid down, 2] cheese layer is laid down, 3] bread and cheese layers are folded, etc.).**

8. **After ten minutes, have the groups trade sandwiches and try to figure out the order of events represented.** Have them draw a cross-section of the sandwich and label the layers numerically, with the oldest layer being "1." Each group should also write a list of events (as in Step 7) so the group that made the sandwich can check their interpretations.

9. **When all the groups have come up with their answers, have them check each other.**

10. **Discuss the activity.** What types of events were the hardest to interpret? Could they apply the same principles when they see rock layers?

Part II

1. **Ask students to look again at the cross-section of the Grand Canyon rock layers (*Grand Canyon Geology Student Copy Page*).** The Grand Canyon is unique because the erosion of the Colorado River has exposed so many layers of rock: over 1 billion years of Earth's history! The cross-section shows basically horizontal layers of rock down to the Tapeats Sandstone, where it suddenly changes. Ask students to come up with an explanation for the difference between the upper and lower layers. In what order did events occur? The oldest rock formations in the canyon are Vishnu Schist and Zoroaster (zo-raster) Granite. The cross-section shows that the schist has been intruded by Zoroaster Granite, similar to the mayonnaise "intrusions" they made in their sandwiches!

2. **Direct their attention to the descriptions of each formation.** Geologists can tell what type of environment was present when the sediment was deposited to form different rock layers. For example, the Kaibab Formation reveals that a warm, shallow sea covered the area, while the Coconino Formation was deposited in a semi-arid coastal environment where sand dunes formed. In this way, the rocks tell the story of the landscape through time.

3. **Tell them that their next task as a group is to create an artistic horizontal timeline showing how the environment in this area changed over time.** They will need to use the information from their *Student Copy Page* to divide the timeline according to millions of years, and then draw a representation of the environment for each period, labeled with the appropriate rock formation. Timelines should start with the Tapeats Sandstone and continue through the Moenkopi Formation.

4. **Give each group a sheet of butcher paper and set of colored pencils or markers.**

5. **Hang each completed timeline in your classroom.**

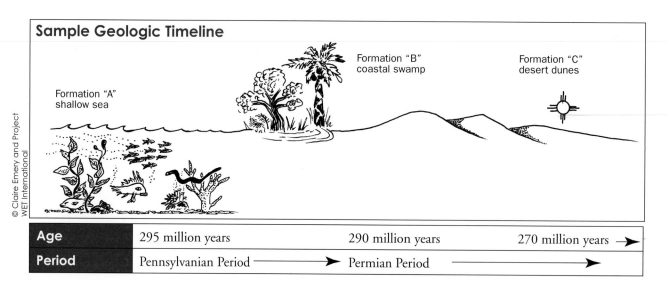

Sample Geologic Timeline

Formation "A"
shallow sea

Formation "B"
coastal swamp

Formation "C"
desert dunes

Age	295 million years	290 million years	270 million years →
Period	Pennsylvanian Period ——→	Permian Period	——————→

Wrap Up

1. **Guide the class in a discussion that encourages them to think about the geology of the Grand Canyon in the context of the whole watershed.** How might sedimentary rocks found in the Grand Canyon relate to other parts of the watershed? Geologists can trace certain rocks and sediments to the surrounding mountains, where they originated before washing into the river and being deposited. These clues help geologists determine how the course of the river may have changed over time.

2. **Direct students' attention to the *Colorado River Watershed Wall Map.*** The Grand Canyon formed as tons of rock were eroded by the river and removed. Where would we look to find the sediments that used to fill the canyon? The Colorado Delta has received millions of tons of sediment over time, including those from the Grand Canyon. By figuring out the age of Grand Canyon sediments found in the delta (and other evidence), geologists know that the river has been flowing to the delta for the past 4–5 million years.

3. **What do they think the sediments at the delta would look like in cross-section?** It is easy to picture them as an upside-down version of the Grand Canyon layers, but in fact the sediments are mixed with eroded material from throughout the watershed (more like a soup than a sandwich!) and reformed in new layers that are distinct to the delta region. How would the age of sedimentary rocks at the delta compare to the age of rocks found in the Grand Canyon?

4. **Studying geology can reveal the history of a landscape including its past climate, geographic position, animals, and plants.** Have students write a paragraph explaining the "big picture" concepts they learned from this activity.

Assessment

Have students:

- discover basic principles of geology that can be used to interpret landscapes (***Warm Up***, Steps 1–4; *Part I*, Steps 1–2);
- construct sandwich models representing a sequence of geologic events (*Part I*, Steps 3–7);
- interpret each others' models based on basic principles of geology (*Part I*, Steps 8–10);
- apply what they have learned to the geology of the Grand Canyon (*Part II*, Steps 1–5);
- create timelines depicting the different environments in which Grand Canyon rock formations originated (*Part II*, Steps 3–5);

- explain how Grand Canyon geology relates to geology in other parts of the watershed, especially the delta (***Wrap Up***, Steps 1–3);
- write a paragraph describing "big picture" concepts they learned from the activity (***Wrap Up***, Step 4).

Extensions

Take students on a field trip to see local geologic formations and ask questions about the type of rock, its age, and the environment in which it was deposited.

Have students bring in rock samples and make predictions about which rock type each represents.

Have students research the geology of another part of the watershed.

Have students research the economic aspects of geology, i.e., the extraction of mineral resources.

Resources

Belknap, Buzz, and Loie Belknap Evans. 2001. *Belknap's Waterproof Grand Canyon River Guide*. Evergreen, CO: Westwater Books.

Chronic, Halka. 1983. *Roadside Geology of Arizona*. Missoula, MT: Mountain Press Publishing Co.

Collier, Michael. 1980. *An Introduction to Grand Canyon Geology*. Grand Canyon, AZ: Grand Canyon Natural History Association.

Plummer, Charles, and David McGeary. 1993. *Physical Geology: Sixth Edition*. Dubuque, IA: Wm. C. Brown Publishers.

Potochnik, Andre. 2001. Paleogeomorphic Evolution of the Salt River Region: Implications for Cretaceous-Laramide Inheritance for Ancestral Colorado River Drainage. In *Colorado River Origin and Evolution*. Eds. R. A. Young and E. E. Spamer. Grand Canyon, AZ: Grand Canyon Association.

e-Links

United States Geologic Service
USGS education page; provides geology resources for teachers and students.
www.usgs.gov/education/index.html

Westwater Books
Informational guides to rivers in the Colorado Basin. You can order a Grand Canyon geology poster or guidebook.
www.westwaterbooks.com

The Rock Cycle

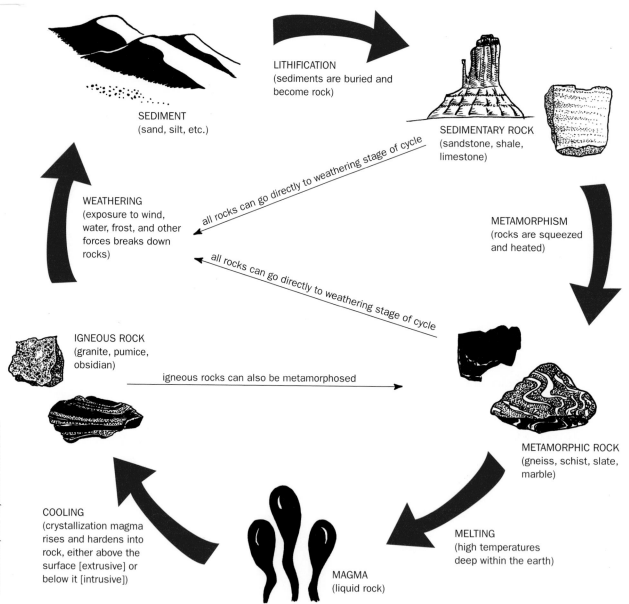

LITHIFICATION
(sediments are buried and
become rock)

SEDIMENT
(sand, silt, etc.)

SEDIMENTARY ROCK
(sandstone, shale,
limestone)

WEATHERING
(exposure to wind,
water, frost, and other
forces breaks down
rocks)

all rocks can go directly to weathering stage of cycle

all rocks can go directly to weathering stage of cycle

METAMORPHISM
(rocks are squeezed
and heated)

IGNEOUS ROCK
(granite, pumice,
obsidian)

igneous rocks can also be metamorphosed

METAMORPHIC ROCK
(gneiss, schist, slate,
marble)

COOLING
(crystallization magma
rises and hardens into
rock, either above the
surface [extrusive] or
below it [intrusive])

MAGMA
(liquid rock)

MELTING
(high temperatures
deep within the earth)

Grand Canyon Geology

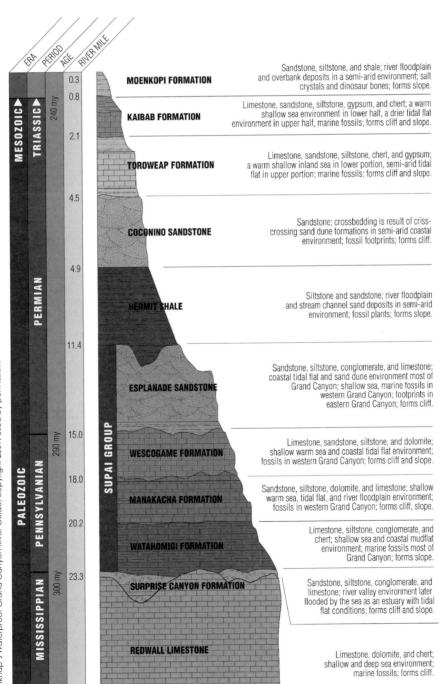

GEOLOGY

ROCK SEQUENCE

The sequence below shows successive rock layers in the Grand Canyon
from oldest at the bottom to youngest at the top.

ERA · **PERIOD** · **AGE** · **RIVER MILE**

MESOZOIC

TRIASSIC

240 my

0.3 — **MOENKOPI FORMATION** — Sandstone, siltstone, and shale; river floodplain and overbank deposits in a semi-arid environment; salt crystals and dinosaur bones; forms slope.

0.8 — **KAIBAB FORMATION** — Limestone, sandstone, siltstone, gypsum, and chert; a warm shallow sea environment in lower half, a drier tidal flat environment in upper half, marine fossils; forms cliff and slope.

2.1

TOROWEAP FORMATION — Limestone, sandstone, siltstone, chert, and gypsum; a warm shallow inland sea in lower portion, semi-arid tidal flat in upper portion; marine fossils; forms cliff and slope.

4.5

PERMIAN

COCONINO SANDSTONE — Sandstone; crossbedding is result of criss-crossing sand dune formations in semi-arid coastal environment; fossil footprints; forms cliff.

4.9

HERMIT SHALE — Siltstone and sandstone; river floodplain and stream channel sand deposits in semi-arid environment; fossil plants; forms slope.

11.4

PALEOZOIC

ESPLANADE SANDSTONE — Sandstone, siltstone, conglomerate, and limestone; coastal tidal flat and sand dune environment most of Grand Canyon; shallow sea, marine fossils in western Grand Canyon; footprints in eastern Grand Canyon; forms cliff.

SUPAI GROUP

PENNSYLVANIAN

290 my

15.0

WESCOGAME FORMATION — Limestone, sandstone, siltstone, and dolomite; shallow warm sea and coastal tidal flat environment; fossils in western Grand Canyon; forms cliff and slope.

18.0

MANAKACHA FORMATION — Sandstone, siltstone, dolomite, and limestone; shallow warm sea, tidal flat, and river floodplain environment; fossils in western Grand Canyon; forms cliff, slope.

20.2

WATAHOMIGI FORMATION — Limestone, siltstone, conglomerate, and chert; shallow sea and coastal mudflat environment; marine fossils most of Grand Canyon; forms slope.

23.3

MISSISSIPPIAN

300 my

SURPRISE CANYON FORMATION — Sandstone, siltstone, conglomerate, and limestone; river valley environment later flooded by the sea as an estuary with tidal flat conditions; forms cliff and slope.

REDWALL LIMESTONE — Limestone, dolomite, and chert; shallow and deep sea environment; marine fossils; forms cliff.

Cut out and tape together the two portions of this geologic sequence (pages 123–124) to make a complete sequence.

Grand Canyon Geology

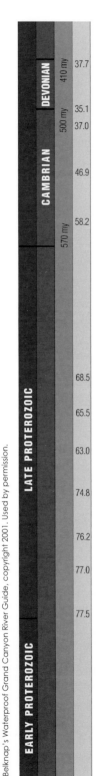

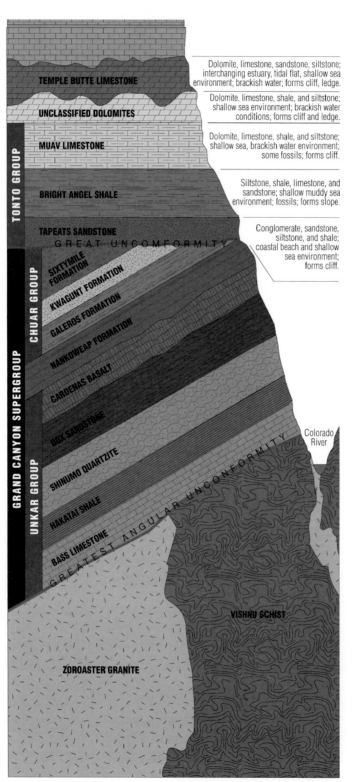

TEMPLE BUTTE LIMESTONE — Dolomite, limestone, sandstone, siltstone; interchanging estuary, tidal flat, shallow sea environment; brackish water; forms cliff, ledge.

UNCLASSIFIED DOLOMITES — Dolomite, limestone, shale, and siltstone; shallow sea environment; brackish water conditions; forms cliff and ledge.

MUAV LIMESTONE — Dolomite, limestone, shale, and siltstone; shallow sea, brackish water environment; some fossils; forms cliff.

BRIGHT ANGEL SHALE — Siltstone, shale, limestone, and sandstone; shallow muddy sea environment; fossils; forms slope.

TAPEATS SANDSTONE — Conglomerate, sandstone, siltstone, and shale; coastal beach and shallow sea environment; forms cliff.

GREAT UNCONFORMITY

SIXTYMILE FORMATION
KWAGUNT FORMATION
GALEROS FORMATION
NANKOWEAP FORMATION
CARDENAS BASALT
DOX SANDSTONE
SHINUMO QUARTZITE
HAKATAI SHALE
BASS LIMESTONE

GREATEST ANGULAR UNCONFORMITY

Colorado River

VISHNU SCHIST

ZOROASTER GRANITE

DEVONIAN — 410 my — 37.7

CAMBRIAN — 500 my: 35.1, 37.0; 46.9; 58.2; 570 my

TONTO GROUP

CHUAR GROUP
GRAND CANYON SUPERGROUP
UNKAR GROUP

68.5, 65.5, 63.0, 74.8, 76.2, 77.0, 77.5

LATE PROTEROZOIC

EARLY PROTEROZOIC

Cut out and tape together the two portions of this geologic sequence (pages 123–124) to make a complete sequence.

Hydrology

Go with the Flow

How can you watch the flow of an entire river without leaving your classroom?

Grade Level:
8–12

Subject Areas:
Environmental Science, Earth Science

Duration:
Preparation time: 60 minutes
Activity time: 120 minutes

Setting:
Classroom

Skills:
Discuss, Problem Solve, Evaluate, Design, Build, Hypothesize, Experiment, Compare

Vocabulary:
active reservoir capacity, competence, current, dead reservoir capacity, deposition, discharge, eddy, erosion, floodplain, gradient, inactive reservoir capacity, inlet, meander, outlet, sediment, sediment load, spillway, streambed, stream channel, stream velocity, wetted perimeter

Summary
Students build a working river model and explore stream dynamics, including erosion, deposition, and the effects of diversions and dams.

Objectives
Students will:
- build river models to explore how the shape of the river channel affects current, sediment deposition, and erosion;
- observe how dams and diversions affect river flow and sediment deposition;
- map the capacity levels of a modeled reservoir;
- compare their river model to rivers and streams in their own communities.

Materials
- *Copies of **River Flow Model Design** Student Copy Page* (1 per student)
- *Copies of **Go with the Flow Observations** Student Copy Pages* (1 per student)
- *Copies of **Go with the Flow Definitions** Student Copy Page* (1 per student)
- *Mixing bucket*
- *Wooden spoon*
- *Sponges for cleanup*
- *Plastic wrap*
- *Salt dough* (2 balls per group)
- *Cafeteria trays or similar water-resistant surface* (1 per group)
- *Two-liter bottles with water* (2 per group)
- *Fine soil* (two cups per group)
- *Stirring straws or small diameter drinking straws* (2 per group)
- *Molding clay* (1½"-diameter ball per group)
- *1½" block* (1 per group)

- *One-gallon water bucket* (1 per group)
- *Blue, red, and green colored pencils* (1 set per group)
- *Rulers* (1 per group)

Background

Stream dynamics play an important role in our lives. Streams carve canyons, erode hills, and deposit sediment where soil can develop. Understanding these dynamics can be difficult because they take place over the entire length of a river. Models can help us to see more of the picture at one time.

Water is one of the most important sculptors of the land: eroding, transporting, and depositing sediment to form shallow ditches, deep canyons, and broad valleys. Even in the dry Colorado River Basin, its effects can be seen everywhere. In the north, glacial valleys lead out of high mountains. In winter, cold silence is sometimes broken when water, freezing in rock cracks, expands and breaks boulders apart. In the central basin, canyons form as water cuts into the bedrock. All along the waterway, this eroded material (now referred to as sediment) is picked up and deposited countless times before finally reaching the river delta or the Gulf of California.

When viewed from the air, the effects of erosion on the Colorado River Basin are seen as a series of gullies, canyons, and rivers spreading across the land like veins in a leaf. On the ground, travelers navigate an endless system of creeks and rivers and are sometimes stopped by vertical walls cut by flowing water. Other times they may find themselves wading through knee-deep sediment, deposited by a nearby river, lake, or reservoir.

The shape, direction, and flow of rivers and streams (geologists use the term "streams" to refer to all flowing bodies of water regardless of size) are dictated by the geologic composition and slope of the land across which they flow. For example, when water flows around sharp bends or large rocks, some of the current is slowed. This change creates an eddy. Sand bars and deep pools are often associated with eddies.

A stream normally stays within its stream channel, a long narrow depression eroded by the stream into the earth. The banks of the channel direct flow and the bed provides a surface over which water flows. During flooding, a river may spill over the riverbanks and into the floodplain.

When viewed in a longitudinal profile, streams typically begin in steep mountains and flow across a broad plain to the sea. Near the headwaters, where the stream is flowing quickly, the river cuts V-shaped valleys. As the land across which the stream flows flattens out, the river slows and deposits sediment. These processes are continual and dynamic.

Stream Erosion

Stream erosion and deposition are primarily controlled by velocity and discharge. Velocity is the speed at which water flows and is controlled by slope, channel shape, and channel composition. Discharge is the volume of water transported by a stream and is primarily influenced by the amount of precipitation into the system.

Channel shape affects velocity by changing the amount of friction between the water and the riv-

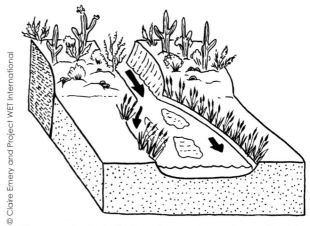

© Claire Emery and Project WET International

Stream velocity is faster when a stream is confined to a narrow channel. When the channel widens, stream velocity will slow, allowing sediment to be more easily deposited. In some cases, the river will seep into the soil where it will flow underground until the river channel becomes confined again.

erbed. Water in a narrow channel will move faster than it would in a wider channel because the contact surface between the water and the riverbed (known as the wetted perimeter) is smaller, resulting in less friction. Channel composition also affects velocity. A stream can flow quickly over a smooth surface, but a rough surface increases friction and slows velocity. Boulders, gravels, and other coarse particles create a rough channel while sand and other small particles create a smooth one.

Streams continually erode the land through which they flow, transporting sediments downstream. Velocity and discharge determine how much sediment can be carried and how large the particles can be. A stream with higher velocity has a higher competence, meaning that it can transport more sediment. As discharge increases, the river is able to transport larger particles. This is referred to as the river's capacity. During floods, a river's capacity and competence increase and can lead to rapid erosion.

Stream Deposition
Sediments carried by a stream are called the sediment load. The load is eventually deposited along the waterway, at the river delta, or in the ocean. Sediments may be picked up and deposited downstream countless times before reaching their final resting place. During a flood, large amounts of sediment are eroded and transported, but as the water slows, the load is deposited. Deposition also occurs when a river's current slows upon meeting obstacles such as dams and diversions.

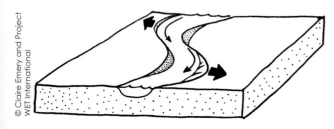

Curves on meandering streams can become exaggerated over time because of erosion on the outside of corners and deposition on the inside.

A common place for sediment to deposit is on the inside of a river bend. This is because velocity tends to be higher on the outside of river curves (or meanders). On the inside of the curve, velocity is lower. As a result, sediment may be deposited. Over time, these curves may become highly exaggerated. Rivers with many meanders are referred to as meandering streams. They are common in places where sediment particles are fine and the river gradient is shallow.

Another common place for sediment to be deposited is at the upper end of lakes or reservoirs. This is a result of reduced stream velocity. As reservoirs age, they become filled with sediment and their ability to use the water stored in them diminishes. Managers discuss the water held in reservoirs in terms of capacity levels. These levels identify how water can be used. The three primary levels are active, inactive, and dead capacities (see illustration).

The dead capacity is first to fill with sediment. The effects of this on the overall operation of the dam are minimal, as unusable water is simply replaced with sediment. Filling of the active and inactive capacities is more detrimental, as it reduces managers' ability to control the flow out of dams for irrigation, household use, industry, and hydroelectric power generation.

Impacts of Dams and Diversions
Today the Colorado River has many dams and diversions that control its flow. They are used for flood control, to store excess water for use in dry times, and to produce hydroelectric power. Their reservoirs provide countless recreational opportunities. Diversions allow water in the river to be used for farms, cities, and other purposes in areas far away from it.

Dams and diversions alter the river's flow in order to make its water more useable by humans. As a result of changing the flow of water, the movement of sediment is also altered. This has its own impacts on ecosystems and human use of the river. One example of this change has to do with the amount of

Reservoir Model

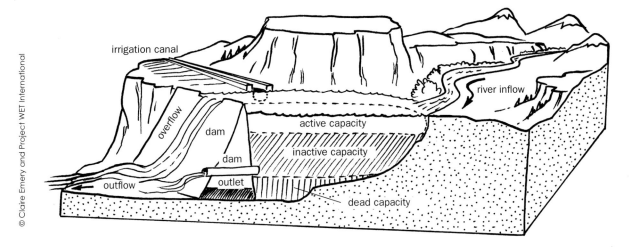

Reservoir capacity can be divided into three levels. Active capacity can be withdrawn from the reservoir by an irrigation canal or other outlet. Inactive capacity can be released from the dam outlet. Dead capacity cannot be released from the dam without pumping.

nutrients carried in the river. The pre-dam Colorado River carried large amounts of organic and inorganic material, which provided food for aquatic organisms (see page 162, "Too Thick to Drink"). Dams trap much of this material in reservoirs, thereby reducing the availability of nutrients. At the same time, the clearer water below dams allows light to penetrate and facilitates the growth of algae, producing food for other life forms.

Another effect of reduced sediment is that sand bars, which rely on new sediment to continually renew them, are disappearing below dams. This changes the river ecosystem by reducing habitat for some species (see page 211, "Chillin' with the Chubs," and page 244, "An Invited Guest in the Colorado Watershed").

The effects of reduced sedimentation may be seen in the Grand Canyon, where sediment that would have rebuilt beaches is trapped behind Glen Canyon Dam. Among other effects, beaches used for camping are disappearing and archaeological sites on riverbanks are being eroded. Resource managers are trying to find ways to reduce the negative effects of dams (see page 211, "Chillin' with the Chubs").

Procedure
Preparation

1. **Make a batch of salt dough and roll into two balls per group.** The following proportions will make enough dough for one group:

    Mix one cup table salt, two cups flour, two cups boiling water, and two tablespoons vegetable oil.

    Multiply by the number of groups you will have, and make some extra in case a group needs more to work with. You can make the dough ahead of time, but it works best if made just before use. If you do make it ahead of time, store it in an airtight container. You can also use commercial clay.

2. **You will also need a cafeteria tray or some other flat and water-resistant surface for each group. Laminated plywood works well.** If you choose plywood, cut a sheet into 24" x 16" rectangles. This will yield twelve platforms.

    If you will be doing this activity over several class periods, you will need to cover partially complete models for overnight storage.

Warm Up

1. **Have students gather around a large table.** Tell them that you will demonstrate how to make a river flow model.

2. **Build a sample river flow model.** Use the same methods and materials students will employ. Demonstrate how to roll the salt dough, make it stick to the platform, construct dams, etc.

3. **Demonstrate how to pour water through the model.** Show students where eddies form and the current is fastest.

4. **Explain that rivers are powerful forces and that over time they can move entire mountains.** We can see where land has been eroded, but where does all that earth go?

5. **Tell students that they will use their models to learn how and where soil (sediment) is moved.**

The Activity

Part I

1. **Pass out the *Go with the Flow Definitions, River Flow Model Design,* and *Go with the Flow Observations Student Copy Pages*.** Students will use these pages to guide construction, identify features, and record observations.

2. **Divide students into groups of two to three.**

3. **Pass out activity supplies.**

4. **Have the students sketch onto the platform the outline of the river channel they will create.** If you are using cafeteria trays, be sure the students use pencils.

5. **After they have sketched the river channel on the platform, students may begin constructing the model.** Have them form the salt dough into long, one-inch diameter pieces. These pieces will form the banks of the river. They can join short pieces by wetting the dough and lightly pressing the ends together.

One student can roll the dough while the other group members press it onto the platform in the shape they have drawn. The dough will stick better if they moisten the entire platform first.

6. **Have students place the secondary outlet at the beginning of the irrigation canal.** The outlet straw should be one-quarter inch above the riverbed.

7. **When students have completed this first stage, have them prop the headwaters end on the block.** The model outlets should hang off the end of the table and be positioned above the water bucket. To minimize splash, have the students place the bucket on a chair. The model is now ready for operation.

8. **Have students slowly pour water into the headwaters from the bottle with clean water in it.** They should be careful not to overflow the banks of the river. Ask them to record their observations and answer the questions on the ***Go with the Flow Observations*** *Student Copy Pages*. When using clean water, students will be able to see how water flows through the irrigation and reservoir dam works. Without the reservoir dam in place, it is unlikely that

water will flow into the irrigation canal except when a higher volume of water is being poured through the model. This is analogous to a spring flood.

9. **Now have students place the reservoir dam in the dam site.** They should be sure that the dam outlet is one-quarter inch above the riverbed and that the spillway is below the banks of the river. Using the Reservoir Diagram on the *River Flow Model Design Student Copy Page* as reference, students should be able to identify the different capacity levels (active, inactive, and dead) of the reservoir they have created.

10. **Once the dam is in place, students should once again pour water into the headwaters using the clean water.** Have them record what they see on the *Go with the Flow Observations Student Copy Pages.*

11. **After students have recorded their observations, have them map the active, inactive, and dead capacity of the reservoir following the steps on the *Observations Student Copy Page*.**

12. **Have students remove the reservoir dam and run water through the model using muddy water.** Have students put two cups of fine soil in one of the two-liter bottles of water. Be sure to have the students agitate the bottles before they pour the muddy water into the model and periodically during the activity. Muddy water will make it easier to see the current. When students stop pouring water, they will be able to see where sediment is deposited in the riverbed. The most common places for sediment to deposit are on the inside of river bends, on the line between eddies and the main current, and in the reservoir. Why is this? Have students record their observations on the *Go with the Flow Observations Student Copy Pages.* Using a blue colored pencil, have students draw the location of sediment deposits on the *River Flow Model Design Student Copy Page.*

13. **Have students replace the reservoir dam and again pour muddy water through the system.** Have them record their observations on the *Go with the Flow Observations Student Copy Pages.* It will not take long for the sediment to fill the reservoir. Have students draw the location of new sediment deposits on the *River Flow Model Design Student Copy Page* using a red colored pencil, labeling these "post-dam deposits." You should note that in this model most of the sediment will collect near the dam. This is because the reservoir is too small for sediment to settle before reaching the dam. In large reservoirs such as Navajo Reservoir and Lake Powell, most sediment is deposited when the river enters the lake. The result is a large fan of sediment on the upper end of the lake and less sediment at the lower end (see page 162, "Too Thick to Drink").

Part II

1. **Have students remove the salt dough from the platforms.** Students will now design a river, predict flow patterns and sedimentation, and build it using the same methods used above. Set criteria such as create one or more eddies, include at least one diversion, and build at least one dam.

2. **Have students design their river by drawing it on a blank piece of paper.** The design should be close to scale and should have enough room to label critical elements of the river. Ask them to predict and draw—using the knowledge they gained in *Part I*—where the current will be fastest, sediment will settle, eddies will form, etc. (refer to the *Current Flow Diagram Teacher Copy Page).*

3. **Ask students to construct their river following the design they made in Step 2.** They should work to match the design with their model as closely as possible, as the model will be used to see if their hypotheses were correct.

4. **Have students build the new model and pour water into the headwaters.** Were their predictions accurate? Why or why not? How is their river model different from the first? What changes would they make next time?

Wrap Up

1. **Ask students to compare the rivers they created with a river or stream near them.** How are they different? How are they similar? Are there any reservoirs near them? What are they used for? How are they important?

2. **Ask the students if they can think of ways sediment can be a problem.** In agricultural areas such as the Imperial Valley in California, sedimentation can fill irrigation ditches, thereby reducing the amount of land that can be irrigated and forcing farmers to spend money on cleaning ditches. Sediment can also reduce the capacity of reservoirs. Lake Powell is an example of a reservoir that has a reduced capacity due to sedimentation. Sediment surveys performed in 1986 determined that about 37,000 acre-feet of sediment enter the lake per year. Even at this rate of sedimentation, however, the reservoir should be able to function and support power generation, water supply, and recreation for hundreds of years. Another effect of sedimentation is that it can kill aquatic organisms by smothering them with mud. In the sediment-laden Colorado River Watershed, many aquatic organisms have developed adaptations that allow them to survive sedimentation. Sedimentation can also be an economic problem, as it increases the cost of treating water for drinking (see page 162, "Too Thick to Drink").

3. **Discuss the benefits of sediment.** As a result of sediment deposition during floods, the floodplain of the Colorado River is highly fertile. Wheat, alfalfa, sugar beets, lettuce, asparagus, and many other crops can be grown in the rich soil. Cattle and other livestock also thrive on grass growing there. These products are sold all over the world and are central to the economy of the basin. Some aquatic organisms also benefit from food found in the rich sediment. And recreationists benefit from broad beaches formed by deposited sand. Can the students think of other benefits?

4. **Discuss the effects of the reservoir dam.** How did it change flow in the irrigation canal? What are the benefits of this change? How did it change flow in the natural riverbed? What are the effects of this change? How did sedimentation patterns change with the "construction" of the dam? What effects would this have on the system?

Assessment

Have students:

- build a model that demonstrates river flow, sedimentation, and current patterns (*Part I*, Steps 3–6);
- observe the effects of river channel shape on flow and current (*Part I*, Step 7);
- test the effects of water storage dams (*Part I*, Steps 8–9);
- map active, inactive, and dead reservoir storage capacity (*Part I*, Step 10);
- test the effects of river channel shape, dams, and diversions on sedimentation and current (*Part I*, Steps 11–12);
- design and build their own river flow model (*Part II*, Steps 2–4);
- predict the effects of model design on flow, sedimentation, and current (*Part II*, Step 3);
- test their hypotheses using a model of their river design (*Part II*, Step 5);
- compare river flow models to rivers or streams near their home (***Wrap Up***, Step 1);
- discuss the costs and benefits of sediment in streams and rivers (***Wrap Up***, Steps 2–3);
- discuss the positive and negative effects of dams on river systems (***Wrap Up***, Step 4).

Extensions

Have the class plan and develop a large-scale model on a 4' x 8' sheet of plywood. To enable the entire class to work on the project, the plywood may be divided into sections with two to three students working on each. The larger scale of this model magnifies eddies, currents, and sedimentation. Have students decorate the platform with plants, animals, and fishes appropriate for each part of the river. Label key parts of the model with permanent markers. The model may then be displayed for viewing by the entire school.

Develop an exhibit of four river flow models that show 1) river flow before construction of the reservoir dam, 2) river flow after construction of the dam, 3) sedimentation before a reservoir dam, and 4) sedimentation after the reservoir dam. Invite other classes to view the exhibit. Have students take turns operating the model and explaining to visitors what each model shows. Students can develop posters that help communicate key concepts.

Have students experiment with different stream characteristics. They may add gravel, sticks, vegetation, sand, and other materials to the bed of their river. They may also build tributaries, experiment with the effects of different volumes of sediment, alter the placement of dams, construct additional irrigation diversions, increase or decrease the slope of the river, etc.

Have students use the Internet or other resources to learn about dams and diversions on their local streams and rivers.

Resources

Brater, Ernest F., Horace W. King, James E. Lindell,. and C. Y. Wei. 1996. *Handbook of Hydraulics: Seventh Edition*. New York: McGraw Hill Professional.

Collier, Michael, Robert H. Webb, and John C. Schmidt. 1996. *Dams and Rivers: Primer on the Downstream Effects of Dams*. Tucson, AZ: U.S. Geological Survey.

Can be obtained for free at:
U.S. Geological Survey
Branch of Information Services
Box 25286
Denver, CO 80225

Plummer, Charles, and David McGeary. 1993. *Physical Geology: Sixth Edition*. Dubuque, IA: Wm. C. Brown Publishers.

e-Links

Army Corps of Engineers
Information and historical perspectives on flood control.
www.usace.army.mil

United States Bureau of Reclamation
Information about the Adaptive Management Work Group, which works to reduce the negative effects of Glen Canyon Dam while maintaining the benefits.
www.usbr.gov/uc/envprog/amp/background.html

United States Geologic Survey
Information about U.S. water resources.
http://water.usgs.gov

River Flow Model Design

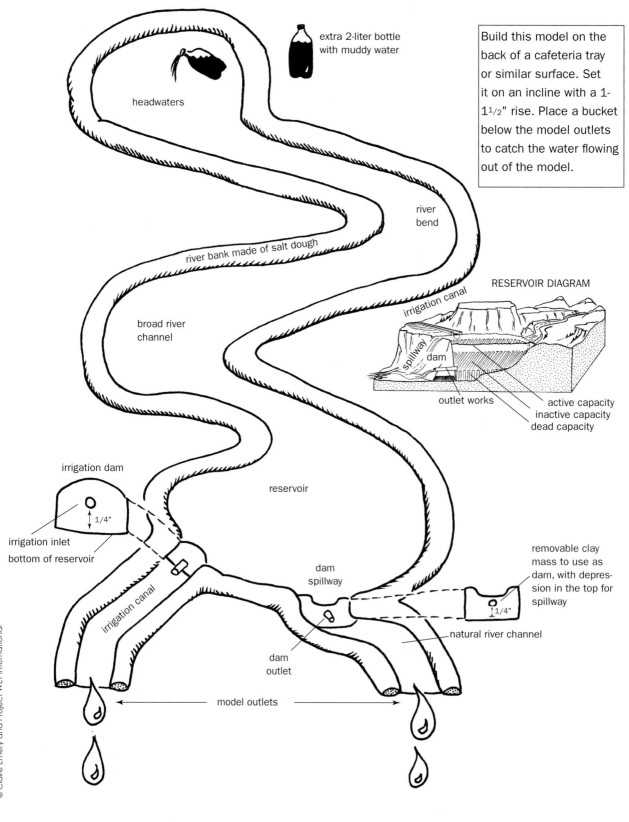

extra 2-liter bottle with muddy water

headwaters

river bend

Build this model on the back of a cafeteria tray or similar surface. Set it on an incline with a 1-1½" rise. Place a bucket below the model outlets to catch the water flowing out of the model.

river bank made of salt dough

RESERVOIR DIAGRAM

irrigation canal

broad river channel

spillway

dam

outlet works

active capacity
inactive capacity
dead capacity

irrigation dam

reservoir

1/4"

irrigation inlet
bottom of reservoir

removable clay mass to use as dam, with depression in the top for spillway

dam spillway

irrigation canal

1/4"

natural river channel

dam outlet

model outlets

Go with the Flow Definitions

active reservoir capacity. The reservoir capacity available for use. It extends from the top of the reservoir to the lowest point from which water can be removed.

current. The flow of water or air.

dead reservoir capacity. The reservoir capacity from which water cannot be removed by gravity.

inactive reservoir capacity. The reservoir capacity from which the water is normally not available due to design or regulation. The inactive capacity extends from the bottom of active capacity to the top of dead capacity.

inlet. The point at which water flows into a canal, spillway, or other structure.

outlet. The point at which water flows out of a canal, spillway, or other structure.

eddy. A swirling pattern of water flow where part of the current moves upstream. Usually the result of water slowing as it moves around an obstacle such as a rock or bend in the river.

floodplain. Any normally dry land that is susceptible to being inundated by water from any natural source; usually low land adjacent to a stream or lake.

meander. An arcing curve along a stream's course.

sediment. Created from natural processes of erosion, where wind, water, frost, and ice slowly break down rocks into finer and finer pieces. Runoff often carries sediment into nearby waterways.

spillway. A channel through which excess water can flow from a dam.

streambed. The bottom of a stream or river.

stream channel. A long, narrow depression, shaped and mostly filled by a stream.

Go with the Flow Observations

Clean Water—No Dam
With the headwaters end of the model propped on a block, pour water into the headwaters.
1. Where is the water current fastest? _____
2. Is water flowing into the irrigation canal? _____
3. What happens when you change the amount of water being poured into the model? _____
_____
_____
4. For how many seconds does the water keep flowing after you stop pouring water? _____

Clean Water—Dam in Place
Use clay to construct a dam to put in the dam site. Follow the diagram to see where to place the outlet works. Pour clean water into the headwaters after the dam is in place.
5. Where does the current begin to slow above the dam? Why? _____
_____
_____
6. Is water flowing to the irrigation canal? Why or why not? _____
_____
_____
7. For how many seconds does the water keep flowing after you stop pouring water? _____
8. Does the natural riverbed or the irrigation canal stop flowing first? Why? _____
_____
_____

Map of Active, Inactive, and Dead Reservoir Capacities
9. **Use the following steps to draw a map of the reservoir capacity levels. Mark the locations on the reservoir map (below).**
   a. Stop flow of water through the reservoir dam outlet works and the irrigation inlet using a piece of clay or dough.
   b. Pour water into the system until it begins to flow over the spillway (stop pouring when the reservoir is full).
   c. On the reservoir map provided below, draw the extent to which the water is backed up. This is the maximum capacity of the reservoir. Label this on your map.
   d. Remove the plug covering the irrigation inlet. The water level will drop to the inlet level. Map the extent to which the water is backed up. The area between the maximum reservoir level and that of the irrigation inlet is the active capacity. Label this on your map.
   e. Next, remove the plug covering the reservoir dam outlet works. Water will fall to the level of the outlet. Again, map the limit of the water. The area between this line and the active capacity is the inactive capacity. Label this on your map.
   f. The water remaining below the outlet works is the dead capacity. Label this on your map.
   g. Finally, color in each of the sections with a colored pencil and create a key next to the map.

Go with the Flow Reservoir Capacity Map

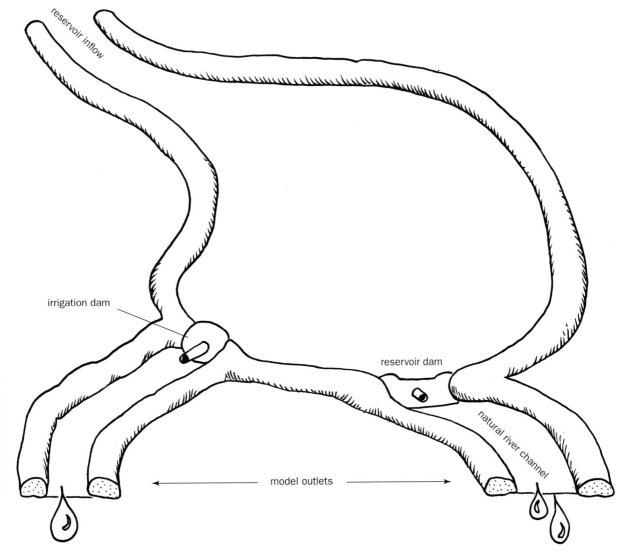

reservoir inflow

irrigation dam

reservoir dam

natural river channel

model outlets

Go with the Flow Observations

Muddy Water—No Dam

Remove the dam and set it aside for later use. Fill the second water bottle with water and add one cup of fine soil. Shake the bottle often to be sure that the soil is suspended. Pour the muddy water into the headwaters.

10. Where do eddies form in the river flow model? Why? _____

_____

11. What happens when you change the amount of water being poured into the model? _____

_____

12. Where do sediment deposits form? Why? _____

_____

13. Draw the location of sediment deposits on the ***River Flow Model Design*** *Student Copy Page* using a blue colored pencil. Create a key that identifies blue deposits as "pre-dam."

Muddy Water—Dam in Place

Replace the dam. Pour muddy water into the headwaters. Shake the bottle often to be sure that the soil is suspended. You may add more water and soil if needed.

14. Where does most of the sediment collect? _____

_____

15. What happens to the channel of the irrigation canal? _____

_____

16. How is the natural riverbed different now that the dam is in place? _____

_____

17. What happens to the dam as sediment builds up? _____

_____

_____

18. What are the effects of the dam? _____

_____

_____

_____

19. Draw the location of sediment deposits on the ***River Flow Model Design*** *Student Copy Page* using a red colored pencil. Create a key that identifies red deposits as "post-dam."

Go with the Flow Current Flow Diagram

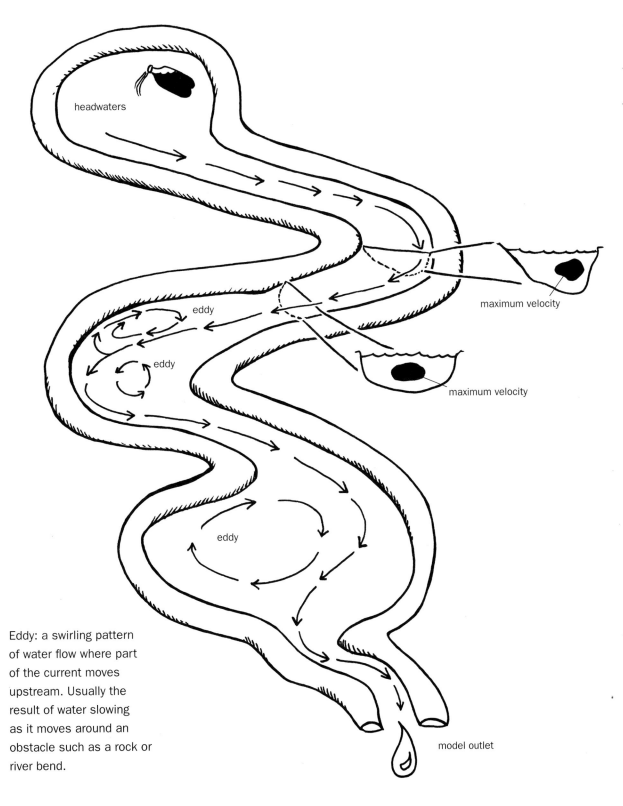

headwaters

eddy

eddy

maximum velocity

maximum velocity

eddy

Eddy: a swirling pattern of water flow where part of the current moves upstream. Usually the result of water slowing as it moves around an obstacle such as a rock or river bend.

model outlet

© Claire Emery and Project WET International

Basin in a Bottle

How does pumping water from below the ground affect rivers and lakes on the surface?

Grade Level:
6–8

Subject Areas:
Life Science, Earth Science, Environmental Science, History/Anthropology

Duration:
Preparation time: 40 minutes (for first time use; subsequent uses will take less time)
Activity time: 60 minutes

Setting:
Classroom

Skills:
Build, Experiment, Analyze, Discuss, Measure

Vocabulary:
aquifer, artesian well, confined aquifer, discharge area, ground water, precipitation, recharge, recharge area, saturated zone, seep, spring, unconfined aquifer, water cycle, water table, well, wo'o

Summary
Students build a ground water model to observe the effects of surface water and ground water pumping.

Objectives
Students will:
- discuss the importance of ground water to desert communities (human, plant, and animal);
- build ground water models using two-liter plastic bottles;
- measure the effect of pumping on ground and surface water;
- investigate the connection between ground and surface water.

Materials
- *Copies of **Ground Water Model Set-Up** Student Copy Page* (1 per group)
- *Copies of **Basin in a Bottle Data Sheet** Student Copy Page* (1 per student)
- *Overhead transparency (or 1 copy per group) of the water cycle diagram* (see page 92, "Incredible Journey of the Colorado River")
- *Two-liter plastic bottles* (1 per group)
- *Plastic drinking straws* (1 per group)
- *Polyester fiberfill* (available at craft or sewing stores) (1 6" x 18" piece, 2" thick, per group)
- *Felt fabric* (1 6" x 18" piece per group)
- *Small plastic or paper cups* (1 per group)
- *Permanent markers* (1 per group)
- *Turkey basters* (1 per group)
- *Rulers* (1 per group)
- *500-milliliter graduated cylinder or other liquid measurer* (1 per group)
- *Construction paper* (1 sheet per group)
- *Scissors* (1 per group)

- *Water*
- *Optional: food coloring to make water more visible*

Background

Water stored in the pores, cracks, and openings of underground rock and soil layers is called ground water. Close to the soil surface, these spaces have little moisture in them, but below a certain depth (which varies according to location), they are filled with water. This is called the saturated zone. The boundary between the saturated zone and the surface layer (or unsaturated zone) is called the water table. When rain or snowmelt soaks into the ground, gravity pulls it downward until it hits an impermeable surface (such as a clay layer). Water collects above that layer, filling porous spaces. As more water percolates into the soil, that water continues to fill the underground basin. The water table rises during times of wet weather and falls during dry periods. To help envision this, imagine pouring milk into a bowl of cereal. The milk filling the spaces acts in the same

This spring-fed pool in the Grand Canyon provides an important water source for plants, animals, and people.

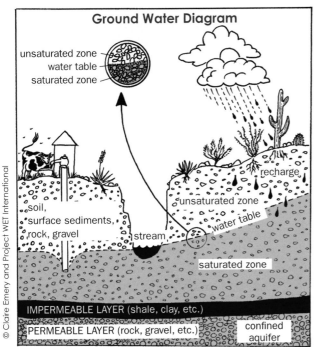

This cross-section shows the relationships between confined and unconfined aquifers, saturated and unsaturated zones, and other key features in the movement and storage of ground water.

manner as water percolating through soil.

Aquifers are underground formations of saturated soil or rock that hold significant quantities of water. These formations are often composed of porous rock such as sandstone, which acts as a sponge to absorb, store, and transport water. Water in aquifers comes from water that has fallen as rain or snow. Aquifers vary in size, depth, and the quality of water they hold. People often pump aquifer water to the surface for drinking, watering crops, livestock, and other uses. In some places, ground water naturally emerges at the surface as a seep (where water slowly seeps out of rock or soil) or a spring (where water flows from rock or soil).

Aquifers are described as confined or unconfined. Confined aquifers are bound by impermeable layers of rock above and below them. Unconfined aquifers have no impermeable layer above them and water can percolate directly into the underground basin. Any area of land through which water flows downward or laterally into an aquifer is called its recharge area. Ground water moves from the recharge area, through the aquifer, and out to a discharge area (well, spring, seep, lake, stream, or ocean) as part of the water cycle (see page 89, "Incredible Journey of the Colorado").

The rate of ground water movement depends on the characteristics of the rock material through which it flows, and the slope it moves down. Ground water typically moves from areas of higher elevation to lower elevation (due to gravity) and from areas of higher pressure (caused by the weight of overlying water and rock) to lower pressure. If a well is drilled into a confined aquifer that is under high pressure, the water will flow to the surface without being pumped. This is called an artesian well. A well drilled into an unconfined aquifer needs a pump to withdraw the water since it is not under as much pressure. The ground water basin created in this activity models an unconfined aquifer.

The "age" of ground water (the length of time it has been underground) varies. An unconfined surface aquifer, for example, may hold water that is only a few days, weeks, or months old. A confined aquifer may contain water that has been there for thousands of years. Surface (shallow) aquifers recharge quickly, while deep aquifers may take centuries. The Navajo Aquifer (sometimes referred to as the N-Aquifer) in northern Arizona is an example of a deep aquifer. Water held there is estimated to be 16,000–39,000 years old.

Ground and surface water are connected. Lakes, rivers, and ponds can be viewed as places where the water table is exposed. If ground water pumping lowers the water table in an aquifer, lakes and rivers can dry up. This is happening on the San Pedro River in southern Arizona. Farms, homes, and cities are withdrawing water from the aquifer below the

Justin Howe

Expedition student Paul Viosca fills a water jug from Matrimony Spring in Moab, UT.

river faster than it can be recharged. As a result, the river is sinking into the sand.

If aquifers are over utilized, the water table drops further below the surface. When this happens, the space between soil particles that was once filled with water becomes empty. The weight of soil and rock above can force the ground down, filling the space. This is called subsidence. It is common in many of the ground water basins in southern Arizona and California. If subsidence persists, deep cracks can develop in the soil, causing damage to fields and structures.

Water managers monitor aquifer depletion using monitoring wells. Monitoring wells allow managers to measure changes in water table depth over time. The goal is to ensure that water is replaced as quickly as it is withdrawn. In Arizona and California, water managers are recharging aquifers with Colorado River water. This is done by spreading river water over aquifer recharge areas where it can percolate into the soil, as well as by using high-pressure wells to inject water underground. This process is sometimes referred to as "water banking" because the water can later be withdrawn for use in cities and on farms.

Ground water that reaches the flows to the earth's surface is known as spring water. These springs support life in regions that would otherwise be dry. People rely on ground water, seeps, and springs for drinking and agriculture, and they have built civilizations around them. Viewed in this way, they are oases of cultural diversity. The Hopi people of northern Arizona have survived in an extremely dry region for thousands of years by using ground water flowing from seeps and springs.

The Tohono O'odham people of southern Arizona also depend on a combination of ground water and surface (rain) water for their survival. *Wo'o* is the Tohono O'odham word for a rainwater pond. Historically, each Tohono O'odham farming village was built near a *wo'o*. Its water was used for drinking, cooking, and washing. Often, these ponds would dry up by fall, and the Tohono O'odham would move to their winter villages, where mountain springs could provide enough water.

In deserts, the perennial (year-round) nature of seeps and springs make them biological hot spots. Some of the greatest biological diversity is found at these special places. Animals travel from miles around to drink water and find food that can grow only in places where water is present year-round. Some species of plants and animals can only live where there is a constant water supply (see page 172, "Hunting for Habitats in the Colorado Watershed"). The Kanab amber snail (*Oxyloma haydeni kanabensis*) is an example. It is found in only two places in the world, both of them at perennial springs.

Many urban areas (including Mexicali,

During droughts, many wo'o (rainwater ponds) dry up, impacting livestock and Tohono O'odham farmers in southern Arizona.

Vasey's Paradise, in the Grand Canyon, is an oasis in the desert. It is one of only two places where the endangered Kanab amber snail is found. Up to 80 percent of desert biodiversity can be found at seeps and springs.

Phoenix, Tucson, and Las Vegas) rely on ground water for drinking. Ground water is also important for farmers in the Mexicali Valley and other agricultural areas in the basin.

Procedure

Preparation

Use the instructions on the ***Ground Water Model Set-Up*** *Student Copy Page* to build a ground water model before the lesson so that you can demonstrate it to the students.

Warm Up

1. **Show students the overhead transparency or hand out copies of the water cycle diagram (see page 92).** Point out how ground water fits into the water cycle. Discuss how water enters the ground (recharge) and how it emerges at the surface (discharge). Familiarize students with the vocabulary of ground water (aquifers, wells, seeps, springs, recharge, etc.).

2. **Ask students whether they know if they use ground water in their homes.** They may have a private well or be connected to an urban water delivery system that uses ground water. The cities of Tucson, Phoenix, Los Angeles, San Diego, Denver, San Luis Rio Colorado, and Mexicali are just a few that use ground water to supplement surface water supplies.

3. **Discuss the importance of ground water seeps and springs for plants and animals in the desert, including humans (see Background).** While surface water sources that depend upon rain or snowmelt for their flow may dry up during drought, ground water springs and seeps may provide more reliable sources of water throughout the year.

The Activity

1. **Show students a completed ground water model.** Explain that the models that they will make in this activity are like unconfined aquifers, with permeable layers above the aquifer, a spring-fed pond that fills when the water table is high, and an impermeable layer at the bottom that holds water in. Show students the surface water pond, pumping well, and monitoring well.

2. **Organize the students into groups of three.** Distribute materials: bottles, scissors, polyester fiberfill, felt, straws, Dixie cups, turkey basters, construction paper, measuring containers, and rulers.

3. **Hand out the *Ground Water Model Set-Up Student Copy Page* and instruct students to follow the directions to build their own "basin in a bottle."**

4. **Observe students and guide them as necessary while they experiment with their ground water models.** Encourage them to experiment with their models.

5. **Have students answer the questions on the *Basin in a Bottle Data Sheet Student Copy Page*.**

Wrap Up

Discuss the activity. What did they learn about ground water? Discuss their answers on the ***Data Sheet***.

Assessment

Have students:

- build ground water models in two-liter plastic bottles (Steps 1–5);
- measure depth to ground water (Steps 4–5);
- observe the changes that take place in their models when ground water is pumped, surface water is added, etc. (Steps 4–5).

Extensions

Have students conduct research to find out what their local water sources are. Do they have a private well at their home? Do they have to haul water to their homes from another source? If the city provides their water, where does it come from? When was the infrastructure developed? How was water obtained before?

If possible, contact local water managers to arrange a field trip to a local ground water pumping station where students can observe how ground water levels are measured.

Obtain ground water measurements for a local aquifer and have students graph the changes over time.

Resources

Arizona-Sonora Desert Museum. 2000. *A Natural History of the Sonoran Desert.* Tucson: Arizona-Sonora Desert Museum Press.

Nabhan, Gary Paul. 1982. *The Desert Smells Like Rain: A Naturalist in Papago Indian Country.* New York: North Point Press (Farrar, Straus and Giroux).

The Watercourse. 2001. *Discover a Watershed: Rio Grande/Rio Bravo Educators Guide.* Bozeman, MT: The Watercourse.

e-Links

Arizona-Sonora Desert Museum
Educational activities teach about desert cultures and ecology.
www.desertmuseum.org

Ground Water Model Set-Up

How to build your own "Basin in a Bottle" ground water model:

1. Tightly screw the cap onto an empty two-liter bottle (peel off the label if there is one).

2. With the bottle on its side, cut out a "window" that is approximately 3" x 6".

3. Cut a piece of quilt polyester fiberfill to fit in your bottle.

4. Cut a piece of felt that is the same size as the polyester fiberfill. This will represent the soil surface.

5. Cut the top off of the cup so that it is about 1" deep, then poke several holes in its sides and bottom. This will represent a spring-fed pond.

6. On the inside of your cup, make marks every ¼" using a permanent marker. This will help you to see changes in the level of the water surface.

7. Cut a hole in the felt and polyester fiberfill that is the same size as the cup.

8. Cut two small Xs in the felt that are big enough for straws to fit through.

9. Place the polyester fiberfill and felt in the bottle. Insert a pencil or pen into each of the Xs and make a hole that goes all the way through the polyester fiberfill.

10. Cut your drinking straw into 3" lengths.

11. Cut a 1" slit in the side of one of the lengths. This will be used for the monitoring well. Cut a 1/4" slit in the side of another of the lengths. This will be used as the ground water well.

12. Insert the first straw through one of the Xs and push it through to the bottom of the polyester fiberfill. This straw represents a monitoring well where you can measure the depth to ground water.

13. Insert the second straw through the other X and push it through to the bottom of the polyester fiberfill. This straw represents a well that pumps water out of the aquifer.

14. Place the cup in the hole you have cut for it. Push it down so that its rim is level with the felt.

15. Follow the directions on the ***Basin in a Bottle Data Sheet*** as you explore your model and answer the questions.

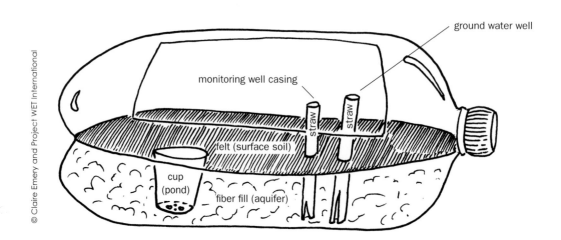

© Claire Emery and Project WET International

Basin in a Bottle Data Sheet

1. Add 400 milliliters of water to your bottle by pouring it onto the felt. This will simulate rainfall. Lift the capped end about 1"–2" so that the model is tilted. What do you observe?

   _____

   _____

   _____

2. Return the bottle to level and measure the depth to ground water by following these steps:

   • Cut a piece of construction paper into six strips that are 1/8" wide and 6" long.
   • Insert one of these strips into the straw (monitoring well casing) and push it to the bottom of the straw.
   • Make a mark on the strip at the top of the well casing.
   • Remove the strip and measure the distance from the water mark to the mark that indicates the top of the well casing.
   • Record your measurement here:

   _____

   • What does the water mark indicate?

   _____

   _____

3. Use the turkey baster (water pump) to withdraw water from the spring-fed pond. This represents water removed and consumed by plants and animals, and evaporation. As you withdraw each amount of water, measure how much you have removed using a graduated cylinder or liquid measuring cup. Then measure the new depth to ground water using

a dry strip of paper and the steps you followed above. Repeat this three times and record your measurements in the chart below.

4. Use the turkey baster to withdraw water from the straw that represents the pumping well. What happens to the water level in the cup as you withdraw more water?

   _____

   _____

5. How did the depth to ground water change as you withdrew different amounts of water?

   _____

   _____

   _____

6. How would the water that you removed be naturally replaced in the "real world"?

   _____

   _____

7. What happens if water is removed from the system at a faster rate than it can be replaced?

   _____

   _____

8. What could happen to people, plants, and animals that need the spring for water if the ground water is removed faster than it is replaced?

   _____

   _____

   _____

	Amount of Water Withdrawn	**Depth to Ground Water**
Test 1		
Test 2		
Test 3		

Reading the Rings

How can we know how the Colorado flowed in 1617? Dendrochronology!

Grade Level:
10–12

Subject Areas:
Environmental Science, Math, Ecology, Earth Science

Duration:
Preparation time: 20 minutes
Activity time: two 60-minute periods

Setting:
Classroom

Skills:
Graph, Add, Subtract, Analyze, Interpret, Discuss, Problem Solve

Vocabulary:
cambium, cross-dating, dendrochronology, growth release, increment borer, increment core, marker ring, master tree-ring chronology, pith, skeleton plot, streamflow

Summary
Students will use the science of dendrochronology to interpret past climate, predict average annual streamflow, and discuss significant climate events such as drought.

Objectives
Students will:
- interpret tree rings to identify past climatic events including dry and wet years;
- use cross-dating to extend a tree-ring record back in time;
- examine how tree rings can be used to reconstruct the climate of the past and therefore predict average annual streamflow for rivers like the Colorado;
- graph annual streamflow and annual precipitation over time;
- interpret graphs to identify periods of drought and wetter-than-average periods;
- discuss the impact of drought on communities, ecosystems, and economies.

Materials
- *Overhead transparency of **1902–1920 Colorado River Streamflow Data Table** (or 1 copy for each student)*
- *Copies of **Tree-Rings Worksheet** Student Copy Pages (1 per student)*
- *Copies of **Colorado Watershed Precipitation and Streamflow Data** Student Copy Pages (1 per student)*
- *Copies of the **Colorado River Average Annual Streamflow** Student Copy Pages (1 per student)*
- *Optional: sanded cross-section of conifer tree (your school's science teachers may have a tree-ring sample, or you can make your own)*
- *Optional: microscopes*

Background

When the Colorado River's water was divided between the U.S. basin states in 1922, policymakers based the allocation for Upper and Lower Basins on the available twenty years of streamflow data. The average annual streamflow from 1902–1920 was 17.3 million acre-feet (maf). With this knowledge and after lengthy negotiations, 7.5 maf per year was allocated to each basin (see page 244, "Sharing the Shed"). State negotiators felt confident that this was a conservative estimate of available water. When Mexico was guaranteed 1.5 maf per year through the 1944 treaty, the United States believed that there would be enough water in the river (with the help of large storage reservoirs) to meet the requirements of the treaty.

Since the 1960s, scientists using dendrochronology (the study of tree rings) have conducted research to reconstruct streamflow for the Colorado Basin over the past several centuries. With this greatly extended view of streamflow variation, scientists have concluded that the average annual streamflow of the Colorado is actually closer to 13.5 maf than the 17.3-maf estimate that the 1922 compact was constructed upon (recent studies of ancient clamshells and fish bones in the Colorado River Delta indicate that the average annual flow may be 12.5 maf). How would things be different today if the 1922 compact negotiators had known that the twenty years prior to 1922 were significantly wetter than average?

Tree rings provide a valuable record of past climate because each ring represents a year of growth and reflects that year's growing conditions. Tree growth is especially sensitive to temperature and precipitation. Since the amount of runoff each year (and thus, streamflow) is also dependent upon precipitation and temperature, the relative width of annual growth rings correlates well to streamflow (Stockton 1975).

When selecting trees to sample for the purposes of reconstructing past climate and/or streamflow, researchers take care to find relatively old trees that are most likely to be sensitive to annual precipi-

tation. An ideal site for such trees has dry, well-drained soils, where a tree's rings will be variable, reflecting the direct precipitation it receives. Trees growing along a stream channel or in a sheltered valley, in contrast, are more likely to have stored soil moisture available to them and their growth rings will not vary as much in response to yearly precipitation. Another factor that can influence the width of a tree's annual rings is the amount of light it receives. When a tree is very young, it is often shaded by larger trees, resulting in narrow annual rings that reflect lack of light rather than moisture. For this reason, rings near the center (pith) of the tree (reflecting the tree's first years of growth) are often not good indicators of annual precipitation.

Tree-ring-width is correlated to streamflow using a complex set of mathematical and statistical formulas, but it is based upon comparing the relative ring-widths of trees from a specific area to known (recorded) streamflow data from the same area. When the relationship between streamflows and ring-widths for a known period of years has been determined, that relationship can be extrapolated to years for which we have ring-widths, but need to know streamflow.

Tree-ring samples are usually collected using two methods: 1) by obtaining a cross-section of a tree's trunk, or 2) by obtaining increment cores from the tree using an increment borer. An increment borer is drilled by hand into the tree and extracts a core sample that is about the diameter of a pencil. Increment cores are often used because they do not result in the death of the tree. Cores or cross-sections are sanded to a high degree and examined using a microscope. When examined through a microscope, even very narrow annual rings are visible.

An annual ring is made up of two layers, one of porous, light-colored springwood and one of dense, darker-colored summerwood. The newest growth ring is found just beneath the cambium, a spongy layer between the tree's bark and its wood. This ring will usually appear incomplete and represents the current year's growth. The oldest ring is found at the pith (center) of the tree. In order to obtain the most accurate count of the tree's age, rings must be counted as close to the tree's base as possible and must be counted all the way to the pith.

In order to extend the tree-ring record back in time as far as possible, scientists use cross-dating. Since trees in a given location or region will respond similarly to climate conditions, distinct "marker rings" can be used to verify specific years. For example, 1934 was an extremely dry year in much of the American Southwest, and many trees record a narrow ring for that year. The ring for 1934 can be considered a "marker" because it is consistently narrower than surrounding rings. The relative width of rings for an entire core can be measured and compared with another tree's rings to match the pattern of narrow and wide rings. By cross-dating the ring sequence from a tree of known age with those of a tree whose age is not known, scientists can determine when the tree of unknown age lived and died. By using progressively older trees, scientists have been able to extend the tree-ring record back almost 9,000 years.

Cross-dating is also valuable in archaeological studies. A master tree-ring sequence dating back 8,700 years has been established in some parts of the Southwest. Archaeologists can match well-preserved timbers found in ancient buildings with the master sequence, thereby allowing them to determine the time of construction of many archaeological sites in the Colorado Basin.

Much of our understanding of the Colorado Basin's long-term climate patterns is based on tree-ring research. Of special importance to resource managers is the duration, intensity, and timing of drought. Drought is defined as a continuous period with precipitation (and thus, streamflow) that is below the long-term average for an area. Sustained drought in the modern Colorado Basin results in

Roof beams inside an ancient dwelling in Mesa Verde National Park, Colorado, can be used to determine the date that it was constructed.

impacts to ecosystems, the depletion of storage reservoirs, and in some communities, the implementation of water rationing.

Based on tree-ring research, the longest, most severe drought in the Colorado Basin during the last four hundred years appears to have been a drought between 1579 and 1598 (Meko et al., 1995). The most severe drought in recent years occurred between about 1943 and 1962. The long-term climate record shows that droughts, while not predictable, are normal occurrences in this region. Interestingly, the brief hundred years of streamflow for which we have recorded measurements have been wetter than most of the last four hundred years studied with tree rings. Scientists believe that the likelihood of severe droughts in the future is high. Studies are in progress to determine the possible impacts of global climate change on the severity and frequency of drought in the Colorado Basin. Future droughts are likely to impact all water users, from farmers to fish.

Procedure
Preparation
Optional: if your school's science lab does not have a sanded cross-section of a tree showing the rings,

Balcony House in Mesa Verde National Park, Colorado.

Justin Howe

you can make your own. Use a handsaw to cut a section from a fallen log, fence post, or piece of firewood. The section should be about an inch thick, and the wood must be free of rot. Conifer trees (e.g., spruce, pine, fir) are better than deciduous trees (e.g., elm, maple, aspen) for this purpose because their annual rings are more distinct. Use sandpaper to sand the cross-section until it is smooth; sanding makes the rings more visible (the finer the sandpaper, the better the result).

Warm Up

1. **Make sure your students understand what is meant by the term "acre-foot."** An acre-foot is a volume of water equal to an acre of land covered with water a foot deep. The average American family of four to five people uses about one acre-foot of water per year (325,851 gallons)!

2. **Write the following numbers on the chalkboard:**
   - 17.3 million acre-feet—estimated average annual streamflow for Colorado River in 1922
   - 7.5 million acre-feet—annual allocation for Upper Basin (determined in 1922)
   - 7.5 million acre-feet—annual allocation for Lower Basin (determined in 1922)
   - 1.5 million acre-feet—annual allocation for Mexico (determined in 1944)
   - 12.5–13.5 million acre-feet—current estimate of average annual streamflow for Colorado River

3. **Ask students to consider these numbers.** Why was the 1922 estimate of average annual streamflow so high compared to the current estimate? (Because it was based on many fewer years of data, which happened to be collected during a wetter-than-average period of years.) Show them the **_1902–1922 Streamflow Data Table_** (overhead transparency or hand-out). How wet was the wettest year, and when was it? How dry was the driest year? What are some of the risks of relying on an average when the difference between wettest and driest years is so great? Have them think about the winters they remember in their lifetime. Do they remember many wet winters or many dry winters, or some of each? The number of years that they remember may be close to eighteen, the number of years of data that was used to determine the 1922 allocation of the Colorado River!

4. **Ask students if they know why the current estimate is lower than the 1922 estimate.** Is it simply because we now have about eighty more years worth of data? Is one century enough time to give us a good picture of how much the river can change? If not, how can we look at a longer period of time in the river's history? What living things may record past precipitation and climate conditions over hundreds of years?

5. **Pass around a sanded cross-section of a tree with visible rings and talk about how tree-rings have been used to reconstruct past climate and annual streamflow for the Colorado River (see Background).** Have students each write down one observation about the tree sample. If possible, use microscopes to look at the rings.

6. **Tell students that they are going to practice interpreting tree rings in order to make estimates of annual streamflow in the past and identify past periods of drought and wet years.**

The Activity

1. **Pass out copies of the *Tree-Rings Worksheet Student Copy Pages*, one for each student.** Have them work independently or in groups to complete the questions. Be available to answer questions (refer to the ***Reading the Rings Answer Key*** *Teacher Copy Pages*).

2. **When the students have completed the questions, discuss their answers as a class.**

3. **Pass out copies of the *Colorado Watershed Precipitation and Streamflow Data Student Copy Pages*, one for each student.** Students will graph the data and compare the two lines to each other (you may have them make the graphs in this exercise by hand, or using a computer program such as Excel).

4. **Pass out copies of the *Colorado River Average Annual Streamflow Student Copy Pages*, one for each student.** Have the students graph the data from Stockton and Jacoby (ten-year intervals) and interpret the graph to answer the questions, working independently or in groups. As a class, discuss their graphs and the more detailed graph by Meko et al. included on the *Student Copy Page*. What was happening in your area in the 1500s, when the oldest trees used for this study were alive? What are some of the most important things we can learn by looking at long-term data?

Wrap Up

1. **Discuss the Meko et al. graph's information about drought and average streamflow.** What are the chances that we will experience future droughts in the Colorado Basin? If the river is already over-allocated, how will we make sure there is enough water for everyone? What will happen when even more people live in the basin?

2. **Have each student write down three solutions to water shortage problems in the Colorado Watershed and hand them in.** Make a list of solutions on the board, based on

their suggestions. Discuss which options would be more expensive than others, which would provide long-term vs. short-term benefits, which might impact the environment, etc. What would they be willing to do personally to make sure there is enough water to go around?

Assessment

Have students:
- interpret tree rings to identify past events including dry and wet years (Steps 1–2);
- use cross-dating to extend a tree-ring record back in time (Step 1);
- examine how tree rings can be used to reconstruct the climate of the past, and therefore average annual streamflow for rivers like the Colorado (Steps 1–4);
- graph annual precipitation and annual streamflow for a specific location in the Colorado Basin and compare the graphs to tree-ring data (Step 3);
- use tree-ring data to graph annual streamflow for the Colorado River in the past (Step 4);
- interpret graphs to identify periods of drought and wetter-than-average periods (Step 4);
- discuss drought and its impacts on communities, ecosystems, and economies (***Wrap Up***, Steps 1–2).

Extensions

If you have access to the Internet, have students go to the Laboratory of Tree-Ring Research Web site (see e-Links) and follow the directions to learn more about cross-dating. They can do an online activity to learn how to make skeleton plots (graphs of relative ring width) from tree-ring data and compare them to a master tree-ring chronology.

Invite a forester from a local Forest Service or Bureau of Land Management office to speak to your class. Have them bring tree-ring sampling equipment and show the students how increment cores are collected. Take the students on a field trip to look for old trees and sample their rings if an increment borer is available. Have the students count the rings and look for patterns of wet and dry years.

Resources

Hobbs, Gregory Jr. 2003. Inside the Drama of the Colorado River Compact Negotiations: Negotiating the Apportionment. *Proceedings of the Fourth Biennial Colorado River Symposium, September 17–19, 2003.* Sacramento, CA: The Water Education Foundation.

Meko, David, Charles W. Stockton, and William R. Boggess. 1995. The Tree-Ring Record of Severe Sustained Drought. *Water Resources Bulletin* (Journal of the American Water Resources Association) 31, no. 5: 789–801.

The Watercourse. 1995. *Project WET: Curriculum and Activity Guide.* Bozeman, MT: The Watercourse.

Stockton, Charles W. 1975. Long-term Streamflow Records Reconstructed From Tree Rings. *Papers of the Laboratory of Tree-Ring Research* 5. Tucson: University of Arizona Press.

Stockton, Charles W., and Gordon C. Jacoby, Jr. 1976. Long-term Surface-Water Supply and Streamflow Trends in the Upper Colorado River Basin. *Lake Powell Research Project Bulletin* 18 (March 1976).

e-Links

Laboratory of Tree-Ring Research, University of Arizona, Tucson
In-depth information about the science of dendrochronology for teachers and students.
www.ltrr.arizona.edu/dendrochronology.html.
> An interactive Web activity that leads students through the process of making skeleton plots from tree-ring samples and cross-dating them to a master tree-ring chronology:
> http://tree.ltrr.arizona.edu/skeletonplot/introcrossdate.htm

National Climate Data Center
Climate data for the United States.
www.ncdc.noaa.gov

United States Geological Survey
Data on U.S. water resources including streamflow, water quality, etc.
http://waterdata.usgs.gov/nwis

The Desert Research Institute's Western Regional Climate Center
Climate data and maps for the western U.S.
www.wrcc.dri.edu

Institute for the Study of Planet Earth, University of Arizona
Links to articles about climate research and drought.
www.ispe.arizona.edu

American Water Resources Association
Links to archived and current scientific articles about water resources.
www.awra.org

Henri D. Grissino-Mayer's Ultimate Tree-Ring Web Pages
Information and photos about dendrochronology for teachers and students.
http://web.utk.edu/~grissino/

Defining Sustained Colorado River Drought (USGS pages)
Paper investigating the impacts of drought in the Colorado Basin.
http://geochange.er.usgs.gov/sw/changes/natural/codrought/define.shtml

1902–1920 Streamflow Data Table

Colorado River at Yuma, Arizona
Drainage Area = 242,000 square miles
(Climatological year = October 1–September 30)

YEAR	ACRE-FEET
1902 (Jan.-Sept. only)	7,110,000
1902–03	11,100,000
1903–04	9,870,000
1904–05	18,900,000
1905–06	19,200,000
1906–07	26,000,000
1907–08	13,600,000
1908–09	26,100,000
1909–10	15,000,000
1910–11	16,200,000
1911–12	19,600,000
1912–13	12,000,000
1913–14	19,900,000
1914–15	15,800,000
1915–16	21,500,000
1916–17	22,100,000
1917–18	13,100,000
1918–19	10,700,000
1919–20	21,400,000
Average	**17,300,000**

(Data from: Hobbs, Gregory Jr. 2003. Inside the Drama of the Colorado River Compact Negotiations: Negotiating the Apportionment. *Proceedings of the Fourth Biennial Colorado River Symposium, September 17–19, 2003.* Sacramento, CA: The Water Education Foundation.)

Tree-Rings Worksheet

1. Approximately how old is this tree?_____
   _____

2. Are there any periods of two or more narrow
   rings next to each other? _____ If so, when?

3. During which year did the tree grow the most?
   _____ Approximately how old was the tree
   in that year? _____

4. Often, a tree will grow slowly at first because it
   is shaded by larger trees. It will then show a
   "growth spurt," called a *growth release*, when
   it grows tall enough to reach the light. These
   early narrow rings often mean that the tree
   is lacking light, not moisture, and are
   not reliable indicators of drought. In
   what year did the tree most likely
   exhibit a growth release? _____
   How would we distinguish the
   growth release from a wet year?
   _____

5. An unusually narrow ring that shows up
   consistently in many trees from the same area
   or region is called a *marker ring*, and usually
   indicates poor growing conditions (often due
   to drought) that are experienced by many
   trees. Find a possible marker ring in the tree.
   _____

Cross Section of a Tree

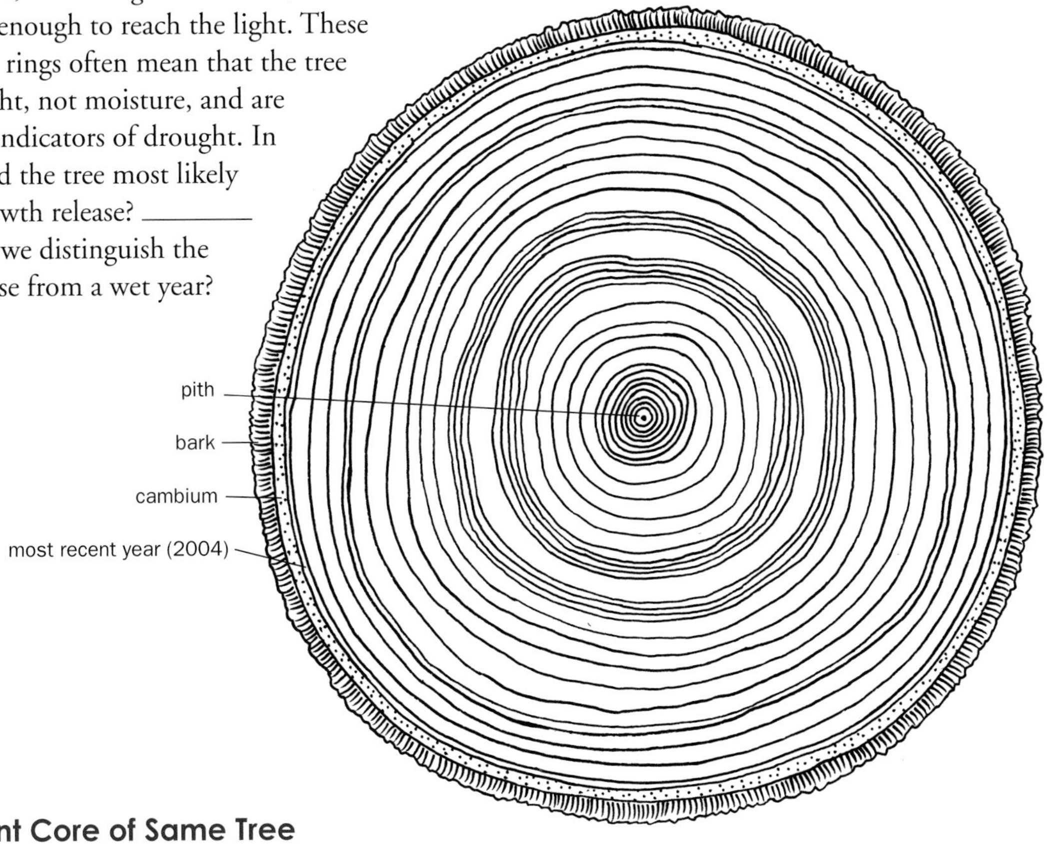

pith

bark

cambium

most recent year (2004)

Increment Core of Same Tree

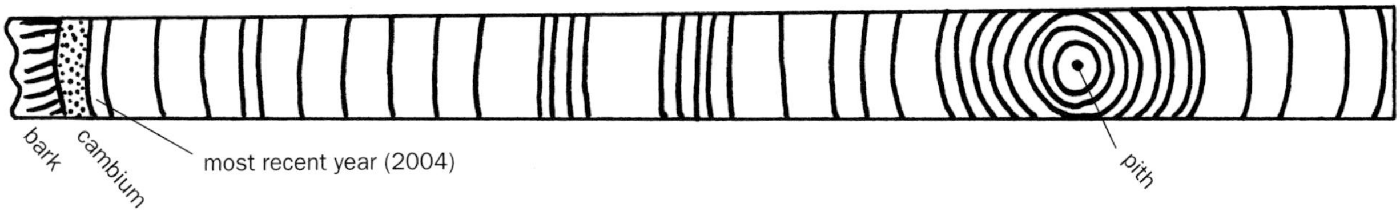

bark

cambium

most recent year (2004)

pith

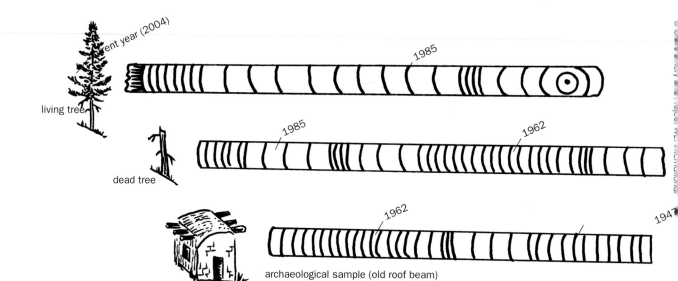

By lining up tree rings on cores of different ages, you can find out how long ago a tree died.

6. *Cross-dating* is used to extend the tree-ring record back in time. Archaeologists often use this method to date old buildings that have well-preserved logs. They start by counting the rings of a tree that is living so that they know exactly which year to count back from. Marker years in this dated core can then be matched with marker rings from a sample that came from an older, dead tree. When we match those marker rings, we now have a year (or more) to count back from to find the oldest ring on the second tree sample. This tree will have marker rings that are older than any from the first core, which can then be matched with the oldest tree core. Finding a marker year that matches will give us a year in the oldest core to count back from and forward from to determine the year the tree was born and the year it died.

This example is simplified; with actual tree samples, hundreds of years would be represented. In this example, in what year was the oldest tree cut down for a roof support?

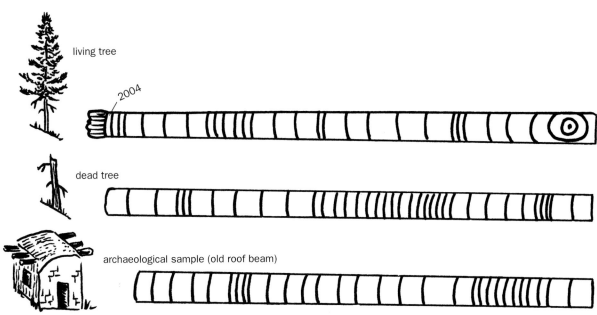

living tree

2004

dead tree

archaeological sample (old roof beam)

Line up these tree cores to cross-date them and find out the age of each core.

7. Cut apart the following three cores so that you can move them next to each other to find the matching ring sequences (cross-dating). Count the rings to find the oldest year represented in the three cores. _____

Colorado Watershed Precipitation and Streamflow Data

Make a graph showing the annual precipitation and streamflow for the years 1934–1958. These data are for the Animas River near Durango, Colorado. The Animas is a tributary of the San Juan River that originates high in the San Juan Mountains of Colorado and joins the San Juan near Farmington, New Mexico.

1. The line for streamflow on your graph doesn't exactly mirror the line for precipitation. What are some reasons why this may be the case? What other variables might be affecting the average annual streamflow besides the amount of annual precipitation?

2. Based on your graphs of precipitation and streamflow, list three years that you think would be likely to show up as marker rings on tree cores from this area:

Year	Total Yearly Precipitation (inches)	Annual Mean Streamflow (100,000 acre-feet)
1934	8.9	2.8
1935	21.4	7.8
1936	17.2	6.3
1937	18.2	6.9
1938	19.4	9.1
1939	13.2	4.6
1940	21.3	4.5
1941	33.6	14.1
1942	12.5	7.9
1943	17.9	6.3
1944	16.6	8.5
1945	9.5	5.9
1946	15.0	4.4
1947	21.8	7.1
1948	18.4	8.2
1949	21.1	9.5
1950	14.4	4.5
1951	15.9	3.7
1952	20.8	9.9
1953	18.3	4.4
1954	17.5	4.5
1955	19.5	4.4
1956	10.2	4.2
1957	32.4	10.5
1958	16.0	9.1

(Data from: Western Regional Climate Center: www.wrcc.dri.edu; U.S. Geological Survey: http://waterdata.usgs.gov/nwis.)

Colorado River Average Annual Streamflow

Year	Colorado River Streamflow at Lee Ferry, Arizona (million acre-feet)
1517	12.9
1527	13.9
1537	14.7
1547	11.2
1557	17.6
1567	11.6
1577	17.3
1587	11.2
1597	14.7
1607	12.4
1617	17.8
1627	11.8
1637	10.7
1647	14.1
1657	16.2
1667	7.9
1677	14.6
1687	11.6
1697	16.0
1707	8.6
1717	9.3
1727	20.8
1737	10.6
1747	18.4
1757	10.2
1767	12.9
1777	12.0
1787	17.7
1797	18.1
1807	14.4
1817	15.8
1827	15.3
1837	16.7
1847	2.8
1857	9.3
1867	19.7
1877	17.6
1887	10.1
1897	18.1
1907	19.2
1917	21.7
1927	17.7
1937	16.5
1947	14.8
1957	17.5

Tree-ring data were used to reconstruct streamflow at Lee's Ferry, Arizona, from 1512 to 1962. Instead of graphing 450 years of data, graph the flow at 10-year intervals.

(Data from: Stockton and Jacoby 1976.)

Historic Streamflow of the Colorado River

Use your graph to answer these questions:

1. During the years represented on your graph, what was the highest flow? _____ In what year did it occur? _____

2. What was the lowest flow? _____ In what year did it occur? _____

3. The lowest flow is _____ percent of the highest flow.

4. What does this data tell us about the variability of flow in the river over the last five hundred years?

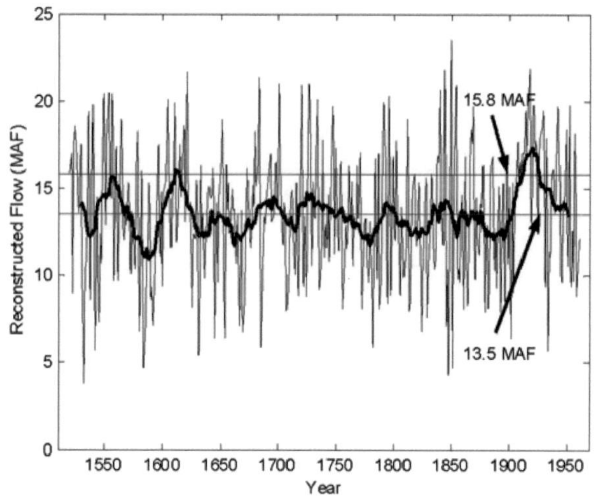

Use the graph below to answer the following questions:

5. Are extended droughts (times when the curve dips below the average line for several years in a row) uncommon?

6. What do you observe about the graph for the period between about 1900 and 1920? What are the implications?

(Graph from Meko et al., 1995. *Annual Series and 20-Year Moving Average of Reconstructed Flow of the Colorado River at Lee's Ferry, Arizona, 1520–1961.* Source of data: Stockton and Jacoby, 1976.)

Reading the Rings Answer Key

Tree-Rings Worksheet

1. This tree is thirty-two years old.

2. Yes: 1972–1980, 1986–1989, 1991–1993.

3. 1990: eighteen years old.

4. 1981: A growth release is usually recognized when a tree shows consistently narrow rings for the first several years of its life, with a sudden increase in ring-width that is then maintained for several years in a row.

5. The year 2000.

6. 1972

7. 1931

Colorado Watershed Precipitation and Streamflow Data

1. Temperature, the timing of precipitation (winter vs. summer), diversions for human use, and other factors may be affecting streamflow so that it doesn't exactly mirror precipitation.

2. 1934, 1945, 1956 (other answers possible).

Historic Streamflow of the Colorado River

1. 21.7 maf, 1917

2. 2.8 maf, 1847

3. 13 percent

4. The river's flow has been highly variable over the last five hundred years.

5. No, extended droughts are common occurrences.

6. This period of time was wetter than average. The 1922 compact is based on data from this time period, which means that the river's average flow was over-estimated and the river is currently over-allocated.

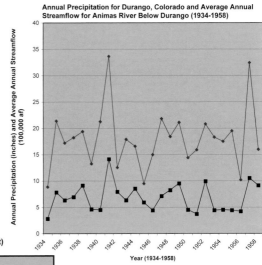

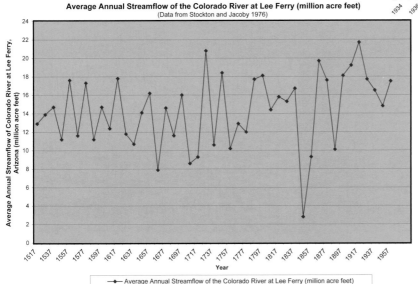

Too Thick to Drink

What did Mormon settlers in the late 1800s call "too thick to drink and too thin to plow"? The Colorado River!

Grade Level:
7–9

Subjects:
Earth Science, Life Science, Environmental Science, Physical Science, Math

Duration:
Preparation time: 20 minutes
Activity time: two 60-minute class periods

Setting:
Classroom

Skills:
Construct, Generalize, Hypothesize, Plot, Compare, Test, Extrapolate

Vocabulary:
detritus, dredge, erosion, germination, macroinvertebrates, nephelometric turbidity unit (NTU), photosynthesis, phytoplankton, riparian, silt, solids, suspension, turbidity

Summary

Students explore the concepts of turbidity and erosion, simulate changes in turbidity at different points along the Colorado River, and explore the effects of turbidity on humans and aquatic life.

Objectives

Students will:
- explore the relationship of erosion to the turbidity of water;
- compare the turbidity of muddy and clear water;
- simulate changes in turbidity at different points along the Colorado River;
- graph changes in turbidity as the river flows to the delta;
- discuss the effects of changing turbidity in the river system as a result of dams and diversions, etc.

Materials

- *Copies of **Too Thick to Drink** Student Copy Pages (1 per student)*
- *4 clear containers (one-quart or larger)*
- *Three cups of fine-grained soil*
- *Measuring cups (one-half cup and one cup) (1 set per group)*
- *6 test tubes or clear juice glasses per group (twenty-five milliliters or greater)*
- *1 test tube rack per group*
- *1 quart of milk*
- *Clear tap water*
- *Eyedroppers (1 per group)*
- *Graphing paper*
- *Pencils*
- *Straight edges*

Background

On its way to the Gulf of California, the Colorado River, with its powerful erosive forces, cuts through thousands of feet of soil and stone, forming such wonders as the Grand Canyon. Each year hundreds of thousands of tons of material are eroded and suspended in the river to be carried toward the delta. Water that carries suspended material is less clear than water that is not.

Flash floods are common in the desert. After floods, water can be highly turbid. Aquatic organisms must be able to adapt to these rapidly changing conditions.

Scientists estimate how much suspended material is in water by measuring turbidity. Turbidity is a measure of how much light can pass through water. Highly turbid (murky) water has a high level of suspended solids. The major sources of turbidity are phytoplankton, silt, and detritus. Phytoplankton are microscopic floating plants (mostly algae) that live suspended in bodies of water. Silts are inorganic mineral matter. Detritus is organic material left over from plants and animals. It may include dead algae, fallen leaves, fecal matter, and other materials.

During certain times, the Colorado River is more turbid than others. During spring runoff, it may be impossible for light to penetrate more than a few inches below the surface (see page 330, "Colors of the Colorado," for a discussion of how turbidity affects the color of water.) When Mormon settlers arrived in the Colorado River Watershed in the late 1800s, they said that the river was "too thick to drink and too thin to plow."

Prior to the construction of dams, the Colorado River was an environment of extremes. Historic spring flows in the Colorado sometimes exceeded 300,000 cubic feet per second (cfs). Boulders the size of houses, hundreds of thousands of tons of sediment, and other material would race toward the Upper Gulf of California each year. By late summer, runoff would decrease and the water temperature would grow very warm. In some places, rivers would stop flowing altogether. This was a problem for human water users, and they built dams to regulate flow. They also reduced turbidity by allowing suspended material to settle into reservoirs.

Reduced turbidity in the Colorado River Watershed has affected aquatic organisms by changing the environment to which they are adapted. Native fish such as the razorback sucker and humpback chub, for example, rely on food and nutrients carried in suspended material. They use sensitive mouth organs to feel for their food. When suspended material is removed, light can penetrate deeper into the water. This allows plants to grow and a different ecosystem to develop. Native fish are not adapted to this new environment. As a result, nonnative fish species such as trout, bass, sunfish, northern pike, and others that are adapted to this new environment have caused a decline in formerly large populations of native fish (see page 211, "Chillin' with the Chubs").

Turbidity is highest near shorelines and is increased by erosional forces such as flood events, dredging, high water velocity, and wind agitation.

Some rocks and soils erode more easily than others. Rivers flowing through areas of hard granite, for example, are usually less turbid because the surface resists erosion. Much of the soil and rock in the Colorado Basin is easily eroded. Limestone, sandstone, and other relatively soft substrates yield more quickly to water flow, creating canyons, caves, and other features. The arid climate and resulting low density of vegetation make the area more susceptible to erosion; the low-density vegetation does not hold soil in place when forces of wind or water act upon it.

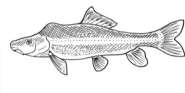

Razorback suckers rely on turbid water to hide and feed in.

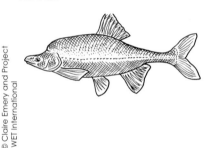

Humpback chubs are adapted to fast, turbid water.

Reduced turbidity and regulated flows in the Colorado River have also decreased the amount of sediment being deposited on the floodplain. When a turbid river floods, much of the rich sediment it carries is deposited outside of the riverbanks. Like the flood plain of the Nile, that of the Colorado is rich in naturally growing and cultivated plants. Humans have used this rich soil to grow crops for thousands of years. As turbidity in the Colorado River has decreased, so too has sediment deposition on the flood plain and along the riverbanks as beaches. Areas such as the Colorado River Delta that used to

Many native riparian plants, including cottonwoods, require spring deposition of sediment from floodwaters for seed germination.

receive massive amounts of sediment now receive much less. Many native riparian plants, including cottonwoods, require spring deposits of sediment from floodwaters for seeds to germinate.

Turbidity can be a problem for water managers because large amounts of suspended solids make water harder to use. For example, to make water safe for drinking, particulate matter must be filtered out because bacteria, heavy metals, and other materials can cling to the particles. Chemical treatment is effective only after the suspended solids have been removed. In the Colorado River Basin, some cities and towns use water pumped from wells or drawn from clear reservoirs. Using water from such sources reduces the cost of providing clean, treated, drinking water.

Turbidity affects farmers and ranchers because sediment carried in the water can clog ditches and canals, making it harder to deliver water. To cope with this problem, some irrigation districts have built settling ponds to remove sediment before the water enters canal systems. By taking this action, managers have been able to reduce the amount of maintenance associated with limiting sediment in the system.

Government agencies such as the U.S. Bureau

Used by permission of Imperial Irrigation District.

Settling ponds used by the Imperial Irrigation District to remove sediment from river water before sending it into the All American Canal (right) to be used for drinking and irrigation.

of Reclamation, U.S. Fish and Wildlife Service, and Mexican Institute of Water Technology, as well as other public and private organizations, are working hard to maintain a balance between the positive and negative effects of turbidity in the Colorado River and its tributaries.

Procedure

Preparation

Test to make sure that the test tubes or juice glasses you have chosen are appropriately sized for the concentrations of milk that will be used. They should not be so large that milk has little effect on turbidity. Similarly, they should not be so small that a few drops of milk will make the turbidity so high that light cannot shine through them—fifteen-milliliter test tubes work well.

Warm Up

1. **Fill the quart containers with clear tap water and number them one through four.** Place them in the front of the class. Tell students that water in the jars is clear because it has been treated and contains very few suspended (floating) solids such as algae, silt, and sand. Explain that most water has some suspended

solids in it and that the solids get into the water through processes of erosion and growth of aquatic organisms. Ask students to list actions that cause erosion (e.g. rainfall, dredging operations, and wave action).

2. **After the discussion, explain that you are going to add suspended solids to the water by placing soil in the quart containers.** Add zero cups of soil to container number one, one-half cup to number two, one cup to number three, and one and a half cups to the fourth (test beforehand to make sure that the soil used will not make all the jars too dark). Place caps on the containers and agitate them to ensure that the material is suspended in water. Note that the water in the containers with more soil is most murky. Explain that this is because particles in the water make it more difficult for light to pass through.

3. **Introduce students to the term "turbidity" and explain that it is a measure of water clarity that is used to estimate the volume of suspended solids present.** Tell the students that they are going to create water samples that mimic the turbidity of the Colorado River at different times and in different places within the watershed. Turbidity is commonly measured in units called Nephelometric Turbidity Units (NTUs). For this activity, a drop of "sediment" (milk) will equal one NTU.

4. **Allow the containers to settle while students do the activity.** You may later refer to the jars to demonstrate how suspended solids settle in still water, thereby reducing turbidity.

The Activity

Part I

1. **Divide students into cooperative groups.**

2. **Distribute beakers or juice glasses and copies of the *Too Thick to Drink Student Copy Pages* to groups.**

3. **Have students follow the procedures on the *Too Thick to Drink Student Copy Page,***

Part A. This first section mimics the turbidity of the river in 1900, before major dams and diversions were placed on the system. As the river flows toward the sea, its volume increases, improving its ability to transport sediment. To illustrate this, the amount of milk (turbidity) required to match the samples increases. Discuss this with students.

4. **Have students perform the turbidity test found on the *Too Thick to Drink Student Copy Page*.**

5. **Using the results from the test, have students graph the turbidity of each sample.**

Part II

1. **Have students follow the procedures on the *Too Thick to Drink Student Copy Page, Part B*.** Students will create turbidity samples that mimic that of the Colorado River in 2000, after large dams and diversions were placed on the system. As before, students should record their interpretation of the results.

2. **Using the results from the turbidity test, have students graph the turbidity of each sample.**

Wrap Up

After students have completed the activity, discuss the results with them. Why has the turbidity of the river changed since 1900? Why do they think some places on the river have higher turbidity? What kinds of aquatic organisms would likely live in the highly turbid water? What about the clear water? How might vegetation growth be affected by murky water? Why? What are some ways to decrease the amount of turbidity in water? What are the effects of decreasing turbidity in water? What would cause turbidity to change even in the modern river system (e.g. season, flash floods, construction sites, etc)?

Assessment

Students will:

- explore the relationship of soil erosion to the turbidity of the Colorado River (***Warm Up***, Steps 1–3);
- create and compare turbid water samples that represent samples taken from the Colorado River in different places at different times (Steps 1–4 and 7);
- graph variations in the turbidity of water samples (Step 5);
- discuss the effects of turbidity on humans, plants, and animals (***Wrap Up***, Step 1).

Extensions

Have students collect water samples from water bodies around your school. Mud puddles, ponds, and rivers are good sources. Compare the turbidity of each of the samples. Can you see the source of the turbidity? What is the main source of suspended solids? Are there aquatic organisms living in the water? What are they? Are there plants living in the water? What are they? Is the water moving? How fast?

Resources

Barzilay, J. L, J. W. Eley, and W. G. Weinberg. 1999. *The Water We Drink*. New Brunswick, NJ: Rutgers University Press.

Freedman, B. 1989. *Environmental Ecology*. San Diego, CA: Academic Press, Inc.

Healthy Water, Healthy People Educators Guide. 2003. Bozeman, MT: Project WET International.

Michaud, J. 1991. *A Citizens Guide to Understanding and Monitoring Lakes and Streams*. Olympia: Washington State Department of Ecology.

Murdock, T., and M. Cheo. 1996. *Streamkeepers Field Guide*. Everett, WA: The Adopt-A-Stream Foundation.

Rinne, John, and W. L. Minckley. 1991. *Native Fishes of Arid Lands: Dwindling Resources of the Desert Southwest.* Gen. Tech. Rep. RM-206. U.S. Department of Agriculture, Forest Service, Rocky Mountain Forest and Range Experiment Station.

United States Environmental Protection Agency (EPA). 1999. *Guidance Manual for Compliance with the Interim Enhanced Surface Water Treatment Rule: Turbidity Provisions.* www.epa.gov/safewater/mdbp/mdbptg.html

Water on the Web. 2003. *Understanding Water Quality: Turbidity.* Retrieved on September 12, 2004, from the World Wide Web: http://waterontheweb.org/under/waterquality/turbidity.html

e-links
United States Environmental Protection Agency Information about volunteer water quality monitoring programs.
www.epa.gov/owow/monitoring/volunteer/stream/vms55.html

Too Thick to Drink, Part A

Turbidity in the Colorado River in 1900

1. Fill six test tubes or glasses three-quarters full with water and label them one through six.

2. Hold the test tube above the corresponding turbidity test circles below. Use an eyedropper to slowly add milk to container. Agitate the container with the addition of each drop. Stop adding milk when you can no longer distinguish between dark and light sections of the circle. The number of drops required is the turbidity reading (one drop = one NTU). Record this number in the chart below and set the sample aside.

3. Repeat the above procedure for each sample.

4. After you have found the turbidity reading for each sample, record your interpretation in the box provided. Which sample is the least turbid? Which is the most? Can you see a pattern in the readings?

5. Make a graph of your findings. Use the site number or location as the X-axis and the number of drops as the Y-axis.

Data Sheet for Part A

Granby, CO, USA (1)	Moab, UT, USA (2)	Lee's Ferry, AZ, USA (3)	Pierce Ferry, AZ, USA (4)	Imperial Dam, CA, USA (5)	Los Algodones, SON, Mexico (6)
# Drops (NTUs): ___	# Drops (NTUs): ___	# Drops (NTUs): ___	# Drops (NTUs): ___	# Drops (NTUs): ___	# Drops (NTUs): ___
Interpretation:	Interpretation:	Interpretation:	Interpretation:	Interpretation:	Interpretation:

Too Thick to Drink Test Circles

Part A – Turbidity in 1900

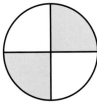

Granby, Colorado (1)

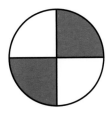

Moab, Utah (2)

Lee's Ferry, Arizona (3)

Pierce Ferry, Arizona (4)

Imperial Dam, Arizona (5)

Los Algodones, Sonora (6)

Part B – Turbidity in 2000

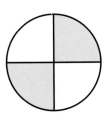

Granby, Colorado (1)

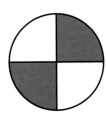

Moab, Utah (2)

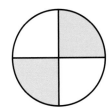

Lee's Ferry, Arizona (3)

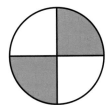

Pierce Ferry, Arizona (4)

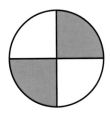

Imperial Dam, Arizona (5)

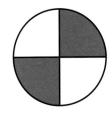

Los Algodones, Sonora (6)

Too Thick to Drink, Part B

Turbidity in the Colorado River in 2000

1. Fill six test tubes or glasses three-quarters full with water and label them one through six.

2. Hold the test tube above the corresponding turbidity test circles below. Use an eyedropper to slowly add milk to container. Agitate the container with the addition of each drop. Stop adding milk when you can no longer distinguish between dark and light sections of the circle. The number of drops required is the turbidity reading (one drop = one NTU). Record this number in the chart below and set the sample aside.

3. Repeat the above procedure for each sample.

4. After you have found the turbidity reading for each sample, record your interpretation in the box provided. Which sample is the least turbid? Which is the most? How has turbidity changed since 1900? Why?

5. Make a graph of your findings. Use the site number or location as the X-axis and the number of drops as the Y-axis.

Data Sheet for Part B

Granby, CO, USA (1)	Moab, UT, USA (2)	Lee's Ferry, AZ, USA (3)	Pierce Ferry, AZ, USA (4)	Imperial Dam, CA, USA (5)	Los Algodones, SON, Mexico (6)
# Drops (NTUs): ___	# Drops (NTUs): ___	# Drops (NTUs): ___	# Drops (NTUs): ___	# Drops (NTUs): ___	# Drops (NTUs): ___
Interpretation:	Interpretation:	Interpretation:	Interpretation:	Interpretation:	Interpretation:

Flora and Fauna

Hunting for Habitats in the Colorado Watershed

Would you expect to find a moose and a Mojave rattlesnake living in the same habitat?

Grade Level:
7–10

Subject Areas:
Life Science, Geography, Ecology, Environmental Science

Duration:
Preparation time: 20 minutes
Activity time: 90–120 minutes

Setting:
Classroom

Skills:
Organize, Analyze, Interpret, Evaluate, Present, Discuss, Synthesize

Vocabulary:
community (biological), conifer, deciduous, dendrogram, ecological niche, ecosystem (ecology), endangered species, generalist species, habitat, riparian, specialist species, species, wetland

Summary
Students learn about ecological communities and animal adaptations and apply this knowledge by matching animal species with their Colorado Watershed habitat/ecosystem.

Objectives
Students will:
- explain the ecological concepts of ecosystems, communities, and habitats;
- identify and describe five major ecosystems of the Colorado Watershed;
- locate the five ecosystems on a map of the southwestern U.S. and northern Mexico;
- predict the locations/ecosystems of specific animals based on their habitat requirements;
- relate diversity of habitats to diversity of species.

Materials
- *Map: Five Ecosystems of the Colorado Watershed Student Copy Pages* (1 per student)
- *Ecosystems of the Colorado Student Copy Pages* (1 per student, plus 1 classroom copy)
- *Hunting for Habitats Cards Student Copy Pages* (5 copies of the complete set of cards, 1 set for each group [each group should have the full set of 25 cards])
- *Dendrogram: Ecological Organizations Student Copy Pages* (1 per student; a dendrogram is a branching diagram that shows the relationships between different categories of things)
- *Dendrogram: Ecological Organizations Answer Key Teacher Copy Page*
- *Scissors*

Background

As the Colorado River flows from its headwaters to its mouth, it passes through an incredible variety of ecosystems. From alpine tundra to the Sonoran Desert, a great diversity of plants and animals make up the Colorado Watershed's flora and fauna. Variations in the physical environment of the watershed relate to elevation, latitude, and many other factors, and this variation contributes to the diversity of ecosystems and the plants and animals that are adapted to them.

All organisms are members of communities, which are groups of different species (plants, animals, fungi, microorganisms, etc.) that live and interact together in particular places. A community together with its non-living environment (the soil, rock formations, water features, etc.) makes up an ecosystem. An ecosystem may be as small as a cup of water, or as large as an entire watershed. Some of the major ecosystems of the Colorado Watershed include conifer forests at the headwaters, the Navajoan Desert of the Colorado Plateau, the Mojave Desert, the Sonoran Desert, and the Upper Gulf of California.

The place in an ecosystem/community where a species lives is called its habitat; for example, an alpine meadow within a conifer forest ecosystem or a marsh within the Sonoran Desert ecosystem. Every habitat is characterized by certain ranges of temperature, precipitation, elevation, vegetation structure, predators, competitors, and the other living and non-living elements that make up the environment; these characteristics determine which organisms can survive and successfully reproduce there. Every organism performs a certain role, or fills a niche, in its community; for example, yucca moths perform the role of pollination for yucca plants.

Species may be called either specialists or generalists, depending on whether their habitat requirements are broad or specific. Yuma clapper rails are specialists, requiring cattail marsh habitats in warm climates. The coyote, on the other hand, is a generalist. It can be found in ecosystems throughout the watershed.

Throughout the world, certain species of plants and animals are becoming rare or extinct due to habitat loss, hunting by humans, competition with invasive species, and other factors. The Colorado Watershed is no exception, and there are numerous species that formerly occupied the watershed, but have become rare in the last century due (at least in part) to human activities. Some of the animals featured in this activity have been identified by the United States and Mexico as species in danger of extinction. The management and recovery of endangered species is an important issue in the watershed.

A dendrogram is "a branching diagram representing a hierarchy of categories based on degree of similarity or number of shared characteristics. . . ." In this activity, a dendrogram is used to illustrate the relationships among ecosystems, communities, and habitats. Of course, as with all living systems, these relationships aren't static. Habitats for certain animals may be found in more than one community. Similarly, an ecosystem may be defined by a single community or collection of communities. The dendrogram presents a visual aid to help students organize the concepts of ecosystems, communities, and habitats. Students may notice that the dendrogram resembles the network of a river system.

Procedure

Preparation

1. **Post the classroom copies of the *Ecosystems of the Colorado Student Copy Pages* so that each of the five ecosystems is in a different area of the room.**

2. **Make five copies of the *Hunting for Habitats Cards* and cut them apart.** Keep each set separate but mix up the cards within each set.

The Colorado River flows through Topock Gorge near Needles, California, creating habitat for birds, fish, and other animals.

Warm Up

1. **Ask students to brainstorm common local plants and animals.** Which plants and animals would they expect to find together in the same place? For example, would you expect to find a moose, desert tortoise, or rainbow trout in the same place?

2. **Discuss the way in which biologists organize species and habitats in the natural world.** Ask students if they know what is meant by an ecosystem. Community? Habitat? What is a species? Give the students the dendrogram (*Ecological Organizations Student Copy Pages*) and describe the concepts of ecosystem, community, and habitat. Explain that a dendrogram is a branching diagram that represents the relationships among ecosystems, communities, and habitats. Emphasize that species are members of all levels of the classification system. For example, the Yuma clapper rail is a member of the greater Colorado ecosystem and, within that ecosystem, the Sonoran Desert ecosystem. Its habitat is freshwater marsh with cattails.

3. **Give each student a copy of the *Map: Five Ecosystems of the Colorado Watershed*.**

4. **Referring to the *Ecosystems of the Colorado Student Copy Pages*, discuss the five major ecosystems (see page XXIX for a map of additional ecosystems) that the Colorado flows through.** Show the students these areas on the map:

   a. The high-elevation conifer forests of the

headwaters in Wyoming's Wind River Mountains, Colorado's Rocky Mountain National Park, and other mountain ranges of the basin.

b. The Navajoan Desert/Colorado Plateau of northeastern Arizona and the Four-Corners region.

c. The Mojave Desert of California, Nevada, and Arizona.

d. The Sonoran Desert of Arizona, Sonora, Baja California, and California.

e. The Upper Gulf of California in northern Baja California and Sonora.

The Activity

1. **Organize students into five groups, one for each ecosystem.** Assign each group to one of the ecosystems (conifer forest, Navajoan Desert/Colorado Plateau, Mojave Desert, Sonoran Desert, Upper Gulf of California).

2. **Have the students sit in the area of the classroom that represents their ecosystem and read the description provided.** They can then move as a group to the next ecosystem and read its description. They should continue on their "tour" of the ecosystems until they have visited each one, staying with their group as they move.

3. **When students have returned to their own ecosystem area, give each group one set of all the animal cards and have them share the cards within their groups.** Based on the descriptions of the ecosystems and the characteristics listed on each animal card, they should decide as a group which ecosystem each animal most likely belongs to. Tell them that some animals may belong to more than one ecosystem, but that there is a "best" ecosystem for each one. They should try to end up with five animals for each ecosystem. Some of the animals will be easy to categorize, but others will have more subtle clues.

4. **After organizing their animal cards into five groups, according to ecosystem, have each group move around the room and place their animal cards in the appropriate ecosystem.** They can visit each ecosystem once and make their final decisions about which animals belong there. Have students place cards in an envelope or box. Tell the students that they can think of this process as "voting"; by placing their animals in each area they are "casting their vote" that it belongs there.

5. **When each group has finished placing their animals in the five ecosystems, lead the class in a comparison of the results.** Start with the conifer forest ecosystem and continue around the classroom to the other ecosystems. There should be twenty-five cards for each if all cards have been correctly placed (there are five different animals in each ecosystem and five groups of students).

6. **Have the students in the group assigned to each ecosystem turn over the cards and report to the class which animals were placed there.** This may be thought of as "counting the votes." If each group of students placed the same cards in that community area, there should be five cards for each of the five species. Are there some species with only one card? If so, they might belong in another community, since most of the class placed them elsewhere.

7. **Lead the students in a discussion to decide which animals belong in each ecosystem and why; continue this comparison and discussion for each of the five ecosystems.** Then use the answer key to check the students' decisions and share the outcomes. Some species may be found in more than one ecosystem, although a certain ecosystem is most likely. The animals that are less likely to be found in an ecosystem are indicated in parentheses in the answer key.

Answers:

Conifer forest: moose, American marten, northern goshawk, American pika, snowshoe hare.

Navajoan Desert: pronghorn, piñon jay, California condor, Hopi rattlesnake, Hopi chipmunk.

Mojave Desert: Amargosa toad, Mojave Desert sidewinder, Mohave tui chub, Ash Meadows Amargosa pupfish, Mojave fringe-toed lizard (California condor, elf owl, Costa's hummingbird).

Sonoran Desert: elf owl, Sonoran green toad, Yuma clapper rail, Costa's hummingbird, lesser long-nosed bat (pronghorn).

Upper Gulf of California: vaquita marina, totoaba, gulf corvina, fish-eating bat, bottle-nosed dolphin.

Wrap Up

1. **Ask students which animals were the most difficult to categorize into a specific community.** Were these species typically generalists or specialists? Which ecosystems had the most overlap of species and why?

2. **Guide a discussion of ecosystems and habitats.** Possible discussion questions may include:

   - What are some important components of habitats? For example, discuss food, water, hiding places, nesting and denning places, temperature, vegetation, etc.
   - What can we deduce about plants and animals by examining the habitats in which they live? Talk about adaptations: for example, cacti are well adapted to desert environments, but wouldn't survive in wet marshlands.
   - What characteristics can we predict a habitat will have if we know something about the characteristics and habits of a plant or animal that lives there? For example, we wouldn't predict that an animal with no hair or feathers that seldom needs to drink would live in the high, snowy mountains!
   - How does the physical environment affect the distribution of species?
   - How does diversity in the physical environment relate to diversity of species? Because organisms are specifically adapted for their physical environment, so too in areas where there is great variation in the physical environment, e.g., from mountains to the gulf in the Colorado Watershed, there is also great diversity of species.
   - Why are some of the animals in the Colorado Watershed on the Endangered Species List? Discuss habitat loss—which is occurring in much of the watershed, especially in wetlands—and its effect on species richness and diversity. Are specialists or generalists more likely to be vulnerable to habitat loss?

3. **Have students fill in the blanks on the dendrogram for one of the communities featured in the activity.** They should include a brief description of the habitat for each of the five animals found in the community they choose. See *Teacher Copy Page* for answer key.

Assessment

Have students:

- locate the five ecosystems on a map of the southwestern U.S. and northern Mexico (***Warm Up,*** Steps 3–4);
- explain the ecological concepts of ecosystems, communities, and habitats (***Warm Up***, Steps 1-2; ***Wrap Up***, Steps 1–3);
- identify and describe five major ecosystems of the Colorado Watershed (***Warm Up***, Step 4; ***The Activity***, Step 2);
- predict the locations/plant communities of specific animals based on their habitat requirements (Steps 3–6);
- relate diversity of habitats to diversity of species (***Wrap Up***, Steps 1–2);
- fill in the blanks on the dendrogram for one of the four plant communities from the activity; the dendrogram should be specific, with habitats described for the animals from the activity (***Wrap Up***, Step 3).

Extensions

If possible, plan a field trip. This can be to a very small natural area near your school. Organize students into teams and have them explore the area to identify the most important physical features that define different habitats (for example, a stream, a south-facing slope vs. a north-facing slope, a marsh, etc.). Have students record their observations and report back to the group. Ask them to identify the dominant plant species in the ecosystem. Have them search for evidence of animals and write down or draw a description of their observations (may be insects, bird calls, animal tracks, etc.). For each animal observed, have the students record their speculations on the animal's niche within the community.

Have students research additional animals that live in the ecosystems featured in this activity, and make new animal cards to add to the activity. They could also research additional ecosystems in the watershed and add these to the activity.

Have students make posters or brochures with information about an endangered species and/or threatened habitat in the watershed.

Resources

Bergman, Charles. 2002. *Red Delta: Fighting for Life at the End of the Colorado River*. Golden, CO: Fulcrum Publishing.

Blair, Rob, ed. 1996. *The Western San Juan Mountains: Their Geology, Ecology, and Human History*. Niwot, CO: University Press of Colorado.

Bowers, Janice Emily. 1993. *Shrubs and Trees of the Southwest Deserts*. Tucson, AZ: Southwest Parks and Monuments Association.

Elphick, Chris, et al., eds. 2001. *The Sibley Guide to Bird Life and Bird Behavior*. New York: Alfred A. Knopf, Inc.

Fisher, Chris, et al. 2000. *Mammals of the Rocky Mountains*. Renton, WA: Lone Pine Publishing.

Gibson, Daniel. 2000. *Audubon Guide to the National Wildlife Refuges, Southwest*. New York: St.

Martin's Griffin, A Balliet & Fitzgerald Book.

Martínez Lozada, Pablo, ed. 2002. *Philips Guides: The Sea of Cortez, Mexico*. Mexico: Editorial Clío, Libros y Videos, S.A. de C.V.

Odum, E. P. 1983. *Basic Ecology*. Philadelphia, PA: Saunders College Publications.

Peterson, Roger Tory, and Edward L. Chalif. 1973. *Mexican Birds*. Boston, MA: Houghton Mifflin Company.

Phillips, Steven J., and Patricia Wentworth Comus, eds. 2000. *A Natural History of the Sonoran Desert*. Tucson: Arizona-Sonora Desert Museum Press.

Sibley, David. 2000. *The Sibley Guide to Birds*. New York: Alfred A. Knopf, Inc.

Tweit, Susan J. 1992. *The Great Southwest Nature Factbook*. Seattle, WA: Alaska Northwest Books.

e-Links

Arizona-Sonora Desert Museum
Information about Sonoran Desert ecosystems.
www.desertmuseum.org

e-Nature
Photos, information, and sound recordings about wildlife species.
www.enature.com

National Geographic Society
Photos and educational information about world geography.
www.nationalgeographic.com

San Diego State University Center for Inland Waters
Information about Colorado River Delta ecology.
www.sci.sdsu.edu/salton/
SaltonBasinHomePage.html

Upper Gulf of California and Colorado River Delta
Biosphere Reserve
Information about Colorado River Delta
ecosystems.
www.cedointercultural.org/conservation.htm

U.S. Fish and Wildlife Service
Information about the Endangered Species
Program.
http://endangered.fws.gov

U.S. Geological Survey
Free online publication: *Status and Trends of the*
Nation's Biological Resources.
http://biology.usgs.gov/s+t/SNT/index.htm

Ecosystems of the Colorado

Headwaters Mountains/Conifer Forests

The headwaters of the Colorado River gather in the Never Summer Mountains of northern Colorado. The Colorado's largest and northernmost tributary, the Green River, originates in a similar environment in Wyoming's Wind River Mountains. The forested slopes of these mountains are covered with conifer trees. Engelmann spruce and subalpine fir are the dominant species at the higher elevations. Aspen groves may be found along the fast-flowing streams and in wet areas. Numerous species of shrubs and wildflowers grow beneath the canopy. Winters are long and very snowy. Summers are short and relatively cool. Cold, rushing streams are home to trout, beavers, and other aquatic life. The forests provide habitat for mule deer, elk, black bears, mountain lions, voles, mice, and numerous other mammals and birds. Similar conifer forest habitat is found at high elevations throughout the watershed.

The conifer forests that surround Green River Lake in northern Wyoming are an example of an ecosystem that is found at high elevations throughout the watershed.

Ecosystems of the Colorado

Navajoan Desert/Colorado Plateau

Between the high elevation mountain forests and the low deserts (Sonoran and Mojave) of the Colorado Basin lie the semi-arid high desert plateaus and canyons of the Navajoan Desert. The Navajoan Desert includes northeastern Arizona and the Four-Corners region of the Colorado Plateau and is sometimes considered an extension of the Great Basin Desert. Its landscapes include grasslands dotted with shrubs, or woodlands of piñon and juniper trees. Common shrubs include sagebrush, rabbitbrush, greasewood, Mormon tea, and others. Piñon-juniper forests have little undergrowth and support many species of birds and mammals with their nutritious seeds. Cottonwood trees, oaks, willows, and tamarisk (an invasive species) grow along streams. Coyotes, mule deer, mountain lions, piñon jays, collared lizards, ravens, jack rabbits, and many other birds, reptiles, mammals, and amphibians make their homes in the high desert canyon country.

Justin Howe

Piñon-juniper forest ecosystems can be found at Navajo National Monument in northern Arizona.

Ecosystems of the Colorado

Mojave Desert

The Mojave Desert is a transitional zone between the Sonoran Desert and the Great Basin Desert. It lies mainly in southeastern California and southern Nevada. Although summer temperatures are usually extremely high (over 100 degrees F), winters are cool and the temperature may drop below freezing. The Mojave yucca is a distinctive and unusual plant of this desert; Joshua trees and teddy-bear cholla cacti are also found here. Much of the desert is sparsely covered with creosote bush. Mesquite trees and tamarisk (an invasive species) grow in the wetter areas. Animals of the Mojave include Gila monsters, desert tortoises, desert bighorn sheep, white-winged doves, and coyotes.

Justin Howe

Teddy-bear cholla is one of the many species of plants that grows in the Mojave Desert.

Ecosystems of the Colorado

Sonoran Desert

The Sonoran Desert encompasses approximately 100,000 square miles (260,000 square kilometers) of the states of Sonora, Arizona, California, and Baja California. Although it is the warmest desert of the Colorado Basin (on average), it is relatively lush, and in the spring or after a summer rain, the land is surprisingly green, with many different plants flowering. Saguaro cacti and mesquite trees distinguish the Sonoran Desert. Paloverde, creosote bush, and ocotillo are other common plants that define the sometimes-surreal character of the Sonoran Desert. Over five hundred species of animals have been identified, including the desert tortoise, kangaroo rat, scaled quail, coati, ringtail, javelina, and chuckwalla lizard. The Sonoran Desert includes the Colorado River Delta with its desert and wetland habitats. One of the delta's few remaining wetlands, La Ciénaga de Santa Clara, is a 12,000-acre cattail marsh that provides habitat for many migratory birds.

Saguaro cacti grow only in the Sonoran Desert.

Ecosystems of the Colorado

Upper Gulf of California

The Upper Gulf of California is a unique ecosystem that has evolved for the last 5 million years with fresh water and sediment from the Colorado River pouring into the salty Gulf of California. With the building of dams on the Colorado, the river's water now rarely flows all the way to the gulf. Because of this change, the ecosystem functions differently now than it used to. Large tidal shifts stir up delta sediments so that the water is the color of coffee with milk rather than the clear blue often associated with ocean water. The huge amount of sediment deposited at the river's mouth creates a relatively shallow and warm marine environment. Low, tide-washed islands are covered with sea grass. There are several small islands made up of millions of ancient clamshells, a species that is believed to be now extinct. Brown pelicans and gulls fish its waters. Fishermen catch rays, sharks, shrimp, and other species.

Cormorants hunt for fish in the Upper Gulf of California.

Hunting for Habitats Cards

moose
Alces alces
- 6–7 feet tall.
- Usually found near streams and ponds where there are willows.
- Eats twigs, bark, roots, and shoots of woody plants.
- Prefers aquatic plants (such as willows) in summer and conifer shoots in winter.
- Lives in forested areas where there is snow cover in the winter; can withstand very cold temperatures.

snowshoe hare
Lepus americanus
- 15–20 inches long.
- Lives in forests, either coniferous or deciduous.
- Eats green vegetation, bark, twigs, and evergreen needles.
- Favors deep winter snowpack, which makes browse available in higher branches of trees.
- Prefers dense, coniferous forests.

American marten
Martes americana
- 19–27 inches long.
- Occurs in isolated areas of the Southwest and Rocky Mountains.
- Prefers dense, mature, spruce-fir forest.
- Dens in rotten logs or rockslides.
- Eats mice, voles, insects, fruit, and seeds.
- Needs dense forest to provide cover while hunting.

American pika
Ochotona princeps
- 6–8 inches long.
- Usually found at high elevations (above 9,000 feet).
- Usually lives in nests within rockslides on high mountains.
- Eats vegetation; dries and stores plants for winter use.
- Sometimes lives in jumbled logs left behind after an avalanche.

Hunting for Habitats Cards

northern goshawk
Accipiter gentilis
- Wingspan of 3 ½ feet.
- Hunts medium-sized birds in ambush attacks through dense forest.
- Builds nest out of sticks, lines it with bark.
- Brings fresh green conifer branches to its nest during breeding season, perhaps to signal to other birds that the nest is occupied.

pronghorn
Antilocapra americana
- 35–41 inches tall.
- Avoids forests.
- Lives in open, semi-arid grasslands and shrub-lands, near the edges of mountains.
- Diet includes sagebrush, rabbitbrush, and grasses.
- Is the fastest North American mammal.

California condor
Gymnogyps californianus
- Wingspan of up to 9 ½ feet.
- Is very rare; now found in several locations where captive-bred birds have been released.
- Eats carrion, prefers large carcasses.
- Does not build nests (lays eggs on bare ground, often on cliff edges).
- Can be seen at the South Rim of the Grand Canyon.

piñon jay
Gymnorhinus cyanocephalus
- 9–12 inches tall.
- Forms nomadic flocks in woodland areas.
- Prefers to eat piñon nuts, but will also eat insects, other seeds, fruit, etc.
- Buries extra seeds in storage caches for later use.
- Has specialized bill for opening pinecones.

Hunting for Habitats Cards

Hopi rattlesnake
Crotalus viridis nuntius
- Usually 2 feet or less.
- Occurs in a relatively small area of northern Arizona, New Mexico, and southern Utah.
- Usually found on the ground, but occasionally climbs into trees or shrubs.
- Occupies mammal burrows, crevices, and caves during cold weather.
- Eats small mammals, birds, lizards, and amphibians.

Hopi chipmunk
Tamias rufus
- 5–8 inches long.
- Stores food, eating juniper seeds, green vegetation, etc.
- Found in canyon habitats with rocky outcroppings and sparse vegetation; also in piñon-juniper woodlands.
- Builds nests in rock crevices or hollow logs.

Amargosa toad
Bufo nelsoni
- 1–3 ½ inches long.
- Found only in the Oasis Valley (Nye County, Nevada).
- Prefers areas with open, clean-flowing water.
- Uses rodent burrows for shelter.
- Has been negatively impacted by wild burros disturbing its pool habitats.

Mojave Desert sidewinder
Crotalus cerastes cerastes
- 3–5 feet long.
- Its side-winding method of travel is adapted for moving over soft sand.
- Eats lizards, kangaroo rats, and other small mammals and birds.
- Burrows under sand for protection from the sun.
- Primary habitat is sandy soils with creosote bushes.

Hunting for Habitats Cards

Mohave tui chub
Gila bicolor mohavensis
- Can be more than 10 inches long.
- Lives in mineral springs, shallow areas of streams flowing out of lakes, and weedy, shallow areas of lakes.
- Is not very tolerant of changes in water temperature and salinity.
- Competes with nonnative, introduced fish for habitat.

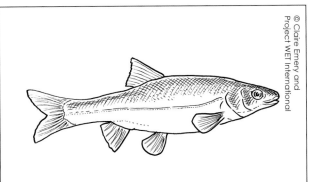

Ash Meadows Amargosa pupfish
Cyprinodon nevadensis mionectes
- About 2 inches long.
- Found only in warm, spring-fed pools and irrigation canals in Ash Meadows National Wildlife Refuge, an oasis in southwestern Nevada.
- Is intolerant of fluctuations in water temperature and salinity.
- Vegetation surrounding its habitat includes mesquite trees and creosote bush.
- Eats algae and small aquatic insects.

Mojave fringe-toed lizard
Uma scoparia
- 5–7 inches long.
- Fringe toes act like snowshoes, allowing it to run rapidly across sand away from predators.
- Has adaptations to protect eyes, ears, and nostrils from sand.
- Burrows in sand to avoid predators.
- Eats insects.
- Found in the Kelso Dunes.

elf owl
Micrathene whitneyi
- About 5 ½ inches tall.
- Nests in holes in saguaro cacti.
- Eats nocturnal insects such as moths, scorpions, and beetles.
- Spends winters on southern coast of Gulf of California in Mexico.
- Can be found in riparian ecosystems in the desert.

Hunting for Habitats Cards

Sonoran green toad
Bufo retiformis
- Up to 2 ¼ inches long.
- Found along washes in mesquite grasslands and creosote bush flats.
- After summer rains, it breeds in temporary rainwater pools.
- Male's call sounds like a combination buzz and whistle.

Costa's hummingbird
Calypte costae
- 3–3 ½ inches tall.
- Lives in desert scrub habitats dominated by saguaro cactus and ocotillo.
- Is well adapted for arid environments.
- Uses spider webs to hold its nest together.
- Eats nectar and small spiders.

Yuma clapper rail
Rallus longirostris yumanensis
- 14–16 inches tall.
- Lives in freshwater cattail marshes.
- Secretive; seldom found on open water.
- Eats aquatic plants and animals.
- The largest population is found at La Ciénaga de Santa Clara, Sonora.

lesser long-nosed bat
Leptonycteris curasoae
- Up to 3 ¼ inches long.
- Is found in Sonora and Arizona, but rarely north of Tucson.
- Requires pollen and nectar from saguaro cacti to provide energy for migration from southern Mexico.
- Also feeds on columnar cactus fruit and agave flower nectar.
- Is an important pollinator for cacti in certain areas of its range.

Hunting for Habitats Cards

vaquita marina
Phocoena sinus
- Less than 5 feet long.
- Eats fish and squid.
- The rarest marine mammal in the world; the population was probably always small, but now only about six hundred individuals remain. Forty to sixty vaquitas die in fishing nets each year.
- Its scientific name means "porpoise of the gulf."

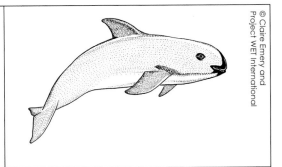

totoaba
Totoaba macdonaldi
- Can grow over 6 feet long.
- Sometimes called a "sea trout."
- Spawns in shallow water near the mouth of the Colorado River.
- Endangered due to habitat changes and over-fishing.

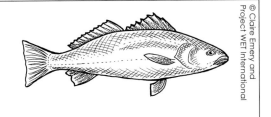

gulf corvina
Cynoscion othonopterus
- Up to 28 inches long.
- Eats other fish.
- Important commercial fish, also valued for sportfishing.
- Inhabits shallow, brackish coastal waters.
- Has been introduced to warm, saline, inland lakes.
- Is endemic to the Upper Gulf of California.

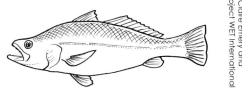

bottle-nosed dolphin
Tursiops truncatus
- Up to 12 feet long.
- Eats fish, shrimp, squid, and other marine animals.
- Lives along most temperate and tropical coasts.
- Is adaptable to many human activities in its habitat and is often seen by fishermen.
- Lives in social groups.

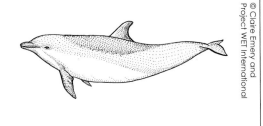

fish-eating bat
Myotis vivesi
- Up to 4 inches long.
- Has large clawed feet for catching small fish at the surface of calm coastal waters.
- Roosts during the day on rocky islands and at night in sea caves.
- Detects fish by the small ripples they cause.

© Claire Emery and Project WET International

Dendrogram: Ecological Organizations Answer Key

vaquita marina

totoaba

fish-eating bat

bottle-nosed dolphin

gulf corvina

UPPER GULF OF CALIFORNIA

elf owl

Sonoran green toad

Yuma clapper rail

Costa's hummingbird

lesser long-nosed bat

SONORAN DESERT

Amargosa toad

Mojave desert side-winder

Mojave tui chub

Ash Meadows Amaragosa pupfish

Mojave fringe-toed lizard

MOJAVE DESERT

pronghorn

piñon jay

California condor

Hopi rattlesnake

Hopi chipmunk

NAVAJOAN DESERT

moose

American marten

northern goshawk

American pika

snowshoe hare

CONIFER FOREST

© Claire Emery and Project WET International

Five Ecosystems of the Colorado Watershed

Dendrogram: Ecological Organizations Worksheet

UPPER GULF OF CALIFORNIA

SONORAN DESERT

MOJAVE DESERT

NAVAJOAN DESERT

CONIFER FOREST

Flight without Borders

How does the flight of birds connect places in the Colorado Watershed?

Grade Level:
6–8

Subject Areas:
Life Science, Geography, Environmental Science, Ecology, Language Arts

Duration:
Preparation time: 30 minutes
Activity time: 80 minutes

Setting:
Classroom; Indoor or Outdoor Open Area (approximately thirty meters by fifty meters)

Skills:
Identify, Simulate, Discuss, Problem Solve, Write, Apply

Vocabulary:
desalination, diurnal, estuary, flyway, Global Positioning System (GPS), habitat, invertebrate, long-distance migrant, migration, Migratory Bird Treaty Act, nocturnal, ornithologist, saline, short-distance migrant, stopover, thermal (air current), waterfowl

Summary
Students play a "choose-your-own-adventure" game to learn about the tradeoffs required in bird migration and to recognize the importance of Colorado Watershed habitats for migrating birds.

Objectives
Students will:
- learn about bird migration strategies and patterns;
- identify important Colorado Watershed stopover habitats;
- simulate seasonal migrations of three Colorado Watershed bird species;
- recognize the value of preserving habitat for migratory birds within the watershed;
- recognize the importance of international cooperation in the management of migratory bird habitats.

Materials
- ***Colorado River Watershed Wall Map***
- ***Migration Routes Map*** *Student Copy Page* (1 per student)
- ***Colorado Watershed Migration Stopovers*** *Teacher Copy Page* (1 set)
- *Backpacks* (1 per group; in larger classes, 2 groups of students may be assigned to the same migratory bird)
- *Weight* (represents food: marbles, gravel, dry beans, etc.)
- *1 box of small zip lock bags* (for holding weight items)
- *String, chalk, or masking tape* (for marking migration routes and stopovers)
- ***Flight without Borders*** *Student Copy Pages* (1 booklet per group of 3 students)
- *Scissors* (1 per group)
- *Stapler*

Background

Each year, millions of North American birds migrate between northern breeding habitats and southern wintering habitats. Many cover vast distances and display amazing navigational strategies to reach the same places year after year. Our understanding of bird migration is still incomplete due to the complexity of this phenomenon.

Bird migration is defined as the seasonal, predictable, annual movement of individuals or groups of birds. Not all individual birds within a species will migrate, nor do all species exhibit migration behavior. For birds to migrate, the benefits gained from it must outweigh the costs. Migration uses much energy and exposes birds to predation, difficult weather, and other dangers.

Some birds must migrate south for the winter because winter conditions are too severe in their northern breeding grounds. But why do birds leave their southern wintering grounds if the weather is favorable there year-round? Ornithologists believe that flying north to breed allows birds to avoid high rates of nest predation and parasites and to take advantage of abundant food supplies and longer days for foraging.

The length of migration routes varies among birds. Long-distance migrants travel between continents from breeding grounds in North America to wintering grounds in Central and South America. Short-distance migrants usually move within the same continent.

Some birds make frequent rest stops during migration, stopping every hundred to two hundred miles to rest and refuel for a few days. Others take the "non-stop flight" approach and stay aloft for long distances during favorable weather. Birds such as hawks usually migrate during the day, using thermal air currents to soar and save energy. Night provides better travel conditions for other migrants (nocturnal migrants) because the air is cooler and less turbulent.

The ability of migratory birds to orient themselves and to navigate without a compass, map, or GPS (Global Positioning System) is astounding!

A combination of complex cues and instincts are believed to be involved, including the position of the sun and stars, magnetic fields, and geographic landmarks. Individual species faithfully follow the same migration routes for generations. Four general migration routes across North America, called flyways, have been identified, but there is a great deal of variability in migratory patterns

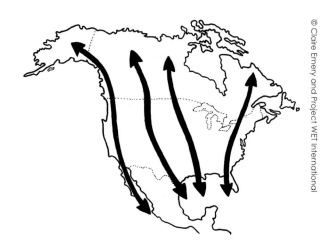

© Claire Emery and Project WET International

Four major migration routes in North America

For all migrating birds, stored fat is essential. Long-distance migrants may build their fat reserves to more than 50 percent of their body weight prior to departure. Other strategies for efficient migration include taking advantage of tailwinds and flying in V-formation to reduce wind drag.

The Colorado Watershed provides important habitat for migratory birds. Wetlands, forests, grain fields, and ponds provide food and shelter. Throughout the watershed, wetland habitats are disappearing due to urban development and an increase in human demands on a limited water supply, so wildlife refuges and reserves provide important protection for bird habitat. Agriculture also plays a role in bird migration patterns by providing abundant food sources (e.g., grain fields) and wetland areas formed by irrigation runoff.

The Salton Sea in Southern California is an example of an agricultural system that has become very important habitat for migratory birds.

Shuzo Yoshihara, Redlands Institute, University of Redlands

Waterfowl forage for grain in fields near the Salton Sea.

However, the Salton Sea is a paradox because, while it provides valuable habitat for birds such as the brown pelican, it can also be an unhealthy environment for them. During summer months, algal blooms related to the high nutrient content of agricultural runoff feeding the sea can cause massive fish die-offs. The dead fish harbor botulism, a serious threat to birds. Biologists at the Sonny Bono National Wildlife Refuge on the sea undertake major rescue operations for brown pelicans that are sick from avian botulism. Resource managers are working to restore and protect habitats for wildlife at the Salton Sea.

Not far from the Salton Sea lies the Colorado Delta. Until the last century, the delta was a 2 million-acre wetland with a variety of habitats used extensively by migratory birds. With the construction of dams on the Colorado River and consumption by water users in the U.S. and Mexico, the water that supplied the delta's wetlands has been reduced to a trickle. As a result, habitat for birds and other species has shrunk dramatically.

La Ciénaga de Santa Clara is the largest wetland area that currently exists in the historic delta. It is formed from agricultural runoff that originates in southern Arizona. This water is too salty for agricultural use or drinking water, so it is carried in a canal to empty onto the delta. The water has created a twelve thousand-acre cattail marsh that provides important habitat for numerous species of birds. However, the future of La Ciénaga is uncertain, since U.S. farmers or urban water users may sometime choose to pay for desalinating the water so they can use it.

Conservationists on both sides of the border are working to find solutions that will preserve habitat for migratory birds and other species while meeting the needs of human communities.

Three Migratory Birds of the Colorado Watershed

The species highlighted in this activity are only three of the numerous species of birds that migrate through and live in the watershed.

American Avocet (*Recurvirostra americana*)

The avocet is found in shallow, marshy, or muddy ponds and feeds by sweeping its bill side-to-side through mud or water to find aquatic insects. Its habitat includes shallow freshwater or saline wetlands, lake shores, and coastal estuaries. Many avocets winter in the Colorado Delta region: at La Ciénaga de Santa Clara, in the Salton Sea, along the coasts of the Gulf of California, and in other wetlands. Wintering ground for avocets extends southward into central Mexico and Central America. They migrate to summer nesting grounds in the central and western U.S. and as far north as Canada and are commonly found in favorable habitats in Colorado and Wyoming. Some populations don't migrate but live year-round along the California coast. Avocets' distinctive orange, black, and white markings and thin, upcurved bills make them easy to identify.

Osprey (*Pandion haliaetus*)

Ospreys are large birds of prey that feed on fish. They find fish visually, hovering high in the air over open water, then diving down into the water head- and feet-first to capture them with their talons. Spiked scales on the bottoms of their feet help them to hold onto slippery, squirming fish. Ospreys build large, sturdy nests of sticks on the tops of dead trees, rock towers, cacti, or nest platforms built by people. The northern breeding grounds of ospreys extend into Alaska, but small populations nest within the Colorado Basin in northern Arizona, southwestern Colorado, and northern Wyoming. They spend the winter along the Lower Colorado River, with some populations living year-round at the Gulf of California.

American White Pelican (*Pelecanus erythrorhynchos*)

American white pelicans live on lakes and shallow lagoons and can be seen throughout the watershed. Many live year-round in the delta region, while others migrate north in the summer to nest in colonies on lakes and rivers in Utah, Wyoming, Idaho, Montana, and as far north as Canada. White pelicans often fish in coordinated groups, working together to "herd" fish into shallow water or to trap them inside a circle of birds where they can be easily caught and eaten. White pelican populations are stable in North America, although some of their winter (southern) habitats are threatened by loss of wetlands and by invasive aquatic plants, such as hydrilla, that choke open waterways and crowd out native species.

During this activity, students will "choose-their-own-adventure" to simulate migration routes and strategies used by three bird species that are found in the Colorado Watershed. They will pack their backpacks with stored energy (fat reserves) and use the ***Flight without Borders*** booklets (*Student Copy Pages*) to guide them. Based on the choices they make along the way, they will use their energy reserves and replenish them, in an effort to reach their migration destinations!

Procedure

Preparation

1. **In an open area of your classroom or outdoor multi-purpose area (about thirty meters by fifty meters), mark one end with a sign that says:**

WINTER HABITAT: Lower Colorado River and Delta (La Ciénaga de Santa Clara, Rio Hardy Wetlands, El Doctor Wetlands, Salton Sea, etc.)

Mark the other end with a sign that says:

SUMMER HABITAT: Northern Nesting Grounds (Upper Green River, Green River Lakes, etc.)

Flight without Borders Activity Set-up

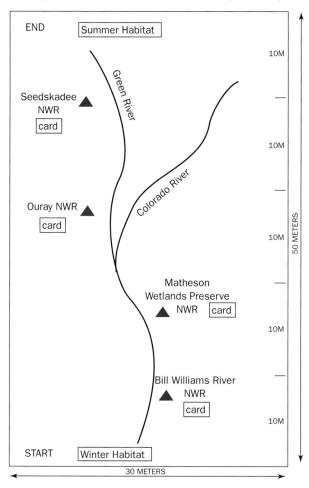

START / END diagram showing:
- END — Summer Habitat
- Green River
- Seedskadee NWR [card]
- Colorado River
- Ouray NWR [card]
- Matheson Wetlands Preserve NWR [card]
- Bill Williams River NWR [card]
- START — Winter Habitat
- 50 METERS (vertical), with 10M increments
- 30 METERS (horizontal)

2. **Between the signs, mark a winding river channel with string, masking tape, or chalk.** Place the *Colorado Watershed Migration Stopovers Cards* (see *Teacher Copy Page*) along the river as marked on the diagram above:

3. **Your students will be working in groups of three for this activity.** Make enough copies of the *Flight without Borders* Student Copy Pages booklets for each group to have one booklet (representing one of the three birds). Try to have each bird represented by at least one group. Students will assemble their booklets in Step 2 of **The Activity**.

4. **Fill small zip lock bags with the weight item you have chosen (e.g., gravel, dry beans).** These represent stored energy that birds need

for migration. Put approximately the same amount (representing one pound) in each bag. Make enough so you have eight to ten bags per group of students.

Warm Up

1. **Ask your students to imagine having a winter home in El Golfo de Santa Clara, Mexico, and a summer home in Pinedale, Wyoming.** Point out these two locations on the *Colorado River Watershed Wall Map.* What would they need to do each season to plan for the trip? What would they take with them? What route would they take? If they chose to drive, could they drive "straight"? What obstacles would determine their route? Where would they want to stop along the way?

2. **Ask them to brainstorm bird species that live in your area.** Which live there year-round, and which are only there for summer or winter? Tell them that many birds migrate through the Colorado Watershed, spending winters in the southern part of the basin and summers in the north. Each species has different habitat needs; ospreys, for example, need open water, high perches to nest on and hunt from, and plenty of fish to eat. White pelicans need open, shallow water, fish to eat, and safe places for their nests, which are on the ground. Avocets need shallow, muddy water to feed in and safe nesting places (they also nest on the ground). The Colorado Watershed provides a variety of habitats, for both summer and winter habitats, and for "rest-stops" (stopovers) for birds that are migrating beyond the watershed.

3. **Discuss the reasons why birds migrate (see Background).**

4. **Use a classroom map of North America and the *Migration Routes Map* (*Student Copy Page*) to illustrate the Pacific Flyway and the routes of the three birds in this activity (see Background).** Talk about the logistics involved for these birds. They must stock up on energy reserves (fat) before the trip;

avoid storms, predators, and human hazards such as power lines; and choose a successful route that provides safe stopovers along the way. Emphasize that individual birds may use different routes. The Pacific Flyway is a general migration corridor. Ornithologists believe that the Colorado Delta wetlands are extremely important for birds migrating along the Pacific Flyway. Migratory birds along the Colorado River provide a strong link between communities in Mexico and the U.S.

The Activity

1. **Divide students into groups of three.** One student will be the bird, wearing the backpack and following directions. One student will read the directions in the group's bird booklet. One student will be responsible for adding and subtracting weight as instructed by the booklet.

2. **Give each group an empty backpack, the copy pages for their species' bird booklet, and a copy of the *Migration Routes Map*.**

3. **Have each group assemble their *Flight without Borders* bird booklet by cutting out the pages and stapling them together in order.** The bird picture should appear on the front and the bird facts should fill the back. Have them read the bird facts listed on the back page to learn about their species.

4. **Lead students to the "migration course" that you set up prior to the activity.** Show them the starting point (Winter Habitat) and ending point (Summer Habitat). Point out the stopover places along the route. Tell them that these represent actual places in the watershed that are used by migrating birds.

5. **Have each group read the first page of their booklet and collect the number of bags of energy that their species starts migration with (for example, white pelicans will need to put seven bags in their backpacks).**

6. **Tell the students that they'll have to make choices along the way to their summer habitats, and each choice will have consequences.** You may want to have a practice run with younger students, reading through sample steps from the booklets.

7. **Let the groups start migrating, reading their booklets and following the instructions.** Remind them that it is not a race; it is a challenge to choose the right steps to make it to their migration destination. When they come to a stopover, they need to read the card that tells about the place and write down three facts about it. Tell them that they will sometimes be instructed to stop between stopovers, as well.

8. **As students drop weight along the way, pick up the bags and move them to stopover spots so that students can pick them up again.** You may want to ask a student volunteer to do this job.

Wrap Up

1. **When all of the groups have completed their migrations, have them return to their desks.** Have each group turn in their three facts from each stopover.

2. **Discuss the activity in the context of an international watershed.** The Colorado River is important to many species, and for them there is no boundary between the U.S. and Mexico. How can resource managers in the two countries work together to ensure that habitats and migration corridors are preserved across the international border? The Migratory Bird Treaty Act is an international treaty prohibiting activities that are harmful to species that migrate across international borders in North America. International conservation groups are seeking to identify habitat needs and develop preservation plans to protect migratory birds.

3. **Have students write up a "Migration Report" or "Recovery Plan" for their species.** If they successfully made it to their summer habitat, they should describe their experience and choices. If they didn't make it,

have them write a recovery plan that will help their species to successfully migrate next time. Explain that recovery plans are similar to the strategies of wildlife managers who seek to help migratory birds succeed.

4. **If time permits, groups can attempt migration again as the same species or trade species with another group.**

Assessment

Have students:
- discuss bird migration patterns and strategies (**Warm Up**, Steps 1–4);
- simulate the migration of three different bird species (Steps 1–7);
- write down three facts about each stopover location from their migration (Step 7);
- discuss the challenges of managing an international watershed for species that migrate between two or more countries (**Wrap Up**, Step 2);
- write reports and/or recovery plans based on their experiences (**Wrap Up**, Step 3).

Extensions

Have students design their own **Flight without Borders** booklets for different species.

Have students design a board game based on this activity.

Have students use the Internet to research organizations and programs that are coordinating international cooperative efforts to protect migratory birds (see **e-Links**).

Contact your local Audubon Society or wildlife management agency to find out about service learning projects in which your students could participate. Planting trees, building nesting sites, and helping with educational outreach are a few possibilities.

Resources

Bergman, Charles. 2002. *Red Delta: Fighting for Life at the End of the Colorado River.* Golden, CO: Fulcrum Publishing.

Elphick, Chris, et al., eds. 2001. *The Sibley Guide to Bird Life and Bird Behavior.* New York: Alfred A. Knopf, Inc.

Gibson, Daniel. 2000. *Audubon Guide to the National Wildlife Refuges, Southwest.* New York: St. Martin's Griffin, A Balliet & Fitzgerald Book.

Phillips, Steven J., and Patricia Wentworth Comus, eds. 2000. *A Natural History of the Sonoran Desert.* Tucson: Arizona-Sonora Desert Museum Press.

Sibley, David. 2000. *The Sibley Guide to Birds.* New York: Alfred A. Knopf, Inc.

e-Links

Journey North
Students across North America share field observations about migration patterns.
www.learner.org/jnorth

National Audubon Society
Bird conservation information and programs.
www.audubon.org

North American Bird Conservation Initiative
An initiative to coordinate bird conservation management efforts from local to international levels.
www.nabci-us.org

Partners In Flight
A cooperative group that works to coordinate international bird conservation efforts.
www.partnersinflight.org

Rocky Mountain Bird Observatory's *Birds Beyond Borders*
An international exchange program that links classrooms in the U.S. with classrooms in Mexico through our shared resource of migratory birds.
www.rmbo.org/education/bbb.html

Colorado Watershed Migration Stopovers

Bill Williams River National Wildlife Refuge, Arizona

The Bill Williams River forms the heart of this refuge in western Arizona. It includes the mouth of the Bill Williams where it flows into Lake Havasu, a major reservoir on the Colorado River that is formed by Parker Dam. The refuge is unique because it preserves some of the last remaining cottonwood/willow woodlands and cattail wetland habitats along the Lower Colorado River. Its Sonoran Desert habitat includes saguaro cacti and mesquite trees. Numerous species of birds, butterflies, bats, mammals, and other animals make their homes here. Many migrating birds also stop here. The river is named after a mountain man who traveled through Arizona in the early 1800s.

Scott M. Matheson Wetlands Preserve, Utah

The Matheson Preserve is a wetlands preserve in the floodplain of the Colorado River near Moab, Utah. In spring and summer, its vibrant green vegetation stands out against the redrock cliffs and canyons that surround it. Boardwalks and blinds allow visitors to observe birds, beavers, frogs, and other animals in their natural wetland habitats. The preserve includes marshes and cottonwood/willow woodlands. It is jointly managed by The Nature Conservancy and the Utah Division of Wildlife Resources and is named in honor of a former governor of Utah.

Ouray National Wildlife Refuge, Utah

The Ouray National Wildlife Refuge was originally established as a refuge for breeding and migrating waterfowl and includes twelve miles of the Green River. Wildlife managers use diversions and flooding to mimic the natural floodplain habitats that existed before the construction of upstream dams on the river. Ponds and marshes provide food and cover for nesting birds, as well as habitat for endangered fish species. A portion of the refuge is used to grow crops, some of which are left behind after harvesting to provide food for wildlife. Many species of migratory birds use the refuge as a stopover and as a summer nesting ground. The refuge is named for Chief Ouray, a well-known Ute leader.

Seedskadee National Wildlife Refuge, Wyoming

Situated along the Green River in western Wyoming, Seedskadee NWR preserves wetland marshes and cottonwood forest for many species of birds and mammals. The river's floodplain creates wetland habitats, and above the flood plain the land is covered with sagebrush and other shrubs and grasses that can survive in arid conditions. Winters are long and cold, but in the summer, the habitats here support many migratory birds that are either passing through or staying to nest. The refuge is named after the Shoshone name for the Green River, "Sisk-adee-agie" or "river of the prairie hen."

Flight without Borders Osprey Booklet

Page 1

The days are getting longer and warmer at La Ciénaga de Santa Clara, where you have spent the winter months fishing and storing fat for your springtime journey north to Wyoming. One morning the weather seems perfect for departure, and you decide to begin your journey. You'll be traveling more than 1,000 miles in two to three weeks. If you spend the day fishing and storing more energy, it will be evening before you fly **(if so, fill your pack with 10 pounds and turn to page 2).** If you leave immediately to take advantage of the daylight and warm breezes, **take 5 pounds and turn to page 3.**

Page 2

It is dusk by the time you lift off. You've had a good day of fishing, but the air is still and it is difficult to gain altitude without the day's rising warm air currents (thermals) to lift you. Instead of soaring between thermals, you flap your wings and quickly become tired. **Flap your arms 50 times and take 5 small steps forward.** You decide to land on top of a telephone pole and rest until morning. **Take 5 pounds out of your pack, count to 60 to recover, and turn to page 3.**

Page 3

You rely on the morning's thermals to carry you northward. As the sun heats the earth, pockets of air begin to rise, lifting you upward. You spiral up and soar northward, saving energy without having to beat your wings. **Turn in circles 5 times and glide 10 long steps forward to the first stopover,** Bill Williams River National Wildlife Refuge on the edge of Lake Havasu in Arizona. You see beautiful cottonwood trees below you, surrounded by desert. **Take 2 pounds of food out of your pack and turn to page 4.**

© Claire Emery and Project WET International

OSPREY

Flight without Borders Osprey Booklet

You spend a good day fishing in Lake Havasu and resting in the top of a cottonwood tree along the Bill Williams River. Rested and refueled, you are ready to fly for several days before your next stopover. **Add 2 pounds to your pack. Turn to page 5.**

Page 4

You've flown steadily for many miles and seen many sights below you, including a section of the Grand Canyon. You're starting to get tired and hungry, but the weather is good for flying. **Take 3 pounds from your pack and fly towards the next stopover.** You see below you a green valley surrounded by dramatic red rock canyons. The Colorado River, which you have tried to stay close to during your flight, flows through Moab, Utah, below you. **If you decide to land at the Matheson Wetlands Preserve for a rest and fishing, turn to page 6. If you decide to keep flying, turn to page 7.**

Page 5

You feel safe roosting in cottonwoods at the Matheson Wetlands Preserve, and decide to try your luck with fishing the river in the morning. You hover over the river until you spot a fish below, fold your wings, and dive in. Your talons close around the fish, but as you struggle to rise from the water with it, a motorboat passes by and startles you. You drop the fish and return to your perch to dry off and try again. **Count to 50 while you wait.** After catching one small fish, you decide it's time to head north again while you still have several hours of daylight. **Add 1 pound to your pack and turn to page 8.**

Page 6

You keep flying, enjoying the strong thermals that are boosting you and saving energy. **Take 10 steps.** By nightfall, you are tired and find a perch along the Green River. **Count to 50 while you rest.** The next morning you're hungry for fish, but a storm has moved in and the water is so choppy it is hard to see your prey. Wet, tired, and hungry, you decide to wait for the storm to pass. **Take 1 pound from your pack.**

The storm is over by the afternoon and you catch a big fish on your first try. **Add 2 pounds to your pack and fly north. Turn to page 8.**

Page 7

Flight without Borders Osprey Booklet

OSPREY
Bird Hints:

Migration:
Ospreys are "diurnal" migrants, using daylight hours to travel.

Flight:
Gliding and soaring flight, using updrafts and thermal air masses to save energy. Average wingspan is 63 inches.

Habitat:
Near open water along lakes and rivers.

Food:
Fish is the major source of food.

Page 11

You are very tired now and feel that it is time to find your nesting site. You've flown a long way from Seedskadee, following the Green River, and now you find yourself on the western slope of the Wind River Mountains. Below you, several mountain lakes beckon. You circle several times and land on a large boulder overlooking your destination, Green River Lakes.

There are many other birds of prey here, but there are also plenty of fish and nesting sites for everyone. **CONGRATULATIONS! You've made a successful migration!**

Page 10

It is clear and cold in the morning, and you decide to fish. You hover over the river and see several fish, choose a big one, and dive for the kill. Success! As you struggle to lift the heavy fish to your perch, the bald eagle swoops in and forces you to drop it. You decide there is just too much competition here and head north. **Take 10 steps and turn to page 10.**

Page 9

The weather stays clear and you are covering many miles of territory. **Flap your wings 10 times, soar in 5 circles, and take 20 steps. Drop 1 pound of weight.**

You are ready to stop for the night. Your instincts lead you to Seedskadee National Wildlife Refuge on the Green River. You circle in to land on a dead tree near the shore. Oh, no! You didn't see the huge bald eagle that was already perched there. Better find another place to rest! **If you decide to stay at Seedskadee NWR for the night, turn to page 9. If you decide to keep going a little further, take 10 steps and turn to page 10.**

Page 8

Flight without Borders Avocet Booklet

AVOCET

Page 1

You are beginning to get restless. You've had a good winter in the El Doctor wetlands, but your instincts are calling you to fly north for the summer to breed and nest. You have spent the winter eating small aquatic insects and other invertebrates that you've picked from the muddy waters of your favorite lagoon. You'll be flying to northern Utah or southern Wyoming, so you have a long way to go. **Fill up your pack with 5 pounds and turn to page 2.**

Page 2

You have stayed with the same group of birds all winter and decide to fly north together. You are ready to go, but the others want to wait until dusk in order to use the stars for orientation and avoid flying when there may be falcons in the sky. **If you convince the others to leave right away, take 5 steps and turn to page 3. If you decide it's better to wait until dusk, count to 60 while you rest and turn to page 4.**

Page 3

You pay for your impatience by fighting a strong headwind all afternoon. **Take 2 wobbly steps north.** You've used a lot of energy but haven't gotten far, and one of the slower fliers in your group almost gets caught by a hunting falcon. **Take 2 pounds from your pack and find a pond to rest on until the winds die down at dusk. Count to 30 and turn to page 4.**

Flight without Borders Avocet Booklet

At dusk you take flight and soon settle into a comfortable rhythm that allows you to cover many miles. **Take 10 steps forward and drop 2 pounds from your pack.** You navigate by the stars and by responding to cues from the earth's magnetic field. You also keep the Colorado River in sight below you so you can easily find safe places to rest and eat when you need to. By morning you are ready to rest. Below you see the cattails that crowd the mouth of the Bill Williams River where it flows into Lake Havasu. You'll be able to spend the day there, resting and foraging. **Count to 50 while you rest and add 2 pounds to your pack. Turn to page 5.**

Page 4

After a good day of resting and refueling, you're ready to move on when the sun sets. **Take 5 long steps.** During the night, you fly into a localized spring storm. You quickly become cold and wet, but don't see any safe places to land until the storm is over. **If you decide to take a risk and land on a neighborhood golf course, turn to page 6. If you decide to keep flying through the storm, turn to page 7.**

Page 5

You find a small pond on the golf course and hesitantly land. Finally, you are out of the storm, but there is no shelter around the pond. As you wearily settle on the shore, you're aware of dogs barking in backyards just a short distance away. You hear one jump its fence and rush towards your pond, and just in time, you take flight. Time to move on. You've used energy flying through the storm. **Drop 1 pound and take 3 steps. Turn to page 8.**

Page 6

As you fly through the storm, it begins to weaken and soon you are flying under clear skies. **Take 5 steps and drop 1 pound.** As the sun rises, you search for a place to land and rest. Below you see a marshy area along the Colorado River. Since you are now in the middle of canyon country in southern Utah, marshes are not easy to find. You find some shallow, muddy water in the Matheson Wetlands Preserve and start to hunt for food. **Add 2 pounds to your pack and count to 30. Turn to page 9.**

Page 7

Flight without Borders Avocet Booklet

AVOCET Bird Hints:

Migration: Avocets migrate as far north as southern Canada and southward into southern Mexico.

Flight: A 31-inch average wingspan and relatively lightweight body help avocets to fly long distances during migration.

Habitat: Shallow muddy or marshy ponds, either freshwater or saline.

Food: Aquatic insects and other small aquatic prey.

Page 11

Using the last of your energy, you fly slowly north, searching for a good place to end your migration and spend the summer. **Take 30 slow steps.** Finally you see below you a welcoming wetland. The Upper Green River has spilled onto its floodplain, creating marshes. This is helped by the work of beavers that build dams and maintain shallow ponds. **Drop off any remaining weight.** You can spend the summer here. CONGRATULATIONS! **You've successfully migrated once again.**

Page 10

After two more nights of flying with a favorable tailwind, you find yourself along the Green River in northern Utah. You remember that there is good nesting habitat somewhere near, but you are tired and hungry. **If you stop now for a few hours to save energy, count to 50 and turn to page 10. If you keep going to find a better place to possibly end your journey and build your nest, turn to page 8.**

Page 9

By now you are really ready for a rest. You've flown all night but are nervous about landing in areas that have houses. Your energy reserves are quickly becoming depleted and you see no safe places to land for resting and refueling. A winter drought in the area means that marshes are still dry and farmers haven't yet begun flooding their fields to irrigate them. **Take 2 pounds from your pack. If you still have stored energy (weight left in your pack), keep going to page 10.**

If, however, you've run out of stored energy, you won't survive migration this year. **WRITE A RECOVERY PLAN.**

Page 8

Flight without Borders White Pelican Booklet

WHITE PELICAN

Page 1

You've spent another good winter on a lagoon in the Rio Hardy wetlands, eating fish and fattening up for your long flight north. You will fly all the way to northern Wyoming to nest on the upper Green River. The lengthening days cue you that it's time to begin your long flight north. One morning, your flock rises from the river and circles upward to 2,500 feet before settling into a V-formation and steadily winging northward. **Put 7 pounds in your pack, take 10 steps, and turn to page 2.**

Page 2

The main flock flies steadily, taking turns "drafting" behind each other and traveling at a steady pace with the help of thermal air currents. Some birds split off from the main flock and fly ahead. **If you're a strong, fast flyer who prefers solitude, run 10 steps and go to page 4. If you're happy sticking with the crowd and being sociable, walk 10 steps and turn to page 3.**

Page 3

The V-formation helps create lift by utilizing the air currents of other birds' wing beats. It makes for efficient flying, with birds in the back of the formation coasting much of the time. **Take 10 steps forward.** Pelicans take turns flying at the front of the formation, and suddenly it's your turn! **Do 5 jumping jacks and take 10 steps. By now you're pretty tired. Take 2 pounds from your pack. As you settle in at the back of the line again, watch for a good place to rest and turn to page 5.**

Flight without Borders White Pelican Booklet

It's almost dark when you take off, joining a small flock of other white pelicans that circles low over the refuge and heads north. Cloudy skies block the moon and stars and force you to fly low. All of a sudden . . . SMACK! You fly right into a set of power lines and get hopelessly entangled. Your migration has come to a sad end. **WRITE A RECOVERY PLAN.**

Page 7

You're feeling strong and energetic after your rest. With a flock of companions, you fly at an easy, steady pace, covering many miles. **Take 15 steps north. Remove 1 pound from your pack.** As you start to descend towards an island you remember in the middle of the Green River, you notice something is different. **Turn to page 8.**

Page 6

You've found a good place to rest and refuel, at the Ouray National Wildlife Refuge in northern Utah. Other flocks of migrating birds, including geese and ducks, have also found the marshes and lakes of this refuge. **Add 2 pounds to your pack.** Some of the flocks take off at sunset, while others settle in to rest for the night. **If you opt for night flight, turn to page 7. If you choose to rest until dawn, count to 60 and turn to page 6.**

Page 5

Although your wings are strong and nearly 9 feet across, it's hard work flying without the flock. You find yourself growing tired without the helpful air currents created by the wing beats of companions. **Flap your arms hard, take 10 slow steps forward, and remove 3 pounds from your pack.** Although you are tired and hungry, you must keep going until you can find a good place to land. Finally, you see your flock on a small lake far below. Although you thought you were flying faster, they arrived before you and are already feeding and resting. You spiral down to rejoin your flock. **Turn to page 5.**

Page 4

Flight without Borders White Pelican Booklet

WHITE PELICAN
Bird Hints:

Migration:
Some white pelicans fly from the Colorado River Delta to northern Wyoming each year. They can be seen on rivers and lakes throughout the Colorado River Watershed.

Flight:
Usually migrates in large flocks, using thermal air currents and V-formations to help conserve energy.

Habitat:
Nests on shores of lakes or lagoons or on islands in rivers. Winters on shallow, open water where fish are plentiful.

Food:
Fish, salamanders, and crayfish.

You finally find a perfect place to stop and build your nest along a stretch of the Green River in northern Wyoming. There are other pelicans here and a large island with low vegetation that will be perfect for nesting. Fish are plentiful.

CONGRATULATIONS on your successful migration!

Page 10

You quickly realize that the river has few fish in it here, and the lack of open water makes you vulnerable to predators. You've wasted precious time and energy by landing. Take half the food from your backpack and take off, flying as hard as you can to the north. **Take 5 giant steps towards your winter breeding grounds and turn to page 10.**

Page 9

The nesting island you've used in the past is no longer surrounded by water. Because of increased irrigating upstream and a recent drought, the river is low and the island is no longer protected from predators. **If you land anyway and try to find a safe place to rest and eat, count to 30 and turn to page 9. If you keep going north to find a better spot, take 5 long steps north and turn to page 10.**

Page 8

Migration Routes Map

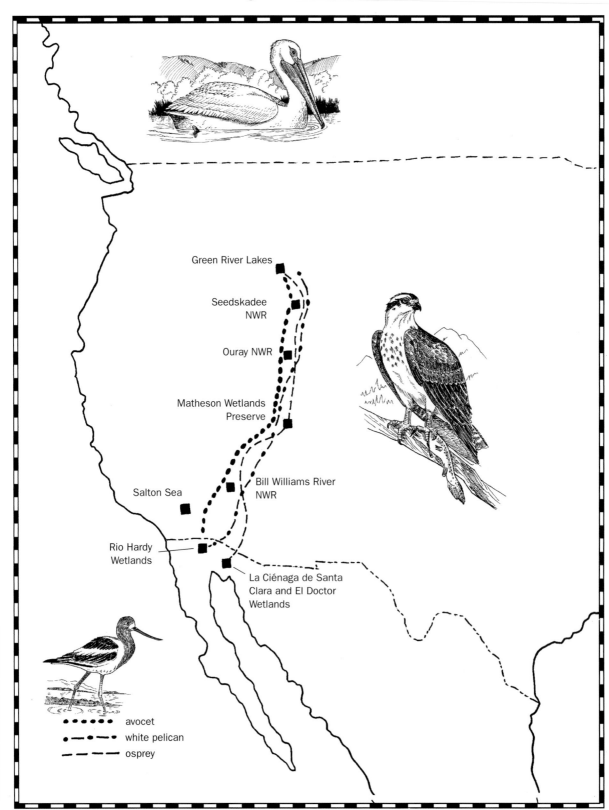

Green River Lakes

Seedskadee NWR

Ouray NWR

Matheson Wetlands Preserve

Salton Sea

Bill Williams River NWR

Rio Hardy Wetlands

La Ciénaga de Santa Clara and El Doctor Wetlands

•••••• avocet
•–•–• white pelican
––––– osprey

© Claire Emery and Project WET International

Chillin' with the Chubs

How do changes in the river environment affect native fish?

~~~~~~~~~~~~~~~~~~~~~~~~~

Grade Level:
6–8

Subject Areas:
Environmental Science, Math, Life Science, Ecology

Duration:
Preparation time: 20 minutes
Activity time: 90 minutes

Setting:
Classroom for *Warm Up, Part II,* and *Wrap Up;* Outdoor Playing Field or Large Indoor Area (gym, cafeteria) for *Part I*

Skills:
Identify, Interpret, Hypothesize, Simulate, Graph, Analyze, Discuss, Problem Solve

Vocabulary:
backwater, cubic feet per second (cfs), crustacean, dam, detritus, diversion, ecosystem (ecology), eddy, estuary, introduced species, invertebrate, native species, nonnative species, riffle, spawn, tail-water, turbidity

Summary
Students play a game to simulate the effects of introduced species and dams on native fish populations in the Colorado River and Upper Gulf of California.

Objectives
Students will:
- identify habitat conditions necessary for the survival of six native fish species;
- compare pre-dam and post-dam habitat conditions in the Colorado and Green Rivers;
- hypothesize about the effects that different environmental stressors (introduced species, dams) will have on various species in the simulation game;
- simulate the change in populations as a result of environmental stressors;
- graph the changes in populations observed in the simulation game;
- discuss management solutions for protecting native fish species.

Materials
- *Chalkboard or large piece of paper for classroom* **Chillin' with the Chubs Survivability Chart**
- *Classroom set of* **Chillin' with the Chubs Fact Cards** *Student Copy Pages*
- *Copies of* **Changing River Conditions** *Student Copy Pages* (1 per student)
- *Copies of* **Fish Habitat Requirements** *Student Copy Pages* (1 per student)
- *Colored pencils or markers*
- *Optional: graphing paper* (can use regular notebook paper)

Background

Native fish were historically plentiful in the sediment-rich waters of the Colorado, and several species were found only in this river system. The Colorado pikeminnow, humpback chub, bonytail chub, and razorback sucker are examples of fish species that were formerly abundant in the river. These four species thrived in the pre-dam Colorado, providing important food sources for other animals in the food chain, including humans. As dams changed their environments, these fish species began to decline.

The construction of dams on the Colorado River and its tributaries has changed the river's flow patterns, water temperature, sediment-carrying capacity, and other environmental conditions. Hoover Dam, completed in 1935, was the first major dam on the main stem of the Colorado. Dams and diversions have now been built on most of the Colorado's major tributaries, resulting in changes to river ecosystems throughout the watershed. Dams and diversions have brought benefits to human populations, providing reliable water sources for agriculture and municipal use, non-polluting energy sources, protection from floods and droughts, and recreational opportunities.

The native plant, animal, and fish species that evolved in pre-dam Colorado River environments had to adapt to extreme conditions. The Colorado's flows varied according to season, with spring floods bringing cold, muddy water to scour riverbanks and deposit sediment, followed by low flows in late summer that were warm. Flash floods in the summer months would carry tons of debris and sediment, causing rapid and short-lived fluctuations in the river environment. Plants that lived along the water's edge included coyote willow, Emory seepwillow, and cottonwood trees. These species are adapted to the changing flows and rely on spring floods for their seeds to germinate.

Justin Howe

A fishing net is poised for the tide to come in on the eastern coast of the Upper Gulf of California.

Another factor that is believed to have influenced the decline of native fish species is the introduction of nonnative fish into the river system. These fish, including rainbow and brown trout, channel catfish, striped bass, and carp, were better adapted for post-dam river conditions than native species. They became new predators for the eggs and young of native fish. Some nonnative fish are more popular with today's fishermen and are routinely stocked in the watershed's reservoirs, streams, and rivers by wildlife management agencies.

The construction of dams affected fish and other species in the river itself and had a great impact on species in the Colorado Delta and in the Upper Gulf of California. The fluctuating flows, periodic floods, and huge amounts of sediment that the river formerly provided to the delta and Upper Gulf were integral to the functioning of these ecosystems. Two species that have declined in the last century are the totoaba, a large fish of the Upper Gulf and lower Colorado River, and the desert pupfish, which lives in shallow, saline lagoons and springs. Totoaba are desirable fish in commercial markets that have been affected by changes to their habitat and by commercial fishing. Desert pupfish have declined due to loss of habitat and predation federal agencies. They meet on a regular basis to develop recommendations on management actions to protect the downstream ecosystem, including endangered fish populations.

Other U.S. agencies (including the Bureau of Reclamation and Fish and Wildlife Service) and state fish and wildlife management agencies are also working to develop management practices that benefit native fish. The Upper Colorado Endangered Fish Recovery Program and the Lower Colorado River Native Fish Work Group are two programs specifically created to address these issues.

In Mexico, the Upper Gulf of California and Colorado River Delta Biosphere Reserve was created in 1993 to protect habitats and species in these important ecosystems. Reserve managers and scientists are working with local fishermen and others to develop management practices that allow economic activities to continue while ensuring the survival of endangered species.

Procedure

Preparation

1. **Using the *Chillin' with the Chubs Survivability Chart* as a guide, draw a large version of the chart on butcher paper, easel paper, or the chalkboard. You won't use the chart until Step 2 of *The Activity*.**

2. **Make copies of the *Chillin' with the Chubs Fact Cards Student Copy Pages.* Divide the number of students by six and make that number of copies of each *Fact Card.* One side of each card should have the information for a native species, while the other side has information about the striped bass or rainbow trout. The back sides of the *Desert Pupfish Fact Cards* and *Totoaba Fact Cards* should say "Environmental Stressor."**

Warm Up

1. **Ask students if they like to fish.** What types of fish do they usually catch? Answers will likely be rainbow trout, brown trout, bass, catfish, carp, tilapia, corvina, and other

Justin Howe

Water releases from Flaming Gorge Dam, on the Green River, are managed to minimize harm to endangered fish living in the river downstream.

by nonnative fish species. When the river flowed to the delta, its flood waters created lakes and pools that provided habitat for desert pupfish.

Scientists and citizens in the United States and Mexico have recognized the importance of protecting these native fish and marine mammal species, and a number of programs have been developed to help improve their chances of survival. For example, in 1997, the U.S. Secretary of the Interior formed the Adaptive Management Work Group to address the impacts of Glen Canyon Dam on the downstream ecosystem. Members of the body include stakeholders from the hydropower and recreation industries, tribes, environmental groups, state governments, and

common fish. Ask them if they've ever heard of a Colorado pikeminnow (Upper Basin areas) or a totoaba (Lower Basin, delta region).

2. **Show students the historic photos of giant pikeminnows and totoaba.** Tell them that these fish were once very common in the watershed and/or Upper Gulf of California and were important food sources for people. Now they are both considered to be endangered species.

3. **Ask students to come up with a few reasons that may explain why populations of these fish have declined so rapidly (e.g., over-fishing, changes in their environment, new predators introduced, natural selection, etc.).** Write their ideas on the board. Explain that a combination of factors has led to the declines in these species and that these factors vary depending on which species is being talked about. Changing conditions in the river due to the construction of dams, introduced fish species that eat the native fish, and over-fishing have all likely contributed to the declines in native fish.

4. **Give students a brief introduction (see Background) about how conditions in the Colorado River and Gulf of California have changed with the construction of dams on the Colorado.** Pass out the ***Changing River Conditions*** *Student Copy Pages*.

5. **Have them examine the two charts to see how conditions have changed with the construction of dams.** Discuss the benefits of dams (reliable, non-polluting energy source; flood control; drought protection; recreational opportunities, etc.).

6. **Pass out the *Fish and Marine Mammal Habitat Requirements Student Copy Pages*.** Explain that, as dams were built, nonnative fish species were introduced into the reservoirs the dams created (e.g., bass and carp) and into the tail-water sections of rivers below dams (trout). These introduced fish species are popular with fishermen.

7. **Ask students to examine the two charts of habitat needs, comparing the native species with the introduced species.** Which species

Blank Survivability Chart for *Chillin' with the Chubs*

Species	Original populations (Year 1800)	Round 1	Round 2	Round 3
Humpback chub				
Bonytail chub				
Razorback sucker				
Colorado pikeminnow				
Totoaba				
Desert pupfish				
TOTAL native species				
TOTAL nonnative species and/or stressors				

do they think will be able to compete best in the new environment?

8. **Have students hypothesize about which species have increased under post-dam conditions, which have decreased, and which have remained the same.** In the columns of the chart labeled "hypothesis," have them draw an "up-arrow" for species they think will increase, a "down-arrow" for those that will decrease, and a "side-ways" arrow to indicate that no change will occur.

The Activity

Part I

1. **Tell students that they are going to participate in a simulation game to demonstrate how populations of the different species have changed in response to different stressors (dams, fishing, predation by nonnative species).** Remind them that habitat conditions include not only physical conditions (water temperature, turbidity, current speed) but also biological conditions (abundance of food, predators, etc.).

2. **Show students the *Chillin' with the Chubs Survivability Chart*.** Data from the game will be recorded in the chart to interpret and graph after the game.

3. **Divide the students into six groups to represent the six native species.** Try to have at least four students in each group; smaller classes can eliminate one or two of the native species from the game. Ask for one volunteer to be the "stressor."

4. **Hand out the *Chillin' with the Chubs Fact Cards*.** Have students paper-clip them to their shirts with the native-species side facing up.

5. **Take the students to a large area to play the simulation game (e.g., outside playing field, gymnasium, or cafeteria).** Bring a copy of the *Survivability Chart* to record the outcomes of each round of the game.

6. **Tell the students that the "stressor" represents three different factors that have led to declines in the native species:**

   a. The construction of dams has changed the physical environment of the river, including variation of flows, water temperature, and turbidity. This has affected all of the native species.

   b. The introduction of nonnative species has changed the ecosystem. They are better able to survive in the new environmental conditions, and they also prey on the eggs and young of native fish. This has primarily affected all but the totoaba.

   c. Over-fishing by humans has reduced the population. This has primarily affected the totoaba.

7. **Tell the students that their goal is to make it across the playing field without being tagged by the stressor.** However, some of them will have hindrances that make it harder to cross. These obstacles represent sensitive native species' intolerance for new environmental stressors.

8. **On the *Survivability Chart*, write down the number of students in each group.** Tell the students that these numbers represent conditions in 1800, before dams were built and nonnative species were introduced, and before commercial fishing in the Upper Gulf of California.

9. <u>Round 1:</u> **Assemble the groups at the starting end of the playing field, with the stressor in the middle of the field.** When the round starts, the fish will try to make it to the end of the playing field without being tagged by the stressor. Students can walk fast (but not run) during the game. Designate a finish line about fifty yards from the starting end so students will know when they are "safe."

10. **Students that get tagged should return to the start and flip their *Fact Cards* to show the nonnative (tolerant) species on the back.**

Intolerant Species and Hindrances

Species	Hindrance
Humpback chub	Must stop every 8 steps and do 3 jumping jacks
Bonytail chub	Must stop every 10 steps and touch the ground for 5 seconds
Razorback sucker	Must hop on 1 foot
Colorado pikeminnow	Must spin in a circle every 5 steps
Totoaba	Must walk sideways
Desert pupfish	Must walk backwards, stopping to touch the ground every 10 steps

Sample Survivability Chart from *Chillin' with the Chubs*

Species	Original populations	Round 1	Round 2	Round 3
Humpback chub	6	6	4	2
Bonytail chub	5	5	2	0
Razorback sucker	6	6	3	1
Colorado pikeminnow	5	5	4	2
Totoaba	5	5	3	1
Desert pupfish	2	2	1	0
TOTAL native species	30	29	17	6
TOTAL nonnative species and/or stressors	0	1	13	24

Students who "survive" (make it to the end of the field without being tagged) return to the start and don't flip their *Fact Cards* over. Groups should re-assemble at the starting line.

11. <u>**Round 2: Record the number of students in each group now, both native and nonnative species.**</u> The students that are now trout or bass should move to the middle of the playing field to become stressors, along with the tagged students who were desert pupfish or totoaba in the first round.

12. **Repeat Steps 9–10.** With more students as stressors, the number of native species left at the end of the round will be reduced.

13. **At the end of the round, repeat Step 11.** Record the number of each species on the *Survivability Chart.*

14. **If there are still native species left, begin Round 3.** Repeat Step 11 and record final numbers. Return to the classroom to graph the data and discuss the results.

Part II

1. **Write the data from the game on the large version of the *Survivability Chart* that you prepared prior to the activity.**

2. **Ask students to look at their hypotheses for increases/decreases of each species that they**

recorded in their *Fish Habitat Requirements Chart.* How do their hypotheses compare with the results of the game?

3. **Have each student make a line graph of the data.** The Y-axis should be labeled "Number of Individuals" and the X-axis should be labeled "Round 0, Round 1,"etc. Total native species and total nonnative species/stressors should each be represented by a line on the graph (see sample graph).

Wrap Up

1. **Have students discuss the results.** Because this is a simplified model of how native and nonnative populations interact, the decrease in native species happens at the same rate as the increase in nonnative species. In actual situations, the rates would probably differ since the factors involved are more complicated.

2. **Ask students to brainstorm ideas to help protect these endangered species.** Ideas may include removing nonnative fish, finding ways to increase water temperature and make flows more similar to pre-dam flows, banning certain types of fishing to protect vaquitas, etc.

3. **Discuss the management practices that are currently being used to protect these species:**

Flaming Gorge Dam:
- releasing water from higher in the reservoir to provide warmer temperatures;
- releasing water at times and levels that more closely mimic natural flow patterns.

Glen Canyon Dam and the Adaptive Management Work Group:
- reducing daily fluctuations in flow to protect fish;
- altering flows to "strand" eggs of

nonnative fish in dry zones;
- mechanically removing nonnative fish from humpback chub spawning grounds in the Grand Canyon.

Upper Colorado River Endangered Fish Recovery Program:
- removing nonnative fish from certain stretches of rivers and reservoirs that are critical to native fish;
- raising hatchery populations of species that aren't reproducing in the wild to restock rivers;
- managing stocking of nonnative fish to limit interference with native fish recovery;
- building passageways around certain diversions and dams to allow fish to migrate, and prevent them from being trapped in irrigation canals.

Lower Colorado River Native Fish Work Group:
- raising hatchery populations of species that aren't reproducing in the wild to restock rivers and lakes;
- supporting scientific studies of endangered fish;
- constructing habitat.

Upper Gulf of California and Colorado River Delta Biosphere Reserve:
- limiting types of fishing and areas of

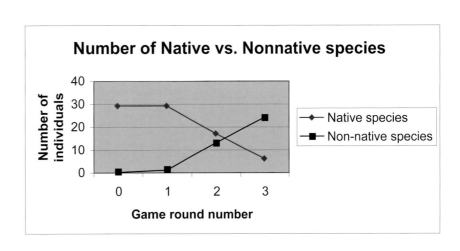

commercial fishing to protect totoaba;

- enforcing protection of endangered species;
- supporting scientific studies of endangered species.

Assessment
Have students:
- compare pre-dam and post-dam habitat conditions in the Colorado and Green Rivers (**Warm Up**, Steps 3–5);
- identify habitat conditions necessary for the survival of six native fish species (**Warm Up**, Steps 6–7);
- hypothesize about the effects that different environmental stressors (introduced species, dams) will have on the various species (**Warm Up**, Step 8);
- simulate the change in populations as a result of environmental stressors (*Part I*, Steps 1–14);
- graph the changes in populations observed in the simulation game (*Part II*, Steps 1–3);
- discuss management solutions for protecting native fish species (**Wrap Up**, Steps 1–3).

Extensions
Have students research other native species in the watershed that have been impacted by the introduction of nonnative species and describe recovery practices for these species.

Have students interview a biologist who is working on a recovery plan for an endangered species.

Resources
Collier, Michael, Robert H. Webb, and John C. Schmidt. 1996. *Dams and Rivers: Primer on the Downstream Effects of Dams*. Tucson, AZ: U.S. Geological Survey. *(**Copies of this report are available free from**: USGS Branch of Information Services, PO Box 25286, Denver, CO 80225.)*

Minckley, W. L. 1991. *Native Fishes of Arid Lands: A Dwindling Resource of the Desert Southwest*. USDA Forest Service General Technical Report RM 206. Fort Collins, CO: USDA Forest Service, Rocky

Mountain Forest and Range Experiment Station.

Upper Colorado River Endangered Fish Recovery Program. 2002. *Historical Accounts of Upper Colorado River Basin Endangered Fish*. Denver, CO: U.S. Fish and Wildlife Service.

e-Links
Glen Canyon National Recreation Area
Information about management of Glen Canyon Dam and downstream resources.
www.nps.gov/glca

Native Fish Work Group
Information about the Native Fish Work Group's efforts to recover razorback sucker populations.
www.mesc.usgs.gov/resources/research_briefs/razorback.asp

Upper Colorado River Endangered Fish Recovery Program
Information about endangered fish recovery efforts in the Upper Basin.
http://mountain-prairie.fws.gov/coloradoriver/

Upper Gulf of California and Colorado River Delta Biosphere Reserve
Official Web site of the reserve.
www.conanp.gob.mx/anp/alto_golfo/altogolfo_ini.php

U.S. Bureau of Reclamation, Glen Canyon Field Division
Facts about Glen Canyon and Lake Powell.
www.usbr.gov/uc/news/gcdfacts.html

U.S. Bureau of Reclamation, Lower Colorado Region
Information about the Endangered Razorback Sucker Program.
www.usbr.gov/lc/region/pao/sucker.html

Chillin' with the Chubs Historic Photos

Totoaba

José Campoy

This totoaba was caught in the Gulf of California near San Felipe, Baja California, in 1989.

Colorado pikeminnow

Courtesy of Sue Mantle and the U.S. Fish and Wildlife Service

Charles and Pat Mantle show off a Colorado pikeminnow caught in the Yampa River around 1935.

Changing River Conditions

Colorado River Facts

Pre-Dam	Post-Dam
Annual flows can vary from approximately 5,000–300,000 cfs.	Annual flows regulated: usually between 5,000–25,000 cfs.
Seasonal fluctuations in flow: High spring runoff, slowing by mid-summer. Low winter flows.	Flows fluctuate daily for optimum power generation, but not seasonally.
Large annual snowmelt floods.	Snowmelt floods moderated by dams.
Water temperature varies from approximately 35º F (2º C) in winter/spring to approximately 85º F (29º C) in summer (Colorado River between Glen Canyon Dam and Hoover Dam).	Water temperature varies between 45º F (7º C) and 50º F (10º C) year-round (for Colorado River between Glen Canyon Dam and Hoover Dam; water is released from deep in the reservoir, which is why it is so cold).
Water is highly turbid in spring and summer.	Water is usually clear.
Fresh water from the Colorado meets the Gulf of California, creating a highly productive wetland and estuary.	Fresh water from the Colorado rarely reaches the Gulf. Much of the wetland and estuary habitats are gone.

Elisabeth Howe

Davis Dam is located on the Colorado River downstream from Hoover Dam. It forms Lake Mojave.

Changing River Conditions

Fish Habitat Requirements

Native Fish	Life History	Hypothesis
Humpback chub	• spawns in spring and early summer. • can live in whitewater sections of canyon rivers. • eats mainly insects found on the bottom of rivers. • lateral stripe is very sensitive to vibrations of insects (can locate prey in muddy water).	
Bonytail chub	• lives in river eddies at the edge of fast currents. • prefers to live in river sections with sandy or gravelly bottoms. • adults eat large terrestrial insects (e.g., mayflies, grasshoppers, etc.). • spawns in late June–early July.	
Razorback sucker	• lives in river sections with slow-moving water. • spawns in late January–April over gravels in relatively shallow water. • young feed in backwater ponds.	
Colorado pikeminnow	• lives in a variety of stream conditions, from riffles to quiet backwaters. • spawns over gravel bars in spring or summer. • optimum spawning temps are 71–77° F (22–25° C). • young feed on insects and crustaceans in backwater areas; adults prey on other fish.	
Totoaba	• spawns in Colorado River estuary. • nursery areas are near the mouth of Colorado River. • lives in Gulf of California. • endangered due to over-fishing.	
Desert pupfish	• lives in shallow, slow-moving water in the southern portion of the Colorado Watershed. • can tolerate high salinity and warm temperatures. • eats algae and detritus. • river floods create pools that are habitat for these fish.	

Introduced Fish	Life History	Hypothesis
Rainbow trout	• usually spawns in spring, but can also spawn in late fall or early winter. • eggs laid in gravelly bottom of small riffles. • prefers cold, clear water (temps of 54°–64° F [12–18° C]). • eats small fish and invertebrates.	
Striped bass	• lives in inland lakes and reservoirs (also in the Atlantic Ocean). • spawns in streams that flow into reservoirs. • lays eggs in rivers with gentle current. • eggs float, which prevents them from being covered by silt on the river bottom. • eats invertebrates and fish.	

Chillin' with the Chubs Fact Cards

Humpback chub (*Gila cypha*)
- Hump behind its head and large fins help it to maneuver in strong currents and whitewater.
- Evolved 3–5 million years ago.
- Lifespan: up to 30 years.
- Length: up to 18 inches.

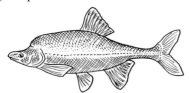

© Claire Emery and Project WET International

F O L D H E R E

Striped bass (*Morone saxatalis*)
- Introduced to reservoirs in the Colorado River system; native to the Atlantic coast.
- Popular game fish because it is good to eat.
- Lifespan: up to 31 years.
- Length: 24 inches or more (up to 60 pounds!).

© Claire Emery and Project WET International

CUT HERE _

Bonytail chub (*Gila elegans*)
- Large fins and streamlined body.
- Rarest endangered fish species in the Colorado Basin.
- Evolved 3–5 million years ago.
- Lifespan: up to 50 years.
- Length: 22 inches or more.

© Claire Emery and Project WET International

F O L D H E R E

Rainbow trout (*Oncorhynchus mykiss*)
- Named for its rosy lateral stripe.
- Popular game fish native to western North America.
- Lifespan: up to 11 years.
- Length: 16 inches or more.

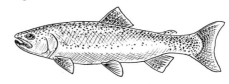

© Claire Emery and Project WET International

CUT HERE _

Razorback sucker (*Xyrauchen texanus*)
- Large, bony ridge behind head.
- Fleshy lips used for feeding on river bottom.
- Evolved: 4 million years ago.
- Lifespan: 40 years or more.
- Length: 36 inches or more.

© Claire Emery and Project WET International

F O L D H E R E

Striped bass (*Morone saxatalis*)
- Introduced to reservoirs in the Colorado River system; native to the Atlantic coast.
- Popular game fish because it is good to eat.
- Lifespan: up to 31 years.
- Length: 24 inches or more (up to 60 pounds!).

© Claire Emery and Project WET International

Chillin' with the Chubs Fact Cards

Colorado pikeminnow (*Ptychocheilus lucius*)
- Torpedo-shaped body and large mouth.
- Largest native minnow in North America.
- Evolved: 3–4 million years ago.
- Lifespan: 50 years or more.
- Length: up to 60 inches.

© Claire Emery and Project WET International

FOLD HERE

Rainbow trout (*Oncorhynchus mykiss*)
- Named for its rosy lateral stripe.
- Popular game fish native to western North America.
- Lifespan: up to 11 years.
- Length: 16 inches or more.

© Claire Emery and Project WET International

CUT HERE —

Totoaba (*Totoaba macdonaldi*)
- Historically a very important food fish for people in the Colorado Delta region.
- Largest croaker in the world.
- Now protected, but still illegally captured for their bladders and meat.
- Length: 84 inches or more.

© Claire Emery and Project WET International

FOLD HERE

ENVIRONMENTAL STRESSOR

CUT HERE —

Desert pupfish (*Cyprinodon macularius*)

- Is adapted to tolerate rapid changes in water temperature and salinity that occur when desert pools shrink due to evaporation.
- Large scales vary in color from brilliant blue to metallic gray.
- Length: 5 inches or less.

© Claire Emery and Project WET International

FOLD HERE

ENVIRONMENTAL STRESSOR

An Invited Guest in the Colorado Watershed

What would you do if your home was taken over by guests, invited and uninvited, who wouldn't leave?

Grade Level:
6–9

Subject Areas:
Life Science, Environmental Science, Ecology, Math

Duration:
Activity time: 100 minutes
 Part I: 50 minutes
 Part II: 50 minutes

Setting:
Classroom, Library, Computer Lab

Skills:
Research, Organize, Interpret, Graph, Demonstrate, Analyze, Discuss, Problem Solve

Vocabulary:
biodiversity, ecosystem (ecology), exotic species, habitat, hydrilla, introduced species, invasive species, microorganism, native species, nonnative species, propagation, riparian, tamarisk, zebra mussel

Summary

Students play a game and graph the results to learn about nonnative plant species in the Colorado River Watershed. They explore the consequences that result from introducing new species to an ecosystem.

Objectives

Students will:
- identify nonnative species in the Colorado Watershed;
- recognize the impacts of nonnative species;
- describe the relationships between native and nonnative species;
- investigate the secondary impacts of invasive species (economic, social, and ecological).

Materials

- *Copies of* **Introduced and Native Species of the Colorado River** *Student Copy Page* (1 per student)
- *Library or Internet access for research*
- *Chairs* (1 per student)
- *Red and green strips of paper* (1 of each per student)
- *Chalk board or large sheet of white butcher paper for graphing*
- *Red and green markers for graphing*
- *Large pitcher of water*
- *Small paper cups* (1 per student)
- *Large cups/mugs* (enough for half the class)

Background

Invasive, exotic, introduced, and nonnative species: these terms have become widely used by resource

Justin Howe

Millions of tamarisk seedlings cover a beach along the Green River in Desolation Canyon, Utah.

managers throughout the country. The Colorado Watershed hosts its own complement of nonnative (introduced) species: plants and animals that did not evolve within the watershed, but have been brought here by humans. Some nonnative species are relatively innocuous, or even beneficial, providing shade, landscaping, food, shelter, and other services to humans without dramatically impacting their new environments. Other nonnative species, referred to as invasive species, have had significant negative impacts on ecosystems, agriculture, recreation, and other systems.

Invasive species are a problem when they take over a habitat or ecosystem, resulting in the elimination of the native species formerly present and impacting biodiversity, food chains, predator/prey relationships, and other ecosystem functions. The species are typically very difficult to eradicate once they have established themselves in an ecosystem.

Tamarisk (salt cedar), an ornamental tree native to Eurasia, is an example of a widespread invasive plant species in the watershed. Tamarisk can be found in lower-elevation watersheds throughout northern Mexico and the western United States and has replaced the native riparian vegetation in many areas.

Introduced species may have been intentionally introduced, as tamarisk was, to provide shade, erosion control, and landscaping. Other species have been accidentally introduced, arriving in imported seed mixes, in the bilge water of boats, as seeds in mud on the feet of migrating birds, or by a multitude of other means. When tamarisk was originally brought to the watershed, people did not foresee that it would quickly invade waterways throughout the basin, use large amounts of water, increase soil salinity, out-compete native plants, and dramatically alter riparian ecosystems. Native riparian cottonwood/willow communities, which support some of the highest numbers of breeding bird species found in any vegetative community type in the United States, have declined as tamarisk has invaded. Now tamarisk is acknowledged as a major economic and ecological problem, and large amounts of money are being spent in an attempt to remove it and restore the native vegetation.

Hydrilla is another example of an invasive plant species that is currently impacting the watershed. It is a floating aquatic plant that can cover the surface of a lake, river, or irrigation canal, clogging boat propellers and irrigation systems and affecting fish, wildlife, and other organisms.

This activity focuses on plants, but introduced species of fish, mammals, mollusks, amphibians, and even microorganisms can also be a problem within the watershed. Different regions have different challenges in managing invasive species. The zebra mussel, a tiny mollusk native to eastern Europe, is a species of major concern as it spreads westward into lakes and reservoirs because of the damage caused when the mussels clog the workings of dams and diversions.

The effects of invasive species are a topic of great concern to resource managers, farmers, recreationists, scientists, and others. Many studies and programs are underway to better understand, control, and manage the complex problems presented by introduced species. For information about native and nonnative fish species in the basin, see page 211, "Chillin' with the Chubs."

Procedure

Warm Up

1. **Divide students into research groups of three and assign each group a wetland plant species that is found in the Colorado Watershed.** See the *Student Copy Page* for a list of species. Assign one group to research tamarisk, while all other groups research other introduced or native wetland plant species. Encourage students to explore library resources and the Internet. They can also contact local management agency experts to find out more about their species.

2. **Have each research group create a simple, three-fold brochure about their species.** Brochures should include photos and/or drawings of the species, along with its distribution, description, habitat, propagation method, importance and/or impacts to other species/wildlife, and importance/impacts to humans.

The Activity

Part I

1. **This activity is similar to musical chairs, except that chairs are not removed after each round.** Before beginning the game, give each student a colored strip of paper that represents either tamarisk or native species. Students who researched tamarisk get a red strip of paper, while all the other students get green strips to represent native species. Have students label their strips with the name of the species they represent.

2. **Arrange chairs (one per student) back-to-back in a curving line to represent a stream or river channel (preferred habitat for wetland plants).** For the first round, there will be enough chairs for all the students to succeed within the environment. For example, if there are twenty students and three belong to the tamarisk group, three chairs will be taken by tamarisk and the other seventeen by representatives of native wetland plants.

3. **As with musical chairs, when the music is playing, students circle the chairs clockwise.** When the music stops, they must find a chair,

signifying that they have acquired enough water and habitat resources to survive. When students leave their chairs for the next round, they should leave their strips of paper on their chairs.

4. **Invasive plant species, like tamarisk, may have a competitive advantage over native species by growing or reproducing more quickly, having fewer predators, or other adaptations.** After the first round, demonstrate this advantage by allowing the students in the tamarisk group to closely circle the chairs, while all the native plant students must circle at a distance of six feet. Tamarisk quickly and aggressively reproduces by dispersing millions of seeds and quickly sprouting in disturbed areas (e.g., riverbanks, burned areas, and washes). Along waterways in the Colorado River system, tamarisk crowds out native plant species as it densely invades riverbanks, its huge root systems sucking up large volumes of water and its fallen leaves increasing the salinity of the soil as they decompose. It is extremely drought tolerant. The construction of dams on the Colorado and its tributaries has also influenced the success of tamarisk, by reducing flood flows. Native wetland species such as cottonwood and willow are adapted to take advantage of spring floods for seed dispersal and germination. Without floods, tamarisk has been able to gain a foothold while cottonwoods and willows have died out. When an area becomes dominated by tamarisk, the diversity of birds and other species dramatically decreases.

5. **In ensuing rounds of the game, if a native plant student sits on a chair marked with a red strip (tamarisk), that student becomes a member of the tamarisk group and gains the advantage of circling the chairs closely.** Hand the new tamarisk students red strips of paper to mark their chairs, replacing the green strips when

they take over (populate) those spots (habitats). At the beginning of each round, count the number of tamarisk students and the number of native plants students. Record these numbers so you can graph them later.

6. **As the game progresses, more and more chairs will be taken over by tamarisk, leaving less and less habitat for the native plants (as well as the animals, birds, and insects that have evolved to depend on those plants).** Play enough rounds so that almost all the chairs are taken by tamarisk students.

7. **Make a line graph showing the number of tamarisk and native plants present at the beginning of each round on a dry erase board or large piece of butcher paper (see sample graph).** Use a red marker to represent tamarisk and a green marker to represent native plants. You'll see that the tamarisk line will start low and rise as the rounds progress, while the native plants will start high and decline.

Part II

1. **Start two hundred years ago with a piece of land along the Colorado River that is undisturbed, and move forward in time, showing the changes that have occurred since tamarisk was "invited" to the Colorado Basin.** Illustrate the historic process by using a classroom

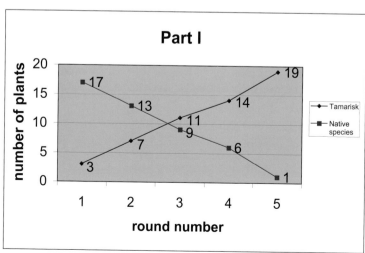

party as a representation of plant species, both native and introduced. The students will graph each round (see sample graph).

2. **Round 1—1800: The piece of Colorado River wetland is in its natural state with regular floods and a full complement of native plant species represented.** In the classroom party, each student represents a different native plant. Each has a small paper cup, and they should all be able to fill their cups with water (habitat resources) from a community pitcher. Graph the number of native plants. After each round, the community pitcher will be refilled and students will empty their cups or mugs.

3. **Round 2—1900: By now, the introduced party guest (tamarisk) has arrived.** However, this guest comes carrying a large mug, not a small paper cup. Have the tamarisk guest fill his or her mug first, then allow the other plants to fill their smaller cups. Those who don't get any water must leave the party. Graph the number of native plants, and the number of introduced plants. Students who are "out" can help complete the graph.

4. **Round 3—1950: Invite several more guests to join in as tamarisk plants, each with a large mug.** Once again, allow the tamarisk guests to fill their mugs before the others, demonstrating their high water consumption and competitive advantages. Ask those who don't get any water this time to leave the party. Graph new plant numbers.

5. **Round 4—2000: By now most of the party will be made up of tamarisk.** Graph the numbers of plants. Ask the students to discuss what is happening to the diversity of plant species in this habitat (classroom).

Wrap Up
1. **Discuss the activity.** What happened to the native plants? How does this activity illustrate what is happening in wetlands along the Colorado and its tributaries? Have the students observed tamarisk and/or other invasive species along rivers and streams? What other habitats in the watershed may be experiencing similar changes from different invasive species? What other examples of invasive species can they think of (e.g., zebra mussels, Russian olives, cheat grass, bullfrogs, carp)?

2. **Explain that the data they graphed is similar to the types of data that a biologist would collect and plot.** Have students brainstorm methods for restoring native plants to riparian ecosystems. Discuss the methods used to eradicate tamarisk: manual (cutting, burning), chemical (spraying herbicides), and biological (insects/pathogens). Many tamarisk-eradication programs use combinations of methods for the best results, and include the re-planting of native plants to take the place of the tamarisk. Ask students to imagine the party in 2050. Will all the guests be tamarisk, or will restoration and management efforts have shifted the balance back towards native species?

Assessment
Have students:
- conduct research to identify and describe invasive species and native wetland species of the Colorado Watershed (**Warm Up,** Steps 1–2);

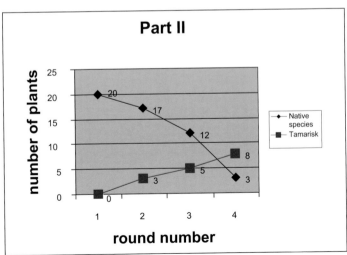

- create brochures to display their research (**Warm Up,** Steps 1–2);
- demonstrate the competitive nature of invasive species (*Part I,* Steps 1–7; *Part II,* Steps 1–5);
- graph the population fluctuations of invasive and native species (*Part I,* Steps 1–7; *Part II,* Steps 1–5).

Extensions

Invite a guest speaker to talk to the class about the impacts of invasive species in your local area. Discuss the impacts on the environment and the economy.

Have students research strategies for controlling invasive species. Encourage additional discussion about why the species were introduced in the first place, what impacts have resulted, and what predictions they might make for the future.

Resources

The Watercourse. 2001. *Discover a Watershed: The Rio Grande/Rio Bravo Educators Guide.* Bozeman, MT: The Watercourse.

Whitson, Tom D., ed. 1991. *Weeds of the West.* Laramie, WY: Western Society of Weed Science and University of Wyoming.

e-Links

National Biological Information Superstructure Information on invasive species of plants and animals. http://invasivespecies.nbii.gov

National Park Service Information on invasive plant species. www.nps.gov/plants/alien/fact.htm

Southwest Exotic Plant Information Clearinghouse Invasive plants of the Southwest. www.usgs.nau.edu/SWEPIC

Introduced and Native Plant Species of the Colorado Watershed

These are a few of the many native and introduced plants that can be found in the Colorado Watershed.

Native Plants	Introduced Plants
Fremont cottonwood (*Populus fremontii*)	Canada thistle (*Cirsium arvense*)
Seep-willow (*Baccharis salicifolia*)	Russian knapweed (*Acroptilon repens*)
Common cattail (*Typha* species)	Giant salvinia (*Salvinia molesta*)
Goodding willow (*Salix gooddingii*)	Hydrilla (*Hydrilla verticilata*)
Horsetails (*Equisetum arvense*)	Russian olive (*Elaeagnus angustifolia*)
Sedge (*Carex* species)	Tamarisk (salt cedar) (*Tamarix ramossisima*)

Fremont cottonwood *(Populus fremontii).*

Common cattail *(Typha latifolia).*

Russian olive *(Elaeagnus angustifolia).*

Tamarisk (salt cedar) *(Tamarix ramossisima).*

History

Colorado River Timeline

Where do you fit in Colorado River history?

Grade Level:
6–10

Subject Areas:
History, Geography, Art

Duration:
Preparation time: 20 minutes
Activity time: 60 minutes

Setting:
Classroom

Skills:
Develop, Discuss, Interpret, Organize, Build, Compare, Predict

Vocabulary:
Ancestral Puebloan, conquistador, 4.4 Plan, Hohokam, hunter-gatherer, nomadic, sedentary, sedimentation, Winters Doctrine

Summary
Students place events in historic context by building a 3-D timeline that highlights important events in the history of water use in the Colorado River Basin.

Objectives
Students will:
- learn important dates and events in Colorado River history;
- recognize that our understanding of history is influenced by the people who write it;
- make connections between historic events and current water use;
- connect historic events to personal experience;
- consider historic events in context;
- predict future events in the watershed.

Materials
- *Copies of **Colorado River Timeline Cards** Student Copy Pages (1 set per group of 2–3 students, plus 1 classroom copy)*
- *Scissors (1 per group)*
- *Glue*
- *Tape*
- *Blank sheets of paper (12 per group)*
- *50 index cards or several large pieces of cardboard*
- *Approximately fifteen feet of string*
- *50–100 paper clips*
- *Optional: 12 clothespins for hanging events on timeline*
- *Optional: markers, crayons, or colored pencils*
- *Optional: magazines with photos of current or historic events*
- *Optional: scissors (1 pair per student)*

Some Hopi farmers still grow corn the same way they have for thousands of years.

Background

For as long as humans have lived in the Colorado Watershed, they have been hunting, gathering, growing, and using resources found here. One of the biggest changes in the way humans interact with land was the gradual shift from nomadic hunter-gatherer societies to sedentary agriculture-based ones. In the Colorado Watershed, this shift began as early as 1,400 years ago. Despite little rainfall and variable growing conditions, the Ancestral Puebloans, Hohokam, and other native people were cultivating plants such as corn, squash, and beans by A.D. 600 (see page 342, "Trading Toss-Up").

The early adoption of agriculture led to highly developed societies such as those at Mesa Verde, Pueblo Grande, and Chaco Canyon. Most of the earliest North American agricultural communities have dispersed, but the Pueblo Indian villages along the Rio Grande and on the Hopi mesas have remained continuously occupied. The Hopi community of Oraibi, established around A.D. 1100, is inhabited by descendants of the original residents.

European exploration and settlement in the United States is often characterized as beginning in the northeast and moving westward. However, European exploration and settlement in the Colorado River Watershed came from the south.

Spanish conquistadors traced the river and its tributaries northward, followed by missionaries and settlers. This pattern of exploration and settlement, with its origins in what is now Mexico, has left an indelible mark on the culture of the basin. Most of the Colorado River Watershed was part of Mexico until the end of the Mexican-American War when, in 1848, the Treaty of Guadalupe Hidalgo ceded the Mexican territory to the United States. Spanish land grants established in the 1700s still exist today.

Though Spanish descendants have a long history in the watershed, it is short when compared to American Indian tribes that have lived there for thousands of years. Interestingly, the ancestors of modern Puebloan people are also thought to have originally migrated northward from Central and South America. Several ancient civilizations had risen, fallen, and risen again by the time the Spanish first explored the watershed in 1540. When the Spanish did arrive, they found nomadic tribes as well as farmers with more permanent settlements. European diseases, coupled with the brutality of the conquistadors, were devastating for tribes, but some were able to avoid Spanish rule. In 1680 and 1700, Pueblo revolts drove the Spanish out of northern Arizona.

During the 1800s, exploration and expansion of European settlement continued. In the 1840s, members of the Church of Jesus Christ of Latter-day Saints (Mormons) began to move into the area to farm, ranch, and escape persecution in the East. Major John Wesley Powell made a historic boat journey along much of the Colorado River, strengthening the idea of the West as a place for future development. It was during this time that the United States government drove American Indians from their lands and forced them onto reservations.

On reservations, American Indians were forced to learn English and abandon their traditional ways of life. Many were told to farm, yet their reservations had little water. It was not until 1908 that the U.S. Supreme Court declared that American Indians on reservations had legal rights to water, creating the Winters Doctrine. The declaration did

The United States of Mexico, before the 1848 Treaty of Guadalupe Hidalgo ceded Mexican territory to the United States. Before that time most of the Colorado River Watershed was Mexican territory.

not, however, address where that water would come from. Currently, many tribes are still fighting court battles to get water delivered to the reservations.

As the pace of growth quickened, some areas of the watershed were identified as needing protection from development. In 1919, Grand Canyon National Park was established in an area that Spanish explorers had once called useless and desolate. In other parts of the basin, agriculture was taking hold and vast areas in the United States and Mexico were being developed.

Growth along the river was slowed, however, by heavy sedimentation and flooding. Water users in the southern basin called for the construction of a flood control dam. Those in the northern basin

feared that such a dam would allow water users in the south to claim rights to river water before the slower-growing Upper Basin states could develop. In 1922, representatives from the seven U.S. basin states signed a treaty that divided the Colorado River among them. This agreement paved the way for major water development projects throughout the watershed.

The flood control structure that southern water users wanted was finally completed in 1935. Originally called Boulder Dam, it was later named Hoover Dam after President of the United States Herbert Hoover. While Hoover Dam facilitated agricultural growth by stopping massive floods and providing reliable water supply through dry periods, it also reduced the flow of water to the river's delta and other parts of Mexico. The United States' ability to stop the flow of the Colorado River was a problem for northwestern Mexico, as the river was their main source of water for a growing agricultural industry.

Numerous management and legal decisions have taken place since the signing of the treaty in 1922. In 1992, the United States Congress passed the Grand Canyon Protection Act to regulate releases from Glen Canyon Dam for the benefit of natural and cultural resources and to facilitate visitor use in the river ecosystem. In 1993, Mexico created a protected area in the Colorado Delta region, the Upper Gulf of California and Colorado River Delta Biosphere Reserve. In 2000, Mexico and the United States agreed to investigate the importance of natural systems in the delta region.

Between 1996 and 2003, the U.S. basin states and the federal government worked on an agreement to help California bring its water use to within its allocated amount (the 4.4 Plan). This agreement is important because California has been using surplus water legally allocated to other states. As those states develop, their need for Colorado River water will increase and less surplus water will be available to California.

The history and prehistory of the Colorado River is complex, and no timeline can address every important event. Each tribe, organization, agency, and individual adds layers of complexity. There are as many perspectives on history as there are people. Therefore, a timeline can be viewed as a starting place for understanding how we fit into the story of the Colorado River (see page XXX, *Colorado River Master Timeline*).

Procedure
Preparation
For *The Activity*: Make enough copies of the

Mauricio Torres Santillan, a student from Tijuana, Baja California, stands on Morelos Dam. Morelos was built with cooperation between the United States and Mexico. Its purpose is to divert the Colorado River into canals for use in Baja California and Sonora.

Colorado River Timeline Cards so that you have one set for each group of two to three students. Cut out the cards from each set and mix cards from all events in that set together. Keep each set separate using paper clips. Keep an uncut copy to use as an answer key and to show how a joined event set will look. Cut out one extra set for making the classroom timeline.

Cut cardboard or index cards into fifty pieces that match the size of the cards made above.

Warm Up
1. **Ask students to list on a piece of paper ten significant events in their lives.** Have them number these events in order of occurrence and place them on a timeline.

2. **Ask students why they chose those ten events.** Did the events affect other things in their lives? How are they interrelated? Do they make sense if placed out of order on the timeline?

3. **Explain that a timeline is a historic account of events in linear sequence.** Timelines can help us to place historic events in context. Just like any history, it is subject to interpretation

and based upon the perspective of the person creating the timeline. Ask students if their parents would list the same events as the students did. Why or why not?

4. **Ask students to brainstorm some important events in the Colorado River Watershed.** These may include the arrival of humans, the development of irrigation, arrival of Europeans, etc. What are some important events in your town? When was it founded? Who were the first people to live there? Why did they come?

The Activity

1. **Tell students that they are going to develop a timeline for the Colorado River that highlights important events in the watershed.** You may want to discuss a few of the events that are discussed in the background section of this activity. Explain that, just as in the students' personal timelines, there are many important events that may or may not have been included.

2. **Divide students into groups of two to three.**

3. **Have each group attach twelve blank pieces of paper together.** Have students use tape to join the twelve sheets of paper together and fold the pages like an accordion. Set these aside to use later in the activity.

4. **Hand out a set of *Colorado River Timeline Cards* to each group.** The cards represent twelve historic events in the Colorado River Watershed. Each event has four cards associated with it, but all the cards have been mixed together.

5. **Organize the cards from one event and show as an example.**

6. **Have students sort the cards by event and place them in the proper order.** When organized correctly, the cards for each activity can be read as a statement. Photos will help in sorting (the card with the date on it is the first card for each event).

7. **After students have completed sorting the cards, have each group read aloud the cards from one event.** Discuss their choices until the class agrees upon the correct cards and sequence for all of the events.

8. **Have the groups work together to create a 3-D classroom timeline.** Use the extra classroom copy and have each group work on one of the twelve events. Have students glue the four cards from each event to index cards or cardboard cutouts. Have them use paper clips to join glued cards from each event to form chains. Once this is done, have them place the chains on the string, evenly spaced apart. *Optional:* Have them color the cards before hanging them to make the timeline more interesting.

9. **Hang the completed class timeline from the ceiling across the front of the classroom.**

10. **Have each group sort and glue all of the cards from their own set onto the twelve sheets of blank paper they attached in Step 3.** Each group will now have their own complete timeline.

© Project WET International Foundation, 2005

Wrap Up

1. **Discuss the Colorado River timeline.** How do the historic events on the timeline affect the way we use water today? How will our actions today affect the history of the Colorado River? Where would important events in your community fit on the timeline? How might cultural perspective affect the selection of events on the timeline? What events might be added to make the timeline more complete? How might time be viewed differently by different cultures?

2. **Have each student predict a possible future event for the Colorado River and write it on a card.** Display cards on the far end of the timeline or in a separate area for further discussion.

3. *Optional:* **Have students place additional events on the class timeline mobile.** These events may include student birthdays, national dates of importance, cultural events, etc. Have them write information, draw pictures, and paste images relating to the chosen events on blank paper. Link images from one event using paperclips and attach them to the timeline.

Assessment

Have students:
- develop a timeline of important events in their lives (*Warm Up*, Steps 1–2);
- discuss how perspective influences history (*Warm Up*, Steps 2–3);
- organize historic Colorado River events into a timeline (Steps 3–10);
- build a 3-D classroom timeline (Steps 4–9);
- discuss how historic events affect the present, and how the present may affect future events (*Wrap Up*, Step 1);
- add important dates to the Colorado River timeline (*Wrap Up*, Step 3);
- predict a future event for the Colorado River (*Wrap Up*, Step 2).

Resources

Hundley, Norris. 1966. *Dividing the Waters: A Century of Controversy between the United States and Mexico.* Berkeley, University of California Press.

Hundley, Norris. 2000. *Las aguas divididas: Un siglo de controversia entre México y Estado Unidos.* Mexicali, Baja California: Universidad Autónoma de Baja California.

Ingram, Helen, Nancy Laney, and David Gillilan. 1995. *Divided Waters: Bridging the U.S.-Mexico Border.* Tucson: University of Arizona Press.

Newcom, Joshua. 2004. *Layperson's Guide to the Colorado River.* Sacramento, CA: The Water Education Foundation.

Powell, John Wesley. 1961. *The Exploration of the Colorado River and Its Canyons.* New York: Dover Publications, Inc.

Waters, Frank. 1963. *Book of the Hopi.* New York: Penguin Books.

e-Links

Center for Desert Archaeology
Publications and programs about archaeology relating to desert cultures.
www.centerfordesertarchaeology.org

Moving Waters
History, essays, and information about the Colorado River Watershed.
www.movingwaters.org/movingwaters

National Museum of the American Indian
Publications and programs relating to the history of American Indians.
www.nmai.si.edu

Smithsonian Institution
A resource for publications, programs, historical information, and art, among other things.
www.smithsonian.org

Colorado River Timeline Cards

Beginning around 600 A.D., Ancestral Puebloan

Justin Howe

In 1100 A.D., the Hopi village of Oraibi is established.

© Claire Emery and Project WET International

and Hohokam Indians

Justin Howe

Oraibi may be the oldest

© Claire Emery and Project WET International

divert water from the Colorado River

Marjie Risk

continuously inhabited settlement

Justin Howe

and its tributaries to irrigate crops such as corn and squash.

Kate Lapides

in the United States.

Justin Howe

Colorado River Timeline Cards

In 1540 A.D., Spanish explorer

Library of Congress

In 1847, Mormon settlers

© Claire Emery and Project WET International

Francisco Vásquez de Coronado and his army

© Claire Emery and Project WET International

begin irrigating in the Salt Lake Valley.

travel through the southwestern United States and northern Mexico,

Library of Congress

Soon they are applying irrigation techniques learned in central Utah

© Claire Emery and Project WET International

becoming the first Europeans to explore the area.

Justin Howe

to farmland in the Colorado River Watershed.

Justin Howe

Colorado River Timeline Cards

In 1869, American explorer and geologist

© Claire Emery and
Project WET International

In 1908, the United States Supreme Court

Library of Congress

John Wesley Powell

Library of Congress

rules that American Indian tribes were granted water rights when their reservations were designated.

Justin Howe

floats small wooden boats along much of the length of the Green and Colorado Rivers

Justin Howe

This ruling gives tribes priority water rights

Justin Howe

and is the first to float through the Grand Canyon.

Justin Howe

on many rivers in the United States.

Colorado River Timeline Cards

In 1919, Grand Canyon National Park

Justin Howe

In 1922, the Colorado River Compact

The Bureau of Reclamation. Courtesy of the Water Education Foundation

is established to protect and manage

Justin Howe

divides water between the seven U.S. Basin states.

Upper Basin:
- Colorado
- New Mexico
- Utah
- Wyoming

Lower Basin:
- Arizona
- California
- Nevada

1,217,403 acres of deep canyons

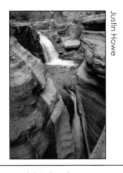

Justin Howe

This agreement paves the way for the construction

Justin Howe

and high plateaus.

Justin Howe

of major water development projects throughout the watershed.

Justin Howe

Colorado River Timeline Cards

In 1935, the construction of Hoover Dam (the first major dam built on the Colorado)

The Bureau of Reclamation

In 1944, the United States and Mexico

Courtesy International Boundary and Water Commission

is completed.

Justin Howe

negotiate a treaty

Its completion makes it possible

Justin Howe

that guarantees 1.5 million acre-feet of Colorado River water

One acre-foot = 325,851 gallons
or
One acre-foot = 1233.5 cubic meters

to irrigate more crops and protects Lower Basin residents from damage caused by flooding.

Justin Howe

will flow to Mexico each year.

Justin Howe

Colorado River Timeline Cards

In 1993, the Mexican government

Robin Kropp

In 2003, U.S. Colorado Basin states help work out the details

Jim Richardson

establishes the Upper Gulf of California Biosphere Reserve

Justin Howe

of California's 4.4 Plan,

Justin Howe

to protect the environment at the delta

Justin Howe

a strategy to bring California's water use

Justin Howe

of the Colorado River.

Justin Howe

to within the amount it is allocated.

Justin Howe

Sharing the Shed

Put yourself in the role of a policymaker in 1922 and 1944. Your job is to fairly divide the waters of the Colorado River among the seven U.S. basin states and with Mexico.

Grade Level:
9–12

Subject Areas:
Geography, Government, Language Arts, History/Anthropology

Duration:
Preparation time: 20 minutes
Activity time: 3 hours
  Part I: 90 minutes
  Part II: 90minutes

Setting:
Classroom

Skills:
Discuss, Problem Solve, Role-Play, Evaluate, Compare, Negotiate, Analyze, Compromise

Vocabulary:
acre-foot, allocation, apportionment, appropriation, beneficial use, commonwealth, compact, doctrine of prior appropriation, impounded, irrigable acreage, policymaker, return flow, silt, stakeholder, streamflow, tributary, water rights, Winters Doctrine

Summary

In *Part I*, students reenact 1922 Colorado River Compact negotiations using quotes taken from proceedings of the 1922 Colorado River Commission. In *Part II*, they reenact the negotiations leading up to the 1944 treaty between the United States and Mexico.

Objectives

Students will:
- examine the water needs of each U.S. basin state in 1922;
- investigate how state allocations in the United States were decided;
- discover how the Colorado River Compact was negotiated through role-playing;
- evaluate the circumstances leading to the development of the U.S.-Mexico Treaty;
- reenact negotiations leading up to the 1944 treaty between the United States and Mexico;
- compare historic water needs with present ones.

Materials

- *16 large index cards or blank pieces of paper*
- *Name tags (1 per student)*
- *Candy (1 piece for each student plus a few extra)*
- *Copies of **1922 Fact Sheet** Student Copy Pages (1 per group)*
- *Copies of **2005 Fact Sheet** Student Copy Pages (1 per student)*
- *Copies of **Sharing the Shed 1922 Stakeholder Cards** Student Copy Pages (1 per group)*
- *Copies of **Sharing the Shed 1922 Negotiation Script** Student Copy Pages (1 per student)*
- *Copies of **Sharing the Shed 1944 Stakeholder***

A farm worker in California's Imperial Valley poses near his home in the 1930s. Mexicans and Americans have lived and worked on both sides of the U.S./Mexico border for hundreds of years.

Card (Mexico) Student Copy Page (1 per Mexican representative)
- *Copies of **Sharing the Shed 1944 Stakeholder Card (United States)** Student Copy Page* (1 per American representative)
- *Copies of **1944 U.S.-Mexico Treaty Negotiations Script** Student Copy Page* (1 per student)
- ***Colorado River Watershed Wall Map***
- *Optional: props such as hats or suit coats*

Background

The Colorado River Compact of 1922 and the U.S.-Mexico Treaty of 1944 are cornerstones of Colorado River water law. The 1922 compact is critical because it helps U.S. basin states predict their water supply and plan its management. According to the United States Supreme Court, when an interstate stream is shared by states gov-

erned by the doctrine of prior appropriation, prior users gain rights to water in the stream regardless of their location ("first in time, first in right": see page 287, "First Come, First Served").

On the Colorado River before 1922, this meant that while most of the river's water originates in Colorado, Wyoming, and Utah, those states did not have an inherent right to that water. This concerned them, as rapid development along the lower river in California and Arizona could potentially claim much of the river's flow. A compact agreement that allocated the river among all of the states would secure northern states' futures by allowing them to develop more slowly without forfeiting rights to Colorado River water.

The Colorado is a powerful river, and unpredictable flows from flooding and drought as well as heavy sediment loads made it difficult for people to use its water (see page 126, "Go with the Flow," and

Negotiators sign the 1922 Colorado River Compact at Bishop's Lodge in Santa Fe, New Mexico.

page 148, "Reading the Rings"). In the early 1900s, water users in Arizona and California called for the construction of large flood- and sediment-control structures. Dams would have to be large enough to withstand floods of up to three hundred thousand cubic feet per second and to trap massive amounts of sediment carried in the river. Such projects would be expensive and federal funding would be required. There was a problem, however, as states in the northern basin felt that such structures would threaten their water rights by allowing the southern basin states to establish priority water rights. The U.S. Congress was unlikely to approve funding for a dam without the consent of the northern states.

The need for a general agreement on the apportionment of Colorado River water led to the idea of creating an interstate treaty (compact) that would guarantee a certain amount of water to each of the Colorado River Basin states. Negotiators would draft the compact, state legislatures approve it, and the Congress enforce it. Negotiators were able to agree upon dividing the watershed into two basins, the Upper and Lower. Each basin would receive 7.5 million acre-feet per year, thus protecting the northern states' water rights while they developed more slowly than the south and paving the way for the construction of dams in the Lower

Basin. Individual states' allocations would be determined later, as well as how to settle water rights claims by American Indian tribes and Mexico (approximately 2 million acre-feet of the estimated average annual flow of the river were left unallocated for future settlements). The Colorado River Compact was signed in 1922 and ratified by all of the U.S. basin states except Arizona in 1923. (See page 8 for more information about state allocations and the history of the compact.)

When the waters of the Colorado River Watershed were divided among the seven U.S. basin states in 1922, little consideration was given to Mexican rights to the river. At that time, American negotiators argued that, since most of the water in the Colorado originated within the United States, Mexico had no legitimate claim to it. Mexico did not agree and argued that, since the waters of the Colorado River flow through both countries, it should be a shared resource.

While Mexico and the United States were debating the allocation of the Colorado River, discussions were being held about uses of the other major shared river—the Rio Grande. On the Rio Grande, the situation was reversed, as much of the water flowing in the lower section of the river originates in Mexico.

Concerned about development projects on the lower Rio Grande in Mexico, the United States sought assurance that water would continue to flow into the river for use north of the border in Texas. Mexico would not agree to this. Just as the United States argued in the Colorado Watershed, Mexico asserted that national sovereignty gave it the right to use all of the water originating in Mexico (Hundley 1966). In part because of control that the United States and Mexico held on the two rivers, treaty talks soon encompassed both the Rio Grande and Colorado Rivers.

Regardless of whether the Rio Grande was to be included in a treaty, giving Colorado River water to Mexico was a difficult task. The U.S. states were concerned that an agreement with Mexico would reduce their respective allocations. In an offer more generous than most, Nevada's Senator Key Pittman suggested that the basin states might agree to give Mexico only 1 million acre-feet, one-third of what Mexico had requested (Hundley 1966).

Despite reservations from stakeholders on both the Rio Grande and Colorado Rivers, Mexico and the United States became anxious to formalize allocations. In 1936, Mexican President Lázaro Cárdenas said in a speech that Mexico either had to develop the Baja Peninsula or see it lost to the United States. He asserted that the central government must be brought into closer contact with the northern part of the country through a colonization program and the construction of highways, schools, dams, and irrigation canals.

Nervous about Cárdenas' vision for growth in the Colorado Delta and concerned that Mexico's plans to build dams in the Rio Grande would reduce flow to the United States, the United States decided to open negotiations over the allocation of the Rio Grande and Colorado Rivers. The Mexicans also had incentive to negotiate, as they watched the construction of the All American Canal just across the border in southern California. This canal would divert large quantities of water before it reached Mexico.

Over several decades, the two nations engaged in talks and finally reached an agreement. Some of the key elements of the treaty follow: On the Rio Grande, Mexico would give the United States one-third of the water flowing from Mexican tributaries above Salinas, Texas, and one-half of any other water reaching the main stem, except for that flowing from the San Juan and Alamo Rivers. Mexico

Irrigation canal carries water to farms in the Mexicali Valley, Baja California.

also guaranteed that its contribution would not be less than 350,000 acre-feet. Provisions were also made for the construction of three international dams for flood and sediment control as well as the generation of hydroelectricity (1944 Treaty).

On the Colorado River, negotiators determined that Mexico should receive 1,500,000 acre-feet with an additional 200,000 acre-feet available when there was sufficient surplus available. Of that amount, 500,000 acre-feet would be delivered through the All American Canal until 1980, after which time 375,000 acre-feet could be sent through the canal (1944 Treaty). This action clause was important to Mexico, as it would help to ensure that some of the water reaching Mexico would be of the same quality as that being used in the United States. After years of failed negotiations and posturing, a treaty governing the Rio Grande and Colorado Rivers was finally complete. On November 8, 1944, the treaty came into effect (Hundley 1966).

Selected Minutes (Amendments) to the 1944 Treaty between the United States and Mexico

Minute	Year	Effect
242	1973	The United States and Mexico agree on the quality (salinity level) of Colorado River water that flows into Mexico as part of its water rights under the 1944 treaty.
248	1975	The United States and Mexico agree to extend the Wellton-Mohawk canal into Mexico where salty irrigation runoff is deposited in the Colorado River Delta, near the town of Ejido Johnson, Sonora.
288	1992	The United States and Mexico establish the first conceptual plan for addressing sanitation issues in Mexicali, Baja California, and Calexico, California.
306	2000	A conceptual framework is established for developing future recommendations about preservation of riparian and estuarine ecosystems in the Colorado River Delta.

The treaty between the United States and Mexico is a living document, and it continues to evolve. Over three hundred minutes (amendments) have been added.

International Boundary and Water Commission

Signing of the 1944 treaty between the United States and Mexico. United States Secretary of State Cordell Hull is signing the treaty. Seated to his right is Mexican Foreign Relations Secretary F. Castillo Najera.

Procedure

Preparation

Part I:

Fold name cards lengthwise to form a tent. In large letters, write the names of the eight delegates to the Colorado River Commission on both sides of the cards. These name cards will be used to identify which delegate to the Colorado River Commission each student is representing. The cards should read:

- Narrator
- Herbert Hoover, U.S. Secretary of Commerce
- Frank Emerson, Wyoming
- Stephen Davis, Jr., New Mexico
- Winfield Norviel, Arizona
- Delphus Carpenter, Colorado
- James Scrugham, Nevada
- W. F. McClure, California
- R. E. Caldwell, Utah

Part II:

As in *Part I*, make name cards for the diplomats involved in the negotiations leading up to the 1944 treaty between the United States and Mexico:

- Narrator
- Fortunato Dozal, chief Mexican negotiator at the 1929 negotiations
- Elwood Mead, chief American negotiator at the 1929 negotiations
- Lázaro Cárdenas, President of Mexico (1934–1940)
- Franklin Roosevelt, President of the United States (1933–1945)
- Manuel Avila Camacho, President of Mexico (1940–1946)
- Lawrence Lawson, American Boundary Commissioner (1927–1954)
- Rafael Fernández MacGregor, chief Mexican negotiator in 1943
- Laurence Duggan, American State Department Advisor on Central and South American Political Relations (1935–1944)
- Adolfo Orive Alba, Mexican representative to the 1943 negotiations

- Royce Tipton, American representative to the 1943 negotiations
- Cordell Hull, American Secretary of State (1933–1944)
- George Smith, University of Arizona professor

Warm Up

1. **Divide the class into groups.** One group should have two students, one should have three, one should have four, and so on.

2. **Have the groups gather around the center of the room.** Dump out the candy on a desk in the middle. Tell the students that they will need to negotiate to divide up all of the candy. The members of each group should work together to negotiate with the other groups. Tell the students not to unwrap the candy until they have decided how to divide the candy among themselves. Give them five to ten minutes.

3. **Sit back and watch while the students negotiate, taking notes on how they proceed.** Try not to be involved in the process. There will not be enough pieces of candy for everyone to have two pieces; how will they divide up the remaining pieces? Does a single student take the lead and divide it for everyone else? Do the groups bicker? Does the largest group take all of the candy for themselves? How smoothly does their negotiation proceed?

4. **Ask students to describe how it felt to be part of this negotiation.** Did the students in the smaller groups feel at a disadvantage? If one student took the lead and made all of the decisions, what was that student's leadership style? Did most of the class feel that the candy was divided fairly, or not? If so, they can eat the candy. If not, ask them to come up with a better solution that can be implemented by the teacher.

5. **Explain that this example provides insight into the issues faced by the United States and Mexico in 1922 and 1944 when they decided that they needed to find a way**

to fairly divide the water of the Colorado River among them. In 1922, the states with smaller populations and slower development (for example, Wyoming and Colorado) were worried that the bigger, rapidly developing states (California and Arizona) would claim all of the river's water by diverting it for beneficial use first. The states needed to find a way to protect the rights of all states to use the water in the future by agreeing on a system to divide the river. One person from each state was sent to represent their state in the Colorado River Commission. The federal government (similar to the teacher in the students' negotiation process) would mediate the negotiations and ratify an agreement once it was reached.

6. **Ask the class to think about what it would be like if the 1922 compact had never been signed?** Do they live in the Upper Basin, the Lower Basin, or Mexico? Would their state or country have a right to use much of the water? What about Mexico's rights? (See *Part II*.)

7. **Tell students that they will be reenacting the negotiations of the 1922 Colorado River Compact and the 1944 treaty between the United States and Mexico.** They will use a script that was developed from quotes, articles, and stories about the negotiations leading to the 1922 compact and 1944 treaty. The negotiations were complex and difficult, as the decisions made would allocate precious water resources and effectively dictate future development of the western United States and northern Mexico.

The Activity

Part I: The 1922 Colorado River Compact

1. **Divide students into eight groups.** Each group will represent one of the seven U.S. basin states or the United States government. Tell each group which state they represent and have these students write the name of their state on a nametag. Ask the students to wear their nametags.

2. **Hand out *Sharing the Shed 1922 Stakeholder Cards* and the *1922 Facts Sheet* to each group.**

3. **Have students read all of the *Sharing the Shed 1922 Stakeholder Cards* and the *1922 Facts Sheets* within their groups.**

4. **Ask each group to elect a student to serve as their representative in the negotiation reenactment.** The remaining members should watch the negotiation from their state's point of view. Ask them to make notes about items with which they disagree. (*Optional*: have the students who will be acting as representatives go into a separate room to practice the script before performing in front of the rest of the class.)

5. **Identify one person to serve as the narrator during the negotiation (it may be the instructor).**

6. **Place nine desks at the front of the room and have participants sit from left to right (as viewed from the front) in the following order: Narrator, Scrugham, McClure, Norviel, Hoover, Caldwell, Carpenter, Davis, and Emerson.** Place the name cards in front of each representative. Have the rest of the class face the commission as an audience. The narrator's desk should be placed apart from the rest of the negotiation actors. If you haven't already passed out the *Sharing the Shed Negotiation Script* to all of the students, do so now.

7. **Allow the narrator to begin the reenactment.**

8. **Following the reenactment, allow groups to reconvene.** Give each group five minutes to develop a list of at least five negotiation outcomes with which they agree or disagree.

9. **At the end of five minutes, ask the class to come together with groups sitting together.** You may want to organize the desks into a circle to facilitate discussion.

10. **Ask each group to report their observations to the class.** Did some states concede more than others to arrive at an agreement? Given information available in 1922, what changes would they have recommended? Why? How do the decisions made at that meeting affect current management of the river?

11. **Ask students to consider the 1922 compact negotiations from Mexico's point of view.** Should representatives from Mexico have been included in the decision-making? Why or why not? Discuss the rationale given by the 1922 negotiators for excluding Mexico from the process, and describe the historical context that eventually led to the development of the 1944 treaty (see **Background**). How did Mexico's position on the Rio Grande motivate the United States to negotiate on the Colorado River?

Part II: The 1944 U.S.-Mexico Treaty

1. **Ask students to imagine that the Colorado River Compact has just been signed and that Mexico is working to develop a treaty agreement that will guide how to allocate rivers that are shared by the United States and Mexico (primarily the Rio Grande and the Colorado).** Students will reenact key parts of the negotiations that led to the 1944 treaty between the United States and Mexico.

2. **Explain that dividing the rivers was not an easy task, as the future of both nations relied on the water they carried.** Much of the area drained by the two rivers is extremely arid, with the Sonoran and Mojave Deserts in the Colorado Watershed and the Chihuahuan Desert in the Rio Grande Watershed. However, the headwaters of both rivers start in wetter areas. On the Rio Grande, mountain snowpack in both the United States and Mexico contributes large amounts of water. In the Colorado River Watershed, 99 percent of the water originates in the United States, but is vital to both countries. In both cases, people,

plants, and animals rely on water flowing in the rivers.

3. **Tell the class that the development of the treaty was done through a negotiation process, similar to the negotiation they reenacted in *Part I* of the activity.** The negotiation of the U.S.-Mexico treaty was completed by representatives from both governments with input from different stakeholder groups. Each country identified when, where, why, and how they needed the water available from the rivers. They then discussed with the other country how best to meet these goals. In reality, much of the "discussion" took place through memos, lawsuits, and phone calls.

4. **Divide the class into two groups, one representing the United States and the other Mexico.**

5. **Hand out the *Sharing the Shed 1944 Stakeholder Card (Mexico) Student Copy Page* (one for each student in the Mexico group).**

6. **Hand out the *Sharing the Shed 1944 Stakeholder Card (United States) Student Copy Page* (one for each student in the United States group).**

7. **Have each group read the stakeholder card for their country and develop a list of goals for the negotiation.** What do they think the terms of the treaty should be, considering both the Colorado River and the Rio Grande?

8. **Hand out the *1944 U.S.-Mexico Treaty Negotiations Script Student Copy Page*.**

9. **Have each group select people to play the parts representing their country.**

10. **Have the students who are role-playing the negotiation sit in desks facing the room, as in *Part I*.** Place each person's name card on the desk in front of them. Have the rest of the class face the negotiators as an audience.

11. **Allow the narrator to begin the 1944 treaty negotiation reenactment.**

12. **After the negotiation is complete, have students return to their groups and review the goals that they had hoped their country would achieve through the negotiation.** Were their needs met? What did they gain or give up by compromising?

13. **Have the class discuss the negotiation and outcome of the treaty.**

Wrap Up
1. **Pass out the *2005 Fact Sheet Student Copy Pages* and review the information as a class.**

2. **Discuss the following:** Given what we now know about the average amount of streamflow, population growth, and agriculture-to-urban water transfers, what would have made the 1922 compact and the 1944 treaty better?

When dividing the river, planners allocated water by acre-feet so that each state or country could plan for a specific amount of water. Unfortunately, these allocations were based upon the belief that the river's average annual flow was 17 million acre-feet (maf). Data now shows that the river's average annual flow is closer to 12–13 maf; the river is over-allocated by 4–5 maf.

Storage reservoirs and return flows have made it possible to satisfy the treaty and compact requirements each year to date, but if there is an extended period of drought, there may not be enough water to meet all water needs. Since it is difficult to calculate the exact flow in a river system and because there is so much annual variability in water volume, planners on some other river systems have allocated the water based on percentages. This system allows users to share the burden of shortages (see page 148, "Reading the Rings").

Another development that the commissioners did not foresee was the growth of urban centers, which has caused a shift in water demand from agricultural to urban. During the 1920s–1940s, planners could not know that Los Angeles, San Diego, Denver, Phoenix, Las Vegas, Tijuana, and other cities would grow so large. They did not recognize the importance of river flow in maintaining ecosystems. Nor did they predict the lucrative recreation industry that now relies on the Colorado River. These changes and more mean that the compact and treaty will be tested as resource managers seek to match new values and demands.

Assessment

Have students:
- negotiate to divide candy among themselves and compare the process to dividing water among states and nations (***Warm Up**, Steps 1–7)*;
- reenact negotiations that took place when dividing the Colorado River among the seven U.S. basin states (*Part 1, Steps 1–7*);
- discuss the outcome of the 1922 Colorado River Compact negotiations (*Part I, Steps 8–11*);
- reenact negotiations that took place while developing the 1944 U.S.-Mexico Water Treaty (*Part II, Steps 1–10*);
- evaluate the outcome of the 1944 treaty negotiations (*Part II, Steps 11–12*);
- discuss the outcome of the 1922 and 1944 negotiations with regard to what is now known about river flow, population growth, and water use (***Wrap Up**, Step 2*).

Extensions

Have students negotiate a new Colorado River Compact or U.S.-Mexico Water Treaty based on current water needs. Students should work in the same groups as above to develop a list of items that they feel are critical. Have each group elect a representative to serve as their lead negotiator. The negotiators should work together to develop a plan that is suitable for their needs. The instructor may want to serve as facilitator of these discussions.

Have students do research on the changes in Colorado River water use from 1922 to the present. How well did the negotiators of the 1922 compact predict future use of the Colorado River? How might negotiators have changed their strategies had they foreseen how water would be used more than eighty years later? What tools do water planners use to predict future growth and water use?

Have students do the activity "Plumbing the Colorado," including the extension on salinity. After students have demonstrated how much salt is in the Colorado River by the time it reaches the United States/Mexico border, have them negotiate an amendment to the agreements developed in this activity that addresses how much salt can be in the Colorado when it flows into Mexico (see page 277, "Plumbing the Colorado").

Resources

Fisher, Roger, William Ury, and Bruce Patton. 1991. *Getting to Yes: Negotiating Agreement without Giving In*. New York: Penguin USA.

Hobbs, Gregory Jr. 2003. Inside the Drama of the Colorado River Compact Negotiations: Negotiating the Apportionment. *Proceedings of the Fourth Biennial Colorado River Symposium, September 17-19, 2003*. Sacramento, CA: The Water Education Foundation.

Hundley, Norris Jr. 1966. *Dividing the Waters: A Century of Controversy between the United States and Mexico*. Berkeley: University of California Press.

Hundley, Norris. 1975. *Water and the West: The Colorado River Compact and the Politics of Water in the American West*. Berkeley: University of California Press.

Martin, Russell. 1999. *A Story that Stands Like a Dam: Glen Canyon and the Struggle for the Soul of the West*. Salt Lake City: University of Utah Press.

Newcom, Joshua. 2004. *Layperson's Guide to the Colorado River*. Sacramento, CA: Water Education Foundation.

e-Links

Colorado River Water Users Association
Information about current uses of Colorado River water.
www.crwua.org

International Boundary and Water Commission
Full-text versions of international water treaties and updates on current international water debates.
www.ibwc.state.gov

International Boundary and Water Commission
List and full text of most recent changes to the treaty governing shared water on the Colorado, Rio Grande, and Tijuana Rivers.
www.ibwc.state.gov/html/body_minutes.HTM

United States Bureau of Reclamation
Links to full-text versions of Colorado River water law documents.
www.usbr.gov/lc/region/g1000/lawofrvr.html

United States Bureau of Reclamation
Full text of 1944 United States/Mexico treaty.
www.usbr.gov/lc/region/g1000/pdfiles/mextrety.pdf

Water Education Foundation
Information about Colorado River water law, history, and allocation.
www.watereducation.org/coloradoriver.asp

1922 Fact Sheet

Policymakers had the following information available to them in 1922 when they negotiated the allocation of the Colorado River within the United States:

- About 90 percent of the water in the Colorado River Watershed originates in the Upper Basin (Colorado, Utah, New Mexico, and Wyoming).
- Data collected between 1902 and 1920 shows the average annual flow in the Colorado River to be 17.3 million acre-feet (maf).
- One acre-foot is enough water to supply a family of four to five people for one year. It is about the amount of water it would take to cover a football field with one foot of water.

- Flow in the Colorado is highly variable. Between 1899 and 1920, flow at Lee's Ferry in Northern Arizona ranged from 9.89 maf to 25 maf. It is expensive to build diversion structures that can withdraw water during low flows and withstand floods.
- The Colorado River carries more silt than almost any other river in the world—carrying about five times that of the Rio Grande, ten times that of the Nile, and seventeen times that of the Mississippi (Hundley 1975).
- The future of the watershed is assumed to be primarily agricultural. Each state has determined the amount of water it would like to have allocated to it, based on estimates of potential agricultural water use in the future.

Sharing the Shed 1922 Stakeholder Cards (Upper Basin)

Colorado 1922: Seventy-five to eighty percent of the water in the Colorado River Watershed originates in Colorado. The entire western part of your state is in the watershed. In 1920, irrigators in Colorado were using Colorado River water to irrigate about 740,000 acres, but experts predict that thousands more can be developed. While much of the state's water is in the Colorado River Watershed, the best agricultural land is in the plains on the other side of the Continental Divide. Most of the state's population growth is also occurring there. State leaders would like to build interbasin diversion projects that would deliver water to the eastern slope from the Colorado River Watershed. You are concerned that rapidly growing California may develop rights to river water before you have a chance to develop. Your representative at the negotiations is Delph Carpenter. He believes that creating a compact between U.S. Colorado River Basin states is critical to secure water for Colorado.

Wyoming 1922: Wyoming is home of the headwaters of the Green River, which contributes more water to the Colorado River than any other tributary. Wyoming residents feel that, although the named Colorado River starts in Colorado, the headwaters of the river system are in Wyoming because they are furthest from the Gulf of California. Most of the land suitable for growing crops is located above 6,000 feet, making a short growing season. Wyoming sees its agricultural future not in farming, but in raising livestock such as sheep and cattle. Like Utah, Wyoming sees potential in building hydroelectric plants on the Green River whose power could be used for railroads and to develop oil shale, coal, and other rich minerals. Your representative at the negotiations is Frank Emerson. He has served as state engineer and is noted as a strong negotiator. Although he has been involved in water litigation against the state of Colorado, he is eager to form an alliance among Colorado, Wyoming, Utah, and New Mexico to strengthen each of their positions.

Utah 1922: Nearly half of Utah is in the Colorado River Watershed. Like the state of Colorado, much of its population growth and arable land is located outside of the Colorado River Watershed. For this reason, Utah wants to ensure that the compact will not limit the state's ability to transfer water out of the basin. Utah's representative to the negotiations is R. E. Caldwell. Like the representative from Wyoming, he sees potential in building hydroelectric plants on the Green River whose power could be used for railroads and to develop oil shale, coal, and other rich minerals. He is also interested in continuing agricultural development along the Colorado River in southeastern Utah. By 1920, about 359,000 acres were being irrigated in this area with potential for thousands more.

New Mexico 1922: New Mexico territory makes up about 10 percent of the Colorado River Watershed. The major tributaries that flow through New Mexico are the Gila, Little Colorado, and San Juan Rivers. Deep canyons on the Gila and Little Colorado make it difficult to use the water for irrigation. The San Juan is the river from which water can be most easily used for irrigation. For this reason, New Mexico would like to ensure rights to all the waters of the San Juan. In 1920, about 34,000 acres were being irrigated in the state. New Mexico's representative to the negotiations is Stephen Davis. Davis is a New Mexico Supreme Court justice and specializes in water law. He argues that an additional 1.5 million acres could be irrigated in New Mexico.

Sharing the Shed 1922 Stakeholder Cards (Lower Basin)

Arizona 1922: About 90 percent of Arizona lies within the Colorado River Watershed. The largest tributaries flowing through the state are the Gila and Little Colorado Rivers. Arizona has big plans for agricultural growth and hydroelectric power. In 1920, there were about 500,000 acres under irrigation. These crops were watered using Colorado River tributary water (such as the Gila, Salt, and Verde) and water pumped from ground water aquifers. Some engineers feel that the state should build projects that would transport Colorado River water to central Arizona, making possible the irrigation of an additional 1.1 million acres. Arizona's topography makes the transportation of water a difficult task, as canals must be built over, around, and through deep canyons and high mountains. Hot and dry conditions mean that large amounts of water must be used to irrigate crops. Flooding on the Colorado River has caused massive destruction in Yuma and other Arizona communities along the lower river. Negotiators would like to secure rights to all tributary water, especially that of the Gila. Arizona's representative to the negotiations is Winfield Norviel.

California 1922: Only 2 percent of the Colorado River Watershed lies within California, and the state contributes almost no water to the river. Beginning at the turn of the century, residents have been diverting large amounts of water from the Colorado River for use in the Imperial Valley and surrounding areas. These low-elevation valleys are very dry but, with the application of water, become highly productive farmlands. Californians argue that, since they were the first major users of the Colorado River, they have the right to use its flow before other users. In 1920, 458,000 acres were being irrigated with an estimated 481,000 more possible (there was no talk of pumping water to Los Angeles and San Diego). Due to high rates of evaporation and sandy soils, the amount of water required to irrigate each acre is about two times greater than in Colorado. Heavy sedimentation and unpredictable flows in the river make diverting water from the Colorado difficult. California would like to construct flood control structures on the river that will regulate its flows. Another problem is that the main agricultural diversion canal for southern California flows south into Mexico before reentering the United States. This situation leaves Californians vulnerable to decisions made in Mexico. California would like to construct a canal that would carry water to the Imperial Valley without entering Mexico. Both flood control and canal construction would be too costly for the state to build without federal support. California's representative to the negotiations is State Engineer W. F. McClure.

Nevada 1922: Nevada has the least interest in the Colorado River. Engineers estimate that only 82,000 acres are good for agriculture, and most of that acreage is along the Virgin River, a tributary to the Colorado River. There are no major cities within the watershed, and the state's primary interest is in hydropower. Nevada's representative to the negotiations is James Scrugham, a man who will later become the state's governor.

United States Government 1922: The United States government is interested in the Colorado River. While most of the basin is desert, application of water can turn it into productive agricultural land. The United States would like to encourage settlement in the sparsely populated region and is prepared to invest in infrastructure that will allow this to happen. Federal representatives are present to show federal support for the negotiations and to direct state representatives toward a solution to which the government can agree. The federal representative at the negotiations is Herbert Hoover, U.S. Secretary of Commerce. He is a strong advocate of taming the river.

Sharing the Shed 1922 Negotiation Script

Narrator:

(Reading to the entire class)

Ladies and Gentlemen, seated before you are eight honorable representatives who are about to reenact the 1922 negotiation of the Colorado River Compact. States represented are Colorado, Wyoming, Utah, New Mexico, Arizona, Nevada, and California. The United States has also sent someone to represent the United States government. Mexico has not been asked to participate in the meetings.

This negotiation is critical, as the outcome will divide the waters of the Colorado River and its tributaries forever. Slower-growing states fear that, if no agreement is reached, the law of prior appropriation—which gives water ownership to those who first develop it—will give senior water rights to faster-growing states. In order to avoid a "race to develop," these states must have a protected water allocation.

Seated at the table before you are: **James Scrugham** of Nevada; **W. F. McClure** of California; **W. S. Norviel** of Arizona; **Herbert Hoover**, the United States Secretary of Commerce; **R. E. Caldwell** of Utah; **Delph Carpenter** of Colorado; **Stephen Davis** of New Mexico; and **Frank Emerson** of Wyoming.

What follows is a condensation of ten months of meetings and negotiations. As narrator, at times I will step in to explain some of the details of the negotiations.

(Gesturing to the student representing Hoover)

It is now my great honor to present to you Mr. Herbert Hoover.

Herbert Hoover (United States): I am glad to have the honor of welcoming the Commissioners to Washington for this meeting. The Commission has been established to consider and agree upon a compact between the seven states of the Colorado River Basin. If achieved, the Compact will be subject to ratification by each state legislature and the United States Congress.

It is fortunate that there is little established right on the river and that we have an almost clean slate to begin our efforts. There is possibly ample water in the river for all—if adequate storage is undertaken. Populations on the lower river are in extreme jeopardy from floods. In fact, flood control has become vital for their very existence.

Narrator: Hoover then asked each of the members to express their views concerning the problems of the commission. The commissioners agree that their work will help decide the division of the Colorado River without costly lawsuits. There are disagreements, however, about whether the commission should develop a flood control plan before allocating Colorado River water.

Herbert Hoover (United States): It may develop in the course of our inquiry that there is a deficiency of water in the Colorado River unless we assume adequate storage [by building dams]. It would seem a great misfortune if we did not give Congress and the country a broad (and specific) project for development of the Colorado River.

Stephen Davis (New Mexico): If we lay down a general plan, we will have a simpler task than if we attempt to work out an entire scheme.

W. F. McClure (California): Mr. Chairman, your remark that there will not be enough water unless it is conserved was quite apropos. The State of California has the largest monetary interest in the Colorado River because of our development in the Imperial Valley, but the area already experiences water shortages during certain parts of the year.

Frank Emerson (Wyoming): In sitting upon

Sharing the Shed 1922 Negotiation Script

the lid, the headwaters, of the basin we recognize that the Imperial Valley needs protection from the Colorado River, but we must have assurance that such projects will not limit the rights to the water flowing in Wyoming. I believe that each state should present to the Commission what it thinks are the possibilities for future growth as well as established rights.

Herbert Hoover (United States): I think Mr. Emerson has hit upon one of the fundamental tasks of the commission. We must understand the claims of each state.

Narrator: The commissioners agreed and each state prepared estimates for the amount of water use that their states would require. This was done and commissioners estimated that about 10 million acres could be irrigated in the Colorado River Basin. Some representatives felt that water allocation should be based on irrigable acreage, but others (particularly in the Upper Basin) were opposed to acreage limitations. This was due in large part to their desire to transfer water to areas outside of the watershed. Such an action would allow them to move water to population centers and irrigate more land.

Herbert Hoover (United States): I believe it has come time to get the various viewpoints in the record. Do you think it is possible to secure an agreement based on acreage limitations?

R. E. Caldwell (Utah): Nothing I have said should be taken as indication that Utah will accept acreage limitations at any time, nor do I consider it the proper basis for allocating the waters of the Colorado River.

Frank Emerson (Wyoming): All Wyoming wants is this: if a large reservoir is constructed on the Colorado River, then such construction and associated water use shall not establish a priority right to

the river and shall not interfere with water development in Wyoming.

Stephen Davis (New Mexico): We have been asked to give up the right to irrigate certain acres, but we get nothing in exchange. It seems to me that the attitude of the lower states ought to be one of extreme liberty toward the upper states. If we can't get sufficient guarantees for the Upper Basin, I think these negotiations fail.

Delphus Carpenter (Colorado): The majority of the water flowing in the Colorado River originates in the upper states and as such those states have the inherent right to use that water for self preservation and development, at least to the extent that they do not injure their neighbors below.

Herbert Hoover (United States) (*disturbed by Carpenter's extreme views*): Do you imply that an equitable division of water is for you to take all you want?

Delphus Carpenter (Colorado): Origin is a concept that runs through international law, specifying that the nation of origin has inherent privileges and benefits that may be denied the lower nation.

Herbert Hoover (United States) (*staring intensely at Carpenter and pushing his authority as chairman of the commission*): Then it comes to this: the upper states want to take all the water they can and be declared immune from litigation by the other states.

Delphus Carpenter (Colorado): We are entitled to freedom of attack from below.

Winfield Norviel (Arizona): He always comes back to the same point—the upper states cannot be limited by anything and are entitled to all that the Maker of the World has put before them, without regard to the rights of anybody else.

Herbert Hoover (United States): We have not been able to get any agreement on a general single

Sharing the Shed 1922 Negotiation Script

idea for a compact. Is it worth having another session or shall we declare that we are so hopelessly far apart that there is no use proceeding?

Winfield Norviel (Arizona): I do not think we should foreclose our meetings at this time.

James Scrugham (Nevada): I believe that we have made a failure thus far.

R. E. Caldwell (Utah) *(rising nearly out of his seat)*: It may not be as hopeless as you think. I do not want the lower states to take home the idea that the commissioners here are not generous and helpful.

W. F. McClure (California): But that is the attitude we are getting.

Delphus Carpenter (Colorado): I think it would be the height of crime to the people who sent us here to adjourn permanently now.

Narrator: It was decided that the meetings should continue and that the next meeting would take place at The Bishop's Lodge in Santa Fe, New Mexico. When the Santa Fe meeting came to order, it became clearer that the conflict over Colorado River allocation was between the upper and lower basins, rather than between states. It was suggested that the watershed be divided into Upper and Lower Basins.

Herbert Hoover (United States): Then we come to whether it is possible to make a division by groups of states. Mr. Norviel, do you think it would be possible to administer the allocation of water under such a division?

Winfield Norviel (Arizona): If we are to divide the river into two basins and require the upper states to send a certain amount of water to the lower states over a given period, the upper states could dry up the river at some times only to send their required water as a flood.

Stephen Davis (New Mexico): Isn't this an objection in detail, rather than in principle?

Winfield Norviel (Arizona): I am willing to discuss the idea, but we do not want to be in a position where we would be dried up for five years and flooded for the next five.

Delphus Carpenter (Colorado): Yes, we will fix a minimum flow to take care of that.

Narrator: The commission continued to discuss the idea of dividing the river between Upper and Lower Basins. After further negotiation, a proposal was drafted.

Herbert Hoover (United States): Gentlemen, I have as follows our proposal for the division of the Colorado River. Under the agreement, the Colorado River system will be divided into Upper and Lower Basins. Each basin shall be allocated 7,500,000 acre-feet per year. The two basins shall operate as separate entities and divide the water among them at a later date. This compact shall not require the construction of flood control structures, but the Commission recommends that Congress pursue at the earliest possible date the construction of such works. All those in favor, say, "aye."

All *(speaking one by one)*: "Aye!"

Narrator: With that, the fundamentals of the agreement were spelled out. On November 24, 1922, the historic compact was signed. Of all the states represented at the negotiations, Arizona was the most reluctant. Representatives did not want to concede any water from Arizona tributaries. Despite Arizona's reluctance, the United States Congress approved the compact. When it came time for states to approve the compact, Arizona refused. The compact went into effect anyway, and it was not until the 1964 court case *Arizona v. California* that Arizona's concerns were finally resolved.

Sharing the Shed 1944 Stakeholder Card (Mexico)

Mexico's Perspective in 1944:

Like the United States, you are pursuing agricultural development in the Rio Grande and Colorado River Basins. Farmers in your territory are cultivating several hundred thousand acres with countless more planned. Much of this water is Colorado River water supplied by the Alamo Canal, a delivery system built as a partnership between the Mexican and American interests. The canal delivers water to both countries. You feel that this and other historic uses give you rights to Colorado River water.

Dams built in the United States have allowed you to utilize more Colorado River water by regulating its flow. You argue that historic usage entitles you to that water regardless of who built the dams.

You are afraid that, without an agreement between the two nations, the United States will claim all Colorado River water.

On the Rio Grande, the situation is the opposite, as much of the river's flow originates within your borders. You would like to increase agriculture in the region. To do so, you are planning the construction of several flood control structures and irrigation diversions. When built, they will allow you to use most of the water in the Conchos River (a major tributary of the Lower Rio Grande) before it reaches the border. If you do this, farms in Texas will lose their water supply. Your analysts tell you that negotiating a treaty is better than having a third party allocate the river.

Sharing the Shed 1944 Stakeholder Card (United States)

The United States' Perspective in 1944:
Like Mexico, you are pursuing agricultural development in the Rio Grande and Colorado River Basins. Farmers in your territory are cultivating over one million acres, and you recently invested millions of dollars to build flood control structures, which will store water and make it easier to get it to water users. Because of these structures, you will be able to grow crops on many more acres. Engineers feel that you will eventually be able to use all the flow of the Colorado River.

Steady flows resulting from the construction of U.S. flood control structures have simplified the diversion of water from the Colorado River. As a result, farmers in the United States and Mexico are rapidly developing more uses for that water. You feel that Mexico's increased usage does not establish a water right because it is American structures that make it possible for them to use the water.

You fear that Mexico will make the same argument on the Lower Rio Grande where most of the water originates south of the border (flowing from the watershed of the Rio Conchos, a major tributary). U.S. farmers in Texas rely on water that reaches the border. You know that Mexico is pursuing projects that will allow it to use almost all Rio Grande water flowing from its territory. If this happens, some Texans will be unable to farm. You want to negotiate a sharing agreement with Mexico. Your analysts tell you that negotiating a treaty is better than having a third party allocate the river.

1944 U.S.-Mexico Treaty Negotiations Script

Narrator: The Colorado River Compact of 1922 divided the Colorado River into Upper and Lower Basins, but more than twenty years after it was established, the United States and Mexico still had not been able to reach an agreement governing how to share the river between them. Both governments recognized that an international treaty would be necessary. The treaty would be important, as it would tell them how much water would likely be available for future growth. In 1929, formal negotiations began.

Seated at the table before you are: **Fortunato Dozal**, chief Mexican negotiator at the 1929 negotiations; **Elwood Mead**, chief American negotiator at the 1929 negotiations; **Lázaro Cárdenas**, President of Mexico (1934–1940); **Franklin Roosevelt**, President of the United States (1933–1945); **Manuel Avila Camacho**, President of Mexico (1940–1946); **Lawrence Lawson**, American Boundary Commissioner (1927–1954); **Rafael Fernández MacGregor**, chief Mexican negotiator in 1943; **Laurence Duggan**, American State Department Advisor on Central and South American Political Relations (1935–1944); **Adolfo Orive Alba**, Mexican representative to the 1943 negotiations; **Royce Tipton**, American representative to the 1943 negotiations; **Cordell Hull**, American Secretary of State (1933–1944); **George Smith**, University of Arizona professor.

This dialog has been compiled from historic documents, letters, and newspaper articles. The actual debate over how to divide the Colorado River took place over decades. It has been compressed to give an overview of the debate. As the narrator, at times I will step in to explain some of the details of the negotiations.

The first negotiation in which progress was made toward dividing the Colorado River between the United States and Mexico was in 1929. We now pick up the treaty negotiations during a conversation between Fortunato Dozal, chief negotiator for Mexico, and Elwood Mead, chief American negotiator.

Fortunato Dozal (Mexico): Mr. Mead, when the United States established the Colorado River Compact in 1922, Mexico was not allowed to participate in the discussions. I am glad that we are finally sitting at the same table to work toward establishing a treaty that will share the waters of the Colorado River between our two great countries.

When the Colorado River Compact was developed, water allocations were decided based on the number of acres that can be irrigated using Colorado River water. The Colorado River delta in Mexico has an estimated 1,500,000 acres ready for agriculture. To grow crops, 3 acre-feet is needed per acre. Based on this calculation, I suggest that Mexico be given rights to 4,500,000 acre-feet of Colorado River water each year.

Elwood Mead (United States): Mr. Dozal, I too am glad that we are beginning this discussion and have high hopes that we will be able to reach an agreement. However, we feel that your request of 4,500,000 acre-feet per year is unreasonable. When we look at your country's historic use, it becomes clear that you use far less than the amount you have requested. The largest volume of water you have ever used in a year is 750,000 acre-feet, and this is 20 percent more than your average use over the last 10 years.

We are concerned that even giving you just 750,000 acre-feet will restrict American development; however, in the name of being good neighbors, we are willing to offer you that amount. In addition, you will receive the benefits of flood and sediment control provided by dams we are building upstream.

Fortunato Dozal (Mexico): But the Colorado's

1944 U.S.-Mexico Treaty Negotiations Script

international geographic nature makes it a commonwealth; it belongs to both countries. The equitable way to distribute its waters is to apportion them according to the irrigable acreage in each country. We can compromise, but we should receive *at least* 3,480,000 acre-feet.

Elwood Mead (United States): If we agree to your demands, we will be required to surrender our resources and restrict our development for reasons that are not required by international law or friendship.

Fortunato Dozal (Mexico): I am sorry to hear you say that. I would like to point out that, in the watershed of the Rio Grande, Mexico contributes about half of the total streamflow. Our water contribution flows to the Rio Grande from tributaries beginning in Mexico. We believe that farmers in our country have the right to use all the water flowing from Mexican streams. If they are to use all the water, there will little water available to American farmers taking water from the Rio Grande.

Elwood Mead (United States): But if you are to use all the water from your Rio Grande tributaries, American farmers in Texas will not have enough water to continue farming.

Fortunato Dozal (Mexico): I recognize that what you are saying is true, but it is not our responsibility to support Texas farmers with Mexican water.

Narrator: The negotiations in 1929 failed in part because neither country was willing to share the water flowing from tributaries starting within their borders. During the next decade, tensions mounted as farmers in the Colorado and Rio Grande Watersheds used increasing amounts of water. In the Colorado River Watershed, agricultural uses rapidly increased. This was due in part to support from Mexican president, Lázaro Cárdenas, who provided funding for irrigation projects in

both watersheds. One of them, the Retamal Canal, would allow Mexico to divert almost the entire flow of the Rio Grande before it could be used by Americans in Texas.

President Lázaro Cárdenas (Mexico): People of Mexico, we have a great nation and it can become greater if we provide agricultural opportunities to more people. This is why I encourage you to take advantage of the rich agricultural areas along the Rio Grande and Colorado Rivers. If we are to settle these lands, we can reduce the risk of losing them to the United States.

On the Colorado River, the United States has been working on the completion of an All-American canal that will allow the Americans to divert greater quantities of water from the Colorado River before it reaches Mexico. This is a threat to our ability to live in the region of the Colorado River Delta. In our country, I propose the construction of the Retamal Canal along the Rio Grande. Like the All-American canal in the United States, the Retamal would give us control of the lower portion of the Rio Grande.

President Franklin Roosevelt (United States): I fear that conflicts over water on the Colorado and Rio Grande Rivers will create divisions between our nations that cannot be bridged. If we are to construct canals with the intention of stopping water before it can be used by our neighbors, conflict may arise between us. As you know, the world war that began in 1941 has brought deep divisions throughout the world. This is a time for us to stand united and put differences behind us. To move toward this goal, I propose that we solve, for once and for all, the question of international water rights on the Rio Grande and Colorado Rivers.

President Manuel Avila Camacho (Mexico): I agree that it is in the best interest of our two countries to reach an agreement on these rivers and

1944 U.S.-Mexico Treaty Negotiations Script

that it is time to take action. Let us settle this issue before it divides our nations in a time when we should be united against evil. Let us now turn the discussions over to our representatives to solve this issue.

Lawrence Lawson (United States): Mr. Fernández, President Roosevelt has asked that we enter into discussions with Mexico to determine how to divide the waters of rivers that are shared by the United States. We would like to divide the Colorado, Rio Grande, and Tijuana Rivers. In previous negotiations, representatives from Mexico have requested 3,480,000 acre-feet of Colorado River water each year. We cannot fulfill that request. We estimate that the Colorado River carries 17.3 million acre-feet per year. Sixteen million acre-feet have already been allocated to American states.

Rafael Fernández MacGregor (Mexico): Along with Canada, Mexico is your closest neighbor and we should share this important resource. As our presidents have communicated to each other, it is in our mutual best interest to settle the division of the rivers you have mentioned. On the Colorado River, there are farms, cities, and citizens in Mexico that rely on Colorado River water. We expect our needs to grow dramatically and insist that we be given rights to the amount of water we have requested. In addition, we still insist on rights to all water flowing into the Rio Grande from Mexico.

Laurence Duggan (United States): Mr. Fernández, you argue that the United States should share water flowing in the Colorado River that originates in the United States, but want rights to all the water flowing to the Rio Grande from Mexico. The United States relies on the water flowing from Mexican headwaters into the Rio Grande. The United States is willing to concede some waters on the Colorado in exchange for flow from the Mexican tributaries to the Rio Grande.

Adolfo Orive Alba (Mexico): If we are to make any progress on this negotiation, we will each have to concede some water.

Royce Tipton (United States): So, we will negotiate how to share these three international rivers between our two nations.

Rafael Fernández MacGregor (Mexico): If you cannot allocate 3,480,000 acre-feet of the Colorado River to Mexico each year, what do you propose?

Cordell Hull (United States): The United States is willing to offer 900,000 acre-feet of Colorado River water per year plus $15,000,000 to be used for construction of dams on the Lower Rio Grande. These dams would store water for use in the United States and Mexico. Mexico would not retain rights to all its rivers that flow to the Rio Grande.

Rafael Fernández MacGregor (Mexico): That offer is still insufficient and fails to acknowledge Mexico's interests and rights that are already established along the Colorado River. Those rights were established by virtue of the original boundary treaties and our historic use of the water. Still, we are glad to see that the negotiations are moving forward.

Narrator: Many citizens were nervous about giving water to the neighboring country and wrote letters and articles trying to stop the process. In the United States, citizens were concerned that Mexico would reap the benefits of dams being built in the United States without having to pay for them. The biggest concern was about Boulder Dam, which was later renamed Hoover Dam.

George Smith (Arizona): I do not believe we should be giving water to Mexico. Americans have rights to all waters of the Colorado River that may be stored or impounded within the United States. Mexico has no right, legal or moral, to Colorado

1944 U.S.-Mexico Treaty Negotiations Script

River water temporarily flowing into their country.

Cordell Hull (United States): Mr. Fernández, I am sure that you recognize that there is much sentiment in the United States portion of the Colorado River Watershed that we should not give any water to Mexico. Still we are willing to increase our offer in the name of being good neighbors.

Rafael Fernández MacGregor (Mexico): Mr. Hull, I am sorry to hear that there is public sentiment against an agreement that gives Colorado River water to Mexico. I must tell you that there is similar sentiment in Mexico on the Rio Grande. Like you, we are still willing to establish a treaty in the name of international peace.

We propose that, on the Rio Grande, Mexico will guarantee the United States 350,000 acre-feet each year of water flowing from Mexico to the Rio Grande. In addition, we would like to work with you on the construction of three major dams that will be used for flood and silt control as well as to generate hydroelectric power.

Lawrence Lawson (United States): I know that I am speaking for all members of the American negotiation team when I say that we are happy with your offer on the Rio Grande. We agree with your offer. Let us consider that issue closed.

In response to your generosity, we propose that, on the Colorado River, the United States guarantee that 1,500,000 acre-feet of water will reach Mexico each year with an additional 200,000 acre-feet in years when additional water is available.

Adolfo Orive Alba (Mexico): Gentlemen, I feel that we are close to reaching a final agreement. However, one of our concerns is that we cannot be assured of the quality of the water reaching Mexico. Though it would not address all of our concerns, we suggest that a portion of Mexico's water be delivered through the All-American Canal. This will insure that some of the water we receive is of the same quality as that being delivered to American users of that canal.

Cordell Hull (United States): We recognize that is a concern for you and are willing to deliver a portion of the water through the All-American Canal.

Adolfo Orive Alba (Mexico): Then it is finally settled. Our two great countries will share the waters of the Rio Grande and the Colorado. The only river we are still to discuss is the Tijuana. I fear that we do not have enough information to make a decision about the division of this river. I suggest that we add a clause to the treaty that will provide for studies that will facilitate a future settlement.

Lawrence Lawson (United States): We agree with you and would like to vote on the decisions we have made. All those in favor of developing the treaty on the Rio Grande, Colorado, and Tijuana Rivers as we have outlined here say "Aye."

All participants: Aye!

Lawrence Lawson (United States): All those opposed, "Nay."

All participants are silent.

Rafael Fernández MacGregor (Mexico): It gives me great pleasure to know that we have finally reached a mutually acceptable agreement that will help us to share these great rivers.

Narrator: And so the foundation for the international management of these rivers was established. Since that time, over three hundred amendments have been added that clarify and update the treaty. It can be seen as a living document, always changing and helping the two countries to share these international waters.

2005 Fact Sheet

The following information about water use in the Colorado River Watershed is available in 2005:

- Based on tree-ring data and on flow data from 1899 to 2001, average annual flow of the Colorado River is about 13 million acre-feet (maf) per year. Analysis of ancient clam shells in the Colorado River Delta indicates that annual average flow may be even less (12 maf)!
- The U.S.-Mexico Treaty has priority over U.S. states' allocations, and Mexico's 1.5 maf must be delivered first in times of shortage. This brings the total number of acre-feet to which the United States and Mexico are allocated to 16.5 maf. The river is 21-27 percent over-allocated.
- There are several outstanding legal disputes between the United States and American Indian tribes. Although American Indian tribes were not included in the 1922 negotiations, their water rights are "reserved," according to the Winters Doctrine. Tribes are starting to develop their water rights in many states.
- Population in the southwestern United States and northwestern Mexico is growing dramatically. Much of this growth has occurred in cities that receive water from the Colorado River, including Tijuana, Mexicali, Los Angeles, Phoenix, and Las Vegas. Twenty-five million people now depend on the Colorado River.
- To solve water shortage problems, some cities have purchased water from farmers so that it can be used in urban areas (about 85 percent of the river's water is currently used for agriculture).

- States in the Lower Basin are using all of the Colorado River water to which they are entitled. California and Nevada also use surplus water that the Upper Basin is not currently using.
- States in the Upper Basin are not using their full allocation, but drought and growing populations have caused them to look at fully developing their Colorado River water rights.
- The environmental movement has raised awareness of the effects that development of Colorado River water has had on species living in the basin. In less than one hundred years, the river ecosystem has been dramatically changed, bringing several species to the brink of extinction. To counteract this, managers try to maintain a minimum flow in some rivers in the basin.
- The United States Endangered Species Act requires water managers in the United States to consider the needs of endangered species when making management decisions.
- The highly productive fishery of the Upper Gulf of California and rich biodiversity of the Colorado River Delta depend on inflows from the river.
- Recreation and tourism have become major industries in the watershed. Fishing, boating, hiking, and hunting bring billions of dollars to the region each year. To meet these new demands, some states and cities have designated instream flows for wildlife and for recreation.

Water Management

8–4–1, One for All: The Colorado River

How many ways do you use the Colorado River? How many different types of water users can you think of?

Grade Level:
6–8

Subject Areas:
Government, Environmental Science, Geography, Economics

Duration:
Preparation time: 40 minutes
Activity time: 60 minutes

Setting:
Large Indoor Area or Outdoors

Skills:
Work with Team, Organize, Communicate, Negotiate, Evaluate

Vocabulary:
consumptive use, direct water use, headwaters, indirect water use, main stem, mouth of stream, nonconsumptive use, nonpoint source pollution (NPS), point source pollution, watershed, water user

Summary
Eight students, representing eight different water users, must safely carry a can of water "downstream" through simulated water management challenges to the next community of water users on the "river."

Objectives
Students will:
- demonstrate the interconnectedness of water users in a community and a watershed;
- demonstrate the complexity of sharing the water;
- negotiate how to move past water management challenges along the river.

Materials
- *1 soup can or small coffee can three-quarters full of water*
- *8 pieces of string of equal length, about 5' each*
- *2 or 3 rubber bands large enough to securely hold the can* (you only need one; the extras are in case it breaks)
- *3 pieces of rope, string, or poles each at least 6' long*
- *4 or more chairs*
- *10 pieces of string of various lengths with pieces of paper* (any size) *tied to one end*
- *Masking tape or chalk*
- *Nametags that hang on necks of students and a marker*

Background
We can't manage the Colorado River Watershed well until we know who the water users are, what their rights are, and how to collectively deal with

Justin Howe

Commercial river trips in the Grand Canyon are a multi-million dollar industry and an important recreational use of water.

Navajo Generating Station, a coal-burning power plant near Page, Arizona, uses water to cool generators as it produces electricity.

common water management challenges (e.g., flooding, drought, population growth, endangered species, etc.).

These challenges affect us all, and any decisions made to solve a water dilemma must consider everyone in the watershed. We recognize that water is important to all water users. We identify eight main categories of water users. They are business and industry, earth systems (e.g. wetlands and forests), energy, fish and wildlife, cultures, recreation, agriculture, and urban (cities and towns).

Water user groups use water in different ways. A shared goal of watershed managers is to meet the water needs of individuals and groups whenever possible. This goal presents a major challenge.

Even tiny insects are water users that require the 4 Rs: the right amount of water at the right cost, the right time, and the right quality.

To satisfy the water needs of any water user, the 4 Rs of water management must be considered. The 4 Rs are the **right amount**, the **right cost**, the **right time**, and the **right quality**. With only one river to support eight water users, communication and teamwork are essential. People, plants, animals, and ecosystems depend on it.

The **right amount** means enough water to sustain life. For humans, this is about eight glasses of water per day. For a cottonwood tree, it may be much more. Recreationists need enough water to raft, kayak, or fish. Agricultural needs vary according to region and crop. Farmers in Grand Junction, Colorado, use less water than those in the Imperial Valley, California, because temperatures are lower and soil types are differ-

ent. Manufacturers of goods from paper to power require water for production. Growing cities use about three hundred gallons per household per day, but this varies by region. Although the quantity needed by each water user may vary greatly on the surface, the interconnections between different users bind us all.

The **right cost** means that water must be inexpensive enough to use. For example, a marina constructs boat ramps, docks, and buildings for recreational boaters. If the river or reservoir level drops significantly, the marina may have to spend money to lengthen or move the ramp. For an industry, the right cost may involve elaborate purification methods to collect, treat, use, and return water back to the river. For animals, the cost might be migration to a new watering hole or dormancy deep in the mud. For a plant, it could mean closing down the stomata and suffering stunted growth due to a lack of carbon dioxide and, therefore, photosynthesis. Some plants, such as the saguaro cactus, are adapted to store water for use when it is scarce. All water users have some cost associated with the water they use directly or indirectly.

The **right time** means water must be available when it is needed. People generally consume water based on thirst, and their bodies are unable to store excess water for use at a later time. People can become dehydrated in just a few hours. It has been shown that test scores improve when students are properly hydrated—even our brains need water! Migrating birds follow the Colorado River and its tributaries so they can drink as they pass through the dry desert. Plants like the honey mesquite need water during the spring so their seeds can germinate. Energy producers require a steady availability of water to rotate turbines and cool motors. Farmers throughout the Colorado River Basin need the right amount of water at the right time: enough to germinate seeds and not so much that they are washed away.

The **right quality** of water is an important factor to water users. All life depends on enough clean water at the right time and right price. Humans need drinking water that is free of bacteria, viruses, and toxins, but not everyone can turn on the tap and know the water is safe. Plants and animals cannot build purification facilities—they must rely on natural processes to clean the water and use that which is available in their environment. Energy producers can often make use of water other users can't, sometimes using recycled water from other users. If water contains a healthy balance of dissolved oxygen and nutrients—and few contaminants—it can support abundant and diverse aquatic life including algae, microscopic organisms, and macroinvertebrates. These organisms form the cornerstone of the aquatic food web that extends to fish, birds, and the mammals that feed on them.

Sometimes conflicts arise between water users.

An example in the Colorado Watershed is the struggle to manage water stored by Glen Canyon Dam and used to generate power when it is released back to the Colorado River. Hydroelectric power generators need to be able to change the amount of water released from the dam according to daily power demand. In contrast, commercial rafting companies on the river in Grand Canyon (below the dam) need the level of flow in the river to remain relatively constant so that they can safely run rapids and camp on beaches. Ecosystems, fish and wildlife, and other water users also have varying needs for the amount, quality, timing, and cost of the water that is released from the dam. These water users must work together to develop solutions and compromises to satisfy multiple needs (see page 35, *Adaptive Management Work Group* sidebar).

Procedure
Preparation
1. **Make eight nametags representing water users.** Label the nametags as follows: Urban Use, Recreation, Earth Systems, Business and Industry, Cultures, Fish and Wildlife, Agriculture, and Energy Production.

2. **Tie eight strings to rubber band.** Water users will place rubber band with strings attached around the can. They will then carry the can by holding the strings and gently lifting together. Test the rubber band to make sure it is the proper tension—too loose and it will not hold the can—too tight and the can will not fall or the rubber band will break (see page 275 illustration).

3. **Lay out a "river" on the floor or ground using a rope, tape, or chalk.** Label communities along the path of the "river." Students exchange the can at each of these communities (see page 276 illustration).

4. **Make water management challenges.** The four obstacles are drought, flood, endangered species, and pollution. Drought is represented by a rope the water users will pass under; flood is

a rope they must travel over; endangered species is a zigzag path between chairs they must pass through; pollution is a rope above their heads holding strings with attached paper that they must pass through. Students whose community is waiting can help hold the "obstacles."

Warm Up

1. **Give students three minutes to list as many ways they use water as they can think of.** Ask for several students to share their answers, and then discuss similarities and differences in the answers. Ask the students how they think riding in a car, reading a newspaper, and turning on a light are connected to water. Discuss direct (e.g., drinking a glass of water) and indirect (e.g., eating vegetables grown using water) uses of water.

2. **Ask students to guess how much water is required to make each of the items listed in the box.** Do not give them the answers until after the activity is completed.

3. **List the eight water user groups on the board (business and industry, earth systems, energy, fish and wildlife, cultures, recreation, agriculture, and urban).** As a class, brainstorm specific water users for each category (for example, coal mine, wetland ecosystem, hydroelectric plant, rainbow trout, American Indian tribe, rafting company, lettuce farm, city swimming pool). Brainstorm examples of how the products in each category relate to the

students' lives.

4. **Ask students if they know what communities are upstream and downstream from them.** How is water use in one community connected to that of another?

The Activity

1. **Briefly discuss with the students the concept of 4 Rs—right amount, right cost, right time, and right quality.** With only one river to support all of the eight water users' needs, teamwork and cooperation are essential. Notify students that in the activity *Wrap Up* they will be asked to consider the 4 Rs and how they relate to the challenges along the river.

2. **Explain the significance of the river and obstacles you have made.**

3. **Divide the class into four groups of eight.** Each group represents a community on the river. Assign remaining students roles as obstacle helpers. Give each group a name. You may number the communities one through four or you may name them according to communities in your area. If you have too few students, you can reduce the number of communities or have one student represent several water users.

4. **In the first community, have each student select one of the eight water user categories that he or she will represent (urban use, recreation, earth systems, business and industry, cultures, fish and wildlife,**

ITEM	AMOUNT OF WATER
A pair of jeans made from cotton	1,800 gallons (6,840 liters)
A two-pound loaf of bread	1,000 gallons (3,800 liters)
A pound of hamburger	4,000 gallons (15,200 liters)
A twelve-ounce can of soda	16.5 gallons (62.7 liters)
Finished steel for one car	32,000 gallons (121,600 liters)
Forty sheets of paper	100 gallons (380 liters)

agriculture, and energy production). Give the students their water user nametags and show them where to stand. As the communities carry the water down the "river," water users will give their nametag to the next water user.

5. **Place Community One before the first obstacle, Community Two between the first and second obstacle, Community Three between the second and third, and Community Four between the third and fourth (see page 276 illustration).**

6. **Direct Community One to stand in a circle.** Place the can three-quarters full of water on the floor in the middle of the circle, with the strings tied to the rubber band that is lying next to the can. There should be eight strings, one end lying in front of each water user. Direct the students to carefully pick up the strings and utilize teamwork to stretch the rubber band, fit it over the can, slowly release tension on their string to tighten the rubber band round the can, and work together to lift the can (see page 275 illustration). Remind them that, if any one water user pulls too hard, the can will fall out of its loop. They must work as a team to pass through the drought (under the rope) and hand off the water to the next community downstream.

7. **Have students from Community One hand off their ropes and nametags to Community Two as the water moves downstream through the flood obstacle.** Do not allow the can to touch the floor. Repeat this process for Communities Three and Four in turn, for endangered species and pollution. Reinforce the concept that working together may be difficult, but if the water needs of community members are going to be consistently met, it will take significant teamwork, effort, communication, and time.

Wrap Up

1. **Discuss the results of the activity.** How much water was left in the can at the mouth of the river? Where did they experience the most trouble? What did they learn about the eight water users, four water needs, and one river? How was communication important for delivering the water? What do they know about specific water users? What are different interpretations of the 4 Rs?

2. **Inform students of the quantities of water used to produce the materials listed in the *Warm Up*.** Do any of the water users from this activity make or use these products? If community water supply and demand are out of balance, how will they resolve the issue? Would they reduce one of the water users' supply? Or would they find another solution?

3. **Have students analyze the challenges that they faced as they moved the can of water down the river.** As a class, discuss which of the 4 Rs relates to each obstacle—right amount, right cost, right time, or right quality.

4. **Finish by having each student write a one- to two-page paper telling what *8–4–1, One for All* means.** They should briefly define each water user, the 4 Rs, and sharing one river. Ask them to add an epilogue discussing their personal feelings about how communities throughout a watershed can improve the ways they share water.

Assessment

Have students:

- analyze their direct and indirect water uses (***Warm Up***, Step 1);
- define eight water users and connect them to their lives (***Warm Up***, Step 3);
- discuss the strategies used by community groups to allow eight water users to meet the 4 Rs and share one river (***The Activity***, Steps 2–7);
- discuss how challenges in one community affect another (***Wrap Up***, Step 1);

- write about how the eight categories of water users must work together when using water (**Wrap Up**, Step 4).

Extensions

Write the names of the eight water users on slips of paper. Have each group draw two to four slips of paper, and eliminate those water users from their group. When they make it past the obstacle to the next community, ask them to discuss how carrying the water was different with fewer water users. Then ask them to list what products or services the community loses along with the missing water users and discuss the impacts.

Change the length of the string to some water users, indicating a greater distance to the river or that a smaller supply of water is going to them. Discuss the effect this creates when the team tries to carry the can.

Resources

The Watercourse. 2002. *Discover a Watershed: Watershed Manager.* Bozeman, MT: The Watercourse.

Wolfe, Mary Ellen. 1996. *A Landowner's Guide to Western Water Rights.* Boulder, CO: Roberts Rinehart Publishers.

e-links

International Boundary and Water Commission, United States and Mexico Section
Information about the management of water between the United States and Mexico.
www.ibwc.state.gov

Mexican National Water Commission (Comisión Nacional del Agua)
Information about water resources in Mexico.
www.cna.gob.mx

United States Environmental Protection Agency
Information about types of water use in the United States.
www.epa.gov/watrhome/you/chap1.html

8–4-1, One for All Set-Up

1. Eight strings tied to a large rubber band.

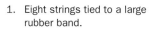

2. Each person steps back to expand opening; then the whole group lowers the rubber band over the can.

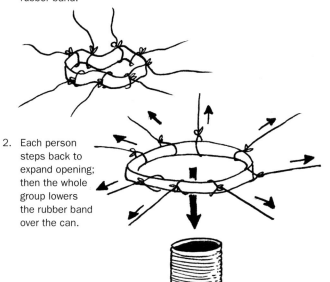

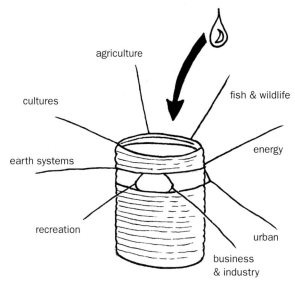

agriculture

cultures

fish & wildlife

earth systems

energy

recreation

urban

business & industry

4. Fill the can 3/4 full of water

3. Each person releases tension on their string to fit the rubber band tightly around the can.

5. Carefully lift the can of water.

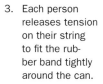

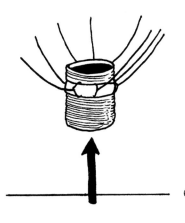

6. As a group, work together to transport the water through the obstacle course.

8–4–1, One for All Set-Up

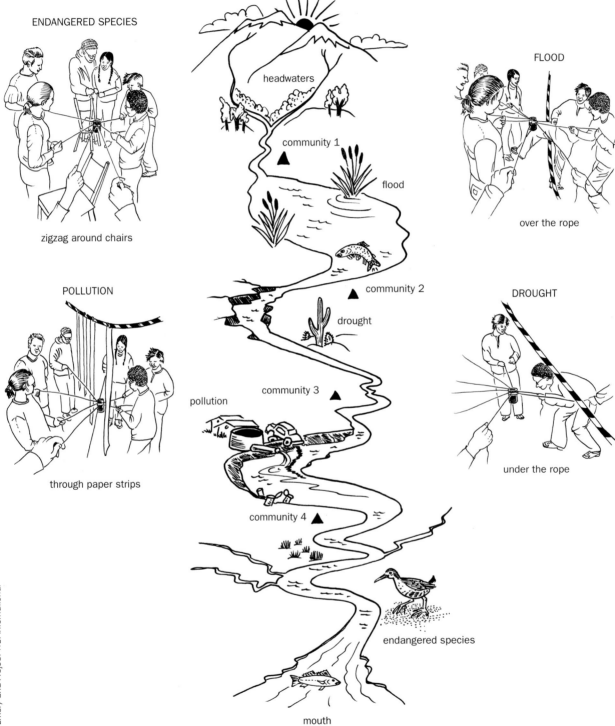

ENDANGERED SPECIES

zigzag around chairs

POLLUTION

through paper strips

headwaters

community 1

flood

community 2

drought

community 3

pollution

community 4

endangered species

mouth

FLOOD

over the rope

DROUGHT

under the rope

Plumbing the Colorado

How does water use in Wyoming affect river flow in Sonora?

Grade Level:
6–12

Subject Areas:
Geography, Government, Environmental Science, Math

Duration:
Preparation time: 40 minutes
Activity time: 60 minutes

Setting:
Classroom or Outdoors

Skills:
Demonstrate, Discuss, Examine, Identify, Measure, Add, Subtract

Vocabulary:
aqueduct, concentration (of a solution), confluence, desalination, delta, dissolve, diversion, evaporation, headwaters, main stem, mouth of stream, reservoir (water), runoff, salinity, snowmelt, snowpack, suspension, tributary

Summary
Students examine the Colorado River system and demonstrate changes in river flow that occur as the river travels from source to sea.

Objectives
Students will:
- demonstrate water inputs and outputs of the Colorado River system;
- gain an increased awareness of water users on the Colorado River, including those outside their geographic area;
- identify the source, tributaries, and mouth of the river;
- recognize that balancing the needs of all water users is difficult.

Materials
- *Copies of the **Plumbing the Colorado** Student Copy Page (1 per student)*
- *5 buckets or storage containers*
- *Index cards (60)*
- *Permanent marker*
- ***Colorado River Watershed Wall Map** or copies of the **Major Dams and Diversions Map** (page XXII)*
- *Masking tape or sidewalk chalk*
- *2 sets of measuring cups (one cup, one-half cup, one-third cup, one-fourth cup)*
- *Water*
- *Optional: several long tablecloths or tarps*

Background
The waters of the Colorado River are hard working. A visit to the Colorado River Delta tells the story of a river that has served the needs of countless people, plants, and animals. Venture to the mouth of the river, and you will see nothing but

Justin Howe

The channel of the Colorado River is usually dry below Morelos Dam, due to the many diversions upstream.

Justin Howe

This structure at the head of the Grand Valley Irrigation Ditch, near Grand Junction, Colorado, diverts up to six hundred cfs from the Colorado River for agricultural, residential, and industrial use.

Salt Lake City, Albuquerque, Los Angeles, San Diego, and Tijuana pump water out of the watershed for the same purpose.

So great is the demand for Colorado River water that water is diverted even before the river begins. In Rocky Mountain National Park, at the head-waters of the Colorado River, the Grand Ditch cuts across the steep slopes of the Never Summer Mountains. Snowmelt and rain runoff are gathered before they reach the river and diverted across the Continental Divide for use on Colorado's eastern slope. Just ten miles further down the Colorado, another diversion, the Big Thompson Project, collects water and sends it to the communities in northern Colorado.

On the Duchesne River, which feeds into the Green River, the Central Utah Project directs water under mountains to provide water for residents of Salt Lake City and Provo. Similar diversions are found throughout the basin. Sonora is the only state in the watershed that does not divert water out of the basin. Every state uses water from the basin to drink, irrigate crops, meet industrial and business needs, provide recreation opportunities, support fish and wildlife, and generate energy. Before dams were built, steamships carried goods and people as far upriver as Black Canyon, near where Hoover Dam stands today.

rippling sand—the "plumbing" system has removed all the water.

Roughly 25 million people rely on the Colorado River, yet much of the watershed is unpopulated. This paradox is explained by the intricate plumbing system that diverts water to waiting cities and farms above the river or outside the watershed. Las Vegas, Phoenix, and Tucson all pump water uphill to supply water users. Denver,

Diversions for irrigation and urban use are found throughout the watershed, but the largest are found in the Lower Basin (see ***Colorado River Watershed Wall Map*** and page XXII, ***Major Dams and Diversions Map***). The All American Canal, Coachella Canal, and Colorado River Aqueduct in California together divert 25 to 30 percent of the annual flow of the river. Arizona has rights to about 19 percent. Most of Arizona's

Justin Howe

Turbines at Glen Canyon Dam use the Colorado River to generate electricity.

Used by permission of the Imperial Irrigation District

Junction of Cerro Prieto Canal (right) and West Side Main Canal (left) in January 1919.

share is taken through the Central Arizona Project, which delivers water to the Phoenix and Tucson areas. Arizona also diverts water for agricultural use by the Colorado River Indian Tribes (near Parker) and irrigators in the Yuma Valley.

Much of Arizona's water use does not come from its Colorado River allocation, but from tributaries to the Colorado. This is because Colorado River water law says that tributaries in Lower Basin states are not part of the compact, so their water

does not have to be included as part of a state's allocation. This has important ramifications, as it means there is more water available to these states. In Arizona's Yuma Valley alone, a total of 6.5 maf is used—more than twice the state's total allocation of water from the Colorado River.

By law, Mexico must receive 1.5 million acre-feet of Colorado River water each year. This water is diverted from the river for use in irrigation and to meet urban needs. About 65,000 acre-feet are pumped to Tijuana each year. The remainder is used to meet water needs in the Mexicali Valley of Baja California and San Luis Valley of Sonora (see page 244, "Sharing the Shed").

As the river makes its way south, diversions reduce its flow. It is also diminished by evaporation due to hot temperatures and low humidity. Reservoirs such as Flaming Gorge, Lake Powell, and Lake Mead spread water and increase the surface area, thus increasing evaporation. Lake Powell alone is estimated to evaporate up to 1 million acre-feet of water per year.

Despite problems like evaporation, dams and reservoirs are an important part of the Colorado River plumbing system. In addition to providing water storage, hydroelectric power, and flood protection, they also contribute to economies by providing recreational opportunities. Indeed, without the water storage provided by reservoirs, there would not be enough water in the river in most years to meet all of the allocations.

The plumbing of the Colorado River has made it possible for humans to live and prosper in the arid southwestern United States and northwestern Mexico. But the benefits of plumbing the river have not come without costs. Dams alter the flow

The Central Arizona Project canal carries water from the Colorado River to central Arizona through a series of canals, tunnels, and reservoirs. The water it carries supports life for people, plants, and animals living there.

of water to which plants, animals, and fishes are adapted. As a result, several species are on the verge of extinction and the ecology of many areas has changed. The ecosystems of the Colorado River Delta, which were created and supported by nutri-ent-rich flows from the Colorado River, are some of the most changed (see page 126, "Go with the Flow," and page 211, "Chillin' with the Chubs").

Procedure
Preparation
1. **In the schoolyard or classroom, create a floor model using the *Plumbing the Colorado Student Copy Page* as a guide.** You may use chalk or masking tape. It is easiest to draw the

main stem of the Colorado River first. Use a color that is different from other features on the model. Blue masking tape is available at most hardware stores. You can also create the model on several long tablecloths or tarps joined together, which will allow you to reuse the model.

2. **Label the Colorado River and the Gulf of California as well as all tributaries, diversions, and reservoirs, using chalk or by writing on index cards taped to the diagram.** It is helpful to number each location to match the chart provided on the *Plumbing the Colorado Student Copy Page*.

3. **Use index cards to make a set of student role cards that matches the labels you have made for the floor model and buckets.** These cards will be divided among the students and will identify which river, diversion, or dam each student will represent.

4. **Make labels for buckets that will transport the water.** They should read: 1) Colorado River, 2) Colorado River Supply Bucket, 3) Green River, 4) Green River Supply Bucket, 5) Colorado River Delta and the Gulf of California. Tape these labels to the buckets.

5. **Use index cards to make student role cards that match the labels made for the buckets (five cards total).** These cards can be intermixed with the other student role cards.

Warm Up
1. **Ask students to brainstorm ways water is used.** Have them write down their ideas.

2. **List eight categories of water use on the chalkboard.** They are: urban, recreation, earth systems (e.g. wetlands and forests), business and industry, cultures, fish and wildlife, rural agriculture, and energy (see page 268, "8–4–1, One for All: The Colorado River"). Discuss how water might be used in each category.

3. **Have students read the water uses they identified during their brainstorm.** Write them on the board under the categories you have listed. Why do some categories have more uses listed than others? Does that mean that some categories are more important than others? Why or why not? Invite class to add more water uses if they see any that are missing.

4. **Explain that the "plumbing" of the Colorado River allows people to distribute and use Colorado River water.** The plumbing system is particularly important in the Colorado River Watershed because much of the area through which the river flows is desert. By using dams and diversions, humans are able to live and grow crops where it would otherwise have been very difficult. For example, the area around the U.S./Mexico border receives three to four inches of rain per year, yet it is one of the most productive agricultural areas in North America. This productivity is made possible by irrigation water diverted from the Colorado River.

The Activity

1. **Introduce the *Colorado River Watershed Wall Map* or hand out copies of the *Major Dams and Diversions Map* (page XXII).** Explain that the map shows some of the major rivers, reservoirs, dams, and diversions of the watershed.

2. **Direct students' attention to the floor model you have made.** Show where major features from the floor model are located on the *Wall Map* or *Dams and Diversions Map.* Point out the main stem of the Colorado as well as the tributaries, reservoirs, and diversions. Explain that tributaries add water to the river and that diversions take water from the river for use in irrigation, drinking, industry, and other uses. Reservoirs are used to store water for use in times of drought. Much of the Colorado Basin is very

hot. This means that some of the water stored in reservoirs evaporates before it is released.

3. **Show students the location of Lee's Ferry and the United States/Mexico border.** These are legal water divisions in the Colorado River Watershed. Lee's Ferry is the dividing line between the Upper and Lower Basins. In the United States, water users above Lee's Ferry are entitled to 7.5 million acre-feet of water each year. American water users below Lee's Ferry have rights to that same amount. The United States/Mexico border is also important in managing flow in the Colorado River, as a treaty between the two countries says that the United States must send 1.5 million acre-feet of Colorado River water to Mexico each year.

4. **Tell students that they are going to simulate the amounts of water that enter and leave the Colorado River Watershed as it flows from its headwaters to its mouth at the Gulf of California.**

5. **Hand out the student cards that correspond to labels on the diagram (one per student).** Some students may need to share or double up on locations, depending on class size. Explain that each card represents a place where water is added to or removed from the Colorado River.

6. **Ask students to gather around the floor model.** Tell them that each branch off of the main stem represents where water enters or exits the river. Branches with arrows pointing toward the river are tributaries that carry snowmelt and rain water to the Colorado. Branches with arrows pointing away from the river represent places where large amounts of water are withdrawn or evaporated from the river.

7. **Direct students' attention to the buckets at the beginning of the Green and Colorado Rivers (the headwaters).** The water in these buckets represents water carried in the Green and Colorado Rivers. Explain that now they are empty, because they need snow or rain to bring water into the system.

8. **Tell students that the buckets at the headwaters will be carried down the river to mimic the flow of water in the Colorado River Watershed.**

9. **Explain how the demonstration will work.** Water will be added and subtracted by students representing places where water enters or exits the river.

10. **Ask the five students with water supply bucket or river bucket cards to find their respective buckets.** These students will carry the buckets along their respective rivers, stopping at each tributary, diversion, or reservoir to allow water to be added to or subtracted from the river buckets. Water added to or taken from the river buckets will be taken from or added to the supply buckets.

11. **At each tributary, diversion, or reservoir, have the students with corresponding card and number add to or subtract water from the river bucket.** Use the measuring cup for this. Note that the Big Thompson Project, Central Utah Project, Colorado River Aqueduct, and All American Canal are all diversions that transfer water out of the watershed. The Central Arizona Project is entirely within the Colorado Watershed, but it pumps water thousands of feet uphill from the river to meet water needs in the Phoenix and Tucson areas.

12. **When the buckets from the headwaters of the Green and Colorado Rivers meet at the confluence, have the student carrying water from the Green River pour it into the Colorado bucket.** The two students carrying river buckets can then carry the Colorado bucket together.

13. **Be sure to note when the buckets pass Lee's Ferry and the U.S./Mexican border.**

14. **When the buckets reach the Gila and San Pedro Rivers, note that no water is added.** This is because most of the water flowing in these rivers is used before it can reach the Colorado. Note also that the San Pedro River begins in the Mexican state of Sonora. Its flow is stopped by ground water pumping before it reaches the Gila River (for more on the interaction between surface and ground water, see page 140, "Basin in a Bottle"). The San Pedro is the only Mexican river that adds water to the Colorado River Watershed.

15. **When the "river" reaches the delta, have students pour the contents of the Colorado River Bucket into the one marked "Colorado River Delta and the Gulf of California."** There should not be any water left for this bucket. All the water has been used upriver. This is what happens to the Colorado River most years. Only during extremely wet years does water flow all the way to the Gulf of California.

Wrap Up

1. **Discuss what might happen as populations in the Colorado Watershed and the cities that rely on its water continue to grow.** Where will the water come from? Currently, some areas are using ground water or water from other watersheds to meet needs, but even these water supplies are limited. Will new technology be used to supply water? Some areas are considering using desalination to remove salt from seawater and salty water from underground aquifers. This process is expensive and energy intensive. Other areas are encouraging conservation to stretch current water supplies. Los Angeles and San Diego, which receive water through the Colorado River Aqueduct, plan on leasing Colorado River water currently being used for agriculture in the Imperial Valley. Since agriculture requires much more water than urban uses, this seems like a good solution for the time being. However, the food grown in the Imperial Valley is important economically and helps feed millions of people.

Still another method used is water banking. In one form of water banking, unused water is allowed to seep into aquifers so that it can be pumped to the surface for use in dry times. In another form of water banking, communities use surface water as much as possible, saving water already in aquifers for use in dry times (see page 140, "Basin in a Bottle").

2. **Ask students to discuss what would happen in wet or dry years.** During wet years, excess water is stored in reservoirs for use during dry periods. This is why, even though some reservoir water is lost to evaporation, reservoirs have been built. During very wet periods, reservoirs can be totally filled. When this happens, water flows all the way to the Gulf of California. Extended drought could empty all the reservoirs, leaving many water users without water. This has not happened since dams were built on the Colorado.

3. **Expand the discussion to talk about the watershed in general.** What are some of the ways that Colorado River water is used? Make a connection between the categories discussed in the **Warm Up** and actual places in the watershed (for example, recreation on Lake Powell). How is the climate different in the Upper Basin than in the Lower Basin? How might this affect the availability and use of water?

4. **Discuss the effects of the plumbing of the Colorado River on fish and wildlife.** Dams and diversions have regulated the flow of the Colorado River. This has changed habitat in and around the river. Below dams, fish that were adapted to river sediment and floods are being forced out by nonnative species that are adapted to the new conditions. Along the banks, new plant species have established themselves. At the delta, aquatic organisms adapted to the sediment carried in the water of the Colorado River are dying out. At the same time, the plumbing of the Colorado has made it possible for millions of people to live in an otherwise desert environment. (See page 126, "Go with the Flow," and page 211, "Chillin' with the Chubs.")

Assessment

Have students:

- identify and categorize water users (**Warm Up**, Steps 1–3);
- examine the geography of the Colorado River with regard to the main stem, tributaries, dams, and diversions (Steps 1–3);
- demonstrate the addition and withdrawal of water from the Colorado River (Steps 4–15);
- discuss how increasing population and corresponding demand for water will affect Colorado River water use and management (**Wrap Up**, Step 1);
- use what they have learned to hypothesize about what would happen during wet or dry years (**Wrap Up**, Step 2);
- discuss where in the basin the water uses identified in the **Warm Up** might occur (**Wrap Up**, Step 3);
- discuss the effects of the allocation of the Colorado River on fish and wildlife (**Wrap Up**, Step 4).

Extensions

Salinity is an important issue in the Colorado Watershed. Demonstrate how salinity increases as the river flows southward. Explain that much of the salt in the Colorado River originates in Colorado and Utah (see Part I, page 58). Water flowing through salty soil dissolves the minerals and carries them in the water. Since the salts are dissolved rather than suspended (floating) in the water, the only way they can be removed is through evaporation or expensive treatment called desalination. This means that, once salt is in the water, most of it remains there. Salt is an important mineral when it is in low quantities, but when there is too much, it can kill plants, fish, and animals. In the Lower Basin, relatively little fresh water is added to the

Colorado River and hot temperatures evaporate lots of water. Since salt remains after evaporation, the concentration of salt in the river goes up.

By the time the Colorado reaches Mexico, salinity is about fourteen times greater than it is at the headwaters. To demonstrate the difference in concentration, show the class two small, clear bottles of water. Place one drop of green food coloring in the first. Although dissolved salt cannot be seen, the food coloring helps visualize how much salt is in the river. Explain that this drop represents the level of salinity at the headwaters. Place fourteen drops of "salt" (color) in the second bottle. Explain that this bottle represents the amount of salt in water at the end of the river.

Ask the students to discuss salinity in the river. How might it affect people, plants, and animals? Humans and animals are affected because salt changes the way their cells store water. They will die if they have too much salt. Plants have varying tolerance to salt. Cattails, for example, can live in saline water (see photo, page 63, Ciénaga de Santa Clara cattails). Wheat, on the other hand, cannot. How might high salinity affect the use of water in the southern basin? As salinity increases, plant growth is stunted and more water is required to achieve the same growth that would occur with water that is less salty. Salt also builds up in soils irrigated with the saline water. To combat this build-up, farmers flush large amounts of water through the fields to remove the salt.

Have students design and conduct an experiment to test how varying levels of salinity in water affects the growth of plants.

Resources

Debuys, William and Joan Mayers. 2001. *Salt Dreams: Land and Water in Low-Down California*. Albuquerque: University of New Mexico Press.

Colorado River Water Map. Sacramento, CA: The Water Education Foundation.

Bergman, Charles. 2002. *Red Delta: Fighting for Life at the End of the Colorado River*. Boulder, CO: Fulcrum Publishing.

The Water Education Foundation. 1999. *Colorado River Project Symposium Proceedings September 16–18, 1999*. Sacramento, CA: The Water Education Foundation.

The Water Education Foundation. 2004. *Hydroexplorer*. Sacramento, CA: The Water Education Foundation.

e-Links

Colorado River Water Users Association
Information about water users in the Colorado Watershed.
www.crwua.org

Comisión Nacional del Agua
Information about water projects and use in Mexico.
www.cna.gob.mx

The Colorado Foundation for Water Education
Information about the Colorado River and other water issues associated with the state of Colorado.
www.cfwe.org

Southern Nevada Water Authority
Information about allocation and use of the Colorado River.
www.snwa.com

The Water Education Foundation
Purchase the Hydroexplorer, a computer program for five- to ten-year-olds that teaches about water conservation, pollution prevention, the hydrologic cycle, and how water gets to the home.
www.watereducation.org/store

Plumbing the Colorado

Number	Place/Role Cards	Add	Remove
	Green River		
1	Green River Bucket		
2	Green River Supply Bucket		
3	Green River Headwaters	4 1/3	
4	Flaming Gorge Reservoir		- 1/2
5	Central Utah Project		- 1/2
6	Duchesne River	1	
7	Price River	1	
	Colorado River above Lee's Ferry		
8	Colorado River Bucket		
9	Colorado River Supply Bucket		
10	Colorado River Headwaters	4 1/3	
11	Big Thompson Project		-1
12	Gunnison River	1	
13	Dolores River	1	
14	Lake Powell Reservoir		-1
15	San Juan River	2	
	Colorado River below Lee's Ferry		
16	Little Colorado River	1	
17	Lake Mead Reservoir		-1 1/4
18	Virgin River	1/3	
19	Las Vegas Intake		- 2/3
20	Lake Havasu Reservoir		-1
21	Colorado River Aqueduct		-1 1/3
22	Central Arizona Project		-1 1/2
23	Colorado River Indian Tribes		-1
24	Yuma Irrigation Districts		- 3/4
25	Coachella Canal		-1
26	All American Canal		-3
27	Gila River	0	
28	San Pedro River	0	
	Colorado River in Mexico		
29	Canal Independencia		-1 1/4
30	Colorado River - Tijuana Aqueduct		- 1/4
31	Colorado River Delta and the Gulf of California		
	Total	16	-16

Plumbing the Colorado

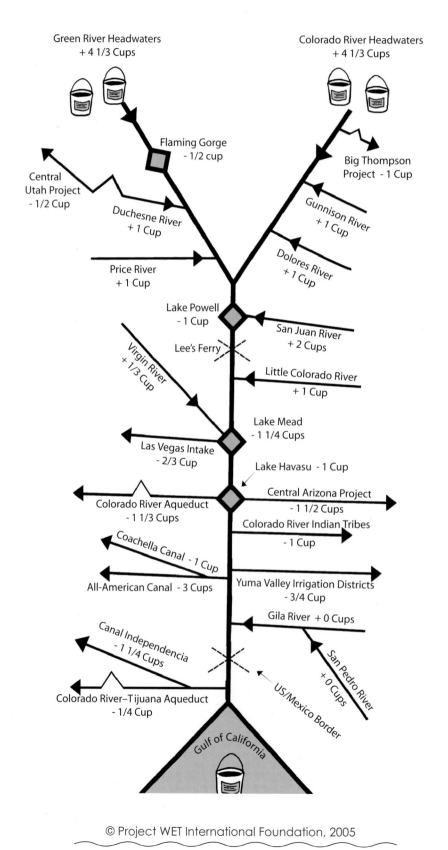

Green River Headwaters + 4 1/3 Cups

Colorado River Headwaters + 4 1/3 Cups

Flaming Gorge - 1/2 cup

Big Thompson Project - 1 Cup

Central Utah Project - 1/2 Cup

Gunnison River + 1 Cup

Duchesne River + 1 Cup

Dolores River + 1 Cup

Price River + 1 Cup

Lake Powell - 1 Cup

San Juan River + 2 Cups

Lee's Ferry

Virgin River + 1/3 Cup

Little Colorado River + 1 Cup

Lake Mead - 1 1/4 Cups

Las Vegas Intake - 2/3 Cup

Lake Havasu - 1 Cup

Central Arizona Project - 1 1/2 Cups

Colorado River Aqueduct - 1 1/3 Cups

Colorado River Indian Tribes - 1 Cup

Coachella Canal - 1 Cup

All-American Canal - 3 Cups

Yuma Valley Irrigation Districts - 3/4 Cup

Gila River + 0 Cups

Canal Independencia - 1 1/4 Cups

San Pedro River + 0 Cups

Colorado River–Tijuana Aqueduct - 1/4 Cup

US/Mexico Border

Gulf of California

First Come, First Served

How do new and old water users share a river? Are some uses more important than others?

Grade Level:
7–12

Subject Areas:
Environmental Science, Math, History/Anthropology, Economics, Government

Duration:
Preparation time: 15 minutes
Activity time: 60–90 minutes

Setting:
Classroom

Skills:
Role-play, Discuss, Analyze, Evaluate, Problem Solve, Graph

Vocabulary:
allocation, beneficial use, compact, consumptive use, diversion, federal reserved water right, instream flow, international water treaty, interstate water compact, Law of the River, Lower Basin, nonconsumptive use, *prelación*, public interest, prior appropriation doctrine, Upper Basin, water rights, Winters Doctrine

Summary
Students role-play various scenarios of competing water use as they learn about water rights, the "Law of the River," the principles of prior appropriation and beneficial use, and the Mexican water distribution system of *prelación*.

Objectives
Students will:
- describe the principles of prior appropriation and beneficial use;
- compare systems of water allocation used by Mexico and the United States;
- discuss how the "Law of the River" affects water users in the United States and Mexico;
- role-play to demonstrate how water is allocated through prior appropriation and *prelación*;
- evaluate current water management practices;
- develop solutions to water management challenges such as drought;
- analyze their individual and collective water-use values.

Materials
- *1 classroom set of **First Come, First Served Water User Cards** Student Copy Pages* (1 card per student)
- *1 set of **First Come, First Served Water Unit Squares*** (2" x 2" squares of blue paper, enough to fill all of the **Water User Cards** allocations, plus 10 extra)
- *1 classroom set of **First Come, First Served Action Cards** Student Copy Pages*
- *Sticky notes* (3 per student)

Background
The Colorado River is one of the most intensively managed rivers in North America. Because it is a

Morelos Dam is the point where Mexico diverts the majority of its share of the Colorado River.

multinational river, shared by two countries and more than thirty American Indian tribes, its management framework is highly complex. Mexico and the United States have very different water management systems.

In Mexico, the constitution establishes water resources as a public good. The federal government manages water rights. Water is distributed according to use (e.g. human consumption, agriculture, industry, support of natural systems, etc.). The Mexican government gives priority to water uses that are in the greatest public interest. This system of allocating water according to use is known as *prelación*.

In 2004, the Mexican congress passed legislation that will decentralize Mexican water law (*Ley de Aguas Nacionales*). The new system will establish watershed-level management. Watershed authorities (*organismos de cuenca*) were created within the National Water Commission, and watershed councils (*consejos de cuenca*) were established to help citizens and local governments participate in water management. Watershed authorities will work closely with watershed councils to determine which

water uses will be given higher priority under the *prelación* of each watershed.

Domestic and urban use will always have first priority, but agriculture, industry, natural systems, etc. can be given varying priority. Under normal circumstances, water will be allocated according to each *prelación*. In the event of disaster, severe drought, overexploitation of aquifers, risks to the environment, etc. the government can impose restrictions in the name of the public interest. This system of management has been adapted from that used by the ancient Romans.

In the United States, the body of rules, treaties, court decisions, and regulations dealing with the management of Colorado River water is referred to as the "Law of the River." There are four basic levels in the Law of the River's allocation scheme. The top level is the U.S.'s obligation to deliver 1.5 million acre-feet of water to Mexico annually. The second level divides water between the Upper and Lower Basins, the third allocates water to each American basin state, and the fourth manages water rights within states.

At the fourth level, water is generally allocated through individual water rights. A water right is defined as the right to use a public resource for a beneficial purpose (e.g., drinking, watering crops, cooling industrial equipment, etc.). Water users in the United States own the right to use a specific quantity of water. That right can be sold, leased, and traded within each state.

Two basic principles underlie water law in the United States' portion of the watershed: beneficial use and prior appropriation. Beneficial use is defined by each state's laws and traditionally has been limited to consumptive uses such as agricultural, domestic, municipal, and industrial. Nonconsumptive uses, including fish and wildlife, recreation, hydropower, and cultural uses, are now

American Water Allocation System

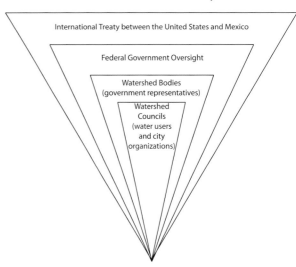

International Treaty between the United States and Mexico

Interstate Compacts (Upper and Lower Basin)

State Allocations
(CO, WY, UT, NM, AZ, NV, CA)

Water Rights
Within States

Mexican Water Allocation System

International Treaty between the United States and Mexico

Federal Government Oversight

Watershed Bodies
(government representatives)

Watershed
Councils
(water users
and city
organizations)

Ground water wells are an important part of water use in the United States and Mexico. In some parts of the watershed, ground water pumping is drying up rivers by lowering the water table. Since it is difficult to determine where well water comes from, managing surface and ground water together can be a challenge.

also considered beneficial uses in some states. Early water rights were established by diverting a certain amount of water from a stream or aquifer and putting it to beneficial use. Today, applications and permits must be filed to establish a new water right.

The doctrine of prior appropriation allocates water according to who first put it to beneficial use. This system is sometimes referred to as "first in time, first in right" because the water user who began using water first has the highest priority, or senior right. In times of shortage, users with senior rights will receive water before those with junior rights. Junior water users may not receive water until senior water users receive their full share. Unlike Mexico, in the United States there is not a set of rules that determines which class of water use must be met first.

If water is not deemed to be put to beneficial use for a certain length of time, the water right may be considered abandoned and terminated. It is important to remember that water right abandonment occurs only at the individual level; if a state in the Colorado Basin is not using its full allocation of water, the allocation is protected by the Law of the River and cannot be taken away or claimed by another state.

Another type of water right that is protected from being considered abandoned if not in use is a federal reserved water right. Federal reserved rights are set aside for federal lands (like national parks) and for American Indian tribes and reservations. The Winters Doctrine of 1908 determined that a tribe's water right date is the same as the date that their reservation was established. Although many tribes have not had their federal reserved water rights quantified, several tribes in the Colorado Basin are in the process of negotiating or have received delivery of water to which they are entitled (e.g., the Navajo Nation, Gila River Indian Community, Tohono O'odham Tribe, Ute Mountain Ute Tribe, and Southern Ute Tribe).

According to the Law of the River, Mexico is allocated 1.5 million acre-feet (maf) per year, the Upper and Lower Basins are each allocated 7.5 maf, and each state within the Upper and Lower Basins is allocated a certain amount. In the Upper Basin, states are allocated water according to the percent of water available. Allocation to states in the Lower Basin is set at a certain amount for each state (see page 11, chart with state allocations).

This difference in the way the river is allocated between Upper Basin and Lower Basin states raises questions for water managers. In the event of a water shortage on the Colorado River, it is not clear whether the shortage would be shared by both basins or whether the Upper Basin would still be required to send the Lower Basin its full allocation. If the latter were the case, states in the Upper Basin would have to reduce their water use while the Lower Basin states would be unaffected.

Most of the river's water is derived from snowmelt in Colorado and Wyoming, so a dry year in these states means that there is less water in the river. So far, storage reservoirs have been able to provide enough water for all states, even in dry years.

On some rivers, the amount allocated to each state varies annually according to the amount of snowpack feeding the headwaters. A state is entitled to a certain percentage of the total amount available. This system has its advantages and disadvantages; in times of drought, water shortages are shared, but it is difficult to administer a fluctuating allocation.

Procedure
Preparation
1. **Cut several sheets of blue construction paper into small squares (approximately 2" x 2").** These are the *Water Unit Squares* (each represents 100 cfs of water from the river). You will need to make enough so that all of the *Water User Cards* can have their allocations met, plus about ten extra water units (the number will vary according to the number of students participating).

2. **Make copies of the *First Come, First Served Water User Cards* so that there are enough for each student to have one card.** Cut the cards into water-user strips and place them in a hat or bag from which students will be able to draw cards. If there are more than ten students in your class, some will need to work together as a team.

3. **Make one copy of the *First Come, First Served Action Cards* and cut the cards into strips.** Keep them separate to give to the Water Commissioner and to new water users.

Warm Up
1. **Tell the students that the basis for water rights in the U.S. portion of the Colorado Basin is the idea of "first in time, first in right."** Everything they need to know to understand this idea, they learned in kindergarten!

2. **Describe the analogy of standing in line to fill your glass at a punch bowl and how it relates to the idea of "first in time, first in right."** The person who got to the bowl first can fill his or her glass first. The person who arrived last can fill his or her glass only if there is punch left after all the other people in line have filled their glasses. In water law,

this system of water allocation is referred to as the doctrine of prior appropriation. Water users that developed uses for water first retain "senior" rights. For example, a farmer that began using Colorado River water in 1899 will have rights that are senior to a farmer that began using Colorado River water in 1950.

3. **Ask students if they think all water uses are equal.** For example, is filling a swimming pool as important as providing water for drinking? What if the first person in line at the punch bowl used half of the drink to cool down? Is that fair to the other water users? To address this problem, water laws in the United States dictate that water must be put to beneficial use. Beneficial uses include drinking, watering crops, cooling industrial machinery, etc. In some states, where recreation is an important part of the economy, instream flows for recreation are considered beneficial use. In Mexico, citizens determine which water uses are most important and allocate water to uses that provide the greatest good (e.g., drinking water would have priority over that used for industry). This rating system is known as *prelación*.

4. **Explain what is meant by the "Law of the River," and how international treaties and interstate compacts have priority over the principles of prior appropriation, beneficial use, and *prelación*.**

5. **Make sure students understand the meaning of the terms cfs (cubic feet per second) and cms (cubic meters per second).** Cubic feet per second and cubic meters per second are used to measure water in motion. One cubic foot contains 7.5 gallons. It is the amount of water that would fill a cube that measures one foot on each side. One cfs is one cubic foot flowing past a certain point each second (100 cfs is 100 cubic feet flowing by per second, and so on). In Mexico, water flow is measured in cubic meters per second (cms). One cubic meter contains 1,000 liters (264 gallons).

The Activity

1. **Tell the students that they are each going to have a role to play in the following water rights game**. Ask for one volunteer to be the Water Commissioner.

2. **Have all students except the Water Commissioner draw *Water User Cards* from the hat or bag.** If you have more than ten students, some will draw the same card and work as a team.

3. **Have students that drew the same *Water User Cards* form teams.**

Colorado River Management in Mexico and the United States

Mexico		United States
The Law of the River dictates Mexico's allocation of the Colorado River.	*(Same)*	The Law of the River dictates the United States' allocation of the Colorado River.
Water rights are a public good, managed by the federal government, which issues water concession titles (water rights) to individuals. Water is allocated according to *prelación*, which assigns priority to different types of use.	*(Different)*	Water rights are held by individual water users (e.g., farmers, cities, irrigation companies, tribes, and homeowners). The principles of prior appropriation and beneficial use are used to administer water rights at the state and local level.

4. **Tell the students that each water user card has a "priority number" based on when their water right was established and a "type of use" classification.** The "priority number" will be used when water (represented by the *Water Unit Squares*) is allocated with the system used in the United States (prior appropriation). The group with priority #1 has the most senior water right (the oldest water right); the student who drew the highest number has the most junior water right. The "type of use" will be used when water is allocated using the Mexican system (*prelación*).

5. **Have students read their cards to determine their role, priority number, type of use, and amount of water to which they are entitled.** Remind the students that these are fictitious water users, but are similar to actual water users in the Colorado Basin.

6. **Round 1 (a year with sufficient streamflow in the United States):** Explain that each blue *Water Unit Square* represents 100 cfs. For the first round, make sure that there are enough *Water Unit Squares* to satisfy the allocation of each water user (represented by an individual or a group) plus ten extra squares (eighty-seven squares total). The extra squares represent water that remains in the stream.

7. **Spread the blue *Water Unit Squares* on the floor to represent the river.** Tell students that they will first allocate the "water" according to the law of prior appropriation as it is applied in the American portion of the Colorado River Watershed.

8. **Have each group collect the number of squares to which they are entitled, according to their *Water User Card*.** Have students representing water users take turns coming forward to collect squares. Water users with senior water rights (lowest priority number) should go first. Two hundred cfs is represented by two squares; three hundred is represented by three squares; and so on.

9. **Ask students what they think of the water rights system so far.** Does everyone feel that he or she is satisfied? Does it seem fair?

10. **Round 2 (a year with sufficient streamflow in Mexico): Have students replace all the *Water Unit Squares*.**

11. **Write on the board which types of water use the citizens of Mexico have assigned highest priority.** Remind students that this system is referred to as *prelación*. The *prelación* for this hypothetical scenario is: 1) drinking water, 2) industry, 3) agriculture, 4) hydroelectric power, 5) natural systems. You may want to explain that these priorities are determined at the watershed level and may change according to needs in different regions. There are many other types of water use that can be given priority ranking in this system.

12. **Have students collect the amount of water their cards dictate.** The water users should take turns collecting the *Water Unit Squares* with users having "types of use" that are first on the *prelación* system going first.

13. **Ask students what they think of this water rights system.** Does everyone seem satisfied? Does it seem fair?

14. **Round 3 (a drought year in the United States): Have students return all of their *Water Unit Squares* to the river, then have the Water Commissioner read the *Drought Card* aloud.** The Water Commissioner should remove about half of the *Water Unit Squares* from the river.

15. **Repeat Step 9.** This time there will not be enough water in the river to satisfy all of the water users, and the junior users will have to go without water while the senior users receive their full entitlements. Do they feel this is fair? Which water users are left without all the water they require?

16. **Round 4 (a drought year in Mexico): Have students return the *Water Unit Squares*.** The

Water Commissioner should not return the ones he or she has removed.

17. **Repeat Step 13.** How does this allocation system compare to the one used in the United States. Is it fair? Which water users are left without sufficient water?

18. **Explain that water law and water use are constantly changing.** To demonstrate, ask three students from groups that have more than one student representing a water user to separate from their groups. Give these students *Action Cards 1, 2,* or *3.* Each *Action Card* represents a new demand for the water.

19. **Have the Water Commissioner replace all the *Water Unit Squares.***

20. **Add recreation as the sixth priority under *prelación* to the list already on the chalkboard.** This will account for the new recreation water user on *Action Card 3.*

21. **In two rounds, have students gather the *Water Unit Squares* as they would under the American and Mexican water allocation systems.** Is there enough water for all users? If not, which ones will go without water under each of the systems? Does one system deal with the new water users better than the other?

Wrap Up

1. **Have students discuss the activity.** What do they see as the pros and cons of each water allocation system? How might each be improved? Under prior appropriation, do holders of senior water rights see a need for change? How about junior water rights holders? Is there a water user group that suffers under this particular organization of *prelación*? What are some of the impacts of the entire river being allocated? How might water be divided if there were no formal allocation system?

2. **Ask students to develop a list of water uses that weren't included in the game** (e.g., **boating, hunting, transportation, and cultural uses**). Ask them to consider non-human water uses such as use by plants, animals, ecosystems, etc.

3. **Have the students write their own lists of water uses that they regard as "beneficial."** Have them rank their lists in order of the uses they value from highest to lowest.

4. **Pass out three sticky notes to each student.**

5. **Have students write their top three water uses on the sticky notes (one per note).**

6. **Make three blank graphs (X- and Y-axes) on the board, large enough so that each sticky note can be one unit on the Y-axis (see illustration below).** Label the graphs #1, #2, and #3.

7. **Label the X-axes with eight categories: the eight major water users (Urban, Recreation, Earth Systems, Energy, Business and Industry, Rural Agriculture, Fish and Wildlife, Cultures) (see page 268, "8–4–1, One for All: The Colorado River").**

8. **Have the students come up to the board and place their sticky notes on the graphs.** Their #1 water use should go on the graph labeled #1, and so on. If their water use is more specific than the eight categories, they should choose the category that they think it best fits (for example, "boating" could go into recreation; "fishing" could go into business and industry, recreation, or fish and wildlife).

9. **When all of the students have placed their sticky notes on the graphs, you will have a visual representation of the class's water use values.** Discuss the results. How can the needs and values of human and non-human water users be recognized and met?

Assessment

Have students:

- demonstrate the principles of prior appropriation and *prelación* by simulating how water is distributed in a hypothetical watershed (Steps 6–21);

- compare Mexican and American systems of water allocation (Steps 6–21);
- demonstrate how water shortages affect water users differently according to their ranking under prior appropriation and *prelación* (Steps 6–21);
- discuss the pros and cons of Mexican and American water allocation systems (**Wrap Up**, Step 1);
- analyze their personal water use values (**Wrap Up**, Steps 2–3);
- make graphs to identify the class's water use values (**Wrap Up**, Steps 4–9).

Extensions

Have the students write their own water user cards and action cards using actual water users, priority

dates, and amounts allocated for local water users in their community/county. They will have to identify several major water users and do research to find out the pertinent facts and figures. Have the class repeat the game using these actual water users or teach it to another class.

Resources

Gleick, Peter, et al. 2002. *The World's Water: The Biennial Report on Freshwater Resources 2002–2003*. Washington, DC: Island Press.

Hobbs, Gregory J., Jr. 2003. *Citizen's Guide to Colorado Water Law*. Denver: Colorado Foundation for Water Education.

Newcom, Joshua. 2004. *Layperson's Guide to the Colorado River*. Sacramento, CA: Water Education Foundation.

Wolfe, Mary Ellen. 1996. *A Landowner's Guide to Western Water Rights*. Boulder, CO: Roberts Rinehart Publishers.

e-Links

Comisión Nacional del Agua
Information about water law and allocation in Mexico.
www.cna.gob.mx

Colorado River Water Users Association
Information about different water users in the Colorado Watershed.
www.crwua.org

San Juan River Basin Recovery Implementation Program
Endangered fish recovery programs in the San Juan Basin.
http://southwest.fws.gov/sjrip

Upper Colorado River Endangered Fish Recovery Program
Information about endangered fish in the Colorado River.
www.r6.fws.gov/coloradoriver

U.S. Bureau of Reclamation
Information about water projects and use in the United States.
www.usbr.gov

Water Education Foundation/Colorado River Project
Information and tours about water use, history, and law relating to the Colorado River.
www.watereducation.org/coloradoriver.asp

First Come, First Served Water User Cards

Water User .... The Republic of Ríos
Priority Number **1**
Type of Use: International Treaty

Your country and the Republic of Ríos, which shares the watershed, signed an international treaty in 1953 that guarantees a water right of **2500 cfs** for the Republic of Ríos. Although there are older water rights on the river, the treaty holds the highest priority and must be satisfied before all other water users receive their water.

Water User .... Goodin Irrigation District
Priority Number **2**
Type of Use: Agriculture

Goodin Irrigation District provides water to farmers for more than 200,000 acres of croplands. The water is used to grow vegetables, alfalfa, cotton, and other products. Goodin was the first irrigation district to formalize its claim to the river, in 1895. The district has rights to divert **2,000 cfs**.

Water User .... Vaca Valley Irrigation Company
Priority Number **3**
Type of Use: Agriculture

Vaca Valley Irrigation Company (VVIC) has the right to divert **700 cfs** to deliver to its shareholders (local farmers, homeowners, and commercial users) for irrigating and landscaping. VVIC has been an important part of the local economy since its establishment in 1897.

Water User .... Flying M Ranch
Priority Number **4**
Type of Use: Agriculture

The Flying M has been owned and operated by the Miller family since it was first homesteaded in 1898. The ranch includes 11,000 deeded acres, plus grazing allotments on public land. It produces beef cattle, hay, and winter wheat, using its **200 cfs** water right.

Water User .... Scheer Mills
Priority Number **5**
Type of Use: Industrial

This small town was founded by Mormon pioneers in 1901 and has historically been a farming community. Now the area has been discovered by tourists and retirees, and the town's economy is thriving on this new source of income. The town's water right entitles it to **600 cfs** from the river.

First Come, First Served Water User Cards

Water User ………. Roessmann Power Company
Priority Number **6**
Type of Use: Hydroelectric Power

The Roessmann Power Company partnered with the federal government to build Massive Dam in 1905, which produces hydroelectric power for thousands of customers in the region. In order to efficiently operate the dam's generating turbines, a minimum of **200 cfs** must flow through the dam at all times.

Water User ………. Page City
Priority Number **7**
Type of Use: Drinking Water

Page City started as a sleepy ranching town, but its population has exploded in the past thirty years. More than 1 million people now call it home, with thousands more moving to the city and surrounding area every year. The city's original water right on the river is dated 1911, and it is entitled to **800 cfs** with this water right.

Water User ………. Fillion Paper Company
Priority Number **8**
Type of Use: Industrial

Fillion Paper Co. was established in 1979 and has one manufacturing plant that is located near the river. The company is a major employer in its county and has a water right of **100 cfs**.

Water User ………. Walker County Water Authority
Priority Number **9**
Type of Use: Drinking Water

Walker County has a relatively large population and limited water supplies. In 1981, it established its water right on the river. The county diverts **500 cfs** to supplement ground water supplies.

Water User ……….Uribe National Wildlife Refuge
Priority Number **10**
Type of Use: Natural Systems

The Migratory Birds Wildlife Refuge was established in 1985 by order of Congress. The refuge has rights to **100 cfs** of instream flow to create habitat for white pelicans, Yuma clapper rails, avocets, osprey, and other migratory birds. Desert pupfish and other endangered fishes also live here.

First Come, First Served Action Cards

Action Card #1
Priority Number **8**
Type of Use: Natural Systems

Recent scientific studies have revealed that a native species of trout is in danger of extinction due to the increased water temperatures that result when the river's flow falls below 300 cfs. In order to stabilize the population as mandated by the Endangered Species Act, at least **300 cfs** minimum instream flow is required.

Action Card #2
Priority Number **2**
Type of Use: Agricultural

The Mesa River Indian Tribe's reservation encompasses approximately four hundred square miles of high desert plateaus. Until recently, the tribe has not received agricultural water to which it is entitled. In the last five years, the tribe has waged successful legal battles to ensure delivery of its water allocation. The reservation was created in 1895, and according to the Winters Doctrine, this is also the tribe's water right date. The tribe has partnered with the state government to build the necessary water delivery infrastructure to serve the reservation and will now start withdrawing their full entitlement of **500 cfs**.

Action Card #3
Priority Number **11**
Type of Use: Recreation

In one of the basin states, recreational users (commercial rafting companies, kayakers, fishermen, and others) have united to lobby the state legislature to guarantee minimum instream flows. A bill has passed that requires **400 cfs** minimum instream flow for recreation, fish, and wildlife. However, this instream flow requirement is a junior water right to all previous water rights and will only come into play if there is sufficient water in the river.

Drought Card

The winter snowpack this year was only 50 percent of normal. More than 90 percent of the river's flow comes from snowmelt, so there is significantly less water in the river. Remove half of the *Water Unit Squares* from the river. This represents the lower snowpack, plus the additional loss of water from the river to evaporation and seepage into the dry soil.

Irrigation Calculations

As a farmer, how will you keep your profits from flowing away from you?

Grade Level:
6–12

Subject Areas:
Math, Life Science, Environmental Science, Economics, History/Anthropology

Duration:
Preparation time: 60 minutes
Activity time: 60–120 minutes

Setting:
Outdoors (a schoolyard or other outdoor area with access to a hose or water source is required; a warm sunny day is ideal)

Skills:
Calculate, Simulate, Analyze, Evaluate, Apply, Discuss

Vocabulary:
conservation, dryland farming, evaporation, irrigation, irrigation efficiency, salinity

Summary
Students become irrigators and learn about the balance of factors that make up irrigation efficiency.

Objectives
Students will:
- define irrigation efficiency;
- explain the costs and benefits of different irrigation systems;
- identify different irrigation systems that are used in the Colorado Watershed;
- evaluate factors that determine which irrigation system will be used in a specific location;
- present a fair policy for water distribution to all water users;
- explain what factors of irrigation efficiency are within the control of irrigators and which are not.

Materials
- *1 fifty-gallon trashcan* (clean)
- *5 five-gallon buckets*
- *5 one-gallon buckets* (gallon ice cream buckets are perfect)
- *Drill and ½" drill bit*
- *$100 in play money for each station* (see **Play Money** Student Copy Page)
- *5 slips of paper numbered 1–5 and a bowl or bag to draw them from*
- *Access to a hose or water source*
- *Change of clothes* (for all students)

Background
Agriculture has been important in the Colorado River Watershed since ancient times. Three thousand years ago, Hohokam and Ancestral Puebloan people began to grow crops in the watershed. Since most of the watershed receives

little rainfall, irrigation has been used in many areas for as long as agriculture has been practiced. Irrigation is defined as the process of acquiring water, delivering it to where it is needed, and applying it to crops at the correct time and in the correct quantity. Some areas are still farmed using dryland farming practices (e.g., pinto bean farms near Dolores, Colorado, that rely solely on precipitation), but the majority of agriculture uses some form of irrigation. Irrigation is so important in the watershed that agriculture uses approximately 80 percent of the Colorado River's water.

Irrigation can range from simply storing rainfall and watering plants by hand, to using complex, computerized drip systems that deliver a specific amount of water to each plant at a certain time. Dams and diversions are used to store and transfer water from rivers and reservoirs to fields. Ditch and canal systems transport water through fields and drain wastewater away from them. Sprinkler systems, drip systems, siphon systems, and flooding are all forms of irrigation that are used in the watershed today.

Irrigating effectively involves careful decisions about money and energy costs. By participating in this hands-on activity, students investigate the relationships between efficiency, cost, and water use as they try to develop the most efficient system possible.

Irrigation efficiency is the efficiency associated with acquiring water, delivering it to fields, and applying it to crops. Efficiency is determined through a combination of factors including how much water is lost between the point of diversion and the point of use (mostly through evaporation and leaky ditches); the cost of delivering the water (mostly through equipment, energy, labor, and other infrastructure costs); and how well the soil holds water once water is applied (for example, clays soils tend to hold water near the surface where plants can reach it longer than sandy soils, which drain quickly). Given this, it is important to note that no two farms, and no two irrigation systems, are exactly alike.

Differences in soils, landforms, distance to water, cost of energy, and other factors make each situation unique, with its own challenges and benefits. Even the most modern irrigation technology combined with outstanding soils can't provide 100 percent efficiency. Water that is "lost" through leaky ditches or rapidly draining soils sometimes results in the creation of wetlands and habitat for wildlife. In addition, water that flows back to rivers and streams after being applied to fields (return flow) is important for downstream water users (see page 307, "Many Happy Return Flows").

In the Colorado Watershed, salinity is a major issue for irrigators. This is because naturally occurring salts in the soils of the basin become concentrated in ground water and rivers when irrigation is used. For this reason, in places like the Imperial Valley, irrigators must apply enough water to fields to force salts lower in the soil away from the roots of plants and install drain systems, called tiles, beneath fields to direct salty water out of the soil and away from the field. The need to mitigate salinity problems also becomes a factor in irrigation efficiency in some places.

The Grand Valley in Colorado, the Imperial and Coachella Valleys in California, the Yuma Valley in Arizona, the Mexicali Valley in Baja California, and the San Luis Valley in Sonora are some of the major agricultural areas in the watershed that rely on irrigation from the Colorado River and its tributaries.

In places like the Coachella Valley, complex computer systems are used to deliver specific amounts of water to specific places at specific times of day. Irrigation systems throughout the watershed range from very simple to highly technological. Hundreds of different crops are grown, from hay to peaches to cattle.

Common Methods of Irrigation in the Colorado Watershed

1. **Center-Pivot Irrigation:** This system uses an electric-powered automatic sprinkler that delivers water via a wheeled rotating boom with a center pivot point. Water is applied uniformly by a progressive increase in nozzle size from the pivot to the end of the line. The rate at which water is applied is determined by how fast the pivot travels. Most units irrigate about 130 acres, and the circles of green they create can be seen from airplanes.

2. **Wheel-Line Sprinkler:** In a wheel-line sprinkler system, water is delivered to crops via sprinkler heads mounted on a pipe that is elevated on moving wheels. Water pressure, generated with electric pumps, propels the system. This system is used for square or rectangular fields.

3. **Flood Irrigation:** Flood irrigation is a process in which the entire surface of the soil is covered (flooded) by water. Water is typically delivered via an irrigation canal or pumped to fields using electric- or gas-powered pumps. In some areas, ditches are unlined and farmers use a shovel to release water from the banks and build small dams with plastic tarps to hold water where it is needed in the field. Hay fields and pastures in Wyoming, for example, are usually irrigated in this way. In other areas, "gated pipe" is used. Water is delivered through large plastic pipes on the ground surface, and gates at each row in the field can be opened or closed as needed for water delivery. Vegetable farmers in California and Arizona often use pipe systems since less water is lost to evaporation or seepage. Fields are typically flooded at intervals throughout the growing season.

4. **Drip System:** A system of pipes and hoses is used to deliver water to individual plants. This system allows the irrigator to closely control the amount of water that is used.

Procedure

Preparation

1. Label five one-gallon buckets with numbers 1–5.

2. Drill the following number of ½" holes in the bottom of the one-gallon buckets:

   - Bucket #1—5 holes
   - Bucket #2—10 holes
   - Bucket #3—20 holes
   - Bucket #4—30 holes
   - Bucket #5—35 holes

3. **Stack the buckets and prevent your students from seeing the holes in them.**

4. **Set up the outdoor playing field in the following way:** Fill the fifty-gallon trashcan with water. Arrange the five-gallon buckets in a circle with the trashcan in the center. The buckets should be about thirty-five feet from the trashcan.

5. **Make copies of the *Play Money Student Copy Page* (enough for each group of five students to have $100).** Cut the bills apart.

Warm Up

1. **Ask students to describe the different types of irrigation systems they know about or that they have seen in their area.** If students are farmers or ranchers, have them explain why their family uses the irrigation system they do.

2. **Discuss the concept of irrigation efficiency.** Do students have opinions about which irrigation systems are the most efficient? Why? Why is irrigation efficiency important in the Colorado River Watershed?

The Activity

1. **Divide students into five groups and pass out $100 in play money to each group.**

2. **Read the following instructions:**

   a. Each group represents a family farm in the Colorado Basin.

   b. Each farm has $100 to get them through the irrigation season.

   c. The goal of this activity is to irrigate your crops for the season (represented by filling a five-gallon bucket to the top) using an irrigation system (the one-gallon buckets stacked next to you). The trashcan represents the water source (irrigation canal, river, reservoir, etc.). The winner is the family who has the most money left after purchasing an irrigation system and paying the costs to irrigate for a season.

3. **With this in mind, tell each group to make a plan to purchase an irrigation system.** Describe the differences between the systems (see **Background**). How much do they want to spend? (In reality, farmers do research to

BUCKET	# OF HOLES	COST	REPRESENTS
Bucket #1	5	$70	State-of-the-art computerized drip system
Bucket #2	10	$60	Electric-powered center-pivot system
Bucket #3	20	$50	Wheel-line sprinkler system
Bucket #4	30	$30	Gated pipe flood irrigation system
Bucket #5	35	$10	Hand-dug flood irrigation system

determine which system makes the most sense for their individual situation.)

4. **Have each group draw a slip of paper (numbered 1–5) to determine the order in which they will have the opportunity to buy an irrigation system.** Proceed to "sell" the "irrigation systems" for the prices shown in the table below. Do not let students see the holes in the buckets. Naturally, students will have different levels of satisfaction with the buckets they receive. Discuss how some irrigation systems are more efficient than others and that their efficiency is often reflected in their cost.

5. **Inform students of the rules of the game:**

   a. Teams use their one-gallon buckets to fill their five-gallon buckets, making trips until they fill their five-gallon buckets or run out of money. Everyone makes their trips to the "river" (trashcan) at the same time.

   b. Each trip to the river costs $5 for energy and labor, which they will pay to the teacher when they are finished irrigating. It is the responsibility of each team to keep track of how many trips they take to fill their buckets and to pay you when they are finished.

   c. The five-gallon buckets must stay in the same place.

6. **Have students take their places at their five-gallon buckets.** Before they begin, have students calculate the number of trips they can afford to make to the trashcan after purchasing their irrigation system. Have them predict whether they will have enough money to fill their five-gallon bucket.

7. **When students are ready to begin, shout "Irrigate!"** The teams begin to fill their five-gallon buckets, some with more success than others. They should haul water (irrigate) until they either fill their buckets or run out of money. WARNING: Depending on the enthusiasm of students, everyone, including

you, could end up very wet!

8. **At the end of the activity there should be a mixture of results.** One or two teams will be soaking wet and gasping for breath. Others will have varying amounts of money and energy remaining.

9. **Have each team tally its irrigation costs and pay its expenses.** Have each briefly describe the pros and cons of their particular system to the entire group.

10. **Ask students to discuss the following:** Who "won" the activity? Why? What factors caused success or failure? Discuss how each delivery bucket represents a different type of irrigation system, with varying levels of efficiency.

11. **Ask students to define irrigation efficiency.** Have them consider the following situations: In real life, not all of the farmers would need the same amount of water to irrigate their crops. If your farm needed only half of a bucket, for example, would it make sense to use the most expensive irrigation system? Imagine that you are irrigating to grow hay for five cows. Your neighbor is irrigating to grow five hundred acres of grapes for winemaking. Would you both want the same system? If the crop you are growing does not have a high market value, would you buy the most expensive system, even if it is more efficient?

12. **Ask students to think about what could make an irrigation system more efficient?** Why don't all farmers use the most efficient system? Regardless of how much money it costs to irrigate, are there other reasons why someone might choose a more efficient system so that they can save water?

13. **Repeat the activity using the following scenarios.** If there is not enough time to perform these steps, take time to discuss the scenarios.

14. **Scenario 1: Energy costs skyrocket and each trip to the river now costs $15!** How does

this change each group's irrigation efficiency? Which system is most attractive now?

15. **Scenario 2: Drought year! Fill the fifty-gallon trashcan only halfway to represent a drought.** Are the leaky irrigation systems fair to other water users when water is in short supply? Why should some irrigators pay for more efficient systems when others "waste" water using inefficient ones?

16. **Scenario 3: Everyone pays a flat rate for water, no matter how much is used.** Rather than paying for each bucketful, have each group pay $20 up front and use as much water as they need. How does this affect their choice of systems?

17. **Scenario 4: Each farm is growing a different crop with differing market value and different water requirements (based on how much water the crop needs, how large an area is being irrigated, etc.).** Assign each group a crop and have them choose their irrigation system. How does this change their decision-making process?

   a. Hay for cattle. Market value = $50. Amount of water = 4 gallons.
   b. Organic asparagus. Market value = $100. Amount of water = 5 gallons.
   c. Cotton. Market value = $70. Amount of water = 5 gallons.
   d. Winter wheat. Market value = $60. Amount of water = 3 gallons.
   e. Peaches. Market value = $80. Amount of water = 4 gallons.

18. **Scenario 5: Each farm has different soils, which retain water for varying amounts of time.** Repeat the activity, but this time drill holes in the groups' five-gallon buckets. Students will use irrigation to fill their buckets, but depending on how many holes are in the bottom, the buckets will empty at varying rates.

Wrap Up

Discuss the activity. What factors do farmers have to consider when selecting an irrigation system? Which of these factors are within their control? What incentives do farmers have to conserve water on their farms? How does this apply to students' own communities?

Assessment

Have students:
- define irrigation efficiency (**Warm Up**, Steps 1–2; Step 10);
- calculate the costs of different irrigation systems and scenarios (Steps 2–4, 8, 13, 15, 16).
- explain the costs and benefits of different irrigation systems (Steps 8–9);
- identify different irrigation systems that are used in the Colorado Watershed (Step 3);
- evaluate factors that determine which irrigation system will be used in a specific location (Steps 10–18);
- explain what factors of irrigation efficiency are within the control of irrigators and which are not (**Wrap Up**).

Extensions

Have students come up with further scenarios to add to the activity. What if the order in which each group withdraws water is predetermined by the priority of their water right?

Have students research specific areas of the Colorado Watershed to identify which types of irrigation systems are the most common. Why is a particular system best for that area?

Have students create irrigation models in clear plastic or glass trays or boxes. Have them use different soil types (potting soil vs. sandy soil, for example) and different water delivery methods (sprinkling, flooding, dripping, etc.). Students can use notebooks to record their observations about the rate of infiltration into the soil, amount of water needed to saturate the soil, and other differences.

Resources

The Watercourse. 2000. *Conserve Water Educators Guide*. Bozeman, MT: The Watercourse.

Project WET International. 2004. *Discover a Watershed: The Missouri Educators Guide*. Bozeman, MT: Project WET International.

The Watercourse. 1995. *Project WET: Curriculum and Activity Guide*. Bozeman, MT: The Watercourse.

e-Links

Arizona Department of Water Resources.
Links to information about water users in Arizona.
www.water.az.gov/adwr

Central Arizona Project
Links to information about irrigation districts in Arizona.
www.cap-az.com

Coachella Valley Water District
Information about irrigation in Southern California.
www.cvwd.org

U.S. Bureau of Reclamation
Information about irrigation projects in western Colorado.
www.usbr.gov/dataweb/html/grandvalley.html

Imperial Irrigation District
Information about irrigation in Southern California.
www.iid.com

San Diego State University
Information about Mexicali Valley and San Luis Valley agriculture.
www.ccbres.sdsu.edu/data/indicators_of_the_month/pdf/agriculture_and_livestock.PDF

Play Money

Many Happy Return Flows

Did you know that water in the Colorado River may get used as many as seventeen times before it evaporates or reaches the Gulf of California?

Summary

Students analyze water quantity and quality as they track diversions and return flows from agricultural, industrial, and municipal users in a hypothetical watershed similar to the Colorado.

Grade Level:
Grades 6–10

Subject Areas:
Environmental Science, Geography, Math, History/Anthropology

Duration:
Preparation time: 15 minutes
Activity time: 90 minutes

Setting:
Classroom

Skills:
Map, Graph, Add, Subtract, Analyze, Discuss, Problem Solve

Vocabulary:
arid, channel, cubic feet per second (cfs), cubic meters per second (cms), confluence, consumptive use, contaminant, cumulative effect, discharge, dissolve, diversion, effluent, erosion, evaporation, gaging station, ground water, instream flow, irrigation, leach, municipal, nonconsumptive use, nonpoint source pollution (NPS), nutrients, point source pollution, precipitation, return flow, sediment, selenium, streamflow, suspension, transpiration, tundra, water rights

Objectives
Students will:
- use addition and subtraction to track changes in water quantity and quality as it is returned to the river by various water users;
- demonstrate the differences between consumptive and nonconsumptive use;
- compare point source and nonpoint source pollution;
- develop solutions for addressing pollution;
- learn about cumulative effects of contaminants such as salts, selenium, heavy metals, and nutrients in a river.

Materials
- *Copies of **Many Happy Return Flows Water Users Scenario Cards** Student Copy Pages* (1 set per group)
- *Copies of **Many Happy Return Flows Worksheet** Student Copy Pages* (1 per group)
- *Copies of **Many Happy Return Flows Hypothetical Watershed Map** Student Copy Pages* (1 per group)
- *Sets of colored pencils or markers* (1 per group)

Background
When water is diverted from a stream or river and used for agricultural, municipal, or industrial purposes, not all of the water is used "consumptively." Consumptive use refers to water that is either absorbed by soil, transpired,

evaporated, or incorporated into a product and thus is not returned directly to a surface or ground water supply (Wolfe 1996). For example, when a farmer diverts water to irrigate a crop, the portion of that water that is used by the plants (consumed) or evaporates is unavailable for immediate further use.

The remainder of the water makes its way (either through surface or shallow ground water flows) back to the stream or river and is then available for downstream users. When a city withdraws water from a river for use by residential and commercial customers, a portion of that water will eventually return to the river after it has been used and treated. The water that returns to a stream or river after it has been applied to a beneficial use is called a return flow. Nonconsumptive uses, such as hydroelectric power generation, return all the water they use.

Return flows are important, especially in rivers like the Colorado that have many demands on a limited supply of water, because they mean that water is available for more users. Although some may see return flows as evidence of inefficiency and waste (in irrigation, for example), return flows have become an integral part of present-day water systems. In arid regions like most of the Colorado Watershed, there are not enough tributaries or precipitation to replace water that has been withdrawn between diversions. Without return flows, there would not be enough water left in the river for downstream users.

Return flows vary in volume depending on the season, soil type, climate, type of water use, and other factors. Since much of a return flow may occur through ground water movement, it can be difficult to quantify. The flow of a stream is typically measured in cubic feet per second (cfs) in the United States and in cubic meters per second (cms) in Mexico. One cfs equals 7.48 gallons per second and one cms is equivalent to 1,000 liters per second. Streamflow is measured at gaging stations located along the stream or river.

Although return flows are important in maintaining the quantity of water in a river, water qual-

ity can be affected. When water is diverted for urban use and applied to lawns, it may run back into the river (untreated) through storm drains, bringing with it fertilizers, herbicides, pet waste, and other contaminants. In agricultural areas, ground water leaching may increase dissolved salts in return flows. A decline in water quality means that more extensive treatment is required before the water can be re-used. Water quality declines can create problems for fish and wildlife, riparian ecosystems, recreation, agriculture and industry, and communities. The water quality of return flows also varies according to soils, climate, season, type of usage, volume of flow, and other factors.

Point Source and Nonpoint Source Pollution

Water pollution is classified in two ways: point source and nonpoint source pollution. Point source pollution can be traced back to a single point, such as a sewage-outflow pipe. Nonpoint source pollution includes sources such as agricultural or urban runoff that don't have a specific point of origin. Materials that impair water quality may be of natural origin (naturally occurring salts in bedrock, sediment, organic material, etc.) or may come from human-caused sources (chemicals, heavy metals, petroleum products, fertilizers, etc.). Forest fires are an example of natural events that can result in lowered water quality as erosion and runoff carry sediment to streams.

Farmers, ranchers, and water managers are working together to improve return flows. The Salinity Control Forum is a group of water users and managers whose goal is to reduce the volume of salt entering the Colorado River through management practices. They have been particularly active in the Upper Basin where geologic deposits such as the Mancos Shale introduce large amounts of salt and selenium. When water flows across the shale, the minerals are dissolved and can end up in the Colorado River. This is a problem for water

New River Wetlands Project, near El Centro, California, uses a man-made wetland to remove sediment and other material from irrigation return flows.

Justin Howe

users in the Lower Basin because the minerals can make the water unusable. The Salinity Control Forum has developed programs to reduce the amount of irrigation water that comes in contact with the shale.

As the Colorado River and its tributaries flow toward the Gulf of California, minerals, sediment, contaminants, and other things collect in the water, creating a cumulative effect. By the time the river reaches Mexico, it is carrying high amounts of dissolved and suspended material that can make it difficult to use the water. This problem is exacerbated by evaporation, which concentrates materials in the water. Levels of dissolved and suspended material must be carefully monitored. If concentration gets too high, the water cannot be used for agriculture or drinking. (See page 58 for more on salinity and its effect on water users.)

One of the ways in which the water quality of return flows can be improved is through the use of wetlands, either natural or man-made. The New River Wetlands Project in Southern California was initiated in the late 1990s to address water-quality problems in the New and Alamo Rivers, both of which drain into the Salton Sea. These rivers acquire nutrients and heavy metals from sewage, and silt, nutrients, selenium, and pesticides from agricultural and urban drainage. Two wetlands have been constructed at sites along the river to reduce pollutants and improve habitat. Water is diverted from the river into a series of ponds and bands of marsh vegetation. In 2001, for the small portion of the river that was treated, total suspended solids decreased by 89–98 percent after flowing through these wetland sites.

Wetlands are highly important for maintaining

Las Vegas Uses Return Flows

Water managers in Las Vegas and the surrounding area use urban return flows to help meet growing water needs. Water is withdrawn from Lake Mead, treated, and delivered to homes and businesses. After use, it flows through the sewer system to a treatment facility before being released into Las Vegas Wash, which flows back to Lake Mead (see page 320, "Faucet Family Tree"). Wetland vegetation in the wash helps to slow the water, acting as a filter to remove sediment before the water reaches Lake Mead. A partnership of public and private entities (the Las Vegas Wash Coordination Committee) has been formed to restore wetlands in the wash and construct erosion control structures to manage increased flows as population growth continues in Clark County.

According to the Colorado River Compact, the state of Nevada is entitled to 300,000 acre-feet of Colorado River water plus 4 percent of any surplus water as declared by the U.S. Secretary of Interior. Through a special arrangement, Nevada is able to take amounts in excess of its allocation and is given credit to its "water account" for the amount of water that returns to Lake Mead. For example, Las Vegas may use 650,000 acre-feet of water, so long as 350,000 acre-feet flow back to Lake Mead. By taking advantage of return flows, Las Vegas is able to meet the water needs of more people.

Justin Howe

Return flows from Las Vegas and the surrounding area are returned to Lake Mead via Las Vegas Wash.

water quality and regulating streamflow. Although natural wetlands have decreased in much of the basin due to development and changes in the river's hydrology, some of the remaining wetlands are protected as wildlife refuges, nature preserves, conservation easements, and in other ways as resource managers and citizens recognize their importance.

The relationships between upstream and downstream water users in a watershed are complex. Water quality and quantity are two of the most important issues that water users face as they seek fair and sustainable water management policies.

Procedure
Preparation

Students can use the *Many Happy Return Flows Watershed Map* provided in the *Student Copy Pages* to complete the activity, or they can cre-

ate their own maps using the *Watershed Map* as a guide. If you would like the students to create their own maps, prepare large sheets of paper (one for each group) and art materials (markers, colored pencils, etc.).

Warm Up

1. **Ask students to discuss the ways in which they use water (in their homes, in school, in growing the food they eat, etc.).** Is all of this water used completely (consumptive use vs. nonconsumptive use)? How does water return to streams and rivers after use? What needs to be done to prevent water quality from declining? What water users are upstream from the students' water source? Would it be better if the water was not returned to the river after it has been used? If the water does not

return, would there be enough for everyone downstream?

2. **Tell students that many uses of water result in some of it returning to the stream or river from which it was originally diverted (for example, Las Vegas; see Background).** Most farms return a portion of the water they divert, through surface runoff and shallow ground water return flows. All of the return flows in a system are important because they make more water available for water users downstream.

3. **Ask the students to write down three ways that they think the quality of water may be changed after it is used (e.g., chemicals added, sediment levels increased, higher concentrations of organic material).** Discuss point source and nonpoint source pollution.

4. **Tell the students that they are going to simulate withdrawals and return flows for a hypothetical river system.** Be sure to emphasize that the numbers used in the scenario cards are only representative and are not related to actual data. Actual river flows and return flows are variable according to season, temperature, soil type, and many other factors. The water quality rating is only a way of indicating change in the system and does not refer to measurable data.

5. **Make sure the students understand the meaning of the term _cfs_ (cubic feet per second).**

The Activity
Part I
1. **Divide the students into groups of three or four.**

2. **Give each group a copy of the _Watershed Map_, a set of _Water User Scenario Cards_, a _Many Happy Return Flows Worksheet_, and a set of markers or colored pencils.**

3. **Ask each group to read their scenario cards aloud within their small groups, using the** information on the cards to make a map of the hypothetical watershed.

4. **Ask students to draw each water user on the map in its correct position along the river and/or its tributaries and label it.**

5. **Tell the students that they will add more information to the maps during the next part of the activity.**

Part II
1. **Direct the students' attention to the _Many Happy Return Flows Worksheet_.** Ask them to carefully read through the scenario cards again. This time, they will need to do math to fill in the _Return Flows Worksheet_. Explain the categories in the table and lead them through the first three scenario cards, filling in all the spaces in the table. When the tables are complete, the final total for instream flow should be ninety cfs and the final total for the Net Water Quality Rating should be negative sixteen points.

2. **In addition to filling in the _Return Flows Worksheet_, the students will need to label their maps with new information.** For each water user, the students will need to label the amount of water diverted, the amount returned, and the amount left instream between water users.

Part III
1. **Tell the students that, after they have completed their worksheet and map, they will need to graph the information in the worksheet.** They will make two graphs, one for water quantity (streamflow) and one for water quality. Both graphs should use the water user number for the X-axis. For the water quantity graph, the Y-axis should be cfs. For the water quality graph, the Y-axis should be Net Water Quality Rating.

2. **Have students compare their graphs side by side.** What is the relationship (if any) between quantity and quality? Why does the water quality rating continue to decline even when the quantity has increased? Talk about cumulative effects and how contaminants in water can add up as the stream moves through a series of water users. Even though each user may treat the water and improve its quality slightly before they return it to the stream, even a few points of lowered quality add up.

Wrap Up

1. **Ask students to discuss the activity.** What are some of the causes of water quality decline as the water moves downstream? If the water quality declines, what does this mean for downstream water users (e.g., more expensive water treatment is required, greater amounts of water must be used to fill the same purpose, etc.)? How should the responsibility for water quality be shared among water users in a watershed?

2. **Review the concepts of point source and nonpoint source pollution.** Write the two categories on the chalkboard, and ask the students to list the pollution sources from their scenario cards as either point source or nonpoint source.

3. **Ask the students to return to small groups and develop water quality solutions for each scenario card that has a decline in water quality rating.** They should write their solution on the card. For example, for Rapidston's urban runoff problem, they could educate citizens about storm drains and the importance of keeping them free of pollutants (i.e., not dumping used oil in them); they could require new parking lots to incorporate natural drainage areas with vegetation to trap runoff so that it didn't run directly into the creek; they could reduce the use of herbicides and fertilizers; they could install pet waste bag dispensers and trash cans in parks, etc.

4. **Have students discuss their solutions.** Would there be additional costs associated with taking action to prevent water contamination? How would these be paid for? Some of the water users in the scenarios contribute more to the decline in water quality than others, but they also may contribute to the local economy in important ways. How do communities balance these issues?

Assessment

Have students:
- create a map of water users in a watershed (*Part I,* Steps 3–4);
- calculate changes in streamflow and water quality as the water moves through a series of water users in a watershed (*Part II,* Steps 1–2);
- graph changes in streamflow and water quality as the water moves through a series of water users in a watershed (*Part III,* Steps 1–2);
- develop solutions to water quality problems (***Wrap Up***).

Extensions

Students may want to do an analysis of upstream and downstream users within their local watershed and calculate diversions and return flows as they track the water's path. They could identify water quality issues in their community and work on solutions to these problems.

Resources

Gleick, Peter, et al. 2002. *The World's Water: The Biennial Report on Freshwater Resources 2002–2003.* Washington, DC: Island Press.

Hobbs, Gregory J., Jr. 2003. *Citizen's Guide to Colorado Water Law.* Denver: Colorado Foundation for Water Education.

League of Women Voters of Colorado. 2001. *Colorado Water.* Denver: League of Women Voters of Colorado.

The Watercourse. 2002. *Discover a Watershed: Watershed Manager.* Bozeman, MT: The Watercourse.

Wolfe, Mary Ellen. 1996. *A Landowner's Guide to Western Water Rights.* Boulder, CO: Roberts Rinehart Publishers.

e-Links
Las Vegas Wash Coordination Committee
Specific information about the Las Vegas Wash restoration efforts.
www.lvwash.org

Citizen's Congressional Task Force on the New River
Specific information about wetlands restoration projects on the New and Alamo Rivers.
www.newriverwetlands.com

Many Happy Return Flows Answer Key

Water User Number	Instream Flow (cfs)	-	Diverted Flow (cfs)	=	Remaining Flow (cfs)	+	Return Flow (cfs)	+	Added Flow (cfs)	=	New Instream Flow (cfs) Move answer to next row down in column 2	Water Quality Rating	Net Water Quality Rating
1	80	-	0	=	80	+	0	+	0	=	80	0	0
2	80	-	10	=	70	+	8	+	0	=	78	-2	-2
3	78	-	10	=	68	+	6	+	0	=	74	-2	-4
4	74	-	5	=	69	+	3	+	1	=	73	-3	-7
5	73	-	0	=	73	+	0	+	20	=	93	5	-2
6	93	-	8	=	85	+	6	+	0	=	91	-3	-5
7	91	-	7	=	84	+	4	+	0	=	88	-4	-9
8	88	-	0	=	88	+	0	+	0	=	88	6	-3
9	88	-	0	=	88	+	0	+	60	=	148	-1	-4
10	148	-	35	=	113	+	28	+	0	=	141	-5	-9
11	141	-	20	=	121	+	13	+	0	=	134	-7	-16
12	134	-	7	=	127	+	2	+	0	=	129	-1	-17
13	129	-	30	=	99	+	7	+	0	=	106	-2	-19
14	106	-	20	=	86	+	20	+	0	=	106	4	-15
15	106	-	100	=	6	+	0	+	0	=	6	-2	-17
16	6	-	0	=	6	+	0	+	85	=	91	-3	-20

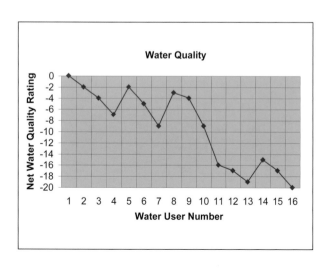

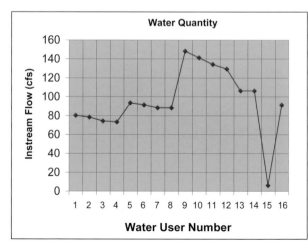

Many Happy Return Flows Water Users Scenario Cards

#1 Rapids Creek
The eighty cfs of cold, clear water in this mountain stream comes from melting snow. It begins as a trickle through tundra, gathering volume as it moves down into the forest below. The water is fast moving, and the stream channel is rocky. The water users are plants, wildlife, and the occasional backpacker, and the quality is virtually pure.

#2 Big Mountain Ski Area
Skiers and snowboarders love the steep slopes and deep snow of the Big Mountain Ski Area. The ski area makes snow in the early and late parts of the ski season, and diverts five cfs from Rapids Creek for snow production. All of this water returns to the creek when the snow melts. Another five cfs is treated and used inside the lodge and other buildings for drinking water and other uses. Three cfs are returned to the creek after treatment; its quality has declined by two points due to increased nutrients in treated effluent.

#3 Bar 7 Ranch
This 1,500-acre ranch encompasses meadows and forested land approximately sixty miles from the headwaters of Rapids Creek. The ranch has senior water rights on the creek and diverts ten cfs to irrigate hay fields. Six cfs return to the creek as shallow ground water return flows and surface runoff from the hayfields, which are flood irrigated. This high return flow results from porous soils that allow water to quickly move through the ground. Fortunately, the soil does not contain salts or selenium, and return flows remain low in these elements.

In addition, the creek is used as the drinking water source for the ranch's hundred head of cattle. The ranch has made an effort to reduce the cattle's contact with the stream, and there is only a slight increase in sediment and nutrients from the cattle's use. Water quality decreases by two points.

#4 Rapidston
This small town was first settled by miners and ranchers in the late 1800s and is situated on the banks of Rapids Creek. Its 576 residents are conscious of the creek's high-quality water and make an effort to preserve it. The local drinking water supply comes from ground water wells. The city pumps from ground water two cfs for in-home use. One cfs of this water is later released to the creek after sewage treatment. Five cfs are diverted from the creek to water landscaping around public buildings and in the city park. Three cfs of this water returns to the creek through storm drains. Water quality decreases by three points due to sewage, parking lot runoff, lawn fertilizers, and pet waste.

#5 Bronco Creek
Bronco Creek enters Rapids Creek just below Rapidston, adding twenty cfs. Its quality is quite pure since it flows through the Granny Smith Wilderness Area and there are no upstream users. The addition of this pure water to Rapids Creek improves its water quality by five points by dilution.

Many Happy Return Flows Water Users Scenario Cards

#6 Waterfall Estates

This new, 150-acre development enjoys a beautiful view of a waterfall on Rapids Creek. New homes are being built at a rate of five to six per year, providing work for people in the construction industry in Rapidston. The county has no regulations on construction sites to prevent erosion, and increased sediment is entering the creek (lowering water quality by three points). The sediment settles in backwater areas of the stream, burying gravels where trout lay their eggs and reducing the trout population. The development diverts eight cfs and returns six cfs to Rapids Creek.

#7 Valley Vista Golf Course

Another new addition to Rapids Creek's valley is the Valley Vista Golf Course. This state-of-the-art eighteen-hole course incorporates many natural features and is highly rated by golfers. The greens are watered with seven cfs from the creek and four cfs returning. The return flows carry varying amounts of pesticides, herbicides, and fertilizers, reducing the water quality by four points.

#8 Hermosa National Wildlife Refuge

Including more than five thousand acres of wetlands and riparian forest, the wildlife refuge provides habitat for nesting birds and other animals. It allows excellent opportunities for bird watching, photography, fishing, and hunting. The wetlands of the refuge are maintained by beavers whose dams slow the flow of the creek and promote the development of willow habitat. The slower flows and dense vegetation serve as a cleaning filter, and the water that flows out of the wetland is of higher quality than that which flowed in (add six points). The amount of water lost to evaporation in the beaver ponds is insignificant; flows remain virtually the same above and below the refuge.

#9 Confluence with Vermillion Creek

Vermillion Creek is a large stream and contributes sixty cfs. Water quality in the Vermillion is variable since numerous tributaries like Rapids Creek have entered it, carrying their own loads of sediment, heavy metals, nutrients, dissolved salts, and other materials. In addition, the river has directly received return flows from farms, towns, and industry upstream. The contaminants in Rapids Creek are diluted by the greater volume of the Vermillion, but the net water quality in the Vermillion Creek decreases by one point.

#10 Vermillion City

This city is home to about one thousand residents. A portion of its municipal water needs are met by water from Vermillion Creek. The city diverts thirty-five cfs and treats it before delivering it to its residential and commercial customers. Twenty-four cfs are returned to the river after treatment, and four cfs return directly to the river through storm drains. Water quality is diminished by five points below the city due to runoff from parking lots and lawns (treated with fertilizers and herbicides) and from treated effluent.

Many Happy Return Flows Water Users Scenario Cards

#11 VR Dairy Farm
The VR Dairy Farm is important to the economy of the area, stimulating business in farm implements, hay production, transportation, etc. Its two thousand cows produce millions of gallons of milk a year, but also produce tons of waste. Since the farm's pens and pastures are located near the river, high levels of nutrients flow into the river, especially after large precipitation events. The farm holds a senior water right on the river and diverts twenty cfs for hay production and the dairy operation. Thirteen cfs return to the river, and its quality declines by seven points.

#12 Valley Orchards
The three-hundred-acre Valley Orchards farm produces primarily peaches and apples. The farm recently installed a drip irrigation system to water the trees, resulting in lower overall water usage and also low return flows to the river. The farm diverts seven cfs and two cfs return to the river through shallow ground water flows. Water quality is diminished by one point due to pesticides and herbicides that run into the river during storm events.

#13 Winhere Casino
The Winhere Casino attracts thousands of visitors from all over the region with its big jackpots and beautiful architecture and landscaping. The casino is owned by an American Indian tribe and diverts thirty cfs for drinking water and landscaping (including a large lake and fountains). Seven cfs return to the river; five cfs have been treated after domestic use; and two cfs are direct runoff flows from the parking lots and landscaping. Water quality declines by two points due to parking lot runoff and fertilizers and herbicides used in landscaping.

#14 Restored Wetland
The tribe that owns the casino, the dairy farm owner, and Vermillion City created a partnership to restore a wetland along the river in order to improve downstream water quality. Although the entire river doesn't flow through the new wetland area, twenty cfs are diverted from the main channel to meander through a series of ponds and marshes before re-entering the river. When the twenty cfs return to the main channel, improved water quality results in an improvement of four points to the overall quality of the river.

#15 Vermillion Creek Canal
This cement-lined canal carries one hundred cfs from the Vermillion Creek to deliver water to irrigation districts and cities more than two hundred miles away. Since the water users who will receive water from the canal are located outside of the Vermillion Creek's watershed, any return flows will enter a different river system. The water quality below the canal is lower by two points because the reduced volume of water means that dissolved salts are more concentrated.

#16 Big Rainstorm
A major rainstorm in the watershed results in an increase in flow of eighty-five cfs, improving water quality by four points through dilution. However, the erosion that resulted from the heavy rain adds sediment, decreasing water quality by three points.

Many Happy Return Flows Worksheet

Water User Number	Instream Flow	-	Diverted Flow	=	Remaining Flow	+	Return Flow	+	Added Flow	=	New Instream Flow (Move answer to next row down in column 2)	Water Quality Rating	Water Quality Index
1	80	-	0	=	80	+	0	+	0	=	80	0	0
2	80	-	10	=	70	+	8	+	0	=	78	-2	-2
3	78	-		=		+		+		=			
4		-		=		+		+		=			
5		-		=		+		+		=			
6		-		=		+		+		=			
7		-		=		+		+		=			
8		-		=		+		+		=			
9		-		=		+		+		=			
10		-		=		+		+		=			
11		-		=		+		+		=			
12		-		=		+		+		=			
13		-		=		+		+		=			
14		-		=		+		+		=			
15		-		=		+		+		=			
16		-		=		+		+		=			

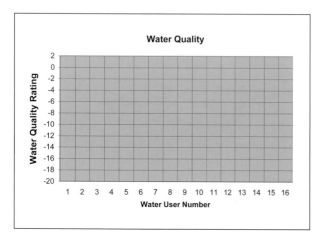

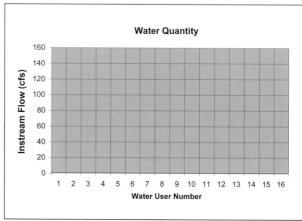

Many Happy Return Flows Watershed Map

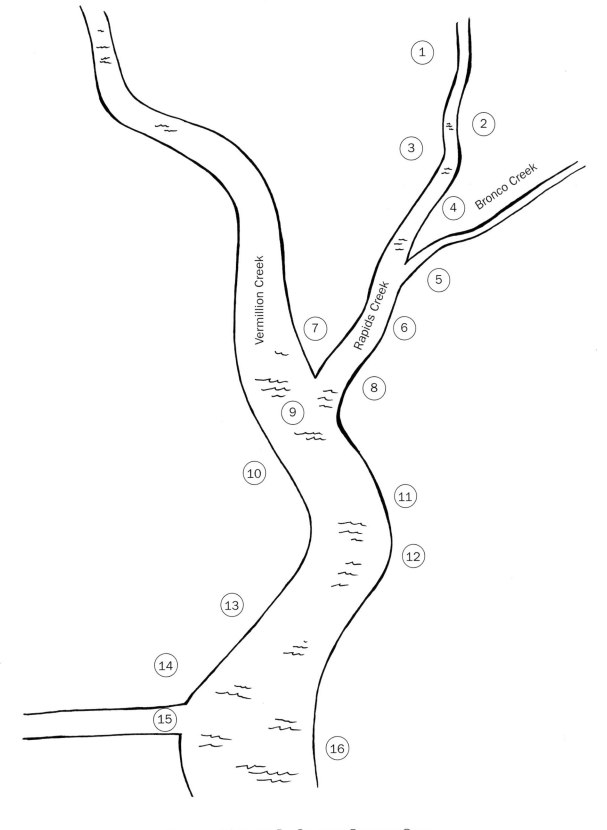

Faucet Family Tree

Do you know the "ancestry" of the water flowing from your faucet?

Grade Level:
8–10

Subject Areas:
Math, Environmental Science, Life Science, Physical Science

Duration:
Preparation time: 15 minutes
Activity time: 75 minutes

Setting:
Classroom

Skills:
Calculate, Discuss, Evaluate, Compare

Vocabulary:
conservation, consumptive use, evaporation, impermeable layer, nonconsumptive use, pathogen, transpiration, tributary, water pressure, water treatment, Xeriscape™

Summary

Students use algebra to trace water use from its sources, through urban developments, and back to a river.

Objectives

Students will:
- develop their understanding of how water is moved to and from household faucets;
- calculate quantities of water as it moves through a municipal system;
- examine the physical construction of a municipal water system;
- calculate indoor and outdoor water use;
- calculate sewer return flows;
- recognize the importance of math in water management.

Materials

- *Copies of* **Faucet Family Tree Instructions** *Student Copy Page* (1 per student)
- *Copies of* **Faucet Family Tree Worksheet** *Student Copy Page* (1 per student)
- *1 set of* **Faucet Family Tree Role Strips** (see **Preparation**)

Background

The movement of water from its source, through drinking-water treatment, to water users, and back out of the system is complex. Much of the movement takes place in buried pipelines, hidden pipes, and the industrial part of cities and towns. It is no surprise that most city residents do not know where their water comes from. A municipal water system may be viewed as a "tree" that expands as water is diverted from major pipelines and then contracts as sewage flows from small pipes into larger ones.

A typical municipal water system. In this illustration, water is diverted from the river and pumped from wells. It is then treated, moved into the water tower to pressurize the water, and delivered to homes and businesses for drinking, cleaning, and fire fighting among other things. After use, the sewage water is piped to the treatment plant. The treated sewage water is returned to the river.

The "faucet family tree" begins where melting snow and rain flow together to form tributary streams, then large rivers. Most of that water seeps into the ground, evaporates, or transpires (is used by plants), but some of it remains above ground and flows as surface water. Some of the surface water is collected in reservoirs to be used for crop irrigation, industrial applications, and household uses. Water that has soaked into the ground continues to move downward until it meets an impermeable layer, emerges from the ground as a spring, or is withdrawn from a well. Water can also flow underground.

Many cities in the Colorado Basin use a combination of well and surface water to meet needs. To do this, they combine water diverted from streams, reservoirs, and canals with that taken from ground water sources. In Arizona, 41 percent of the water is drawn from wells (Arizona Water Resources Research Center, 2002). Some water has high levels of contaminants such as heavy metals, bacteria, and other organisms. Most water must be treated before it can be used as drinking water. Proper water treatment and delivery are critical to human health.

Water Delivery

Before water can be delivered, it must be pressurized. This is achieved by storing water at an elevation above the water users. For every thirty-two feet water is raised above a given point, water pressure is increased by one atmosphere (atm) or 14.7 pounds per square inch (psi). Once the water is pressurized, it can be moved to waiting towns, subdivisions, houses, and factories. The distribution systems of some cities have thousands of miles of water pipes. Phoenix, Arizona, has five thousand miles of pipes, some as large as nine feet in diameter! Throughout the system, chemists take samples to ensure that the water meets water quality standards. Taste, smell, and the presence of aquatic organisms are just a few of the things they test for.

Once water reaches subdivisions, a medium-sized pipe connects to the main water line, and smaller pipes take it to individual houses. These individual lines enter houses where they are connected to toilets, sinks, dishwashers, washing machines, outside watering faucets, etc.

Water use varies according to fixtures used, conservation practices, type of landscaping, and climate, among other things. Residential water use may be divided into inside and outside use. This is an important distinction, as much water use that occurs indoors is nonconsumptive (the water is not removed from the system entirely). For example, when you wash dishes, most of the dirty water flows down the drain. From there, sewage lines carry the dirty water to a treatment facility where grease, organic material, pathogens, and other undesirable materials are removed. Often, treated water is then returned to a nearby stream or river where it can be reused.

In the Lower Basin, about 70 percent of residential water is used outside for landscaping, swimming pools, car washing, etc. (Water Use Facts, 2003); this amount is less in the Upper Basin. This variation is a result of differences in temperature and soil type. Most outdoor water use is lost to transpiration, evaporation, and seepage. It is not reclaimed by the sewage system. Some types of landscaping use more water than others. For example, Kentucky blue grass grown in Las Vegas or Phoenix (which have year-round growing seasons) requires up to six feet of water per year. In the same areas, some cacti can grow with less than one foot of moisture per year. Planting grass in shaded locations can also help reduce the amount of water required to keep it alive. Some cities, including Las Vegas, Tucson, and Denver, are working to reduce outdoor water use by encouraging homeowners to Xeriscape™ (landscape using plants that require less water). In 2003, Las Vegas initiated a program that credits home owners with one dollar for every square foot of grass they remove.

Procedure

Preparation

1. **Copy and cut strips of paper into the following set of twenty-seven delivery steps.** If you have more than twenty-seven students, you may have students double up or you may add more role strips. If you have fewer, you can remove tributaries, snowfall, or rain. Delivery steps:

- Snow falling in watershed headwaters → Tributary carrying water to the Colorado River
- Snow falling in watershed headwaters → Tributary carrying water to the Colorado River
- Snow falling in watershed headwaters → Tributary carrying water to the Colorado River
- Snow falling in watershed headwaters → Tributary carrying water to the Colorado River
- Rain falling in watershed → Tributary carrying water to the Colorado River
- Rain falling in watershed → Tributary carrying water to the Colorado River
- Rain falling in watershed → Tributary carrying water to the Colorado River
- Tributary carrying water to the Colorado River → Colorado River flowing toward urban area
- Colorado River flowing toward urban area → Pumping station diverting water from the Colorado River to a storage reservoir
- Pumping station diverting water from the Colorado River to a storage reservoir → Reservoir storing river water for use during dry periods
- Reservoir storing river water for use during

dry periods → Canal returning water from the storage reservoir to the Colorado River
- Canal returning water from the storage reservoir to the Colorado River → Water well bringing ground water to the surface for drinking
- Water well bringing ground water to the surface for drinking → Drinking water intake diverting water from the reservoir canal
- Drinking water intake diverting water from the reservoir canal → Drinking water aqueduct carrying water from the reservoir canal and water well to urban areas
- Drinking water aqueduct carrying water from the reservoir canal and water well to urban areas → Pipeline carrying water pumped from wells toward urban areas
- Pipeline carrying water pumped from wells toward urban areas → Water treatment plant treating dirty water so it can be used for drinking
- Water treatment plant treating dirty water so it can be used for drinking → Pipeline carrying water to town's fresh-water delivery system
- Pipeline carrying water to town's fresh-water delivery system → Pipe carrying town water to subdivision distribution
- Pipe carrying town water to subdivision distribution → Pipe directing water from subdivision distribution to individual house
- Pipe directing water from subdivision distribution to individual house → Pipe carrying water from house intake to sink faucet
- Pipe carrying water from house intake to sink faucet → Sewer pipe directing water from sink to house sewer outlet
- Sewer pipe directing water from sink to house sewer outlet → Sewer pipe from house outlet to subdivision sewer system
- Sewer pipe from house outlet to subdivision sewer system → Sewer pipe from subdivision sewer system to town sewer collection
- Sewer pipe from subdivision sewer system to town sewer collection → Sewer pipeline carrying water from town sewer collection to sewer treatment facility
- Sewer pipeline carrying water from town sewer collection to sewer treatment facility → Sewer treatment facility removing harmful waste
- Sewer treatment facility removing harmful waste → Pipeline carrying treated wastewater from sewer treatment to river
- Pipeline carrying treated wastewater from sewer treatment to river → River carrying unused water and treated wastewater downstream to next community

Warm Up

1. **Explain to the students that they will assume roles in the "faucet family tree" to help them visualize the steps involved in bringing water to their household faucets and carrying it away.**

2. **Have each student draw a delivery step role strip from a hat.** Students should then copy the delivery steps onto a blank piece of paper. Each of the two steps on the strip should be copied onto opposite ends of the student's paper. Have them use big letters so the writing can be read from across the room. Markers work best.

3. **Have students line up in the proper order from "Snow falling in watershed headwaters" to "River carrying unused water and treated wastewater downstream to next community."** Students having pages with matching roles should line up next to each other. Students receiving water from "Tributary carrying water to the Colorado River" will have several students that match to their card. This represents tributaries adding water to the larger river. Two students will be left without proper

matches. They are either "snow falling on the headwaters" or "River carrying unused water and treated wastewater downstream to the next community."

4. **Time the activity to see how fast students can line up.** After students have organized themselves (it may take ten minutes), check to see how well they did.

5. **Beginning with "Snow falling in the headwaters" have students read their cards to the group.** Why there are so many cards that represent snow or rain? How would water be used while it is in a house? Are students surprised by the number of steps required to get water to the faucet and back to a river? What might happen if the reservoir dried up? What about the water well? What might happen if everyone turned on their faucets at the same time? What happens to the treated water after it flows downstream? Unless a community is at the end of the river, much of the treated sewer water will be used by communities downstream. Before it is reused, any harmful material in the water will be removed. Why is it important to treat water before drinking it?

The Activity

1. **Explain that human and environmental health as well as economic stability depends on a well-developed water treatment and delivery system.** The water treatment process removes many harmful things. This includes sediment, pathogens, bacteria, viruses, chemicals, and minerals. Without treatment, water can make people sick. In Europe during the fifteenth century, people using untreated water caused cholera epidemics. A well-designed water delivery system is also important. If pipes have leaks or if water pressure is too low, people are left without the water they need to survive.

2. **Hand out the *Faucet Family Tree Instructions Student Copy Page* and the *Faucet Family Tree Worksheet Student Copy***

Page. Tell students that they will use math to trace the flow of water from its source, through water treatment facilities, into distribution pipes, through houses, into wastewater return pipes, through treatment and back to a river.

3. **Using the *Faucet Family Tree Instructions Student Copy Page* as a guide, explain how this "faucet family tree" is constructed.** This discussion should help students connect the *Warm Up* with the activity worksheet.

4. **Have students use algebra to fill in the blanks on the *Faucet Family Tree Worksheet Student Copy Page*.** This will be done by manipulating the formula $A \cdot B = C$. The formula can be changed to $A = C / B$, $B = C / A$, etc. (e.g., $2 \cdot 3 = 6$; $2 = 6 / 3$; $3 = 6 / 2$). These are some of the same formulas used by water managers to determine how much water to process and where to send it! To determine how high the water tower should be, students can use standard math. They will need to convert pounds per square inch (psi) to atmospheres (atm). Once this is done, they will be able to multiply the number of atmospheres by thirty-two feet (a column of water thirty-two feet high has a pressure of one atm) to determine the required height of the tower.

Answers to questions 1–5 on the *Faucet Family Tree Worksheet Student Copy Page*:
1) 893,116 gallons; 2) 130.61 when two decimal places are used; 3) 260,000 gallons; 4) 123,000 gallons; 5) 427,000 gallons

Wrap Up
1. **Ask students to discuss their findings.** How much water is diverted from the river and pumped from the well? How much is returned to the river? What happened to the water that does not return? Why might one house use more water than the other? Outside water use and landscaping cause the biggest difference between households. Houses with large lawns will use substantially more water than will

those that use drought-tolerant landscaping (often native plants and other low water-use features). There is also a big difference between the types of grass used in lawns in terms of how much water they require (see **e-Links** for more information about desert landscaping).

2. **Have students discuss the importance of water treatment in the faucet family tree.** What would happen if we did not treat our drinking water? Does all water we use need to be treated? Many cities use "gray" water that is not as pure as drinking water to irrigate golf courses and parks.

3. **Ask the students if they know where their water comes from.** If they live in a rural area, many of the homes will be supplied by wells. In smaller towns and cities, water may be drawn directly from the river. Some cities use a combination of river and well water to meet water needs, e.g., Mexicali. Large cities such as Las Vegas, Phoenix, Los Angeles, Denver, and others also get their water from a variety of sources. To get specific information about your town, call the city or county water manager. Resources for a few of the larger cities are included under **e-Links**.

Assessment

Have students:
- role-play to learn about the various steps involved in delivering water to faucets (***Warm Up***, Steps 2–5);
- trace the movement of water through a municipal water system (***Warm Up***, Steps 2–5);
- calculate consumptive and nonconsumptive water use with algebraic equations (Step 3);
- use math to determine water pressure and water use in acre-feet (Step 3);
- discuss the results of their findings (***Wrap Up***, Step 1);
- investigate the source of their household water (***Wrap Up***, Step 1);
- discuss the importance of water treatment in the faucet family tree (***Wrap Up***, Step 3).

Extensions

Have students research and present to the class the costs, benefits, and challenges associated with the water delivery stage they represented during the role-play.

Have students make puzzles of a water delivery system.

Have students perform a water audit of their household water consumption. Create a chart that shows the class average for water consumption.

Have students prepare a presentation on the steps in drinking water and wastewater treatment.

Resources

Arizona Game and Fish Department. 2001. *Landscaping for Desert Wildlife*. Phoenix: Arizona Game and Fish Department.

Arizona Water Resources Research Center. 2002. *Arizona Water Wall Map*. Tucson: Arizona Water Resources Research Center.

Binnie, Chris, et al. 2002. *Basic Water Treatment*. London: Thomas Telford.

Culp, Gordon, and Russell Culp. 1974. *New Concepts in Water Purification*. New York: Van Nostrand Reinhold Company.

Gleick, Peter et al. 2003. *The World's Water: The Biennial Report on Freshwater Resources 2002–2003*. Washington, DC: Island Press.

Wastewater Treatment Principles and Regulations. 2003. Retrieved on December 10, 2003, from the Ohio State University Extension Office Web site: http://ohioline.osu.edu/aex-fact/0768.html

Water Use Facts. 2003. Retrieved on December 10, 2003, from the Southern Nevada Water Authority Web Site: www.snwa.com/html/ws_water_use_facts.html

Water Smart. 2004. Retrieved on September 6, 2004, from the Southern Nevada Water Authority Web site: www.snwa.com/html/ws_index.html

Tijuana Water Treatment Plant. 2003. Retrieved on December 10, 2003, from the Water-Technology Web site: www.water-technology.net/projects/tijuana

e-Links

Arizona Water Resources Research Center
Information about water use and conservation in Arizona.
http://ag.arizona.edu/AZWATER

City of Phoenix Water Information
Information on water issues in and around the Phoenix area.
http://phoenix.gov/WATER

Las Vegas Springs Preserve
Information about desert landscaping.
http://www.springspreserve.org/html/index.html

Metro Wastewater Treatment District
Information about Denver wastewater treatment.
www.metrowastewater.com

Metropolitan Water District of Southern California
Links to educational resources and information about water sources for Los Angeles and San Diego.
www.mwdh2o.com

San Diego County Water Authority
Information about water use and supply in San Diego.
www.sdcwa.org

Southern Nevada Water Authority
Information about water use and conservation (including desert landscaping) in Las Vegas and surrounding areas.
www.snwa.com

United States Environmental Protection Agency
Information about household water use in the United States.
www.epa.gov/watrhome/you/chap1.html

Faucet Family Tree Instructions

The ***Faucet Family Tree Worksheet*** is the simplified water plan for a new city that is being built. Water managers have estimated how much water households and swimming pools will use, but the figures are incomplete. Your job is to complete the sheet to determine how much water will be treated, used, and returned to the river.

The "faucet ancestry" of this new town begins at the top of the page where water is pumped from a well and is also diverted from the nearby river. It then enters the treatment facility where sediment is removed and chemicals such as chlorine are added.

Treated water is pumped into the water tower. Since the tower is above town, gravity will pull the water toward houses and create water pressure.

Households, businesses, and public water users get their water from the pressurized water lines. Within a house, water is piped to faucets and appliances. In hot regions, about 70 percent of household water is used outdoors. This water evaporates, transpires (is used by plants), or seeps into the ground. Water that is used indoors is collected and removed through a series of sewer pipes. That water is treated at the wastewater plant and returned to the river.

Residential Water Use

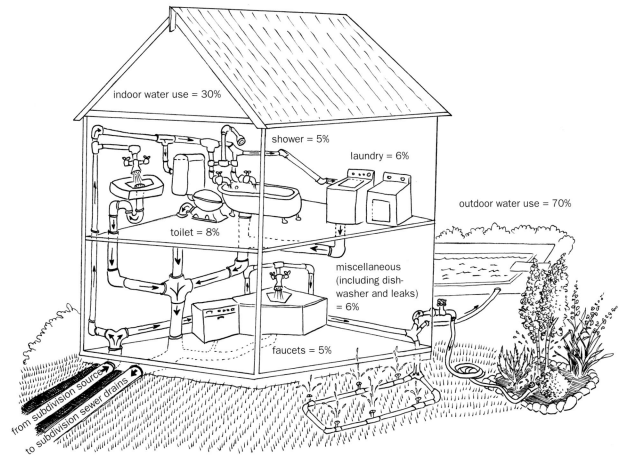

Water that flows from faucets has been carried there by an elaborate system of water treatment and pipes. After use, sewage pipes gather the water and carry it to a sewage treatment plant. After treatment, it will be returned to surface water supplies.

Faucet Family Tree Worksheet

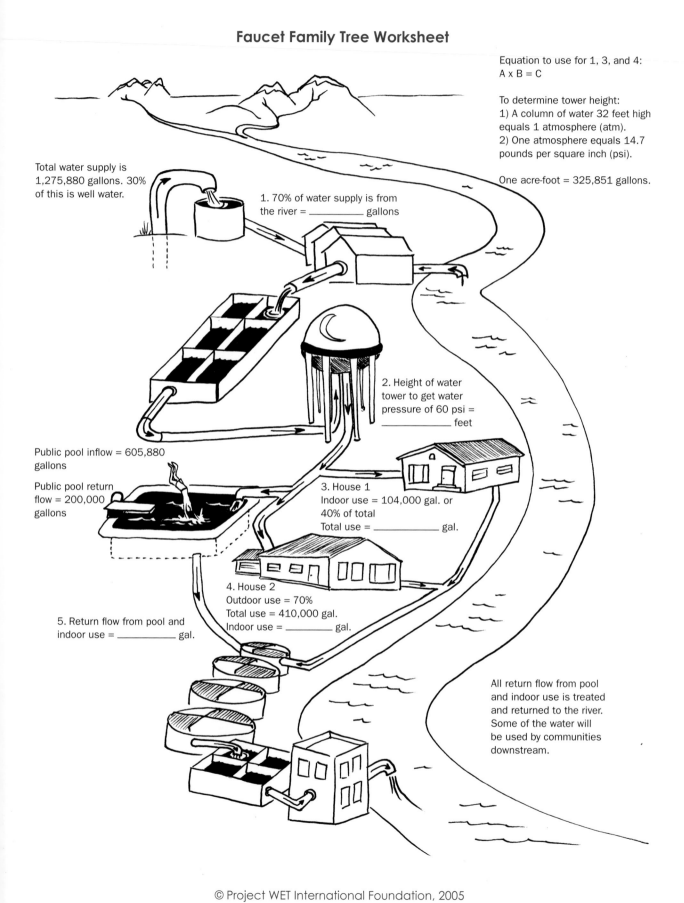

Equation to use for 1, 3, and 4:
A x B = C

To determine tower height:
1) A column of water 32 feet high equals 1 atmosphere (atm).
2) One atmosphere equals 14.7 pounds per square inch (psi).

One acre-foot = 325,851 gallons.

Total water supply is 1,275,880 gallons. 30% of this is well water.

1. 70% of water supply is from the river = _____ gallons

2. Height of water tower to get water pressure of 60 psi = _____ feet

Public pool inflow = 605,880 gallons

Public pool return flow = 200,000 gallons

3. House 1
Indoor use = 104,000 gal. or 40% of total
Total use = _____ gal.

4. House 2
Outdoor use = 70%
Total use = 410,000 gal.
Indoor use = _____ gal.

5. Return flow from pool and indoor use = _____ gal.

All return flow from pool and indoor use is treated and returned to the river. Some of the water will be used by communities downstream.

© Project WET International Foundation, 2005

Art

Colors of the Colorado

The Green River, the Vermillion Cliffs, and Black Canyon: what colors do you see in your watershed?

Summary

Students develop skills of observation by examining and painting landscapes in the Colorado River Watershed. These skills can then be applied to science, language arts, and other disciplines.

Grade Level:
6–12

Subject Areas:
Art, Environmental Science, Earth Science

Duration:
Preparation time: 60–90 minutes
Activity time: 2–3 hours
  Part I: 60–90 minutes
  Part II: 60–90 minutes

Setting:
Classroom/Multi-Purpose Art Room

Skills:
Observe, Discuss, Compose, Draw, Paint

Vocabulary:
background, center of interest, complementary color, composition, cool colors, foreground, horizon line, landscape, media, minerals, opaque, perspective, pigment, primary color, reflected light, refracted light, saturate, secondary color, sediment, transparent, warm colors, white light

Objectives
Students will:
- learn how minerals in rock and soil, sediment in water, and reflected and refracted light create the colors we see;
- observe the colors of water, earth, and sky in the Colorado River Watershed;
- paint landscapes seen in photographs, paintings, and outdoor observation;
- demonstrate understanding of basic watercolor techniques.

Materials
- *4" x 6" pieces of watercolor paper* (6 per student; cold press 140-pound paper is suggested, but any good quality art paper 80 pounds or more will work)
- *5" x 8" cardboard squares* (1 per student)
- *Masking tape*
- *Scratch paper* (4–6 pieces per student)
- *Watercolor paints with 8 colors* (1 set per student)
- *Small, medium, and large watercolor brushes* (2–3 per student)
- *Water containers for rinsing brushes* (1 per student)
- *Paper towels*
- *Pencils*
- *Ruler*
- *Copies of **Watercolor Tips and Techniques** Student Copy Pages* (1 per student)
- *Picture file* (paintings, photos, magazine

photos, Web print-outs, etc., of Colorado River Watershed images)

Background

The landscape of the Colorado River Watershed displays a rich palette of color, from red and purple cliffs to green valleys to golden grasslands speckled with silver sage. The river itself is named for its color, which is often red because of sediment eroded from the surrounding land (in Spanish, *colorado* means red or reddish). Many other features of the watershed are named for their distinctive colors, including the Green River, White River, Verde River (Spanish: green), Black Canyon, Havasu Creek (Havasupai: blue-green water), the Vermillion Cliffs, and the Chocolate Mountains. It is no surprise that numerous generations of artists have been inspired by the natural beauty of the watershed's vivid colors and contrasts. Thomas Moran, a famous American painter of the nineteenth century, is one of many artists known for imparting his sense of awe and wonder towards the natural world in magnificent landscape paintings.

Color originates in light but remains invisible until it is refracted through a prism or reflects off a surface. Rainbows are an example of refracted light. Light passes through water droplets and is separated into the full spectrum of visible light (red, orange, yellow, green, blue, indigo, and violet). Other colors that we see are examples of reflected light. For example, when the sun shines on red rocks, all colors except for those that correspond to red are absorbed by the rock. The reds are then reflected into our eyes. Light that has all colors combined (i.e. has not been refracted or reflected) is referred to as white light.

The many "Colors of the Colorado" are a result of how the minerals in the soil reflect light. These minerals include iron oxides (reds, yellows, and purples), chlorite and copper (greens and blues), and others. Soils in the Red Desert, located in central Wyoming and northern Colorado, are an example. As in many other parts of the watershed, these soils have high concentrations of iron oxide. Iron oxide reflects the red spectrum of light. When the minerals in the soil are dissolved in water, the dissolved pigments give the water a characteristic color. Suspended particles in the water affect the way it reflects light. Particles deposited on the bottom of a lake or stream also influence the color water is perceived (see page 162, "Too Thick to Drink").

Learning about color and art can help students of all ages become more keen observers of the geology, ecology, weather, and light of their surroundings. Painting is a way for students to express what they see and learn. From the headwaters to the delta, the spectacular landscapes, flowing rivers, and diverse

Dory in the Grand Canyon.

Elisabeth Howe

Chrissy Jaworsky and Christine Newell painting with watercolors at the El Golfo Biosphere Reserve Field Station, Sonora.

animals and plants of the Colorado Watershed offer limitless inspiration. Watercolor is just one of many media available to use when painting landscapes.

Procedure
Preparation
In order for students to feel successful at creating art with watercolors, a few techniques are helpful. The first key to working with watercolors is using watercolor paper (rather than regular office or construction paper). Watercolor paper is absorbent enough to resist buckling or tearing when paint is applied. A good-quality cold-pressed 80–140-pound watercolor paper is an excellent choice and is available at most craft stores.

Use masking tape to temporarily attach the paper to cardboard while painting. This will help the paper retain its shape during painting and, when removed, leaves a white frame around the image (tip: wait until the paper is completely dry before removing the tape).

It is ideal to have a variety of watercolor brushes in different sizes and shapes, but not necessary. It is also not necessary to purchase expensive paints with a wide variety of colors; students can mix the full color spectrum using an eight-color watercolor set. Refer to the **Watercolor Tips and Techniques** *Student Copy Pages* for detailed information about the vocabulary of watercolor painting and tips on how to create a beautiful landscape image.

1. **Cut watercolor paper into 4" x 6" pieces.** Use the ruler to help tear the paper.

2. **Cut cardboard into 5" x 8" pieces.**

3. **Make copies of the *Watercolor Tips and Techniques Student Copy Pages.***

4. **Collect images for students to use as reference when painting.** Several books with images from the basin are listed in the reference section. Many students will also have their own good photos of landscapes in the basin. Pictures without people are best. You can download and print photos from the basin at www.discoverawatershed.org/activities/colorado. You may choose to focus the lesson by using only images from a certain geographic location (e.g., the Grand Canyon).

5. ***Optional*: download and print a copy of a completed color wheel (see www.discovera watershed.org/activities/colorado).**

6. **Just before you begin, place a drop of water on each color in your watercolor palette except black.**

Warm Up
1. **Ask students if they can identify all the colors of the rainbow.** They are Red, Orange, Yellow,

Green, Blue, Indigo, and Violet. (You can use the name acronym, Roy G. Biv to help students remember these colors.) Explain that these colors make up the visible spectrum of light.

2. **Discuss the relationship between light and color.** Explain that light contains the entire color spectrum, but that we cannot see these colors until light shines on an object or is refracted through a prism (e.g., a water droplet). Light that has not been separated is known as white light (all colors are present). When it shines on certain objects, some of the color spectrum is absorbed. The colors not absorbed are reflected and can be seen with the human eye. White objects appear that way because all colors of the spectrum are reflected. Black objects are that color because they absorb all colors.

   The composition of an object affects which colors are absorbed. Oxidized copper, for example, is blue-green. This means that all colors of the visible spectrum are absorbed except for blues and greens. Geologists looking for copper will sometimes watch for soil with a blue-green tint. Soils with oxidized iron, which absorbs all colors except reds, yellows, and purples, can be identified in a similar way. What colors are being absorbed by some objects in the classroom?

3. **Focus students' attention on the landscape images you have gathered.** Remind them that the colors they are seeing are those that are not being absorbed. Colors that are not exactly red, orange, yellow, green, blue, indigo, or violet appear that way because several colors are being reflected at once. When viewed together, a new color is created.

4. **Encourage students to look closely at the images.** What color are the shadows? Many students will say that they are black, but a closer look will show that there are other colors present. Many shadows are purple or are simply a darker shade of the colors around them. Look

at the clouds. What color are they? There may be white, but it is likely that there is also pink, grey, blue, red, and other colors.

The Activity
Part I

1. **Tell students that they are going to use watercolor paints to improve their skills of observation.** They will use the pictures you have collected as guides for their paintings. Tell students to pay attention to shapes, colors, and textures. There is no need to copy the pictures exactly; they can be used as a guide for creating an entirely new landscape image.

2. **Pass out watercolor paper and show how it is different from regular paper.** Watercolor paper is absorbent and will give students more control over their paints, help prevent paint from pooling, and keep paper from warping or tearing.

3. **Direct students to label the back of each of their six paper squares:** 1) Wash, 2) Wet-on-Wet, 3) Wet-on-Dry, 4) Dry Brush, 5) Practice, 6) Final Landscape.

4. **Direct students' attention to the color wheel in the *Watercolor Tips and Techniques Student Copy Pages.*** If you wish, have the students paint the color wheel. To save time, you can download and print a completed color wheel at www.discoverawatershed.org/activities/colorado. Explain that by combining specific colors in different amounts, students can make any color they desire. For example, by combining yellow and blue, students can make a variety of shades of green. Similarly, by combining red and blue, students can make violet. Encourage them to mix their own colors rather than simply using the pre-mixed colors in their paint set, which will allow them to create more accurate and interesting colors.

5. **Using your own paper, demonstrate each of the following four techniques as students observe.** You can also demonstrate how to mix

colors at this time. When applying colors, paint with light colors before dark. There is no need to fasten these practice pages to cardboard.

- **Wash Technique:** A wash is a very thin layer of paint put down on wet paper. A wash is a good technique to use for large light areas such as sky or water. Take a clean brush and paint clean water evenly across the paper square. The paper should be wet, but not dripping. Select a color with a wet brush and paint across the paper with bold horizontal strokes. Continue with the same color, or choose another color and show students how the colors bleed together where they meet on the paper.

- **Wet-on-Wet Technique:** This simply means painting with a wet brush on wet paper. Moist paint applied to a shiny wet surface will flow freely and create soft, feathery patterns. Paint a wash of one color on wet paper. Rinse the brush and select another color. Load the brush with paint and apply to the color wash. Colors will mix and mingle on the paper spontaneously. This is a good technique for painting skies. Let the paint blend and see what happens!

- **Wet-on-Dry Technique:** A wet brush on dry paper allows for greater control, crisp lines, and saturated colors. Paint abstract shapes and lines with a loaded brush (lots of paint and water) on dry paper. Colors stay put when applied to dry paper. Encourage students to experiment with the amount of paint and water used with this technique.

- **Dry Brush Technique:** A semi-dry brush on dry paper can create hard edges and saturated colors. This technique provides the most control of all. Load the brush with paint and blot it dry on a paper towel before applying it to dry paper. Try different amounts of paint and different brushstrokes to discover the effects that Dry Brush Technique provides.

6. **Pass out the *Watercolor Tips and Techniques Student Copy Pages*.**

7. **Have students experiment with each of the four techniques using the paper they have labeled.** Encourage students to be abstract and experiment with different amounts of water and paint. The instantaneous interaction between the paper, the water, and the watercolor pigments is where the beauty of watercolor painting lies. Let the paints and water do the work.

8. **Set paper squares aside to dry.**

Part II

1. **Show students more photos from your file of landscape paintings.** Ask students to discuss what they see. What is in the foreground and background? What are the lightest and darkest colors? What are the most prominent colors? What shapes can be seen? Point out the horizon line, center of interest (subject), and other important parts of the painting. Direct students' attention to the ***Watercolor Tips and Techniques*** *Student Copy Pages* to help reinforce the concepts and vocabulary discussed.

2. **Have students select images they would like to paint.** They can paint the entire scene or a small part of it.

3. **On scratch paper, have students use pencil to sketch what they would like to paint.** Have them experiment with having the horizon line in the top third or bottom third of the paper. When the horizon is in the top third, the center of interest will be the land. When it is in the bottom third, the center of interest will be the sky. Advise students to avoid horizon lines that are directly in the center of the paper. These sketches do not need to be realistic or detailed.

4. **Have students choose a favorite sketch and transfer it to watercolor paper using light pencil.** This drawing will help guide the painting. Explain that watercolor paints are transparent and that dark pencil lines will show through. They can also dent the paper, making it difficult to paint on. Discourage excessive erasing, which will change the way paint absorbs.

5. **Have students place a drop of water on each color in their watercolor box except black.** Remind them that even very dark areas are rarely black. Instead, they are very dark shades of other colors. Using pure black paint will overpower the other colors.

6. **Tell students that they have enough paper for two paintings.** They can view the first painting as a practice painting and use the second to refine skills. There is no need to attach the first painting to the cardboard. When they do attach the second painting, have them cover the outer ¼" with masking tape. When applying colors, have them start with the lighter areas, as you can cover light color with dark, but not dark with light.

7. **Provide feedback as necessary.** Remind students that their paintings do not need to be perfect. If they make a mistake, suggest using a brush with clean water to remove the paint.

8. **Tell students to rinse their brushes often and to avoid contaminating one color with another.** Remind students to sign and title their paintings before setting them aside to dry. Once their paintings are dry, they can carefully remove the tape from the edges.

9. **Give specific directions for cleaning brushes, water containers, and paint sets.**

Wrap Up
1. **Display student landscapes.**

2. **Have students observe and identify the different watercolor techniques in each other's paintings.** Another option is to display the paintings anonymously and assign a number to each one. Have students silently walk around the display and write a positive comment for each painting including their own. Cut the comments apart and return them to the student whose painting matches the number. Each student ends up with a collection of comments to keep in response to his or her painting.

3. **Discuss how painting can improve observation skills.** What did students notice about the landscapes that they had not seen at first? How are colors in the background and foreground different from each other? Why is this? In some landscapes, the background is obscured by haze or mist. This sometimes gives it a purple appearance. What did students notice about plants in the landscape images? How many types of plants did they see? How did the students include this diversity in their paintings?

Assessment
Have students:
- demonstrate four different watercolor techniques (*Part I*, Step 7);
- create watercolor landscape paintings of places in the Colorado River Watershed (*Part II*, Steps 3–6);
- observe and identify watercolor techniques (*Wrap Up*, Steps 1–2);
- discuss how painting can improve observation skills (*Wrap Up*, Steps 1–3).

Extensions
Have students write short narratives about their landscapes to display. Topics could include creative or informative descriptions of the landscape they decided to paint.

Have students write a poem or find a poem already written about a special place in the Colorado River Watershed to display with their paintings.

Show students how prisms separate light into visible colors and have them research how this happens.

Have students go outside to paint in the field. Students should bring the following materials: small water container, set of watercolor paints and a brush or two, paper of various sizes and shapes, sketch pad, pencil, and camera (to record the scene for later reference). Painting in the field presents some challenges. First, students must avoid the temptation to paint everything around them, which can be difficult when faced with 360 degrees of scenery; choose a composition with limited boundaries. Second, the changing position of the sun can alter the way a scene looks. Painting scenes that are entirely in shade can help solve this problem. If time is limited, students can combine quick pre-drawings and photographs to create a final work of art.

Resources

Collier, Michael. 1999. *Water, Earth, and Sky: The Colorado River Basin*. Salt Lake City: University of Utah Press.

Durham, Michael. 1990. *The Smithsonian Guide to Historic America: the Desert States; New Mexico, Arizona, Nevada, Utah*. New York: Stewart, Tabori & Chang.

Fielder, John. 1998. *Colorado Skies*. Englewood, CO: Westcliffe Publishers.

Hucko, Bruce. 1996. *Where There is No Name for Art: The Art of Tewa Pueblo Children*. Santa Fe, NM: School of American Research Press.

McQuiston, Don and Debra. 1995. *The Woven Spirit of the Southwest*. San Francisco, CA: Chronicle Books.

Smith, Ray. 1993. *Watercolor COLOR*. New York: Doring Kindersley, Inc.

e-Links

Arizona Highways Magazine
Color photographs of scenic landscapes in Arizona.
www.arizonahighways.com

Color Matters
Information about how humans see light and color.
www.colormatters.com

Discover a Watershed: The Colorado
Color photographs of Colorado Watershed landscapes and a completed color wheel.
www.discoverawatershed.org/activities/colorado

National Geographic
Photographs and stories from around the world.
www.nationalgeographic.com

Watercolor Tips and Techniques I

Color Mixing Practice

1. Fill in the red, blue, and yellow circles of the color wheel with pure, saturated color. These are the **primary colors**.

2. In your paint tray, mix red and yellow in equal parts to make orange, blue, and yellow in equal parts to make green, and red and blue in equal parts to make purple. Fill in the squares on the color wheel. These are the **secondary colors**.

Cool Colors include the family of related colors that range from green through blue and violet. Cool colors remind us of cool things like water, shadows, and night.

Warm Colors include the family of related colors that range from yellow through orange and red. Warm colors tend to remind us of warm places such as desert rocks, sunshine, and canyon walls.

Complementary Colors are colors located opposite each other on the color wheel (e.g., yellow and violet). They provide maximum contrast when placed next to each other, and when mixed will dull each other, making various shades of gray and brown.

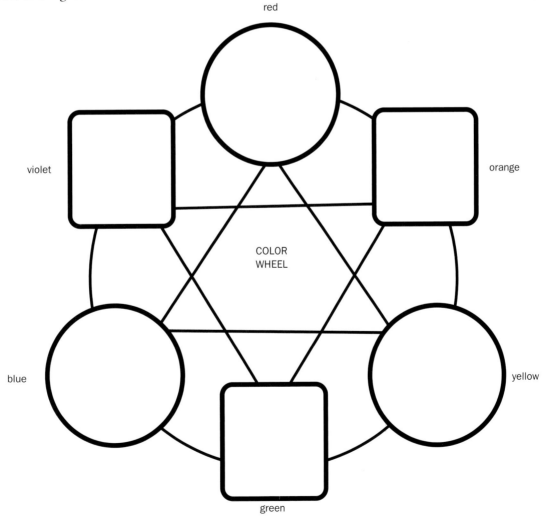

red

violet

orange

COLOR
WHEEL

blue

yellow

green

Watercolor Tips and Techniques II

Colors of the Earth

You can create earthy browns and rich shadow colors by combining complementary colors. Blends of yellow, orange, and red will "wake up" earthy browns and add warmth and light to rock faces and distant cliffs. Blue, gray, and violet will "cool down" brown mixtures, resulting in perfect hues for deep shadows on cliff walls and cool dark stones. Begin studying the colors of the earth by taking a walk and observing color with an artist's eye, and collect a few stones to set by your palette.

Colors of the Sky

The sky is often portrayed as a calm, seamless sea of blue. However, throughout the Colorado River Basin, the sky offers an array of extremes: from blue and cloudless to gray thunderheads, and from delicate pinks of sunrise to burning reds and oranges of sunset. Start with **Wet-on-Wet Technique** and add darker values to create spontaneous cloud shapes with soft edges. Remember that areas intended to be white (such as clouds) must be left unpainted. Wash on a pure blue sky using a loaded brush (loaded with equal amounts of blue paint and water) with even horizontal strokes from one edge of the paper to the other. Overworking a wet wash can result in a muddy, unclear affect. When you are painting the sky and something happens that you like, stop.

Colors of the Water

Water and its translucency are challenging to depict with paints. It is the reflective quality of water that gives it such spectacular color and light. Bodies of water reflect the color of the sky; therefore, it is best to paint the sky first. Greens, blues, and grays will mix on wet paper to create the diverse colors we see in water. Pinks and oranges depict the reflection of sunrise or sunset. Landforms are often reflected as a mirror image in a calm body of water. Pay attention to the direction of the water flow and apply watercolor in the same direction. Surface reflections can be painted in a horizontal direction.

Watercolor Tips and Techniques III

Four Important Techniques

1. **Wash Technique:** A wash is a very thin layer of paint put down on wet paper. A wash is a good technique to use for large light areas such as sky or water. Take a clean brush and paint clean water evenly across the paper square. The paper should be wet, but not dripping. Select a color with a wet brush and paint across the paper with bold horizontal strokes. Continue with the same color, or choose another color and notice how the colors bleed together where they meet on the paper.

2. **Wet-on-Wet Technique:** This simply means painting with a wet brush on wet paper. Moist paint applied to a shiny wet surface will flow freely and create soft, feathery patterns. Paint a wash of one color on wet paper. Rinse the brush and select another color. Load the brush with paint and apply to the color wash. Colors will mix and mingle on the paper spontaneously. Let the paint blend and see what happens!

3. **Wet-on-Dry Technique:** A wet brush on dry paper allows for greater control, crisp lines, and saturated colors. Paint abstract shapes and lines with a loaded brush (lots of paint and water) on dry paper. Colors stay put when applied to dry paper. Experiment with the amount of paint and water to use with this technique.

4. **Dry Brush Technique:** A semi-dry brush on dry paper can create hard edges and saturated colors. This technique provides the most control of all. Load the brush with paint and blot it dry on a paper towel before applying it to dry paper. Try different amounts of paint and different brushstrokes to discover the effects that **Dry Brush Technique** provides.

Key Terms:

Composition: the arrangement of the elements of a scene (line, color, value, space), organized in a way to create a unified, balanced piece of art.

Center of interest: the visual focal point of a composition.

Horizon line: the line where land meets sky in a composition. For an interesting and balanced composition, the horizon line should be in the top or bottom third of the paper, not in the center.

Landscape: a work of art that shows the features of the natural environment (e.g., rivers, lakes, canyons, sky, mountains, light, and shadow).

horizon line in top third

horizon line in bottom third

horizon line in center

© Claire Emery and Project WET International

Moving the location of the horizon line in a composition will change the effect of the painting.

Cultures

Trading Toss-Up

How far would you travel to buy a seashell? How much would you pay for it?

Summary

Students play a trading game and use maps and artifacts to explore the trade network established by ancient cultures living in the southwestern United States, northern Mexico, and Central America.

Grade Level:
6–12

Subject Areas:
History/Anthropology, Economics, Geography

Duration:
Preparation time: 20 minutes
Activity time: 60 minutes

Setting:
Classroom

Skills:
Analyze, Apply, Compare, Discuss, Hypothesize, Evaluate, Write

Vocabulary:
amaranth, Ancestral Puebloan, anthropology, archaeology, exchange, Hohokam, obsidian, resource center, trade, turquoise

Objectives

Students will:
- identify the origin of common classroom items;
- examine the importance and function of trade networks in the prehistoric Southwest;
- compare prehistoric trade with modern distribution of goods.

Materials

- *12 sheets of 8 ½" x 11" paper* (2 sheets each of 6 different colors)
- *Scissors or paper cutter*
- *Tape*
- *Felt tip pen*
- *Overhead transparency of the* **Hohokam Trade Network** *Teacher Copy Page*

Background

Beginning at least two thousand years ago, the Hohokam, Mogollon, Ancestral Puebloans, Cucapá, and other groups in and around the Colorado River Watershed were trading with each other. Throughout the region, these peoples traded each other for non-consumable items such as turquoise, pottery, cotton textiles, copper, parrot feathers, mosaic mirrors, seashells, and obsidian. Some of these items (such as turquoise necklaces) were traded as finished goods. They traded others (like obsidian) in their raw form. Groups receiving the raw goods would use them to make jewelry, tools, and other items. The Mogollon culture, for example, received raw obsidian from the Hohokam

An artist's depiction of Hohokam villiage life, circa A.D. 1200. Irrigation was an important tool the Hohokam used to grow crops in the desert.

Courtesy Pueblo Grande Museum

and used it to make arrowheads and other tools. The Hohokam received raw seashells and used them to make intricate shell jewelry.

They also exchanged consumable goods such as corn, squash, beans, tobacco, and salt. Trade of these items was important because, at times, drought, floods, and frost destroyed these in some areas. When this happened, groups would engage in trade with groups living in areas where the items were available. Prices for traded items depended on the difficulty of procuring or producing them. A finished piece of turquoise was worth more than a piece of raw turquoise. Similarly, a seashell had a higher value in Colorado than in Baja California.

Trade can be viewed as organized around "resource centers." Concentration of a given resource will be highest where the item is extracted, grown, or produced. As you move away from the resource center, the item will become less common. In general, rare items are worth more in trade than

common ones. As a result, resources may have a lower value near the resource center than they will where the resource is rare. To take advantage of this, groups often carry their common goods away from the resource center to trade.

The Hohokam people, whose culture flourished in the Phoenix area between A.D. 700 and 1400, were highly productive farmers, potters, weavers of textiles, and makers of jewelry. They grew cotton, squash, beans, corn, and other crops, using water from the thousands of miles of irrigation ditches that they built.

Some archaeologists have referred to the Hohokam as middlemen in southwestern trade (Crown and Judge 1991). This makes sense, as they were located near the center of the Colorado Basin and between North American and Mesoamerican tribes. This was an important position, as there was much exchange of culture and goods between regions. Mesoamerican influence can be seen in Ancestral Puebloan communities like Chaco Canyon

Parrot feathers found at Chaco Canyon in northern New Mexico indicate that the people who lived here engaged in trade with communities far to the south.

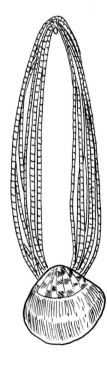

Seashell necklaces are one of many items that were traded throughout the Colorado River Watershed.

and Mesa Verde, as well as many other places.

The Hohokam likely moved goods through community-to-community trade, trade expeditions, and other methods (Crown and Judge 1991). In community-to-community trade, goods exchange hands in each community along the trade route. Goods may stay in a community for some time before being traded again, and it may take years for them to travel a few hundred miles. Trade expeditions distribute goods more quickly than community-to-community trade. It is likely that this method of trade was used with more expensive and perishable items. For example, parrots from Mesoamerica are found throughout the Southwest. These parrots may have been carried from Paquimé, a trading center in what is now the state of Chihuahua, directly to the final buyer in the American Southwest.

Procedure

Preparation

For the *Warm Up* and *Wrap Up*:
Make an overhead transparency of the *Hohokam Trade Network Teacher Copy Page.*

For *The Activity*:

1. **You will need two sets of six sheets of paper in six different colors.** One set will be used as a key to be posted at the front of the classroom. The second set will be cut up as follows: cut four sheets into 2" squares; use only half-sheets of the remaining two colors and cut them into 2" squares. Keep squares of each color separate. Tape the uncut set to the wall or chalkboard at the front of the room.

2. **Use a felt tip marker to label these sheets: 1) obsidian, 2) seashell, 3) turquoise, 4) salt, 5) parrot, and 6) copper bell.** The two half-sheets should be labeled as parrot and copper bell. These sheets will serve as a legend to tell students what resources they have collected. You may want to draw or find pictures to represent each of the items. If samples of each item are available, you can place these with the legend.

3. *Optional:* **Bring a sample of as many of the traded items as you can find.** The earth science teacher will likely have samples of most of the minerals.

Warm Up

1. **Have students (in groups of two) find the origin of several items in the classroom, e.g., books, calendars, computers, food, clothing, etc.** Each group reports the origin of the items for the class. How could all of these items have gotten to this classroom? Use a map or globe to determine which item came the farthest distance. Is there a connection between the cost of an item and how far it has traveled? Why or why not?

2. **Show the *Hohokam Trade Network* overhead transparency and explain that trade has been occurring in the Colorado River Basin and beyond for thousands of years.** Often this trade occurred between groups that were far apart. Talk about the Hohokam and their system of trade. They were involved in trade in the Southwest between A.D. 700 and 1400 and were well situated for trade because their central location gave them access to goods from the mountains, desert, and ocean. Items they traded can be found in Arizona, California, New Mexico, Sonora, and Baja California. Archaeologists have found artifacts from as far away as southern Mexico buried in Hohokam sites. Since there were no cars, horses, or mass transportation, these items had to be carried on foot.

3. *Optional:* **If you have brought samples of each of the traded items, show them to the students and pass them around the room.**

The Activity

1. **With students in their seats, select six students who are evenly distributed around the room.** These students will represent "resource centers" or places where certain resources are most concentrated. Give each of these "resource centers" a pile of paper pieces that are uniform in color. Explain to the class that each piece of paper represents a trade item. To see which trade item is represented, students can compare the color of the cards to the labeled sheets at the front of the room.

2. **Explain that people often engage in trade to obtain items that they need or want.** Often they will give something of which they have adequate supply to get the rarer thing that they need or want. They may trade a resource (such as gold), knowledge (such as the ability to forge steel), or a service (such as raising vegetables to send to places where they cannot be grown).

For example, farmers in the Imperial Valley, Yuma, and Mexicali areas are able to grow vegetables year round, whereas farmers in Wyoming cannot. If people in Wyoming want to eat fresh vegetables during the winter, they can "trade" with farmers on the Lower Colorado to get them.

3. **Explain that trade items are often dispersed from a single place.** This can be likened to a drop of food coloring placed on a wet piece of paper; the color will be darkest where the drop hits the paper and become lighter as it spreads away from that point. Like the food coloring, trade items may have the highest density near the source (resource center) and become less common as you move away from that point. Students holding paper pieces represent resource centers.

4. **With the students still in their seats, ask the volunteers to throw their stacks of paper straight up so that they spread evenly around them.** Some students may note that it is difficult to make paper spread evenly. The same is true with real trade items because cultural and physical barriers can prevent trade items from moving freely in all directions.

5. **Have all students pick up only the pieces of paper that they can reach from their desks.** Some students will end up with only one type of "resource" while others may have several. This will depend on their proximity to resource centers. Have them count and record the number of each resource they collect.

6. **Explain that, in many situations, diversity of resources is critical.** For example, people may have a food source, but they also need a diversity of tools to harvest and cook their food. Similarly, people place more value on things that are rare. For example, a group living by the seashore may place little value on seashells, while a group living in the mountains may give them a higher value because they are not common there.

7. **Tell the students that they will engage in trade to get the highest diversity of resources possible.** To do this, they will need to trade with their neighbors. They may not leave their seats and can only negotiate with the people around them. This means that, in order to get resources from students across the room, those resources will need to be traded through other students in a trading chain. To help motivate students, it may help to give a prize to the students with the greatest diversity of resources (the most pieces of different colored paper).

8. **Tell students to make a slash mark on the resources each time they are traded.** This will record the number of times the resource has changed hands and will demonstrate the amount of effort and cost required to move a resource from one point to another. A resource that is moved from one side of the room to the other will have more marks on it than one that remained in the same region. Point out that there are fewer parrots and copper bells and that this is likely to affect how they are traded. Economists talk about the law of supply and demand. The law says that the greater the supply of one item, the lower its price will be. Conversely, rare items will be more expensive. Periodically remind students to mark their items, as it is easy to forget in the trading frenzy.

9. **Ask the students to begin trading.** Give them ten minutes to complete all transactions. Each student will set the "price" of his or her resources. Some resources may be traded on a one-for-one basis, while other, more rare items may be more expensive.

© Project WET International Foundation, 2005

Wrap Up

1. **After trading is complete, ask students to count the total number of each resource they have.** Is there one resource that they have more of? Why? Were there some resources that were harder to obtain? Why? Did the pricing of items follow the law of supply and demand? Why or why not?

2. **Have each student identify the resource that has the most slash marks (went through the most trades).** Select a few students and have them identify which of their resources have the most slash marks. Have the student that originally dispersed that resource raise his or her hand. What can be noted about the position of resource centers and the most traded resource? Which student has the resource that was traded the greatest number of times? Why?

3. **Ask each student to identify their four resources that have the greatest number of slashes.** Have them count the total number of slashes on those resources. Which students

have the greatest number of slashes? Which students have the least? Why is this and what does it mean for this system of trade? Does the number of times an item is traded depend on where students are in the room or the rarity of the resource?

4. **Ask students what made this system of trade work.** What made it difficult? What changes would make the system more efficient? How is it similar to or different from the way items are traded today? How is it similar to how we price water? How might transportation costs of water change the price people are charged to use it? For example, in the Phoenix and Tucson areas, water pumped form local aquifers is cheaper than that transported from the distant Colorado River.

5. **Return students' attention to the *Hohokam Trade Network Teacher Copy Page*.** How do the trades that took place in the classroom compare with those of the Hohokam? Why? You may want to draw a map of your

classroom on the board. On this map, you can show the location of resource centers and the distance trade items traveled through trade.

Assessment
Have students:
- identify the origin of common classroom items (***Warm Up***, Step 1);
- demonstrate how trade items in the prehistoric Colorado River Watershed were disseminated from their points of origin to the final user (Steps 4–9);
- discuss how resource availability and difficulty to obtain items affected their price (***Wrap Up***, Steps 1–3);
- compare simulated trade patterns to those of the Hohokam (***Wrap Up***, Steps 4–5).

Extensions
Have students write a brief essay comparing prehistoric trade with the modern distribution of items.

Have students identify ten items that they regularly trade at school and at home. How are these items valued? With whom do they trade? Where were these items made?

Resources
Covey, Cyclone. 1993. *Adventures in the Unknown Interior of America*. Albuquerque: University of New Mexico Press.

Crown, Patricia, and James Judge. 1991. *Chaco & Hohokam: Prehistoric Regional Systems in the American Southwest*. Santa Fe, NM: School of American Research Press.

Gabriel, Kathryn. 1992. *Marietta Wetherill: Reflections on Life with the Navajo in Chaco Canyon*. Boulder, CO: Johnson Books.

Lister, Robert and Florence. 1981. *Archaeology and Archaeologists in Chaco Canyon*. Albuquerque: University of New Mexico Press.

Nobel, David. 1999. *The Hohokam: Ancient People of the Desert*. Santa Fe, NM: School of American Research Press.

Stuart, David. 1984. *Glimpses of the Ancient Southwest*. Santa Fe, NM: Ancient City Press.

e-Links
Center for Desert Archaeology
Publications and programs about archaeology relating to desert cultures.
www.centerfordesertarchaeology.org

National Park Service
Information about Chaco Culture National Historical Park.
www.nps.gov/chcu/index.htm

National Park Service
Information about Mesa Verde National Park.
www.nps.gov/meve/index.htm

Project Archaeology
Information and educational materials about archaeology.
www.projectarchaeology.org

Pueblo Grande Museum and Archaeological Park
Information about the Hohokam and the Pueblo Grande Museum and Archaeological Park.
www.ci.phoenix.az.us/PARKS/pueblo.html

University of Arizona Press
Full-text book: *Hohokam Indians of the Tucson Basin*.
www.uapress.arizona.edu/onlinebks/hohokam/titlhoho.htm

Hohokam Trade Network

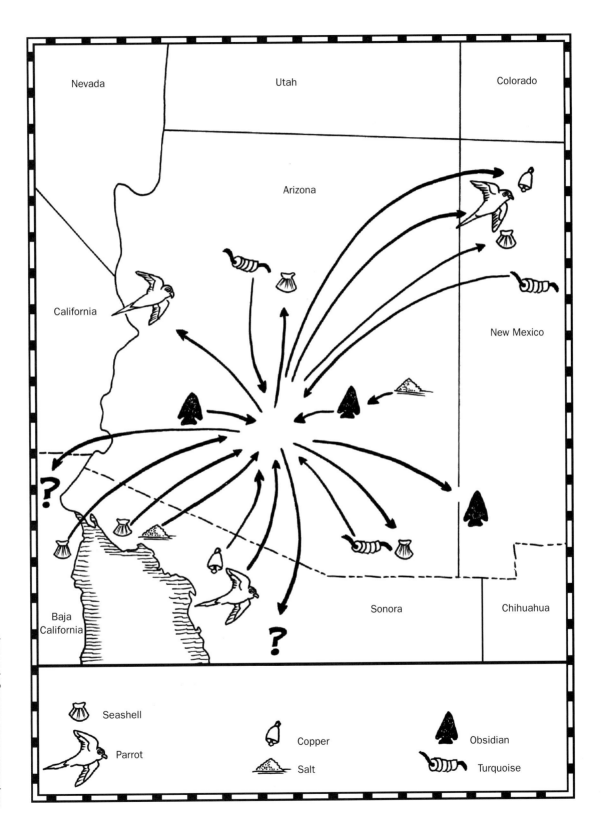

Adapted from Crown and Judge (1991:240).

One River, Many Voices of the Colorado Basin

What is your Colorado River voice?

Grade Level:
10–12

Subject Area:
Language Arts, History/Anthropology, Environmental Science

Duration:
Preparation time: 15 minutes
Activity time: 120 minutes

Setting:
Classroom

Skills:
Analyze, Interpret, Evaluate, Discuss, Write, Interview, Present

Vocabulary:
water user

Summary

Students analyze and interpret excerpts written by diverse water users of the Colorado River, matching each water user with his or her "River Voice." Students also read excerpts from well-known authors who have written about the Colorado and then write their own River Voices.

Objectives

Students will:
- compare and contrast excerpts written about the Colorado Watershed by different water users and authors;
- identify the different values, attitudes, and beliefs about the Colorado that the writings express;
- recognize that cultural, historical, social, political, and economic contexts help determine how people think about the Colorado;
- interpret the work of authors from the watershed to expand their knowledge of the watershed's literature and history;
- write personal essays or poems to express their relationships to the watershed;
- interview a classmate to write a brief biography;
- present their writing and biographies to the class.

Materials

- *Copies of **One River, Many Voices Water User Cards** and **River Voices Cards** Student Copy Pages* (1 classroom set to cut apart, plus 1 copy per student)
- *Copies of **One River, Many Voices Author Cards** Student Copy Pages* and ***Author's Voice***

Larissa Conte finds a quiet spot to write in her journal, Elves Chasm, Arizona.

Cards Student Copy Pages (1 classroom set to cut apart, plus 1 copy per student)
- *Pencils and paper* (for making notes and for creative writing)
- *Optional: selection of books about the Colorado River or Watershed* (see **One River, Many Voices Author Cards** *Student Copy Pages* for suggestions of books and authors)

Background

Of all the rivers in North America, few have been written about more than the Colorado. From scientific papers detailing its ecology, to historical journals recounting adventures in its exploration, to novels and poetry, the body of literature inspired by the Colorado is as vast and varied as its watershed.

Throughout history, people have interacted with the river, using its water and its fertile floodplains for agriculture, following its course as a pathway through the landscape, and incorporating its spirit into stories. Contemporary relationships with the river differ from those of ancient times, as we divert its water miles from the river itself to use in cities; vacation on its shores; and use its water to grow crops that will be shipped to countries around the world. These new relationships are important and vibrant, and when expressed in writing, they convey the ever-evolving story of the river.

Geography, community, and culture may influence a person's relationship with the watershed; someone living in Grand Junction, Colorado, has a different experience of the Colorado River than one living in Los Algodones, Sonora, yet it is the same river. Different water users place value on different aspects of the river, some primarily appreciating its function, while others highly value its spiritual qualities.

Investigating the literature of the Colorado

Watershed, both past and present, can help students understand their own relationship with the river. Becoming fluent in the literature of a place enriches one's understanding of its meaning throughout history. Students may connect to the watershed by creative writing, adding their own "river voices" to the historical chorus.

The following tips and techniques may be helpful as students explore their own creative writing:

Procedure
Preparation
1. **For *Part I*, cut up one copy of the *One River, Many Voices Water User Cards* and *River Voices Cards.*** They are listed in order on the *Student Copy Pages*, with each water user's writing following his or her biography. Make note of which excerpt goes with each water user before you mix up the cards.

Tips and Techniques for Writers

Writers who effectively communicate their understanding of and relationship to a specific place generally share the following characteristics:
- They write about places they know well and appreciate.
- They include details about the way the place looks, smells, feels, sounds, etc.
- They describe how the place makes them feel, as well as its physical features.
- They create an image in the reader's mind.
- They use their own experiences and voice to tell a story.
- They often include facts to teach readers more about the place.

Getting the creative writing process started:
- Begin with action to hook your readers.
- Start with four facts about the place, person, or event you will be describing.
- Create a scene.
- Borrow a first line or quote from another author.
- Describe an interesting character.

Tips for developing a memorable piece of writing:
- Ask yourself, "So what?" What about this scene/event/character is important and will be meaningful to your audience?
- When describing a character, include details that go beyond simple physical description (e.g., their job, pet, favorite time of day, greatest fear, etc.).
- Write about experiences or settings that are familiar to you personally.
- Use metaphors and similes to create images in your readers' minds.
- Use all of the senses in your descriptions; how does the place feel, smell, sound?
- Revise. Rewrite from different points of view, different points in time, or with a different tone. Tone means how the piece feels to your reader: angry, serious, funny, warm, whimsical, scientific, dry, engaging, lively, etc.
- Make your language beautiful. Nothing needs to be dull to read, no matter how factual it is.
- READ. Nothing improves writing more than reading others' good writing and taking time to analyze why it is good writing.

---

2. For *Part II*, cut up one copy of the *One River, Many Voices Author Cards* and *Author's Voice Cards.* They are listed in order on the *Student Copy Pages*, with each author's work following his or her biography. Make note of which excerpt goes with each author before you mix up the cards.

3. *Optional:* check out the selected books from your local library, or other books by these authors (see *One River, Many Voices Author Cards Student Copy Pages*).

Warm Up
Ask students to list the diverse water users within the Colorado Basin. Ask them to select one or two of these water users and discuss how they think these individuals (or groups) relate to the Colorado. Do students believe that water users have different attitudes about the river? If so, why? Are there certain stereotypes we can identify when we generalize about different water users' perceived attitudes, and how valid are/aren't these stereotypes?

The Activity
Part I
1. **Give each student one of the *River Voices Cards* or one of the *One River, Many Voices Water User Cards*.** In smaller groups you may need some students to take more than one card. Make sure that all of the cards are used. Larger classes may need to work in groups.

2. **Tell the students that by using clues from the *River Voices Cards* and the *One River, Many Voices Water User Cards*, they are going to deduce which water user wrote which "river voice."**

3. **Have students read their cards to themselves.** Then ask them to move around the room, sharing their information with each other in order to match each *Water User Card* with the corresponding *River Voice*. You may want to set a time limit.

4. **When students think they have a match,**

have both students bring their cards to the teacher to confirm their match.** If they are correct, they may wait together for the rest of the group to finish. If they are incorrect, send them to search some more.

5. **Once all the *Water User Cards* are correctly matched with their *River Voice Cards*, pass out complete sets of both cards to each class member.** Before they listen and read, ask students some organizing questions. You may wish to have the students answer some or all of these questions on paper after discussing them. Here are some suggestions:

Ask students to:
- listen for common themes or needs among the voices;
- listen for perceptions of the Colorado that are similar or different among the different water users;
- analyze the values expressed by different water users and how each water user's personal background may influence his/her values;
- identify striking images or language used by the writers;
- list facts or opinions with which they agree or disagree;
- list something new they learned from the *River Voice;*
- decide which of the individuals they would like to meet and why.

6. **Have students take turns reading their *River Voices* aloud followed by the reading of the matching *Water User Card*.** Students may follow along on their own sheets. After reading, discuss the writings and questions.

Part II
1. **The *One River, Many Voices Author Cards Student Copy Pages* contain brief biographies of several authors who have written about the Colorado.** In this part of the activity, students will repeat *Part I* using the

writings of well-known authors from diverse backgrounds.

2. **Tell the students that they are going to repeat the process using the writings of well-known authors who have written about the watershed.** Ask them to pay attention to the diverse backgrounds of the authors as well as the variety of writing styles.

3. **Repeat *Part I* using the *One River, Many Voices Author Cards* and the *Author's Voice Cards*.**

4. **The following questions may be used to guide a discussion about these authors and their work:**

   - What are common themes among the writings?
   - How have perceptions of the Colorado changed through time?
   - Ask students to listen for agreement and disagreement among the authors.
   - What different values do different authors express, and how might each author's personal background influence his/her values?
   - What are some striking images or language used by the authors?
   - Ask students to list facts or opinions with which they agree or disagree?
   - Did they learn something new from the **River Voices?**
   - Which of the authors would they like to read more of and why?

Wrap Up

1. **Using the writing tips described in the Background section, have students write their own *River Voice* about their personal relationship to the Colorado, a tributary, or some aspect of the watershed.** If possible, take the students on a field trip to a river and have them record their experiences and observations in a journal before writing. If this cannot be done, have the students write about their favorite place in the watershed. *River Voices* can be personal essays, fictional stories, or poems.

2. **Have each student choose a partner and write a one-paragraph biography of each other, modeled after the biographies of the water users and authors from this activity.**

3. **Have students share their own or each other's writings and biographies with the class.** Compile the students' biographies and *River Voices* in a book or display them in your classroom.

Assessment

Have students:

- match water users and authors with their writings as they compare and contrast the writings (*Part I*, Steps 3–6; *Part II*, Steps 2–4);
- identify the different values, attitudes, and beliefs about the Colorado that the writings express (*Part I*, Steps 5–6; *Part II*, Step 4);
- discuss how cultural, historical, social, political, and economic contexts help determine how people think about the Colorado (*Part I*, Steps 5–6; *Part II*, Step 4);
- write their own *River Voice* (*Wrap Up*, Step 1);
- interview a classmate to write a brief biography (*Wrap Up*, Step 2);
- present their writing and biographies to the class (*Wrap Up*, Step 3).

Extensions

Have students create their own *River Voice* and *Author Cards* based on library research and repeat the activity, perhaps with a focus on voices from minority perspectives.

Invite a local author to class and have him/her talk with the students about his/her approach to writing.

Have students collect songs relating to the river, and share them with the class using the same format as this activity. They could also look for paintings, photographs, and other visual art that relates to the river and make "Artist Cards" for the activity.

Resources

Abbey, Edward. 1968. *Desert Solitaire: A Season in the Wilderness*. New York: Ballantine Books.

Domínguez, Fray Francisco, and Fray Silvestre Veléz de Escalante. 1995. *The Domínguez-Escalante Journal: Their Expedition Through Colorado, Utah, Arizona, and New Mexico*. Ed. Ted J. Warner, trans. Fray Angelico Chavez. Salt Lake City: University of Utah Press.

Fleck, Richard F., ed. 2000. *A Colorado River Reader*. Salt Lake City: University of Utah Press.

Lamott, Anne. 1994. *Bird by Bird: Some Instructions on Writing and Life*. New York: Pantheon Books.

Leopold, Aldo. 1949. *A Sand County Almanac, and Sketches Here and There*. New York: Oxford University Press, Inc.

Powell, J. W. 1961. *The Exploration of the Colorado River and Its Canyons*. New York: Dover Publications, Inc.

Reisner, Marc. 1993. *Cadillac Desert: The American West and Its Disappearing Water*. New York: Penguin Books.

Ryan, Kathleen Jo, ed. 1998. *Writing Down the River: Into the Heart of the Grand Canyon*. Flagstaff, AZ: Northland Publishing Company.

Waters, Frank. 1946. *The Colorado*. New York: Rinehart and Company.

Williams, Terry Tempest. 1994. *An Unspoken Hunger: Stories from the Field*. New York: Pantheon Books.

Zepeda, Ofelia, ed.. 1982. *Mat Hekid O Ju:/When It Rains: Papago and Pima Poetry* (*Sun Tracks* 7). Tucson: University of Arizona Press.

Zwinger, Ann. 1975. *Run, River, Run: A Naturalist's Journey Down One of the Great Rivers of the American West*. Tucson: University of Arizona Press.

e-Links

Poets and Writers Magazine
Book lists, teacher resources, and more information for writers and poets.
www.pw.org/mag

River of Words
A program using art and literature to connect kids to their watersheds.
www.riverofwords.org

One River, Many Voices of the Colorado Basin
Water User Cards and River Voice Cards

Cathy Scheer is a middle-school science teacher in Green River, Wyoming. She has been awarded numerous honors as an educator. Cathy enjoys fishing, canoeing, water skiing, snow skiing, and other water-related recreational activities.

Standing atop Mansface Rock, deeply breathing the clean, cool air, twirling 360 degrees, and gazing across the vast expanse of landscape carved by the forces of weathering, I rejoice—I'm present! At this moment all else seems trivial! Far in the distance and whipped into the jagged peaks are the mountains—the Uintas to the south, the Wyoming Range to the northwest, and the Wind Rivers to the northeast. Pilot Butte, a flat-topped marker for weary, uneasy travelers of the 1800s, stands alone. Low clouds streak midway between the steaming, winding river below and the adjacent cliff tops dusted with the overnight snow. Spectacular are these many varied, yet brief, moments in time along the Green, and the thankful heart skips a beat.

One River, Many Voices of the Colorado Basin
Water User Cards and River Voice Cards

Michael Wilde is a high school science teacher in Glenwood Springs, Colorado. He does numerous outdoor educational activities with his students, including the Riverwatch program for water-quality monitoring. Mike is an outdoorsman who has lived in Glenwood Springs for over twenty years and is well acquainted with the rivers, canyons, and mountains of that area.

Colorado . . . Mother of Rivers . . . a place of beginnings. It is a brisk April day and I sit on the banks of Grizzly Creek. I have come here with my Riverwatch class to spend an hour in quiet reflection on the banks of this pristine mountain stream in the midst of Glenwood Canyon. We have been here before to study the geology of the area, to monitor the health of this stream, to kick bugs, and to observe the rainbow trout in their spring spawn. But today is different, today is about connections, today is about taking the knowledge that is in our heads and moving it to our hearts. I have done this many times with my students and I am still awed by the power that the river exerts over our moods, thoughts, and emotions.

The canyon is alive with sounds . . . birds, rustling leaves, and of course, the thunder of the creek. The water is bitter cold and crystal clear. It crashes over granite boulders in frothy whitewater falls, only to slow down again; how much like life this creek is. But it isn't so caught up in the moment as it is in the journey. This is the lesson I learn today: take a deep breath, enjoy the ride, slow down, speed up, cherish the journey. The destination will take care of itself. Like the river, I have little knowledge of what will lie around the next bend, but the certainty of moving downstream is a constant reminder that the journey has just begun!

One River, Many Voices of the Colorado Basin
Water User Cards and River Voice Cards

Gregory Hobbs is a Justice of the Colorado Supreme Court, poet, water lawyer, author, and student of history. He is a frequent writer and speaker on water and environmental matters. He has backpacked many times along the Great Divide and has rafted the Grand Canyon with his brother, Will Hobbs, the young-adult author.

A Colorado River View
Look out on the western side of the Great Divide from the heart of Rocky Mountain National Park. You're at the top of the watershed destined for the Sea of Cortez. All that lies before you, all you can hope for, is a chance to serve, to be of use, to share tumbling through the sublime. This is what it means to be the Colorado River. This is what it means to be a member of the Great Divide Community.

THE GREAT DIVIDE COMMUNITY

To each of us
The land, the air, the water,
Mountain, canyon, mesa, plain,
Lightning bolts, clear days with no rain,

At the source of all thirst,
At the source of all thirst-quenching hope,
At the root and core of time and no-time,
The Great Divide community

Stands astride the backbone of the continent,
Gathering, draining, reflecting, sending forth
A flow so powerful it seeps rhythmically
From within,

Alive to each of us,
To drink, to swim, to grow corn ears
To listen to our children float the streams
Of their own magnificence,

Out of their seeping dreams,
Out of their useful silliness,
Out of their source-mouths
High and pure,

The Great Divide,
You and I, all that lives
And floats and flies and passes through
All we know of why.

One River, Many Voices of the Colorado Basin
Water User Cards and River Voice Cards

Pat Page is Water Management Team Leader for the U.S. Bureau of Reclamation's Western Colorado Area Office. He is deeply familiar with water management issues of the San Juan River, the second-largest tributary to the Colorado River. He is involved in numerous water-related educational projects and activities in his community of Durango, Colorado.

The San Juan: The Epitome of Competing Water Uses in the West

Throughout the arid West, the scarcity of water and the demand for that precious resource, run head on into each other. The issues in the San Juan River Basin, located in the Four Corners area, could be considered a microcosm of the West regarding the ongoing and intensifying struggle to meet the growing demands on a limited resource.

It's not hard to see why conflicts over water occur in the San Juan Basin, a drainage area roughly the size of the state of West Virginia, which contributes 14.6 percent of the annual volume of water in the Colorado River system. Like other places west of the 100th Meridian, water is the lifeblood of the San Juan Basin. We drink it, and we eat food grown by it. We work it, and we make it work for us. We play in it, and we play on it.

The issues on the San Juan River are really the epitome of competing uses for water throughout the West. Its values are of great agricultural, industrial, municipal, cultural, environmental, and recreational significance. The extreme drought conditions that southwest Colorado and northwest New Mexico have experienced the last few years have only served to intensify the challenge to ensure an equitable water supply to the varying and sometimes conflicting water uses in the basin. Reclamation and other water managing entities are committed to working with the various water interests to ensure that the precious water supply is managed in a way that maximizes the benefits to all users, while still complying with state and federal laws. It is a challenge that won't go away, it will only grow. And it is a challenge that I, as a federal water manager, look forward to facing.

One River, Many Voices of the Colorado Basin
Water User Cards and River Voice Cards

Nancy Wade is an educator for the University of California, Davis Desert Research and Extension Center in El Centro, California. She conducts numerous educational programs to increase awareness of agricultural topics, including bi-national education projects with students in the border area. Nancy grew up on a farm in Casa Grande, Arizona.

My grandfather was a farmer and my father and son are farmers, working the same land as my grandfather at 11-Mile Corner near Casa Grande, Arizona. I was born and raised there and remember watching my grandfather irrigate. When my hands were big enough to cover the end of a siphon hose, my father taught my sister Patty and me how to start hoses. Our farm, like many others in the area, was solely reliant on water from San Carlos Lake on the Gila River. During times of drought there was no water available and sometimes we would lose crops. My grandparents and parents told us stories of San Carlos Lake and Coolidge

Dam. In December 1941, a boating accident on San Carlos Lake claimed four of our family members. Despite the tragedies, that very lake stored valuable water for the livelihood of our family. In the early 1980s an abundance of rain filled the lake beyond capacity and water was running over the spillways. We packed a picnic and went to the dam to enjoy this spectacular sight!

Whenever I stand on the banks of the Gila or the Colorado River, I feel a great sense of pride because I am Arizona born and raised and these waters are truly the lifeblood of the West!

One River, Many Voices of the Colorado Basin
Water User Cards and River Voice Cards

R. J. Johnson is a hydrogeologist in Boulder City, Nevada. He has been involved in numerous scientific studies in the Colorado Basin, including the Grand Canyon. R. J. is also a veteran river guide who has run most of the whitewater rivers in the Colorado River system.

I have just come off a twenty-one-day Grand Canyon river trip with exuberant friends. Seeing what a trip like this can do for people, I started thinking about what it would be like if there was no Colorado River. Without the river there are no canyons, plateaus, spires, mesas, or buttes. Without the river how would we see those beautiful old fluted Precambrian rocks in Westwater and Grand Canyons, the Canyonlands slickrock country, or the high mountain lakes and streams teeming with life? But with the river, we have water, life, sounds, diversity, a future, change, history, waste and growth, growth and conservation, river dynamics, floods, droughts, controversy, management . . . and life-changing experiences. All in a nice, neat package: the Colorado River system. What else could one wish for?

One River, Many Voices of the Colorado Basin
Water User Cards and River Voice Cards

Joe Kahl is a Biological Science Technician for the U.S. Bureau of Reclamation in Boulder City, Nevada. He is an ornithologist and spends much of his time exploring wetlands along the Lower Colorado River, especially Topock Gorge and the Havasu National Wildlife Refuge. He has conducted surveys for endangered Yuma clapper rails since 1996.

In the half-light before dawn, the water is calm and black. It's chilly out here, not a breeze. The birds are calling and have been for a while. The marsh wren buzzes and chatters as he moves about the cattails and bulrushes advertising his territory. The little fellow with the black mask, the common yellowthroat, calls out from his spot in the marsh. Pied-billed grebes, coots, great-tailed grackles, red-winged and yellow-headed blackbirds along with an occasional Virginia rail, least bittern, and hopefully an endangered Yuma clapper rail are all adding their voices to the dawn chorus. It's quite a way to greet the day.

The marshes in Topock Gorge, which are part of the Havasu National Wildlife Refuge, are one of my favorite places on the Lower Colorado River to visit. During spring migration, I have observed over sixty-five species of birds during a morning's survey. I've seen over three thousand tree swallows sweep by me. I've observed cliff swallows building their mud nests on the cliff faces and later watched them feed their young. Flocks of white-faced ibis, red-headed ducks, and double-crested cormorants fly over. I am always in amazement and awe every time I visit the marshes, and if I'm lucky, I may even get to see that elusive Yuma clapper rail.

One River, Many Voices of the Colorado Basin
Water User Cards and River Voice Cards

Greg Walcher is the former Executive Director of the Colorado Department of Natural Resources. He has been active in water policy and management at a variety of levels in the state of Colorado and is a strong advocate for water storage and protection of the state's water rights. He comes from an agricultural background; his family owns a peach orchard in Palisade, Colorado.

We live in a Colorado transformed. Once labeled the "Great American Desert," Colorado now abounds with wetlands, riparian areas, meadows, and farms. We have streams that historically ran dry in summer and fall that now sustain valuable fisheries year-round. There is one thing that has made this transformation possible—water storage.

A full 80 percent of Colorado's water comes from snowmelt. Additionally, Colorado is one of only two states that depend entirely upon water that originates here in our state, and every year, Colorado's rivers lose up to two million acre-feet of our entitled water to other states.

Were it not for water storage, spring flood-waters would rage through our streams to thirsty downstream states, never to be seen again. But capturing, conserving, and wisely using Colorado's water in reservoirs helps supply clean water for drinking, hydroelectric power, irrigation, and recreation, such as fishing. In fact, all of the state's gold medal trout water is directly below water storage because of clear and consistent flows.

Water storage is critical for present and future generations to mitigate against drought and protect the environment, and I am proud of the steps that Colorado is taking to do just that.

One River, Many Voices of the Colorado Basin
Water User Cards and River Voice Cards

Phil Aurit is an Environmental Awareness Specialist for the U.S. Bureau of Reclamation in Boulder City, Nevada. He coordinates Nevada's Project WET (Water Education for Teachers) program for the southern region. A former Hoover Dam tour guide, Phil has spent most of his life fishing, hiking, skiing, surfing, and reading about the West.

River Voice from the Hoover Dam Tailbay

The solid concrete, downstream-pointing tailbay at the base of Hoover Dam is the one place in the structure where the uncontested power of water can best be felt. During peak power generating periods the tailbay is flooded and awash in just-released, cold, green, Colorado River water. The force of the 30,000 cfs of water used to spin up to seventeen 117-ton stainless steel turbines makes the entire tailbay and powerhouse quiver and hum with energy. Huge boils and eddies swirl where swimming pools full of water jet out of the turbine draft tubes every second—back into the unnaturally cold and clear Colorado River.

It is a time-limited demonstration of the power of water. Peaking periods last only a few hours during summer afternoons and evenings. Visitors to the dam ask, "If hydroelectric power is clean, cheap, and renewable, why aren't the generators run at full capacity all the time?" The unqualified answer is—"there isn't sufficient water." If all the generators were run full-out, they would drain Lake Mead in a matter of months. And more importantly, what would people in the Southwest then drink?

One River, Many Voices of the Colorado Basin
Water User Cards and River Voice Cards

Deborah Johnson is a professional archaeologist and high school science teacher in Phoenix, Arizona. She is fascinated by the early history of the Southwest and has explored many of its natural wonders, especially in Arizona. Her husband, Michael, is the grandson of Colorado River pioneer Art Greene.

I came to Tucson in 1971 to study archaeology, never dreaming how intimately I would become tied to the Colorado Watershed in both my private and professional life. I met and married the grandson of Colorado River pioneer Art Greene; Michael Johnson and I were married in a church overlooking Lake Powell, and our reception was held at Wahweap Lodge, a part of the world-famous Canyon Tours Resort that was founded by his family. I have turned the Ethel G. tour boat around with six inches to spare in Forbidding Canyon, hiked the inner recesses of Antelope Canyon, and explored the far reaches of the San Juan as an assistant tour guide. I have held stone tools a thousand years old in my hand—a link to the ancient Hohokam and Anasazi who depended on the waters of the Colorado River and its tributaries for their lives. I have been humbled by the extensive canal systems that delivered life-giving water to agricultural crops grown by the Hohokam in the Salt and Gila River Valleys. We still use them today to deliver water to lawns and fields in an area with a population one hundred times as large. And I have watched in awe as that same river hurled huge stone bridge abutments and girders past as if they were a child's toys. We live in a desert, and that makes the waters of the Colorado Watershed as important to all of us today as they were to the Hohokam one thousand years ago—may we be as thankful and conservative of those waters and the watershed ecosystems as they were!

One River, Many Voices of the Colorado Basin
Water User Cards and River Voice Cards

Michael Collier is a professional photographer, geologist, family physician, author, and Grand Canyon river guide. His photographs include breathtaking aerial views of the Colorado Basin. Michael lives in Flagstaff, Arizona.

Lessons from the River

If the river didn't teach me all that I know, at least it put everything into perspective. The Colorado, through most of its Grand Canyon, is a smooth powerful python gliding past sandstone and schist. I grew out of adolescence and into manhood on that river, an oar in each hand. I'd tuck those oars under my knees and lean back against my raft's load. I was intoxicated, watching the walls spin circles around an impossibly blue sky.

My pulse still quickens to think of the river sliding into Hance or Horn, Serpentine or Sockdolager Rapids. The water's muscular surface flexed and freshened as it accelerated over the debris fan that forms Crystal Rapid. I'd already memorized every rock and wave that loomed downstream. We were quickly swept past the last point where I could have rowed to shore and reconsidered this madness. The boat was perfectly positioned on the rapid's tongue. For now, there was absolutely nothing to be done. The water's surface heaved and shuddered, but still I took no strokes. To start rowing even a second too soon was to court disaster. This dynamic suspension in a rushing river of time is what I live for.

NOW! I pull downstream and to the right. The boat cuts in to the slack water behind a granite boulder. The passengers don't know it, but we've already run the real rapid. The titillation of waves and water will follow soon enough. But for me, the most breathtaking part of river-running was always that moment out on the tongue, oars suspended above the water, waiting for the instant when I could start rowing. I've moved downstream since those days. Twelve thousand miles on the river, four thousand hours in the air, twenty years now as a doctor. I never begin a descent into stormy turbulence, never walk into the maelstrom of an emergency room without remembering how it was to slide down the tongue, take a deep breath, and hold the oars motionless before it's time to row.

One River, Many Voices of the Colorado Basin
Water User Cards and River Voice Cards

Francis Manuel is an elder of the Tohono O'odham tribe. She now lives on the reservation in Sells, Arizona, but lived for many years of her life in Tucson. She is noted as an expert in traditional basket weaving. Her **River Voice** was recorded during a conversation with Justin Howe.

My Grandfather already knew that it was going to be like this. He said that someday the language (Tohono O'odham) is going to be gone. It is like traveling and then you hit something. And then you turn back and remember what the old people say. They will look for it, but they can't find it because it is going to be gone. It's about time now. My grandchildren, my great-grand children don't even talk Indian. That's what he meant, but I didn't understand.

I wanted to go to school. I was twelve years old and I went to school at the Phoenix Indian School. But I worked hard to learn and I learned even more than I expected to learn. And then I woke up and saw that the earth was given to us to be there and everything is already planted for us and we are

not doing it. We depend on someone else to do the work and then we are fed on that. And so I guess I was grown up that day that I thought how beautiful whoever it is that gave us all those things on this earth. And I went back and I thought, that is what I am going to do.

I learned a lot on my own. It was my Grandfather that used to say that everything that is crawling on the ground or anywhere, they have their own job to do. They have their own ways. That whatever put this earth, made the rain, made whatever is crawling on the ground. They are not just there and we are not just there. We have our job to do. And so I am thankful for whoever it was that woke me up.

One River, Many Voices of the Colorado Basin
Water User Cards and River Voice Cards

Judy Maben is the Education Director for the Water Education Foundation, a nonprofit water resources education organization. She also is the California coordinator for Project WET (Water Education for Teachers). Judy is an experienced middle and high school science teacher. She considers Hoover Dam to be one of the most inspiring features of the Colorado Basin.

The Elegant Arch

Hoover Dam sits between the dark walls of Black Canyon, holding back the waters of the Colorado with its elegant arch. The dam was built in another era, a time of hope in the face of depression, by desperate men who came from everywhere, looking for work, willing to brave the heat and the seemingly impossible task of stopping one of the mightiest rivers in the world.

And yet the dam's design doesn't speak of utilitarian taming, but is a model of artistic architecture and Art Deco details. Seen from below on the deck by the generators, the face of the dam swoops over you like a vertical wing against the sky. The floors of the powerhouse are beautiful terrazzo, created by Italian artisans using Navajo designs for their inspiration.

And against the wall of the canyon stand the two winged statues, guarding the dam. Their creator, Oskar Hansen, said they express "the immutable calm of intellectual resolution and

the enormous power of trained physical strength equally enthroned in placid triumph of scientific accomplishment." We must have thought we could do anything then.

But it is only when you view the dam from an airplane that you understand it, that "sliver of thumbnail" as Marc Reisner described it, holding back the waters of the Colorado. That water generates power to light southwestern cities, and flows into the irrigation canals of Arizona, and the desert valleys of California. It made coastal California the Mecca of the West.

When I stand over the star chart built into the top of the dam that marks its day of dedication, I think that the hubris of that dam-building generation was tempered by the knowledge that nothing is permanent. Like hieroglyphics on the pyramids, they wanted to leave a sign that said, "We were here once, and look what a fabulous thing we made."

One River, Many Voices of the Colorado Basin
Water User Cards and River Voice Cards

Carlota Monroy Lopez participated in the 2003 Colorado River Expedition, exploring the river from its headwaters in Colorado and Wyoming to its delta in Mexico. During the expedition, she found that spending time with the Colorado River helped to restore her sense of well-being. She studies tourism at the Centro de Estudio Superiores del Estado de Sonora in Hermosillo, Sonora.

Río Colorado, to be here with you, to listen to life, and interact with everyone who lives here: to be here is to feel happiness, love, energy, spirituality. It is to feel all the goodness that we have.

Why do we not know you? Because we have forgotten love. Because we have lost our equilibrium.

Río Colorado, you carry in your name the color of our blood that boils in each turn and in each part of you. This colored blood that runs through our body and in each special place—this marvelous river. Each rock formed in these great mountains invites us to dream and imagine and is an important part of everything. Everything that we have begun to break apart with egotism, ambition, and malice.

Everything that lives in this paradise shows us how to be civilized and we have not taken the time to listen to them and to learn from these things; because in our desperation to advance and become more civilized we have forgotten them and ourselves.

Río Colorado, give me time to listen to you and to each of my brothers that lives with you, leave me with a sense of love, happiness, spirituality, and everything good that you carry.

One River, Many Voices of the Colorado Basin
Water User Cards and River Voice Cards

Martha Román Rodríguez is a biologist and educator who has worked to support conservation in the Upper Gulf of California and Colorado River Delta region for fourteen years. She and her fellow researchers have found that only a small amount of river water is needed to support life in the Colorado River Delta. She and her family live in San Luis Rio Colorado, Sonora.

Each time that I cross the bridge on my way to Mexicali my heart sinks. I see the dry river and hear my little son, Emiliano, say, "Look Mama, the Colorado River!" My imagination flies to the headwaters and back to the delta. I think about Lake Mead, Lake Powell, and Lake Havasu and I am certain that the delta was a paradise with plenty of water when the river flowed freely to the sea.

I would like to see my river marching sand to the sea as it did before the dams, just as the old people that live from Yuma, Arizona, to El Golfo de Santa Clara, Sonora, saw in their youth. I think that if the river were as it was before dams, shrimp and totoaba would thrive.

The most surprising thing about the dammed Colorado River is that it still brings life. Its delta is noble—with only a small amount of fresh water, it can maintain life for birds, fish, mesquite, and for people . . . my people here in the delta and in the Upper Gulf of California . . . here in Sonora and Baja . . . here in Mexico.

One River, Many Voices of the Colorado Basin
Author Cards and Author's Voice Cards

Alvaro Aldama is director of the Mexican Institute of Water Technology. He believes that the Colorado River is the bloodstream that has given rise to an interdependent and transboundary civilization.

The Colorado River basin: a place where two countries and many cultures have met, clashed, and intermingled, giving rise to an interdependent and transboundary civilization. A civilization so closely linked to a precious and scarce resource: water. A resource that has been debated upon and fought over, and that has fueled the development of a desert, transforming it from an inhospitable territory into a prosperous land.

A resource that has been used and abused, exploited and overexploited, almost to its last drop; jeopardizing the sustainability of the basin and of the ecosystems that depend on the supply of the liquid in sufficient quantity and quality. Amongst those, most notably, the ecosystems located at the river's delta and beyond it, at the Sea of Cortez

(Gulf of California). The river system is the sustenance of life in the basin and therefore, metaphorically, constitutes its bloodstream. Accordingly, it is almost poetic that the river conveys water with a reddish color, given by the minerals contained in the sediment that it transports, hence the name "Colorado," which means red in Spanish.

Only a vision based on public awareness and common will, geared towards the conservation, preservation, and sharing of water and other natural resources related to it, may protect the blood of this arid but living land. Educators will play a critical role in instilling and spreading such vision among the present and future generations. Therein lies the Colorado's hope.

One River, Many Voices of the Colorado Basin
Author Cards and Author's Voice Cards

Father Silvestre Vélez de Escalante and Father Francisco Domínguez

In 1776, the Catholic Church in Mexico City sent an expedition led by Father Domínguez and Father Escalante to find a direct route from the missions of Santa Fe to those on the California coast at Monterey. The expedition faced many hardships as it attempted to find its way through the rugged canyon country of the Colorado Plateau without a guide. Although they were forced to return to Santa Fe because of severe winter weather while still in the Grand Canyon region, the group was able to cross the Colorado River in Glen Canyon. Father Escalante recorded their adventures in his journal, which has since been translated into English.

Source: *The Domínguez-Escalante Journal: Their Expedition Through Colorado, Utah, Arizona, and New Mexico.* 1995. Ed. Ted J. Warner, trans. Fray Angelico Chavez. Salt Lake City: University of Utah Press.

November 7.—We got down to the canyon, and after going a mile we reached the river [the Colorado] and went along it downstream for about as far as two musket shots, now through the water, now along the edge, until we came to the widest part of its currents where the ford appeared to be. One man waded in and found it all right, not having to swim at any place. We followed him on horseback . . . although with some peril . . . and we successfully passed over without the horses on which we were crossing ever having to swim. . . . [The rest of the group] finished crossing the river about five in the afternoon, praising God our Lord and firing off some muskets in demonstration of the great joy we all felt in having overcome so great a problem, one which had caused us so much labor and delay. . . .

One River, Many Voices of the Colorado Basin
Author Cards and Author's Voice Cards

Aldo Leopold

Aldo Leopold is one of the best- known naturalists and conservationists in American history. In 1922, he and his brother explored the Colorado Delta by canoe. He wrote about the trip in his famous book, *A Sand County Almanac,* which was published in 1949. By this time Hoover Dam and others had been constructed on the river and the delta was changing. His idyllic memories of the delta are shadowed by his dark regret over its decline: "All this was far away and long ago. I am told the green lagoons now raise cantaloupes. If so, they should not lack flavor. Man always kills the thing he loves, and so we the pioneers have killed our wilderness. Some say we had to. Be that as it may, I am glad I shall never be young without wild country to be young in. Of what avail are forty freedoms without a blank spot on the map?"

Source: *A Sand County Almanac, and Sketches Here and There,* pp. 141–142. 1949. New York: Oxford University Press, Inc.

Dawn on the Delta was whistled in by Gambel quail, which roosted in the mesquites overhanging camp. When the sun peeped over the Sierra Madre, it slanted across a hundred miles of lovely desolation, a vast flat bowl of wilderness rimmed by jagged peaks. On the map the Delta was bisected by the river, but in fact the river was nowhere and everywhere, for he could not decide which of a hundred green lagoons offered the most pleasant and least speedy path to the Gulf. So he traveled them all, and so did we. He divided and rejoined, he twisted and turned, he meandered in awesome jungles, he all but ran in circles, he dallied with lovely groves, he got lost and was glad of it, and so were we. For the last word in procrastination, go travel with a river reluctant to lose his freedom to the sea.

One River, Many Voices of the Colorado Basin
Author Cards and Author's Voice Cards

Major John Wesley Powell

John Wesley Powell is still a household name in the Colorado Basin, famous for his explorations of the Green and Colorado Rivers. His first expedition took place in 1869, when he and his group of nine men set out from Expedition Island in Green River, Wyoming. They were the first whites to see many sections of the river, and Powell's 1895 compilation of his journals, *The Exploration of the Colorado River and Its Canyons*, dramatically describes the awesome scenery and imminent danger that he felt constantly surrounded them.

Source: *The Exploration of the Colorado River and Its Canyons*, p. 247. 1961. New York: Dover Publications, Inc.

August 13.—We are three quarters of a mile in the depths of the earth, and the great river shrinks into insignificance as it dashes its angry waves against the walls and cliffs that rise to the world above; the waves are but puny ripples, and we but pigmies, running up and down the sands or lost among the boulders.

We have an unknown distance yet to run, an unknown river to explore. What falls there are, we know not; what rocks beset the channel, we know not; what walls rise above the river, we know not. Ah, well! we may conjecture many things. The men talk as cheerfully as ever; jests are bandied about freely this morning; but to me the cheer is somber and the jests are ghastly.

One River, Many Voices of the Colorado Basin
Author Cards and Author's Voice Cards

Marc Reisner

Cadillac Desert: The American West and Its Disappearing Water was written by Marc Reisner in 1986, and it has become popular reading for people interested in western water resources and environmental issues. In his lively writing style, Reisner documents water resources issues and describes the history of development of the major rivers of the American West. The book extensively examines the Colorado River, which Reisner calls, "unrivaled for sheer orneriness."

Source: *Cadillac Desert: The American West and Its Disappearing Water*, p. 120. 1993. New York: Penguin Books.

The Colorado is neither the biggest nor the longest river in the American West, nor, except for certain sections described in nineteenth-century journals as "awful" or "appalling," is it the most scenic. Its impressiveness and importance have to do with other things. It is one of the siltiest rivers in the world—the [pre-dam] Colorado could carry sediment loads close to those of the much larger Mississippi—and one of the wildest. Its drop of nearly thirteen thousand feet is unequaled in North America, and its constipation-relieving rapids, before dams tamed its flash floods, could have flipped a small freighter. The Colorado's modern notoriety, however, stems not from its wild rapids and plunging canyons but from the fact that it is the most legislated, most debated, and most litigated river in the entire world. It also has more people, more industry, and a more significant economy dependent on it than any comparable river in the world.

One River, Many Voices of the Colorado Basin
Author Cards and Author's Voice Cards

Edward Abbey

Ed Abbey's writings are notoriously opinionated, and his writing style is distinctive. A strong advocate for the preservation of land and rivers in the Southwest, his writing has captured the imaginations of many in the environmental movement. His controversial opinions include strong disapproval of dams and reservoirs on the Colorado, especially Glen Canyon Dam and Lake Powell. His book *Desert Solitaire* has been recognized as a classic in southwestern literature.

Source: *Desert Solitaire: A Season in the Wilderness,* pp. 173–174. 1968. New York: Ballantine Books.

The beavers had to go and build another . . . dam on the Colorado. Not satisfied with the enormous silt trap and evaporation tank called Lake Mead (back of Boulder Dam) they have created another even bigger, even more destructive, in Glen Canyon. This reservoir of stagnant water will not irrigate a single square foot of land or supply water for a single village; its only justification is the generation of cash through electricity for the indirect subsidy of various real estate speculators, cotton-growers and sugarbeet magnates in Arizona, Utah and Colorado. . . .

The impounded waters form an artificial lake named Powell, supposedly to honor but actually to dishonor the memory, spirit and vision of Major John Wesley Powell, first American to make a systematic exploration of the Colorado River and its environs. Where he and his brave men once lined the rapids and glided through silent canyons two thousand feet deep motorboats now smoke and whine, scumming the water with cigarette butts, beer cans and oil, dragging the water skiers on their endless rounds, clockwise.

One River, Many Voices of the Colorado Basin
Author Cards and Author's Voice Cards

Annick Smith

Annick Smith is most well known for her writings about her home state of Montana. At the age of sixty-one, she was one of a group of women writers who rafted the Colorado River through the Grand Canyon. The essay she wrote about her experiences on that trip describes her encounter with one of the river's most notorious rapids, Hermit Rapid.

Source: *Writing Down the River: Into the Heart of the Grand Canyon*, p. 87. 1998. Ed. Kathleen Jo Ryan. Flagstaff, AZ: Northland Publishing Company.

First, as always, is the roar. "Forward," shouts Megan. We drop from calm into havoc, attacking Hermit's wave-train head on. One, two, three, four giant waves lift us. . . . Then comes the fifth wave. We climb up and up, but we do not cut through. The wave grows. It's a demon curling above us. Its foaming dragon breath is distinct as a Japanese painting, alive. . . . The raft is hanging vertical in air. Then the crest breaks. We are thrown back. The boat flips. We are flying.

I go down a long way. Buried in brown deep, I'm a pebble in a maelstrom. This is power pure, power strong enough to drive turbines. I am holding my paddle. I let it go. I push up through the icy turbulence until breath leaves me and I am choking, swallowing water. A gulp of air, blessed air, then I am driven down in a whirlpool. Up and down and up again. The river roars past rock walls and I'm still helpless.

One River, Many Voices of the Colorado Basin
Author Cards and Author's Voice Cards

Frank Waters

Known as the "Grandfather of Southwestern Literature," Frank Waters is famous for his fiction and nonfiction books about American Indian culture, including the classics: *Book of the Hopi* and *The Man Who Killed the Deer*. His 1946 book, *The Colorado*, includes a description of his 1925 trip from the delta village of El Mayor, Baja California, to Guaymas, Mexico, aboard a small steamship named the *Rio Colorado*.

Source: *The Colorado*. 1946. New York: Rinehart and Company.

Under the moon the river took on an aspect of serenity and mellowed age, and its broad gentle windings seemed like a road that has been long abandoned. Far out midstream a fish rose leaping, and its splash might have been a tuft of dust. . . . And steadily, hour after hour, a boy sitting on a water cask kept taking soundings of the river. We heard the splash of lead, its bump against the rail, and in a moment his soft voice rising into the night. "Cinco brazas, capitán."—"Cuatro y media."—"Cuatro!"—"Seis, capitán."

The massive Indian [captain] was still awake and waiting. One night it came. The river rose rapidly. The Rio Colorado *jerked at her anchor chain. The capitán stirred for the first time. The anchor was brought up and the engines started,*

though we did not move. Greasy lanterns were lit, and in their dim flicker the crew lounged restlessly, rolling cigarettes. Far downstream sounded a low resounding boom. Swiftly it advanced upstream upon us, clearly visible in the moonlight: a wall of water some four feet high sweeping round the bend. The Rio Colorado, *unfettered and with engines running, met it squarely. She went nose down until her decks were washed and came up with a dizzy roll streaming torrents from every passageway. . . .*

What we had experienced was one of the tide bores of the Colorado. And what we had escaped, due to the capitán's caution in waiting far up the channel until its full force was spent, was the fate of the Topolobampo *three years before.*

One River, Many Voices of the Colorado Basin
Author Cards and Author's Voice Cards

Ofelia Zepeda

Ofelia Zepeda writes about the Sonoran Desert, her homeland. She is a member of the Tohono O'odham (Papago) nation and is a linguist, poet, editor, and community leader devoted to maintaining and preserving American Indian languages and to revitalizing tribal communities and cultures. A major theme in Tohono O'odham literature and art is the importance of rain to their culture and survival.

Source: *Mat Hekid O Ju:/When it Rains: Papago and Pima Poetry* (*Sun Tracks* 7). 1982. Ed. Ofelia Zepeda. Tucson: University of Arizona Press.

Rain

The sun has moved down that way a bit,
And yet it is so hot.
All movement has almost stopped.
A fly goes by so slowly,
    everything has slowed down.
My father is sitting there,
His head is tilted back and he's asleep.
My sister is laying over there asleep.
The dog passed by, he is looking
    for shade,
    everything has slowed down.

And yet the clouds have slowly settled in.
    It's raining, it's raining!
My father jumps up
    "Run and cover my grain!"
    "Run and get the clothes on the line!"
Everything is now moving and alive.
My sister is up.
The dog is up.
    everything is now moving and alive.

One River, Many Voices of the Colorado Basin
Author Cards and Author's Voice Cards

Terry Tempest Williams

Terry Tempest Williams' Mormon ancestors settled in Utah in the 1850s, and her passionate story-telling clearly conveys her strong connection to the landscapes and people of the Southwest. Since childhood she has camped and hiked in the canyons of the Colorado Basin, including the Grand Canyon. She is considered a leader in efforts to conserve wilderness, especially in the canyon country of Utah.

Source: *An Unspoken Hunger: Stories from the Field.* 1994. New York: Pantheon Books.

Few know her, but she is always there—Stone Creek Woman—watching over the Colorado River. Over the years, I have made pilgrimages to her, descending into the Grand Canyon, passing through geologic layers with names like Kayenta, Moenave, Chinle, Shinarump, Toroweep, Coconino, and Supai to guide me down the stone staircase of time. It is always a pleasant journey downriver to Mile 132—Stone Creek, a small tributary that flows into the Colorado. We secure our boats and meander up the side canyon where the heat of the day seeps into our skin, threatens to boil our blood, and we can imagine ourselves as lizards pushing up down on the hot, coral sand.

They watch us step from stone to stone along the streambed. The lizards vanish and then we see her. Stone Creek Woman: guardian of the desert with her redrock face, maidenhair ferns, and waterfall of expression . . . .

Since that hot June day, I have made a commitment to visit Stone Creek Woman as often as I can. I believe she monitors the floods and droughts of the Colorado Plateau, and I believe she can remind us that water in the West is never to be taken for granted. When the water flows over the sandstone wall, through the moss and ferns, she reveals herself. When there is no water, she disappears.

One River, Many Voices of the Colorado Basin
Author Cards and Author's Voice Cards

María Cárdenas

María Cárdenas is a poet who has written about dry lands in Baja California. In one poem about flowers, she writes about *pitahayo* blooms and stems of the thorny *biznaga*.

Source: *Panorama Historico de Baja California*. 1983. Ed. David Piñera Ramírez. Mexicali, Baja California: Centro de Investigaciones Históricas UNAM-UABC.

Flowers of the Desert

Wasted and hostile the panorama extends . . .
indomitable and dry the land groans,
and its lacerating voice that implores
submerges itself in the anguish of its drama.

And the water drops that it reclaims,
when merged into its blood, are bartered
in the savia *that ascends through the hollowed,*
thirsty vein of the shriveled branch.

And when the hefty pitahayo *blooms,*
or the biznaga, *of lonesome stem,*
trembling amongst its rough thorns,
purple flowers break their calyx,

and in its sprout, barely opened,
wet is the blood of the desert!

Part III

Appendices

National Science Standards

© Project WET International Foundation, 2005

Page	Activity	Systems, order and organization	Evidence, models, and explanation	Change, contancy, and measurement	Evolution and equilibrium	Form and function	Abilities necessary to do scientific inquiry	Understandings about scientific inquiry	Properties and changes of properties in matter	Motions and forces	
268	8-4-1, One for All: The Colorado River	●	●	O			O				
224	An Invited Guest in the Colorado Watershed	●	●	O	O	O	O				
140	Basin in a Bottle	●	●	●	O	●	●	O			
211	Chillin' with the Chubs	●	●	O	O		O				
Internet	Colorado Art Festival										
232	Colorado River Timeline										
330	Colors of the Colorado						O				
Internet	Desert Gardens										
320	Faucet Family Tree	●		●		●	●	O			
287	First Come, First Served	●	●	●		●	O	O			
193	Flight without Borders	●	●			O	O	O			
126	Go with the Flow	●	●	●	●	●	O	O	O	●	
172	Hunting for Habitats in the Colorado Watershed	●			●		O				
89	Incredible Journey of the Colorado River	●	●		O	●	O		O	O	
299	Irrigation Calculations	O		O			O				
307	Many Happy Return Flows	●	●	O		O	O				
350	One River, Many Voices of the Colorado Basin						O				
277	Plumbing the Colorado	●	●	●		●	O				
148	Reading the Rings	●	●	●	●	●	●	●			
114	Rock Sandwich, Stone Soup		●	●	●	O	O	●			
80	Seeing Watersheds and Blue Beads: The Colorado	●	●	●	O	●				O	
224	Sharing the Shed						O				
100	String of Pearls: The Colorado Watershed	●									
162	Too Thick to Drink		●	●	●	●	O	O	O		
342	Trading Toss-Up		●	●	●	●	O	O			

● = Fully Meets Standard   O = Partially Meets Standard

	Life Science						Earth and Space Science			Science and Technology		Science in Personal and Social Perspectives					History and Nature of Science		
Transfer of energy	Structure and function in living systems	Reproduction and heredity	Regulation and behavior	Populations and ecosystems	Diversity and adaptations of organisms	Structure of the earth system	Earth's history	Earth in the solar system	Abilities of technological design	Understandings about science and technology	Personal health	Populations, resources, and environments	Natural hazards	Risks and benefits	Science and technology in society	Science as a human endeavor	Nature of science	History of science
		O	O	O								●			O			
	O	O	O	O	●							●	●	O	O			O
O				O	O	●				O	O	O	O	●	O			
	O			●	●							●	O	●				
										O		●			O	●		●
										O		O				O		O
O																O	O	O
O			O		O				O	O	O	●	●	O	O	O		O
	O			O						O	O	O	O		●	O		
				O					O	O		●	●	O	O			
	O	O	●	●	●					O		●	O	●				
O				O	O	O	O		●	O		●	O	●	●	O	●	
	O		O	●	●							●						
O						O												
									●	●		●	O	●	●	O		
			O	O	O					O	O	●	O	O	O			
										O		●	O		O	O	O	O
			O							O	O	●	O	O	●			
	O		●	O			O			O		●	●		O		●	●
						●	●							O				
O			●									●	●					
											O	●	O	O	O	O	O	O
			O									O						
O		O	O	●	●	O						O	●	O	O			O
			O							O		●			●	●	●	●

DISCOVER A WATERSHED: THE COLORADO EDUCATORS GUIDE

Content Standards, Grades 9-12

Page	Activity	Systems, order and organization	Evidence, models, and explanation	Change, contancy, and measurement	Evolution and equilibrium	Form and function	Abilities necessary to do scientific inquiry	Understandings about scientific inquiry	Structure of atoms	Structure and properties of matter	Chemical reactions	Motions and forces	Conservation of energy and increase in disorder	Interactions of energy and matter
		Unifying Concepts and Processes					**Science as Inquiry**		**Physical Science**					
268	8-4-1, One for All: The Colorado River	●	●	O			O							
224	An Invited Guest in the Colorado Watershed	●	●	O	O	O	O							
140	Basin in a Bottle	●	●	●	O	●	●	●						
211	Chillin' with the Chubs			O										
Internet	Colorado Art Festival													
232	Colorado River Timeline													
330	Colors of the Colorado						O			O				O
Internet	Desert Gardens													
320	Faucet Family Tree	●		●		●	●	●			O	O		
287	First Come, First Served	●	●	●		●	O	O						
193	Flight without Borders	●	●		O		O							
126	Go with the Flow	●	●	●	●	●	O	O				O		O
172	Hunting for Habitats in the Colorado Watershed	●			●		●							
89	Incredible Journey of the Colorado River	●	●		O	●	O					O		O
299	Irrigation Calculations												O	
307	Many Happy Return Flows	●	●	O			O	O						
350	One River, Many Voices of the Colorado Basin						O							
277	Plumbing the Colorado	●	●	●		●	O							
148	Reading the Rings	●	●	●	●	●	●	●						
114	Rock Sandwich, Stone Soup		●	●	●	O	O	O	●					
80	Seeing Watersheds and Blue Beads: The Colorado	O	O	O	●	O						O		
224	Sharing the Shed						O							
100	String of Pearls: The Colorado Watershed	●												
162	Too Thick to Drink		●	●	●	●	O	O			O			O
342	Trading Toss-Up		●	●	●	●	O	O						

	Life Science					Earth and Space Science				Science and Tech		Science in Personal and Social Perspectives						History and Nature of Science		
The cell	Molecular basis of heredity	Biological evolution	Interdependence of organisms	Matter, energy, and organization in living systems	Behavior of organisms	Energy in the earth system	Geochemical cycles	Origin and evolution of the earth system	Origin and evolution of the universe	Abilities of technological design	Understandings about science and technology	Personal and community health	Population growth	Natural resources	Environmental quality	Natural and human-induced hazards	Science and technology in local, national, and global challenges	Science as a human endeavor	Nature of scientific knowledge	Historical perspectives
			O									●	●	●	●	●	O	●		
		●	O	O	●							O	O	●	O	O	O	O		O
						O								O	O	O	O			
		●		●											O	●	O	O		
																	O	O		●
																		O		●
																		O		O
		O										O		●		O	O	O		●
O			O									●	O	●	O	●	●			O
			O							O	O	O	O	●	O	●	●			O
		●	O		●						O			O	O	O	O			
			O	O		O	O	O		●	O			●	●	O	O	O		O
		●	●		●									●	O	O	O			
				O		●									●	●	●			O
										●	O		O		O	●	O	●		O
			O							●		O	O	●	●	O	O			
												O		●	O	O	O	O	O	O
			O								O	O	O	●			O			
				●	O	O								O		●	O		O	O
		O					●	●			O			O		O		O	O	O
				O		O		O				O		O	O	●				
												O	O	O	O	O	O	O	O	O
												O								
			O	●	O	O						O		O	●	●	O			O
											O			●			O	●	●	●

Subject Areas

© Project WET International Foundation, 2005

Glossary

acre-foot. The quantity of water required to cover one acre of land to a depth of one foot (325,851 gallons).

active reservoir capacity. The reservoir capacity available for use. It extends from the top of the reservoir to the lowest point from which water can be removed.

adjudicate. To settle or determine (an issue or dispute) judicially.

agriculture. The occupation of cultivating land, raising crops, and feeding, breeding, and raising livestock; farming or ranching.

algal bloom. An overproduction of algae due to nutrient overloading.

alignment. The act of arranging in a straight line.

allocation. The act of allocating; apportionment; the share or portion allocated.

amaranth. Any plant of the genus *Amaranthus*. Some species of amaranth are cultivated as food and some for their showy flower clusters or foliage.

Ancestral Puebloan. American Indians living in the southwestern region of the United States from 2,500–700 years ago. (Source: *Discovering Archaeology in Colorado*)

anthropology. The science that studies the origins, physical and cultural development, biological characteristics, and social customs and beliefs of humankind.

apportionment. The act of distributing or allocating something (water) proportionally.

appropriation. The act of setting something (water) apart for a specific purpose or use.

aqueduct. A pipe, conduit, or channel designed to transport water from a remote source, usually by gravity.

aquifer. A geologic formation(s) that is water bearing. A geologic formation or structure that stores and/or transmits water, such as to wells and springs.

arable. Land fit or used for the growing of crops; also, a plot of such land.

archaeology. The study of past cultures through the study of artifacts and sites.

arid. Being without moisture; extremely dry; parched; barren or unproductive because of lack of moisture.

artesian well. A water well drilled into a confined aquifer where enough hydraulic pressure exists for the water to flow to the wellhead without pumping.

atmosphere. A conventional unit of pressure, the normal pressure of the air at sea level (about 14.7 pounds per square inch).

backwater. Water held or forced back, as by a dam or flood.

basin. (1) A geographic area drained by a single major stream; consists of a drainage system comprised of streams and lakes. Also called river basin, drainage basin, and watershed. (2) A natural or artificial hollow place containing water.

beneficial use. The use of water for the benefit of the appropriator, other persons, or the public, defined more specifically within each state's water law. It may include (but is not limited to) water used for agricultural, domestic, fish and wildlife, industrial, mining, municipal, power, and recreational uses. (Source: Wolfe 1996)

biodiversity. Diversity of plant and animal species in an environment.

brackish. Containing a mix of fresh and salt water.

branching pattern. A branching figure or marking resembling a tree. Found in both natural and man-made systems such as neural networks, highways, and rivers.

browse. To graze or feed on tender shoots, leaves, or other soft vegetation.

cambium. The delicate, spongy layer of tissue between a tree's bark and its wood.

canal. A constructed open channel for transporting water from the source of supply to the point of distribution.

cfs. (See **cubic feet per second**).

channel. The bed of a stream.

check-dam. A structure built of natural materials and intended to prevent soil erosion and retain water.

climate. The sum total of all atmospheric or meteorological influences, principally temperature, moisture, wind, pressure, and evaporation, which combine to characterize a region and give it individuality by influencing the nature of its land forms, soils, vegetation, and land use. (Source: *Resource Conservation Glossary*)

closed basin. A hollow or depression in the earth's surface from which water cannot flow (like the Salton Sea). Any water trapped in such a basin can only be lost through evaporation.

cms. (See **cubic meters per second**).

commonwealth. Any group of persons or nations united by some common interest.

community (biological). A group of different organisms (plants, animals, microorganisms, etc.) that live and interact together in a particular place or environment.

compact. A formal agreement between two or more parties, states, etc.

competence. The capacity of a stream for carrying sediment. A stream with higher velocity has a higher competence, meaning that it can transport more sediment.

compost. A mixture of various decaying organic substances, used for fertilizing soil.

concentration (of a solution). Amount of a chemical or pollutant in a particular volume of water.

condensation. The process by which a gas or vapor changes to a liquid or solid; also the liquid or solid so formed. The opposite of evaporation. In meteorological usage, this term is applied only to the transformation from vapor to liquid.

confined aquifer. A water-saturated layer of soil or rock that is bounded above and below by impermeable layers.

confluence. (1) The act of flowing together; the meeting or junction of two or more streams; also, the place where these streams meet. (2) The stream or body of water formed by the junction of two or more streams; a combined flood.

conifer. An evergreen tree or shrub that bears both seeds and pollen on dry scales arranged as a cone.

conquistador. One of the Spanish conquerors of Mexico and Peru in the sixteenth century.

conservation. The use of water-saving methods to reduce the amount of water needed for homes, lawns, farming, and industry, thus increasing water supplies for optimum long-term economic and social benefits.

consumptive use. The use of a resource that reduces the supply (e.g., removing water from a source such as a river or lake without returning an equal amount). Examples are the intake of water by plants, humans, and other animals and the incorporation of water into the products of industrial or food processing.

contaminant. Any substance that when added to water (or another substance) makes it impure and unfit for consumption or use.

cross-dating. Measuring and comparing the relative width of tree rings, and especially distinct "marker-rings," from a tree whose age is not known with those from a tree of known age, thereby determining when the tree of unknown age lived and died.

cross-section. (1) A graph or plot of ground elevation across a stream valley or a portion of it, usually along a line perpendicular to the stream or direction of flow. (2) A section made by a plane cutting anything transversely, especially at right angles to the longest axis.

crustacean. Any chiefly aquatic arthropod typically having its body covered with a hard shell, including lobsters, shrimps, etc.

cubic feet per second (cfs). Units typically used in measuring streamflow that express rate of discharge. The measurement is equal to the discharge in a stream cross-section one foot wide and one foot deep, flowing with an average velocity of one foot per second; 1 cfs = 44.8 gallons per minute (gpm).

cubic meters per second (cms). Units typically used in measuring streamflow that express rate of discharge. The measurement is equal to the discharge in a stream cross-section one meter wide and one meter deep, flowing with an average velocity of one meter per second; 1 cms = 1,000 liters per second.

cultivate. 1) To work on (land) in order to raise crops. 2) To promote the growth of (a plant or crop).

cumulative effect. (1) Such as is formed by accumulation or heaping on (as opposed to organic growth). (2) Constituted by or arising from accumulation, or the accession of successive portions or particulars; acquiring or increasing in force or cogency by successive additions.

current. A portion of a large body of air or water moving in a certain direction.

dam. A structure of earth, rock, or concrete designed to form a basin and hold water back to make a pond, lake, or reservoir. A barrier built, usually across a watercourse, for impounding or diverting the flow of water.

dead reservoir capacity. The reservoir capacity from which water cannot be removed by gravity.

deciduous. Shedding the leaves annually, as certain trees and shrubs do.

delineate. To trace the outline of, sketch or trace in outline, represent pictorially, or portray in words. To describe or outline with precision.

delta. A landform created by alluvial deposits at the mouths of rivers or at the mouths of tidal inlets.

dendrochronology. The science of dating past events and environmental variations by comparative study of growth rings in trees and aged wood.

dendrogram. A treelike diagram that graphically represents the hierarchy of categories based on number of common characteristics or degree of similarity.

depletion. The loss of water from surface water reservoirs or ground water aquifers at a rate greater than that of recharge.

deposition. The process of laying down sediment or accumulating layers of material carried in suspension.

desalination. The process of removing salt from sea or brackish water.

desert. An area of almost barren land in which less than ten inches of rain per year results in sparse vegetative cover. (Source: *Resource Conservation Glossary*)

detritus. (1) The heavier mineral debris moved by natural watercourses, usually in the form of bed load. (2) The sand, grit, and other coarse material removed by differential sedimentation in a organic material that form the base of food chains in wetlands and many other kinds of habitats.

dilution. The reduction of the concentration of a substance in air or water.

discharge. The volume of water that passes a given location within a given period of time. Usually expressed in cubic feet (or meters) per second.

discharge area. Any area of land to which water flows from an aquifer is called its discharge area; this can include wells, springs, seeps, lakes, streams, or oceans.

dissolve. To make a solution of, as by mixing with a liquid.

diurnal. (1) Of or belonging to the daytime, the opposite of nocturnal. (2) Active during the daytime.

diversion. The removal of water from a natural watercourse by canal, pipe, well, or other conduit for transfer to another watercourse or for application on the land; also called withdrawal. (Source: Wolfe 1996)

downstream. In the direction of a stream's current; in relation to water rights, refers to water uses or locations that are affected by upstream uses or locations.

drainage basin. The land area drained by a river. Also called river basin, basin, catchment, or watershed.

drainage divide. The line of highest elevation(s) separating two or more drainage basins, thus distinguishing water flows into each basin. For example, the Continental Divide is the largest drainage divide in North America. From this divide, water flows east to the Atlantic Ocean, west to the Pacific Ocean, or north to Hudson Bay.

dredge. To clean, deepen, or widen with a mechanical scoop.

drought. An extended period with little or no precipitation; often affects crop production and availability of water supplies.

dryland farming. The process of growing crops in semiarid regions without the aid of irrigation.

ecology. The study of relationships of living things to one another and to the environment.

ecological niche. Total way of life or role of a species in an ecosystem. It includes all physical, chemical, and biological conditions a species needs to live and reproduce in an ecosystem. (Source: Miller 2001)

ecosystem (ecology). A community of animals, plants, and bacteria and its interrelated physical and chemical environment. An ecosystem can be as small as a rotting log or a puddle of water, but current management efforts typically focus on larger landscape units, such as a mountain range, a river basin, or a watershed.

eddy. A current of water or air moving counter to the main current.

effluent. (1) Flowing out or flowing away; something that flows out or forth, especially a stream flowing out of a body of water. (2) A stream that flows out of a larger stream, a lake, or another body of water. (3) A waste liquid discharge from a manufacturing or treatment process, in its natural state or partially or completely treated, that discharges into the environment. The outflows from sewage or industrial plants, etc.

elevation. The variation in the height of the earth's surface as measured by the vertical distance from a known datum plane, typically *Mean Sea Level (MSL)*.

endangered species. Life forms that face extinction.

endemic species. An organism or species peculiar or restricted to a certain area or region.

environment. All of the external factors, conditions, and influences that affect an organism or a biological community.

erosion. The process in which a material is worn away by a stream of liquid (water), often due to the presence of abrasive particles in the stream.

estuary. The lower course of a river where the current is met by ocean tides.

evaporation. (1) The physical process by which a liquid (or a solid) is transformed to the gaseous state. (2) When water from land areas, bodies of water, and all other moist surfaces is absorbed into the atmosphere as a vapor.

evapotranspiration. The loss of water from the soil through both evaporation and transpiration from plants.

exchange. To give and receive reciprocally, to barter or trade goods or services.

exotic species. An organism or species that is not native to the area in which it is found. A nonnative or non-indigenous species usually introduced as the result of human activities.

extinct. No longer in existence; that has ended or died out.

fault. A break in the community of a body of rock or of a vein, with dislocation along the plane of the fracture.

fauna. The animals characteristic of a region, period, or special environment.

federal reserved water right. Water rights set aside for federal lands (like national parks) and for American Indian tribes and reservations. See Winters Doctrine below.

filtration. The mechanical process that removes particulate matter by separating water from solid material, usually by passing it through sand.

flash flood. Flood of very high discharge and short duration; sudden and local in extent. (Source: Plummer and McGeary 1993).

flood. Any relatively high streamflow overtopping the natural or artificial banks of a stream.

floodplain. Any normally dry land area that is susceptible to being inundated by water from any natural source, usually low land adjacent to a stream or lake.

flora. Plant or bacterial life characteristic of a region, period, or special environment.

fluctuation. Continual change from one point or condition to another; wavelike motion; undulation.

flyway. Generally fixed route along which waterfowl migrate from one area to another at certain seasons of the year. (Source: Miller 2001)

4.4 Plan. An agreement drafted between 1996 and 2003 by the Colorado River Basin U.S. states and the federal government that will help California bring its use of Colorado River Watershed water to within its allocated amount. This agreement is important because California has been using surplus water legally allocated to other states.

fresh water. Water with less than 0.5 parts per thousand dissolved salts.

gage (gauge). (1) An instrument used to measure magnitude or position; gages may be used to measure the elevation of a water surface, the velocity of flowing water, the pressure of water, the amount of intensity of precipitation, the depth of snowfall, etc. (2) The act or operation of registering or measuring magnitude or position. (3) The operation, including both field and office work, of measuring the discharge of a stream of water in a waterway.

gaging station. A site on a stream, lake, reservoir, or other body of water where observations and hydrologic data are obtained. The U.S. Geological Survey measures stream discharge at gaging stations.

garden. A plot of ground where flowers, shrubs, vegetables, fruits, and/or herbs are cultivated; to cultivate a garden.

generalist species. Species with a broad ecological niche. They can live in many different places, eat a variety of foods, and tolerate a wide range of environmental conditions. (Source: Miller 2001)

geologic formation. A body of rock of considerable thickness that has a recognizable unity or similarity, making it distinguishable from adjacent rock units. (Source: Plummer and McGeary 1993).

germination. The development of a seed into a plant.

glacial till. Unsorted and unlayered rock debris carried by a glacier. (Source: Plummer and McGeary 1993).

Global Positioning System (GPS). A global system of U.S. navigational satellites developed to provide precise positional and velocity data and global time synchronization for air, sea, and land travel.

gradient. A measure of a degree of incline; the steepness of a slope.

gravity. The natural force of attraction exerted by Earth on objects or materials on its surface that tends to draw them down toward its center.

Great Uncomformity. A famous geologic feature in the Grand Canyon, where almost 1 billion years of the rock record are missing.

ground water. (1) Water that flows or seeps downward and saturates soil or rock, supplying springs and wells. The upper surface of the saturated zone is called the water table. (2) Water stored underground in rock crevices and in the pores of geologic materials that make up Earth's crust.

growth release. When a slow-growing tree shaded by other trees shows a "growth spurt" that allows it to reach the light.

habitat. The environment where a plant or animal grows or lives.

headward erosion. The lengthening of a valley in an uphill direction above its original source by erosion. (Source: Plummer and McGeary 1993)

headwaters. The source of a stream or river.

herbaceous. Having the qualities of an herb; a flowering plant whose stem above ground does not become woody.

high desert. Desert climate in a high-elevation environment.

Hohokam. Ancient indigenous culture in the southwestern United States that built hundreds of miles of irrigation canals in southern and central Arizona between 300 B.C. and A.D. 1450.

humidity. The degree of moisture in the air.

hunter-gatherer. A member of a group of people who subsist by hunting, fishing, or foraging in the wild.

hydrilla. An invasive floating aquatic plant that can cover the surface of a lake, river, or irrigation canal, clogging boat propellers and irrigation systems and affecting fish, wildlife, and other organisms.

hydroelectric. Having to do with production of electricity by waterpower from falling water, often from a reservoir behind a dam.

hydrograph. A representation of water discharge over time.

hydrologic cycle. The cyclic transfer of water vapor from Earth's surface via evapotranspiration into the atmosphere, from the atmosphere via precipitation back to Earth, and through runoff into streams, rivers, and lakes and ultimately into the oceans.

hydrology. The study of Earth's waters, including water's properties, circulation, principles, and distribution.

hypothesis. A potential explanation for a condition or set of facts that can be tested through further investigation.

igneous intrusion. Where melted igneous rock has forced its way into existing rock and hardened; the intrusion, therefore, is younger than the rock it intruded. See also Principle of Cross-cutting Relationships.

igneous rock. A rock formed from solidification of magma. (Source: Plummer and McGeary 1993)

impermeable layer. A layer of material (e.g., clay) in an aquifer through which water does not pass.

impounded. To confine or store within an enclosure or within limits (e.g., water impounded in a reservoir).

inactive reservoir capacity. The reservoir capacity from which the water is normally not available due to design or regulation. The inactive capacity extends from the bottom of active capacity to the top of dead capacity.

increment borer. A tool that is drilled by hand into a tree to obtain a core sample (called an "increment core").

increment core. A core sample, about the diameter of a pencil, that can be examined through a microscope. Increment cores are preferred over cross-sections of a tree because they do not result in the death of a tree.

indigenous. Originating in and characteristic of a particular region or country; native.

inlet. The point at which water flows into a canal, spillway, or other structure.

instream flow. The minimum amount of water required in a stream to maintain the existing aquatic resources and associated wildlife and riparian habitat.

instream water use. Uses of water within a stream's channel (e.g., by fish and other aquatic life, or for recreation, navigation, and hydroelectric power production).

international water treaty. An agreement between two nations dealing with a shared water resource. Such treaties supersede state law. The United States has treaties with Mexico and Canada relating to shared water resources. (Source: Wolfe 1996)

interstate water compact. An agreement between two or more states dealing with competing demands for a water resource beyond the legal authority of one state alone to solve. Such agreements require the consent of Congress. (Source: Wolfe 1996)

introduced species. Species that are not native to a specific area.

invasive plant. A plant that moves in and takes over an ecosystem to the detriment of other species (often the result of environmental manipulation).

invertebrate. An animal without a backbone or spinal column.

irrigable acreage. Agricultural land capable of being irrigated.

irrigation. The controlled application of water to cropland, hay fields, and/or pastures to supplement that supplied by nature.

irrigation efficiency. The efficiency associated with acquiring water, delivering it to fields, and applying it to crops. Efficiency is determined through a combination of factors, including how much water is lost between the point of diversion and the point of use; the cost of delivering the water; and how well the soil holds water once water is applied.

lagoon. A shallow body of water, often separated from a sea by sandbars or reefs.

Law of the River. The body of laws, policies, rules, and regulations that govern the management of the Colorado River.

leach. To remove soluble or other constituents from a medium by the action of a percolating liquid, as in leaching salts from the soil by the application of water.

limestone (geology). A sedimentary rock composed of calcite, or calcium carbonate ($CaCO_3$), and sometimes containing shells and other hard parts of prehistoric water animals and plants. When chemical conditions are right, some calcite crystallizes in seawater and settles to the bottom to form limestone.

lithification. The consolidation of sediment into sedimentary rock. (Source: Plummer and McGeary 1993)

litigation. The act of carrying on a legal contest through a judicial process.

long-distance migrant. A bird that travels between continents, as from breeding grounds in North America to wintering grounds in Central and South America.

Lower Basin. One of two legally defined management basins of the Colorado River Watershed; includes the American states of Arizona, Nevada, and California. The division of the watershed into two management basins was authorized by the 1922 Colorado River Compact.

macroinvertebrates. Invertebrate animals (animals without backbones) large enough to be observed without the aid of a microscope or other magnification.

magma. Molten material beneath or within the earth's crust, from which igneous rock is formed.

main stem. (1) The major reach of a river or stream formed by the smaller tributaries that flow into it. (2) The principal watercourse of a river, excluding any tributaries.

mano and metate. Stone tools used to grind seeds to make flour. The metate is a flat, smooth stone upon which the seeds are ground; the mano is a rounded stone that is used to grind them.

marine. Of the sea.

marker ring. A distinct tree ring that can be used to verify specific years. A marker ring among trees from a particular locale or region will be consistently narrow or wide, reflecting, respectively, drought or abundant rainfall and streamflow in a given year.

marsh. A wetland characterized by soft, wet, low-lying land, marked by herbaceous vegetation.

master tree-ring chronology. A timeline constructed from previously cross-dated samples from trees in a locale or region. Such a chronology can span hundred, or even thousands, of years and can be used to date, for example, well-preserved timbers found in ancient buildings.

meander. A pronounced sinuous curve along a stream's course. (Source: Plummer and McGeary 1993)

metamorphic rock. A rock produced by the transformation of preexisting rock into texturally or mineralogically distinct new rock as a result of high temperature, high pressure, or both, but without the rock melting in the process. (Source: Plummer and McGeary 1993)

microorganism. An organism too small to be viewed by the unaided eye.

migration. The periodic movement of animate things from one area to another, often in response to seasonal change.

mitigate. To lessen; moderate; alleviate; to make less severe. For example, the policy of constructing or creating wetlands to replace those lost to development.

Mojave Desert. Covers more than 35,000 square kilometers of Southern California and parts of Utah, Nevada, and Arizona. It receives less than 6 inches (150 millimeters) of rain a year and is generally between 3,000 and 6,000 feet (1,000 and 2,000 meters) in elevation. The Joshua tree is a species that is found only in the Mojave Desert. (Source: Online encyclopedia: www.wordiq.com)

mortar and pestle. A receptacle of hard material (mortar), having a bowl-shaped cavity in which substances are reduced to powder with a tool intended for pounding or grinding (pestle).

mouth of stream. The point of discharge of a stream into another stream, a lake, or the sea.

mulch. A covering, as of straw or compost, spread on the ground around plants, especially to prevent evaporation or erosion and to enrich the soil.

municipal. Of or pertaining to a town or city or its local government.

municipal water system. A network of pipes, pumps, and storage and treatment facilities designed to deliver potable water to homes, schools, businesses, and other water users in a city or town and to remove and treat waste materials.

native species. A species originally living, growing, or produced in a certain place or ecosystem; indigenous.

natural resource. A material source of wealth, such as timber, fresh water, or a mineral deposit, that occurs in a natural state and has economic value.

Navajoan Desert. A sub-region of the Great Basin Desert centered in northeastern Arizona and including the adjacent Four Corners region of Utah, Colorado, and New Mexico. It is relatively high in elevation, and the dominant vegetation type is piñon-juniper woodland.

nephelometric turbidity unit (NTU). Unit of measure for the turbidity of water. Essentially, a measure of the cloudiness of water as measured by a nephelometer. Turbidity is based on the amount of light that is reflected off particles in the water. (Source: www.texaswater.org/water/facts/glossary/glossary5.htm)

niche. (See **ecological niche**).

nocturnal. 1) Of or occurring in the night, the opposite of diurnal. 2) Active at night.

nomadic. Of or pertaining to a people or tribe that has no permanent abode but moves about from place to place, usually seasonally.

nonconsumptive use. Instream use of water that does not reduce the supply; or, removing water and returning it to the source without reducing the supply (e.g., navigation and fisheries).

nonnative species. Species that migrate into an ecosystem or are deliberately or accidentally introduced into an ecosystem by humans. (Source: Miller 2001)

nonpoint source pollution (NPS). Pollution discharged over a wide land area, not from one specific location. Nonpoint source pollution is contamination that occurs when rainwater, snowmelt, or irrigation washes off plowed fields, city streets, or suburban backyards. As this runoff moves across land surface, it picks up soil particles and pollutants, such as nutrients and pesticides.

nopales. The edible pads of the prickly pear cactus.

nutrients. As a pollutant, any element or compound, such as phosphates or nitrates, that fuels abnormally high organic growth in aquatic ecosystems.

obsidian. Volcanic glass, usually black; excellent raw material for making stone tools.

organic. Related to or derived from living organisms. Organic substances contain carbon.

ornithologist. A biologist who specializes in the study of birds.

outlet. An opening through which water is released.

oxbow. A U-shaped bend in a river, or the land within such a bend.

parts per million (ppm). Units typically used in measuring the number of "parts" by weight of a substance in water; commonly used in representing pollutant concentrations. Equal to milligrams per liter (mg/l).

pathogen. A microorganism that can cause disease.

per capita water use. The amount of water used by each person each day, expressed in gallons.

percolation. (1) The slow seepage of water into and through the ground. (2) The slow seepage of water through a filter medium. (3) The movement, under hydrostatic pressure, of water through the interstices of a rock or soil.

permeable layer. A layer of porous material (rock, soil, unconsolidated sediment); in an aquifer, the layer through which water freely passes as it moves through the ground.

petroglyph. An image pecked or chiseled into a rock surface with a hard stone and bone tools; the earliest form of pictograph.

pH. Is generally referred to as the concentration of hydroxide ions when a substance is dissolved in water; used to express the acidity or alkalinity of a solution. Mathematically it is defined as the negative of the logarithm of the hydrogen ion concentration.

photosynthesis. The process in green plants and certain other organisms by which carbohydrates are synthesized from carbon dioxide and water using light as an energy source. Most forms of photosynthesis release oxygen as a byproduct. Chlorophyll typically acts as the catalyst in this process.

phytoplankton. Microscopic floating plants (mostly algae) that live suspended in bodies of water.

pictograph. A picture that was painted on stone by prehistoric peoples to represent a word or idea.
pith. The cylinder of tissue at the center of a tree.

plate tectonics. A theory that the earth's surface is divided into a few large, thick plates that are slowly moving and changing in size. Intense geologic activity occurs at the plate boundaries. (Source: Plummer and McGeary 1993)

point source pollution. Water pollution coming from a single point, such as a sewage-outflow pipe.

policymaker. A person responsible for making policy, especially in government.

pollution. An alteration in the character or quality of the environment, or any of its components, that renders it less suited for certain uses. The alteration of the physical, chemical, or biological properties of water by the introduction of any substance that renders the water harmful to use.

potable water. Water suitable, safe, or prepared for drinking.

practicably irrigable acreage (PIA). A standard used to determine the extent of a federal reserved water right on Indian reservations that was established to "transform the Indians into farmers." The PIA standard was established in *Arizona v. California* (1963). (Source: Wolfe 1996)

precipitate (from solution). To separate a solid substance from a solution, as when minerals precipitate out to form sedimentary rock.

precipitation. The downward movement of water in liquid or solid form from the atmosphere following condensation in the atmosphere due to cooling of the air below the dew point. Includes rain, snow, hail, and sleet.

prelación. The system of water allocation used in Mexico that assigns priority to different types of water use. Human consumption is always the first priority.

Principle of Cross-cutting Relationships. A basic geologic principle where melted igneous rock has forced its way into existing rock and hardened, with the igneous intrusion being younger than the rock it intruded.

Principle of Original Horizontality. A basic geologic principle in which the rock layers were originally horizontal, but may have been later folded, bent, tilted, or overturned by geologic forces like faulting.

Principle of Superposition. A basic geologic principle in which rock layers were originally laid down one on top of the other with the oldest layer on the bottom.

prior appropriation doctrine. The doctrine of prior appropriation is the law dominating water allocation and use in the western United States. Basically, the law says that the first person in time to divert water from a river or stream and put it to beneficial use is entitled to continue that use without interference from other users who make subsequent claims. The law says "first in time, first in right" and is based on use rather than land ownership.

propagation. Multiplying by natural reproduction.

public interest. Welfare or well-being of the general public. This is a form of water legislation in Mexico. Public interest appears in cases of scarcity, drought, aquifer overdraft, or the need to reserve water for a specific use. The federal government of Mexico has established that human consumption of available water is the first priority.

recharge. Refers to water entering an underground aquifer through faults, fractures, or direct absorption.

recharge area. Any area of land allowing water to pass through it and into an aquifer. (Source: Miller 2001)

reserved water right. A water right recognized by judicial decision to have been created under federal law by a federal reservation of land in an amount sufficient to meet the purposes of the reservation, whether for Indian reservations or for other federal reservations of lands (e.g., national parks). The right is not lost by nonuse, and its priority date is the date the land was set aside. (Source: Wolfe 1996)

reservoir (water). (1) A pond, lake, or basin, either natural or artificial, for the storage, regulation, and control of water. (2) An artificially created lake in which water is collected and stored for future use. (3) Any natural or artificial storage place from which water may be withdrawn as needed.

resource center. The place or region where a given resource is most concentrated, because the item is extracted, grown, or produced there.

respiration (biology). (1) The process in which an organism uses oxygen for its life processes and gives off carbon dioxide. (2) The oxidative process occurring within living cells by which the chemical energy of organic molecules (i.e., substances containing carbon, hydrogen, and oxygen) is released in a series of metabolic steps involving the consumption of oxygen (O_2) and the liberation of carbon dioxide (CO_2) and water (H_2O).

restoration. The process of bringing back to existence, or reestablishing, the original condition of a degraded environment.

return flow. The portion of withdrawn water that is not consumed by evapotranspiration and that returns to its source or another body of water. (Source: Wolfe 1996)

ridge line. A point of higher ground that separates two adjacent streams or watersheds; also known as a divide.

riffle. A shallow, gravelly section in a stream where the current breaks over rocks or other partially submerged organic debris. Used for spawning by certain species of fish. (Source: www.wvwrc.org/glossary/)

río. Spanish for river.

riparian. Pertaining to the banks of a river, stream, waterway, or other, typically, flowing body of water as well as to plant and animal communities along such bodies of water. This term is also commonly used for other bodies of water, e.g., ponds, lakes, etc., although littoral is the more precise term for such stationary bodies of water. Also refers to the legal doctrine (Riparian Doctrine and Riparian Water Rights) that says a property owner along the banks of a surface water body has the primary right to withdraw water for reasonable use.

river. A natural stream of water of considerable volume, larger than a brook or creek.

rivulet. A small stream; a brook or creek.

rock cycle. A theoretical concept relating tectonism, erosion, and various rock-forming processes to the common rock types. (Source: Plummer and McGeary 1993)

runoff. That portion of precipitation, which is not intercepted by vegetation, absorbed by the land surface, or evaporated and thus flows overland into a depression, stream, lake, or ocean. Often carries sediments or pollutants.

saline. Salty or saltlike; salty water.

salinity. Amount of various salts dissolved in a given volume of water.

salt water. Water that contains a relatively high percentage (over 0.5 parts per thousand) of salt minerals.

sandstone. A sedimentary rock formed by the consolidation and compaction of sand and held together by natural cement such as silica.

saturated zone. The part of a ground water system in which all of the spaces between soil and rock material are filled with water. Water found within the zone of saturation is called ground water. The water table is the top of the zone of saturation.

sedentary. Abiding in one place, not migratory.

sediment. Created from natural process of erosion, where wind, water, frost, and ice slowly break down rocks into finer and finer pieces. Runoff often carries sediment into nearby waterways.

sediment load. Sediment carried by a stream, including particles in suspension as well as larger material.

sedimentary. Rocks formed by the deposition of sediment.

sedimentation. The process of suspended solid particles settling out of water onto the bottom of a stream channel, canal, reservoir, or other body of water.

seep. A wetland that forms in areas where ground water discharges to the land surface, often at the base of steep slopes, but where water volume is too small to create a stream or creek. These wetlands have a perpetually saturated soil but may have little or no standing water. (Source: www.ag.iastate.edu/centers/iawetlands/Glossary.html)

selenium. Selenium is a naturally occurring element that is present in soil and water.

sewage treatment. (See **wastewater treatment**)

shale. A fissile rock composed of layers of claylike, fine-grained sediments.

short-distance migrant. A bird that only travels from one part of a continent to another.

silt. Sediment composed of particles with a diameter of 1/256 to 1/16 millimeter. (Source: Plummer and McGeary 1993)

skeleton plot. A graph of relative tree-ring width based upon ring data, that can then be compared to a master tree-ring chronology.

snowmelt. Water from melting snow.

snowpack. A field of naturally packed snow that ordinarily melts in early summer months.

solids. Materials that have relative firmness, coherence of particles, or persistence of form; matter that is not a liquid or gas.

Sonoran Desert. Covers approximately 100,000 square miles (260,000 square kilometers) of the states of Sonora, Arizona, California, and Baja California. It is distinguished from other North American deserts by the presence of legume trees (i.e., mesquite) and large columnar cacti (i.e., saguaro).

spawn. To produce or deposit eggs; the eggs of aquatic animals.

specialist species. Species with a narrow ecological niche. They may be able (1) to live in only one type of habitat, (2) tolerate only a narrow range of climatic and other environmental conditions, or (3) use only one or a few types of food. (Source: Miller 2001)

species. A category of taxonomic classification, consisting of related organisms capable of interbreeding.

spillway. (1) The channel or passageway around or over a dam through which excess water is diverted. (2) A series of gates used to control reservoir levels and to make releases of flow that exceed the capacity of the powerhouse water evacuation.

spring. A place where water flows naturally out of rock onto the land surface. (Source: Plummer and McGeary 1993)

stakeholder. Any party that has an interest ("stake") in an issue or resource.

stomata. Tiny pores in the epidermis or surface of plant leaves or stems through which gases and water vapor are exchanged with the environment.

stopover. A resting place for migrating birds.

storm drain. Constructed opening in a road system through which runoff from the road surface flows into an underground sewer system.

stream. Any body of running water moving under gravity's influence through clearly defined natural channels to progressively lower levels.

streambed. The channel through which a stream flows or has flowed. The bottom of a stream or river.

streamflow. The discharge of water from a river.

stream capacity. The total load that a stream can carry. (Source: Plummer and McGeary 1993)

stream channel. A long, narrow depression, shaped and more or less filled by a stream. (Source: Plummer and McGeary 1993)

stream velocity. The speed at which water in a stream travels. (Source: Plummer and McGeary 1993)

sub-basin. (1) A portion of a sub-region or basin drained by a single stream or group of minor streams. (2) The smallest unit into which the land surface is subdivided for hydrologic study purposes.

substrate. A layer of material beneath the surface soil.

surface water. Water that is on Earth's surface, such as in a stream, river, lake, or reservoir.

suspension. The state in which the particles of a substance are mixed with a liquid but are not dissolved. Pepper in water or snow globes (round glass containers that are shaken to distribute glitter representing snow) are examples of suspension.

sustainable. Capable of continuing for the foreseeable future, as in a level of timber harvest.

tail-water. Outflow from a dam.

tamarisk. An ornamental tree native to Eurasia, also known as salt cedar, which has invaded the Colorado River Watershed, replacing the native riparian vegetation in many areas.

tepary bean. A bushy plant, *Phaseolus acutifolius latifolius,* of the legume family, native to Mexico and Arizona and grown as a food plant in dry regions.

terrestrial. 1) Of or representing the earth. 2) Of land as opposed to water; growing or living on land.

thermal (air current). A rising current of warm air.

topography. A description, model, or drawing of mountains, valleys, hills, rivers, roads, bridges, and other things found on the surface of a place.

trade. Voluntary exchange of goods and services with the expectation of gain.

transboundary. On or to the other side of a boundary; across a boundary.

transpiration. (1) The movement of water from the soil or ground water reservoir via the stomata in plant cells to the atmosphere. (2) The process by which water vapor escapes from a living plant, principally through the leaves, and enters the atmosphere. Transpiration, combined with evaporation from the soil, is referred to as evapotranspiration.

treaty. A formal agreement between two or more nations.

tributary. A stream that contributes its water to another stream or body of water.

tundra. A treeless area between the icecap and the tree line of Arctic regions, having permanently frozen subsoil and supporting low-growing vegetation.

turbid. Having sediment or foreign particles in suspension or stirred up, creating a muddy look.

turbidity. The cloudy appearance of water caused by the presence of suspended and colloidal matter. Technically, turbidity is an optical property of the water based on the amount of light reflected by suspended particles.

turquoise. An opaque mineral (a basic hydrous copper aluminum phosphate often containing a small amount of iron) that is sky-blue or greenish-blue in color and can be cut as a gem.

unconfined aquifer. A partially filled aquifer exposed to the land surface and marked by a rising and falling water table. (Source: Plummer and McGeary 1993)

unsaturated zone. The unsaturated surface layer of the ground in which some of the spaces between soil particles are filled with water and others are filled with air. Some of the water in the zone of aeration is lost to the atmosphere through evaporation.

Upper Basin. One of two legally defined management basins of the Colorado River Watershed; includes the American states of Wyoming, Colorado, Utah, New Mexico, and part of Arizona. The division of the watershed into two management basins was authorized by the 1922 Colorado River Compact.

upstream. Toward the source or upper part of a stream; against the current. In relation to water rights, refers to water uses or locations that affect water quality or quantity downstream.

waffle garden. A type of garden associated with the Zuni Indian tribe in which plants are separated by mounds of soil, forming a grid pattern. Used to conserve water and soil.

wastewater treatment. Any of the mechanical or chemical processes used to modify the quality of wastewater in order to make it more compatible or acceptable to humans and the environment.

water (H_2O). An odorless, tasteless, colorless liquid made up of a combination of hydrogen and oxygen. Water forms streams, lakes, and seas and is a major constituent of all living matter. The word **water** and important concepts related to water appear on almost every page of this text.

water allocation. In a hydrologic system in which there are multiple uses or demands for water, the process of measuring a specific amount of water devoted to a given purpose.

water cycle. The path water takes through its various states—vapor, liquid, and solid—as it moves throughout Earth's systems (oceans, atmosphere, ground water, streams, etc.). Also known as the hydrologic cycle.

water molecule. The smallest unit of water; consists of two hydrogen atoms and an oxygen atom.

water pressure. The downward force of water upon itself and other materials; caused by the pull of gravity.

water quality. The chemical, physical, and biological characteristics of water with respect to its suitability for a particular use.

water right. A legal right to use a specified amount of water for beneficial purposes.

water table. The uppermost level of water in the saturated part of an aquifer.

water treatment. A series of steps that purify water so that it can be put to a specific use (e.g., drinking, irrigation, industrial use).

water user. Anyone who uses water. Water users include: domestic (e.g., drinking, cooking, washing); public uses (e.g., fire fighting, street cleaning); industry (e.g., producing food products, textiles, paper, and chemicals); commercial (e.g., businesses, motels, restaurants); agricultural (e.g., irrigation, livestock); energy production (e.g., electricity); earth systems (e.g., the water cycle, ecosystems); cultures; mining; recreation; fish and wildlife; and navigation.

water vapor. The state of water in which individual molecules are highly energized and move about freely; also known as the gaseous phase.

waterfowl. An aquatic bird.

watershed. The land area that drains water into a particular stream, river, or lake. It is a land feature that can be identified by tracing a line along the highest elevations between two areas on a map, often a ridge. Large watersheds, like the Mississippi River Basin, contain thousands of smaller watersheds.

weathering. Physical and chemical processes in which solid rock exposed at the earth's surface is changed to separate solid particles and dissolved material, which can then be moved to another place as sediment. (Source: Miller 2001)

well. A hole drilled or bored into the earth to obtain a natural deposit, as water or petroleum.

wetland. Land that is covered all or part of the time with salt water or fresh water, excluding streams, lakes, and the open ocean. (Source: Miller 2001)

wetted perimeter. The contact surface between the water in a stream and the streambed.

Winters Doctrine. A ruling in 1908 by the United States Supreme Court in the case of Winters v. United States that allocated water to American Indian reservations. The ruling has also been applied to set aside water rights for national parks, national monuments, protected areas, and any other land that is reserved from the public domain. The doctrine ties the water rights for these lands to the date they were established.

wo'o. The Tohono O'odham word for a rainwater pond.

Xeriscape™. A form of landscaping that utilizes a variety of indigenous and drought-tolerant plants, shrubs, and ground cover.

zebra mussel. A tiny mollusk native to eastern Europe that is a species of major concern within the United States as it spreads westward into lakes and reservoirs and clogs the workings of dams and diversions.

Bibliography

Abbey, Edward. 1968. *Desert Solitaire: A Season in the Wilderness*. New York: Ballantine Books.

Alexander, Gretchen. 1989. *Water Cycle Teacher's Guide*. Hudson, NH: Delta Education, Inc.

Athearn, Fredric J., et al. *Discovering Archaeology in Colorado*. Dolores, CO: BLM's Heritage Education Program

Aton, James, and Robert McPherson. 2000. *River Flowing from Sunrise: An Environmental History of the Lower San Juan*. Logan: Utah State University Press.

Arizona Game and Fish Department. 2001. *Landscaping for Desert Wildlife*. Phoenix: Arizona Game and Fish Department.

Arizona-Sonora Desert Museum. 2000. *A Natural History of the Sonoran Desert*. Tucson: Arizona-Sonora Desert Museum Press.

Arizona Water Resources Research Center. 2002. *Arizona Water Wall Map*. Tucson: Arizona Water Resources Research Center.

Bahti, Tom and Mark. 1999. *Southwestern Indian Arts and Crafts*. Las Vegas, NV: KC Publications.

Barzilay, J. L, J.W. Eley, and W. G. Weinberg. 1999. *The Water We Drink*. New Brunswick, NJ: Rutgers University Press.

Belknap, Buzz, and Loie Belknap Evans. 2001. *Belknap's Waterproof Grand Canyon River Guide*. Evergreen, CO: Westwater Books.

Bergman, Charles. 2002. *Red Delta: Fighting for Life at the End of the Colorado River*. Golden, CO: Fulcrum Publishing.

Binnie, Chris, et al. 2002. *Basic Water Treatment*. London: Thomas Telford.

Blair, Rob, ed. 1996. *The Western San Juan Mountains: Their Geology, Ecology, and Human History*. Niwot: University Press of Colorado.

Bowers, Janice Emily. 1993. *Shrubs and Trees of the Southwest Deserts*. Tucson, AZ: Southwest Parks and Monuments Association.

Braniff Cornejo, Beatriz. El Norte de México: La Gran Chichimeca. *Arqueología Mexicana* I, núm. 6 (Febrero–Marzo 1994).

Brater, E., H. King, J. Lindell, and C. Wei. 1996. *Handbook of Hydraulics: Seventh Edition*. New York: McGraw Hill Professional.

Cargile, Ellen Yeager. 1976. *Understanding and Executing Arts of the Southwest*. Durango, CO: Ellen Y. Cargile.

Caudto, Michael, and Joseph Bruchac. 1996. *Native American Gardening: Stories, Projects, and Recipes for Families*. Golden, CO: Fulcrum Publishing.

Chronic, Halka. 1983. *Roadside Geology of Arizona*. Missoula, MT: Mountain Press Publishing Co.

Clavijero, Francisco Xavier. 1975. *Historia de la Antigua o Baja California*. México: Editorial Porrúa, S. A.

Collier, Michael. 1980. *An Introduction to Grand Canyon Geology*. Grand Canyon, AZ: Grand Canyon Natural History Association.

Collier, Michael, R. Webb, and John Schmidt. 1996. *Dams and Rivers: Primer on the Downstream Effects of Dams*. Tucson, AZ: U.S. Geological Survey.

Collier, Michael. 1999. *Water, Earth, and Sky: The Colorado River Basin*. Salt Lake City: University of Utah Press.

Colorado River Water Map. Sacramento, CA: The Water Education Foundation.

Covey, Cyclone. 1993. *Adventures in the Unknown Interior of America*. Albuquerque: University of New Mexico Press.

Crown, Patricia, and James Judge. 1991. *Chaco & Hohokam: Prehistoric Regional Systems in the American Southwest*. Santa Fe, NM: School of American Research Press.

Culp, Gordon, and Russell Culp. 1974. *New Concepts in Water Purification*. New York: Van Nostrand Reinhold Company.

Debuys, William, and Joan Mayers. 2001. *Salt Dreams: Land and Water in Low-Down California*. Albuquerque: University of New Mexico Press.

DeYonge, Sandra Chisholm. 2000. *Spring Waters, Gathering Places*. Bozeman, MT: The Watercourse.

Domínguez, Fray Francisco, and Fray Silvestre Veléz de Escalante. 1995. *The Domínguez-Escalante Journal: Their Expedition Through Colorado, Utah, Arizona, and New Mexico*. Ed. Ted J. Warner, trans. Fray Angelico Chavez. Salt Lake City: University of Utah Press.

Durham, Michael. 1990. *The Smithsonian Guide to Historic America: the Desert States; New Mexico, Arizona, Nevada, Utah*. New York: Stewart, Tabori & Chang.

Eliot, T. S. 1943. *Four Quartets*. New York: Harcourt Brace & Company.

Elphick, Chris, et al., eds. 2001. *The Sibley Guide to Bird Life and Bird Behavior*. New York: Alfred A. Knopf, Inc.

Fielder, John. 1998. *Colorado Skies*. Englewood, CO: Westcliffe Publishers.

FindLaw. U.S. Supreme Court 207 *U.S.* 564

Fisher, Chris, et al. 2000. *Mammals of the Rocky Mountains*. Renton, WA: Lone Pine Publishing.

Fisher, Roger, William Ury, and Bruce Patton. 1991. *Getting to Yes: Negotiating Agreement Without Giving In*. New York: Penguin USA.

Fleck, Richard F., ed. 2000. *A Colorado River Reader*. Salt Lake City: University of Utah Press.

Fletcher, Colin. 1997. *River: One Man's Journey Down the Colorado, Source to Sea*. New York: Alfred A. Knopf.

Foster, Nelson, and Linda S. Cordell, eds. 1996. *Chilies to Chocolate: Food the Americas Gave the World*. Tucson: University of Arizona Press.

Fradkin, Philip L. 1995. *A River No More: The Colorado River and the West*. Berkeley: University of California Press.

Freedman, B. 1989. *Environmental Ecology*. San Diego, CA: Academic Press, Inc.

Gabriel, Kathryn. 1992. *Marietta Wetherill: Reflections on Life with the Navajo in Chaco Canyon*. Boulder, CO: Johnson Books.

Gibson, Daniel. 2000. *Audubon Guide to the National Wildlife Refuges, Southwest*. NY: St. Martin's Griffin, A Balliet & Fitzgerald Book.

Gleick, Peter, et al. 2003. *The World's Water: The Biennial Report on Freshwater Resources 2002-2003*. Washington, DC: Island Press.

Grahame, John D., and Thomas D. Sisk, eds. 2002. *Canyons, Cultures and Environmental Change: An Introduction to the Land-Use History of the Colorado Plateau*. Retrieved on February 4, 2004, from the World Wide Web: www.cpluhna.nau.edu/.

Hobbs, Gregory Jr. 2003. *Citizen's Guide to Colorado Water Law*. Denver: Colorado Foundation for Water Education.

Hobbs, Gregory Jr. 2003. Inside the Drama of the Colorado River Compact Negotiations: Negotiating the Apportionment. *Proceedings of the Fourth Biennial Colorado River Symposium, September 17-19, 2003.* Sacramento, CA: The Water Education Foundation.

Hucko, Bruce. 1996. *Where There Is No Name for Art: The Art of Tewa Pueblo Children.* Santa Fe, NM: School of American Research Press.

Hughes, Donald J. 1978. *In the House of Stone and Light.* Denver, CO: University of Denver.

Hundley, Norris Jr. 1966. *Dividing the Waters: A Century of Controversy Between the United States and Mexico.* Berkeley: University of California Press.

Hundley, Norris. 1975. *Water and the West: The Colorado River Compact and the Politics of Water in the American West.* Berkeley: University of California Press.

Hundley, Norris. 2000. *Las aguas divididas: Un siglo de controversia entre México y Estado Unidos.* Mexicali, Baja California: Universidad Autónoma de Baja California.

Ingram, Helen, Nancy Laney, and David Gillilan. 1995. *Divided Waters: Bridging the U.S.-Mexico Border.* Tucson: University of Arizona Press.

Kennedy, Roger. 1998. *The Smithsonian Guide to Historic America: The Rocky Mountain States.* New York: Stewart, Tabori & Chang.

Lamott, Anne. 1994. *Bird by Bird: Some Instructions on Writing and Life.* New York: Pantheon Books.

League of Women Voters of Colorado. 2001. *Colorado Water.* Denver: League of Women Voters of Colorado.

Leopold, Aldo. 1949. *A Sand County Almanac, and Sketches Here and There.* New York: Oxford University Press, Inc.

Levin Rojo, Danna Alexandra. Las Siete Ciudades de Cíbola. *Arqueología Mexicana* XII, núm. 67 (Junio–Julio 2004).

Lister, Robert and Florence. 1981. *Archaeology and Archaeologists in Chaco Canyon.* Albuquerque: University of New Mexico Press.

Martin, Russell. 1999. *A Story that Stands Like a Dam: Glen Canyon and the Struggle for the Soul of the West.* Salt Lake City: University of Utah Press.

Martínez Lozada, Pablo, ed. 2002. *Philips Guides: The Sea of Cortez, Mexico.* Mexico: Editorial Clío, Libros y Videos, S.A. de C.V.

Mayes, Susan. 1989. *What Makes It Rain?* London: Usborne Publications.

McClurg, Sue. 2000. *Water and the Shaping of California.* Sacramento, CA: The Water Education Foundation.

McQuiston, Don and Debra. 1995. *The Woven Spirit of the Southwest.* San Francisco, CA: Chronicle Books.

Meko, David, Charles W. Stockton, and William R. Boggess. 1995. The Tree-Ring Record of Severe Sustained Drought. *Water Resources Bulletin* (Journal of the American Water Resources Association) 31, No. 5: 789-801.

Michaud, J. 1991. *A Citizens Guide to Understanding and Monitoring Lakes and Streams.* Olympia: Washington State Department of Ecology.

Miller, G. Tyler, Jr. 2001. *Environmental Science: Eighth Edition.* Pacific Grove, CA: Brooks/Cole.

Minckley, W. L. 1991. *Native Fishes of Arid Lands: A Dwindling Resource of the Desert Southwest.* USDA Forest Service General Technical Report RM 206. Fort Collins, CO: USDA Forest Service, Rocky Mountain Forest and Range Experiment Station.

Moreno de los Arcos, Roberto, et al. 1983. *Panorama Historico de Baja California.* Méxicali, Baja California: Centro de Investigaciones Históricas UNAM–UABC.

Murdock, T., and M. Cheo. 1996. *Streamkeepers Field Guide*. Everett, WA: The Adopt-A-Stream Foundation.

Nabhan, Gary Paul. 1982. *The Desert Smells Like Rain: A Naturalist in Papago Indian Country*. New York: North Point Press (Farrar, Straus and Giroux).

Nabhan, Gary Paul. 1997. *Cultures of Habitat*. Washington, DC: Counterpoint.

National Academy Press. 1996. *National Science Education Standards*. Washington, DC: National Academy Press.

Newcom, Joshua. 2004. *Layperson's Guide to the Colorado River*. Sacramento, CA: The Water Education Foundation.

Niethammer, Carolyn. 1999. *American Indian Cooking: Recipes from the Southwest*. Lincoln: University of Nebraska Press.

Nobel, David. 1999. *The Hohokam: Ancient People of the Desert*. Santa Fe, NM: School of American Research Press.

Odum, E. P. 1983. *Basic Ecology*. Philadelphia, PA: Saunders College Publications.

Peterson, Roger Tory, and Edward L. Chalif. 1973. *Mexican Birds*. Boston, MA: Houghton Mifflin Company.

Phillips, Stephen. 1998. *Desert Waters: From Ancient Aquifers to Modern Demands*. Tucson: Arizona-Sonora Desert Museum Press.

Phillips, Steven J., and Patricia Wentworth Comus, eds. 2000. *A Natural History of the Sonoran Desert*. Tucson: Arizona-Sonora Desert Museum Press.

Plummer, Charles, and David McGeary. 1993. *Physical Geology: Sixth Edition*. Dubuque, IA: Wm. C. Brown Publishers.

Pontius, Dale. 1997. *Colorado River Basin Study: Report to the Western Water Policy Review Advisory Commission*. Tucson, AZ: SWCA, Inc. Environmental Consultants.

Potochnik, Andre R. 2001. Paleogeomorphic Evolution of the Salt River Region: Implications for Cretaceous-Laramide Inheritance for Ancestral Colorado River Drainage. In *Colorado River Origin and Evolution*, pp. 17–22. Eds. R.A. Young and E.E. Spamer. Grand Canyon, AZ: Grand Canyon Association.

Powell, J. W. 1961. *The Exploration of the Colorado River and Its Canyons*. New York: Dover Publications, Inc.

Project WET International. 2004. *Discover a Watershed: The Missouri*. Bozeman, MT: Project WET International.

Reisner, Marc. 1993. *Cadillac Desert: The American West and Its Disappearing Water*. New York: Penguin Books.

Rocha, Benjamin. 1997. *The State of Sonora*. Hermosillo, Sonora: El Colegio de Sonora.

Rinne, John, and W. L. Minckley. 1991. *Native Fishes of Arid Lands: Dwindling Resources of the Desert Southwest*. Gen. Tech. Rep. RM-206. Fort Collins, CO: U.S. Department of Agriculture, Forest Service, Rocky Mountain Forest and Range Experiment Station.

Ryan, Kathleen Jo, ed. 1998. *Writing Down the River: Into the Heart of the Grand Canyon*. Flagstaff, AZ: Northland Publishing Company.

Schmid, Eleonore. 1990. *The Water's Journey*. New York: North-South Books.

Sibley, David. 2000. *The Sibley Guide to Birds*. New York: Alfred A. Knopf, Inc.

Silko, Leslie Marmon. 1999. *Gardens in the Dunes*. New York: Simon and Schuster.

Smith, Ray. 1993. *Watercolor COLOR*. New York: Doring Kindersley, Inc.

Sprinkel, Douglas, et al., eds. 2000. *Geology of Utah's Parks and Monuments*. Salt Lake City: Utah Geological Association.

Stockton, Charles W., and Gordon C. Jacoby, Jr. 1976. Long-term Surface-Water Supply and Streamflow Trends in the Upper Colorado River Basin. *Lake Powell Research Project Bulletin* 18 (March 1976).

Stockton, Charles W. 1975. Long-term Streamflow Records Reconstructed From Tree Rings. *Papers of the Laboratory of Tree-Ring Research* 5. Tucson: University of Arizona Press.

Stuart, David. 1984. *Glimpses of the Ancient Southwest*. Santa Fe, NM: Ancient City Press.

Teiwes, Helga. 1996. *Hopi Basket Weaving: Artistry in Natural Fibers*. Tucson: University of Arizona Press.

Tweit, Susan J. 1992. *The Great Southwest Nature Factbook*. Seattle, WA: Alaska Northwest Books.

The Watercourse. 1995. *Project WET: Curriculum and Activity Guide*. Bozeman, MT: The Watercourse.

The Watercourse. 2000. *Conserve Water Educators Guide*. Bozeman, MT: The Watercourse.

The Watercourse. 2001. *Discover a Watershed: Rio Grande/Rio Bravo Educators Guide*. Bozeman, MT: The Watercourse.

The Watercourse. 2002. *Discover a Watershed: Watershed Manager Educators Guide*. Bozeman, MT: The Watercourse.

The Watercourse. 2003. *Healthy Water, Healthy People Educators Guide*. Bozeman, MT: The Watercourse.

The Water Education Foundation. 1999. *Colorado River Project Symposium Proceedings September 16–18, 1999*. Sacramento, CA: The Water Education Foundation.

The Water Education Foundation. 2001. *Colorado River Project Symposium Proceedings September 11–12, 2001*. Sacramento, CA: The Water Education Foundation.

The Water Education Foundation. 2003. *Colorado River Project Symposium Proceedings September 17–19, 1999*. Sacramento, CA: The Water Education Foundation.

United States Environmental Protection Agency (EPA). 1999. *Guidance Manual for Compliance with the Interim Enhanced Surface Water Treatment Rule: Turbidity Provisions*. Retrieved on April 2, 2004 from the World Wide Web: www.epa.gov/safewater/mdbp/mdbptg.html.

Upper Colorado River Endangered Fish Recovery Program. 2002. *Historical Accounts of Upper Colorado River Basin Endangered Fish*. Denver, CO: U.S. Fish and Wildlife Service.

Water on the Web. 2003. *Understanding Turbidity*. Retrieved on April, 2, 2004, from the World Wide Web: http://wow.nrri.umn.edu/wow/under/parameters/turbidity.html.

Waters, Frank. 1946. *The Colorado*. New York: Rinehart and Company.

Waters, Frank. 1963. *Book of the Hopi*. New York: Penguin Books.

Western Resource Advocates. 2003. *Smart Water: A Comparative Study of Urban Water Use Efficiency Across the Southwest*. Boulder, CO: Western Resource Advocates.

Whitson, Tom D., ed. 1991. *Weeds of the West*. Laramie: Western Society of Weed Science and University of Wyoming.

Williams, Terry Tempest. 1994. *An Unspoken Hunger: Stories from the Field*. New York: Pantheon Books.

Wolfe, Mary Ellen. 1996. *A Landowner's Guide to Western Water Rights*. Boulder, CO: Roberts Rinehart Publishers.

Zepeda, Ofelia, ed. 1982. *Mat Hekid O Ju:/When it Rains: Papago and Pima Poetry* (*Sun Tracks* 7). Tucson: University of Arizona Press.

Zwinger, Ann. 1975. *Run, River, Run: A Naturalist's Journey Down One of the Great Rivers of the American West*. Tucson: University of Arizona Press.

Copyright Page Extension

Index